RUSSIA
AND THE WORLD

RUSSIA
AND THE WORLD

New Views on Russian Foreign Policy

Edited by Ambassador Boris Pyadyshev
Editor in Chief of *International Affairs*

A Birch Lane Press Book
Published by Carol Publishing Group

A Birch Lane Press Book
Published by Carol Publishing Group
Birch Lane Press is a registered trademark of Carol Communications, Inc.

Editorial Offices: 600 Madison Avenue, New York, N.Y. 10022
Sales & Distribution Offices: 120 Enterprise Avenue, Secaucus, N.J. 07094
In Canada: Musson Book Company, a division of General Publishing Company, Ltd., Don Mills, Ontario M3B 2T6

Queries regarding rights and permissions should be addressed to Carol Publishing Group, 600 Madison Avenue, New York, N.Y. 10022

Carol Publishing Group books are available at special discounts for bulk purchases, for sales promotions, fund raising, or educational purposes. Special editions can be created to specifications. For details contact: Special Sales Department, Carol Publishing Group, 120 Enterprise Avenue, Secaucus, N.J. 07094

Manufactured in the United States of America
10 9 8 7 6 5 4 3 2 1

Library of Congress Cataloging-in-Publication Data

Russia and the world : new views on Russian foreign policy / edited by Ambassador Boris Pyadyshev.
    p. cm.
    "A Birch Lane Press book."
    ISBN 1-55972-087-5
    1. Soviet Union—Foreign relations—1985- 2. Perestroĭka.
3. Soviet Union—National security.   I. Piadyshev, Boris Dmitrievich.
DK289.R88   1991   91-33289
327.47—dc20   CIP

Contents

Conversation With Eduard Shevardnadze After the Coup, September 6, 1991

Remember August 1991

B. Pyadyshev. Had it still been Eduard Shevardnadze occupying ministerial office 708 in the Foreign Ministry building on Smolenskaya Square on August 19, what would have been his public stand vis-à-vis the State Emergency Committee? What words would he have addressed to his colleagues at the ministry and to the Soviet ambassadors and diplomats abroad?

E. Shevardnadze. The way I have acted since last fall, as well as my resignation itself, allow me to claim that had I remained foreign minister, I probably would have tried to stick to my own ideas and principles. Not only would I have refused to join the State Emergency Committee, I would have appealed to the people, found a way to do it. The papers were shut down; there was no access to TV. Still,

EDUARD SHEVARDNADZE was Minister of Foreign Affairs from 1985 to January 1991.

I did manage, using foreign press and other media, to tell people about the threat of a coup and its dangerous implications. I think I have the right to talk about it now, since my actions before resigning and afterward, my resignation itself, and everything that followed put me in a position to say this much.

This would have determined my instructions and directives to the ambassadors.

B. Pyadyshev. The attitudes and the conduct of some of our ambassadors who acted under the instructions their embassies received on August 19 and 20, and who did not take the risk of exposing the unconstitutional nature of the State Emergency Committee to leaders of their host countries, bring to mind the perennial dilemma of government officials: professional versus civic duty.

E. Shevardnadze. Your know, Boris Dmitrievich, this question is very complex. What I have just said about my probable reaction should be seen rather as an exception, since not everyone had the opportunity to act this way. You will recall the President's reaction to my statement. All subsequent events vindicated that statement, proved that my warning was indeed well-founded. Yet, back then, many people, including top leaders, dismissed it as an emotional outburst, the words of a man who had gotten tired, who was under stress, and so on. There was no junta, no danger of a putsch.

I don't want to hurt anyone, but a certain lightness in the assessment of everything that followed after my statement kept our ministers and our ambassadors from taking a critical approach and bracing themselves for some kind of unusual or, shall I say, extreme situations. This is why ministries, as well as ambassadors, were caught by surprise at the very outset. No one had told them of any serious threat, any real danger. And when the coup came, look at the key figures who were involved in it: the Vice-President—the country's second highest official, the prime minister, the President's closest aides—the minister of defense, chairman of the KGB, the interior minister, etc. Any ambassador would be hard put to believe this had not been sanctioned by the President. Hence, the hesitation, the ambiguity, the uncertainty both inside the ministry and among the ambassadors.

Now if we in the center make mistakes in picking people like the Vice-President and cabinet ministers, if we have elevated the individuals that were in fact nothing short of traitors to the top of the government, should we actually level accusations at the ambassadors or the Ministry of Foreign Affairs? Not if we cannot even act sensibly in filling the top government jobs. This is how I see it. I would rather not blame it on the ambassadors. Some of them moved fast. Others were more cautious, biding their time. Perhaps they were right. I wouldn't accuse those who were too hasty.

B. Pyadyshev. When you announced your resignation last December some believed that one of the reasons for this decision was personal differences between you and the President. "Both sides" demonstrated that quite clearly later on. At what juncture did you first notice differences or disagreements between your opinions and attitudes and those of the President?

E. Shevardnadze. Over the past few years, starting in 1985, the President and I have not had any particular problems. Naturally, we had discussions and disputes, in particular, because other leaders participated in making major political decisions. Still, mutual understanding prevailed between the President and myself in formulating foreign policy and defining various negotiating positions. But lately certain alarming trends have appeared. In particular, this applies to the negotiations involving the conventional forces in Europe (CFE). The decision on the withdrawal of large amounts of equipment beyond the Urals led to complications with our negotiating partners in the West. For the sake of honesty, trust, and confidence we should have informed them. It so happened that I myself, as foreign minister, was faced with a fait accompli. This was basically regarded as a kind of manipulation, a ploy, some kind of dishonest behavior on our side. I was alarmed, and quite seriously so. I told Mikhail Sergeyevich and others about it.

A significant number of tanks, APCs, and other equipment was reassigned by the Soviet military command to the marines at a stage where this should not have been done. This was the subject of heated discussions with Mr. Baker and other partners with whom we had established businesslike relations. The same happened to aircraft which were repainted and reassigned. And all this came up after the agreement had been signed in Paris.

By the way, the moment I knew about it I sent to the President a special memo that contained my arguments. It said that the issues under negotiation could not be treated in such an uncompromising and reckless manner at a time when a new atmosphere and a new situation had emerged and a partnership was being formed. We ourselves suggested that military confrontation was drawing to an end, and all this would require new attitudes of greater honesty, openness, and frankness. I made it clear in my memo that what had happened ran counter to our principles.

B. Pyadyshev. Did any reaction follow?

E. Shevardnadze. Yes, there was a reaction. The letter was passed over to Marshal Akhromeyev, adviser to the President. Consequently, action followed on his part. Of course, Akhromeyev cited the arguments supporting the Ministry of Defense point of view. The President later called me to say that I was not completely right and that nothing dramatic was in fact going on. I cannot say I reacted quietly and took no offense. This was a major fundamental issue in terms of what we should do and what our future attitudes would be. Whether we would henceforth be guided by new principles which had been quite helpful in looking for major solutions. Or else, whether we would keep playing tricks and manipulating as we did back in the good old times. Who outsmarts whom? I thought we had done away with this rotten old practice, but this time I met with failure, to put it bluntly. We have gained exactly nothing as a result; it was a net loss.

B. Pyadyshev. At the 45th session of the United Nations General Assembly in September 1990, the final words of your address—this is a surmise, of course—sounded like a farewell to your colleagues, the foreign ministers of other states with whom you had met in five General Assembly sessions.

Were you really thinking of abandoning foreign politics back in September 1990?

E. Shevardnadze. Actually, the idea did cross my mind. As you know, in 1989 units of the armed forces dispersed a people's demonstration in Tbilisi, Georgia, and killed about twenty citizens. The affair in Tbilisi came up at the Congress of People's Deputies shortly thereafter. I can never accept dishonesty. We had done a great deal to establish high standards of morality in politics, and I cannot come to terms with any other approach.

This is how it was all orchestrated. We had come to an agreement that Anatoli Sobchak, who headed a parliamentary team investigating the circumstances of the event, would present his findings. Sobchak had everybody's prior agreement to the main points of the report. It was decided that there would be no debate, but a resolution would be adopted containing the assessments and everything else. They asked for my opinion, and I endorsed that approach. After Sobchak had spoken, suddenly the chairman of the USSR Supreme Soviet, A. Lukyanov, gave the floor to the military procurator Katusyev. It came as a complete surprise to me. After all, we had agreed that nobody would take the floor. Well, Katusyev went to the rostrum and read out what sounded like a guilty verdict to the people. I was alarmed, because I had promised to the the people who had ended a protest action and returned to their studies that there would be a fair and objective inquiry.

There was a stir, an outrage and bitterness, because what Katusyev was saying did not correspond to the reality and contradicted the statement made by Anatoli Sobchak on behalf of the parliamentary team.

Then we all gave our accounts, including Gorbachev and other Politbureau members, which caused a bit of a row. I insisted that Lukyanov give me the floor. A delegation left the room, then another and another. I remember Boris Yeltsin rising, all the intellectuals rising, to protest against the report. As it happened, they did not give me the floor.

It was then that I left the Congress to dictate a letter to Mikhail Gorbachev later that evening. He phoned me a number of times, and we had a meeting later. The conflict was settled somehow or other. The Congress adopted a resolution which was a fair one. Still, I had some misgivings even then. It occurred to me that somebody must have been up to something if a thing like that should happen after an agreement had been reached at all levels, with republics, the military, etc. Why would anyone want to do a thing like that?

I saw it as a provocation and a conservative backlash. The provocative report brought the house down, drawing resounding applause and a show of support from many of those present, including members of the government. This made me wonder who those people actually were.

As for my address before the General Assembly to which you referred, it did contain some elements I had worked out with my aides during a brief vacation. It did in a way suggest that it was going to be my last statement there as foreign minister.

B. Pyadyshev. What is your attitude in cases when somebody is labeled "an enemy of the people," as it was done in respect to you and some other Georgian leaders by the president of Georgia, Zviad Gamsakhurdia, in September 1990?

E. Shevardnadze. I cannot accept the use of force against people. I just cannot. This, you may recall, was the attitude I expressed in relation to Tbilisi and to other occasions when force was used, military force in particular. I deplored the decision to send in army vehicles when the Congress was in session. I compared the events that occurred in Tbilisi in the first week of September with what happened there on April 9, 1989, when the decision to use force was taken by the armed forces commander in Trans-Caucausia. The second time it was done by a democratically elected government, which makes it a setback for democracy, which is even worse. It was an actual treason committed under the guise of democracy and humanism. The government had no right to fire on its own people. As to being called "an enemy of the republic" or "an enemy of the people," similar labels have been stuck in the past on a good many authors, artists, and politicians. Incidentally, I was remembering it just yesterday, and I don't think those people are bad company.

B. Pyadyshev. That group of people whom President Gamsakhurdia has denounced as "enemies of the people" includes Zurab Tsereteli, a famous sculptor, who created the monument *Good Defeats Evil* in the United Nations park in New York.

E. Shevardnadze. Yes, Tsereteli is one of them. There are people who must have an enemy image. And once an enemy is there, it gives them reason enough to shoot, destroy, or incarcerate other people. Communists used to believe that if a real threat does not exist, it must be invented. Now that we are building a democracy, those who are out looking for enemies are committing a crime.

The Military, the KGB, The Party Apparatus

B. Pyadyshev. When we flew to New York in September 1990 to attend the 45th General Assembly, I remember you came out several times to join your "team" in our area of the plane. On the evening before our departure, top-ranking military commanders who attended a Kremlin conference took an uncompromising stance on a number of issues which, if left unresolved, could make it impossible to proceed toward the Conventional Forces in Europe (CFE) Treaty, and, hence, the summit for the Conference on Security and Cooperation in Europe (CSCE) scheduled for November. It was apparent that you were upset over the attitude adopted by the generals and marshals.

What were your relations with the leadership of the Ministry of Defense and military–industrial complex and, in a broader sense, between diplomatic and military circles?

E. Shevardnadze. Maybe one example shows the way it was. The delegation received instructions according to the established order. These instructions did not allow our delegation at the final stage of negotiations to solve the major issues; e.g., aviation, etc. The Military and Industrial Commission headed by Lev Zaikov was of great help to me. The commission consisted of high-ranking representatives of the defense ministry, the KGB, foreign ministry, and ministers involved in military production. Though some questions in this commission were not solved, I had an agreement that when I went to negotiate with Mr. Baker or others, I would send to this commission, on the basis of preliminary agreement, information or an explanation of my position.

The commission would quickly hold a meeting, and if possible, make a decision. That time I had an agreement with Mikhail Sergeyevich. I told him that the instructions I had been given would not permit us to get any results. There was no solution. Then we agreed on my sending a telegram to Zaikov, who would report to him, and, if necessary, the President would become involved and would help me.

There were solutions on five to six key issues. I sent a telegram that the old position was not acceptable and not conducive to the solution but it was vital for us to conclude this treaty and reach parity reductions. I told them I would make my own decision if there were no new instructions. That was the way I acted sometimes on certain key issues, and it was quite daring.

One can find these telegrams. I wrote in them that, in my opinion, it was an absolutely right option concerning our national interests and those of security and that it was the right way to act. In this situation the question was like that. As for the relationship with the Ministry of Defense, it was not easy. I was always surprised at the narrow-mindedness of some of the people working in contact with us. I don't want to hurt anybody. For example, we worked together with presidential adviser Marshal Akhromeyev on the treaty over the reduction of conventional armed forces in Europe, and he was often helpful. But there were other people who did not realize the overall trend, that we could not remain a militarized state, that we were not able to endure it, and that we were devastating the country. For decades we have truly been the most militarized country, with enormous expenditures, gigantic armed forces. We needed to take the initiative to cut arms and armed forces and, consequently, spending on a mutual basis. This most important point was not understood. Our military always disputed why we should cut, for instance, by ten or sixteen units more than the Americans.

However, the point was to stop an arms race. Indeed, in some types of armaments the Americans were ahead. But if there were no treaty, it would be impossible to stop the Americans. We, therefore, considered that they might sometimes, preserve certain superiority since we also had some guarantees of security. But many of the military did not understand this obvious truth. There were some debates conducted by Zaikov's commission that proved useful. We democrats tried to come to terms but often did not succeed. That resulted in real tension. When new people chanced to observe our meetings, they saw that not everything ran smoothly.

B. Pyadyshev. As far as I remember, the Foreign Ministry Board chaired by you discussed at one of the meetings a question concerning the fate of two young diplomats from one of our Western European embassies who were engaged in unpermitted commercial business. The first one was punished while the second turned out to be a "neighbor" from the KGB. He was reprimanded by his superiors, and he continued his service "under the roof" of the embassy.

Now, the issue of the excessive number of KGB agents working in various ministries and missions is widely discussed. The issue directly concerns the Ministry of Foreign Affairs. In your opinion, how detrimental is this practice for external policy?

E. Shevardnadze. I have always felt deep concern about this issue. I thought and considered a lot and tried to find the way out. As for concrete, specific facts and situations, I have to admit that I didn't probably follow the right principles till the very end. From the global point of view, I was thinking a lot, making plans to find the right moment to discuss the issue in principle with our foreign partners, in particular with U.S. Secretary of State Baker.

It is no secret that U.S. intelligence also operates under the roof of embassies; we are not the only ones. As to who has more agents, that is another question. The proportions typical for our corps are unacceptable, an anachronism. It is necessary to introduce proper order here. I meant to organize a meeting with Mr. Baker, a special one as we had on Lake Baikal. The environment itself made it possible to discuss many issues that could not be raised earlier.

I wanted to touch on this point. Today the excessive penetration of foreign policy by the KGB raises an atmosphere of suspicion. We have opened cities, enterprises, and plants. Although we and the Americans are controlling now what were top secrets in the past, the world has not collapsed. Everything goes well.

If we say that we are not enemies, that we are not going to fight, then why can't we make it clear? Let's set an example for the entire world. You need intelligence and information that diplomats are unable to provide. We also are in need of this. So let's come to terms on this issue. Everything is known: The Americans are quite aware of who is a diplomat and who works for the KGB. And they know these people in person. We also know everything about everybody; e.g., this one is a diplomat and that one is an intelligence officer. It's a game. We have reached a completely new level. I suggest as an experiment opening not just our strong boxes but certain files. Let's disclose them and say to each other honestly: here are five, they are from our intelligence service. Intelligence is required to obtain information and to lower risk. I made an attempt to do so, and now I want to raise this issue again.

Look how much trouble we had with the British! Our relations were disrupted in 1971 and again after that. I had a lot of trouble, too, with the Americans. Big problems. I think it is time to discuss the point seriously. This issue might even be appropriate for the Security Council, for the United Nations. It is possible to prepare a convention on condition of openness. Everybody wants to have such information. It is also necessary to think over the information itself, its volume and its orientation. Nowadays the mass media is so open and capable that the press and television penetrate all fields of life.

What do many intelligence agents do? They rewrite news from the latest issues and send reports. We need some classified information but not in such volume. Are we really in need of such intelligence? I would put this question up for discussion and consideration if we are talking about a new world and the establishment of a new world order. I realize that it might cause a stormy negative reaction now. Again, there will be malicious attacks, but who cares?

B. Pyadyshev. Do you think that the number of intelligence officers in the Ministry of Foreign Affairs headquarters and abroad has increased during the last fives years?

E. Shevardnadze. I cannot talk of any increase. But the number has not diminished. Nobody raised this issue. As for the headquarters, I have no idea who is who, because, in the case of a skilled official, I consider him to be a diplomat. Whether he serves for the KGB or any other organization, I do not know. I have not met any official in Moscow representing state security who would not fit his diplomatic post professionally. As for the embassies there, I saw at once who was who. When the minister arrives, the chief of the resident network naturally comes to report. As for the rest, even minor KGB officials, I also recognize them. Once you talk to any one of them, you know immediately he is not on diplomatic service.

B. Pyadyshev. There is one more category of people in diplomatic service. It is clear now that what we once considered to be a virtue— the appointment as ambassadors of party leaders who failed in their previous work—proved to be a disaster, especially in relationships with socialist countries. Till the very last days there were efforts to appoint to diplomatic services high-ranking party or state officials. There are more than enough such examples. The practice is a target of pointed public remarks that range from irony to indignation. Eventually it throws a shadow on the whole diplomatic service. So, isn't the diplomatic service capable of functioning even if it is fully manned only by professional diplomats?

E. Shevardnadze. In general, that is typical for any state. For example, there is no lack of these kinds of diplomats in the United States. The American ambassador now working in Moscow has never been engaged in diplomacy. He is a politician, a big businessman, and a specialist in economics. In my view he is a right choice. Today these are the problems which are most urgent. I mean investments and business. So what? Do we criticize the White House decision? I think they made the right one.

Another problem seemed to me a sort of distortion, especially in the first year, when I did not know and did not understand everything. For example: An ambassador to a socialist country should only be a party official. I have no question about assigning party officials to such work. There are no doubts here.

Another question concerns making an appointment after a person is retired or fired. When this was done on a massive scale and when only regional and republic central committees' party secretaries were sent to socialist countries, it proved most unfortunate. It was not because they missed some processes in those countries. The right information was coming from the intelligence officers as well as from the ambassadors.

But the truth is different. We probably came to a conclusion that we did not need professionals in those countries—that they were almost our Union republics, so let a person go there and work. Unfortunately, many of those party officials were in the habit of commanding, administering, and giving orders. The practice and habits they acquired in our country while administering the largest party organizations and ministries were automatically transferred to diplomacy.

For instance, they rarely visited the ministries of foreign affairs in the host countries. Almost every day they visited the general secretaries, and they considered everyone else of minor importance. That was establishing their arrogance of power.

It Will Be a Different Civilization

B. Pyadyshev. Eduard Amvrosiyevich, since you have a firmly established reputation of man who is capable of predicting future events quite precisely, let us try to imagine that we meet in ten years, in 2001. What kind of country and what society shall we have, based in particular on decisions made by the Congress of People's Deputies, in September 1991?

E. Shevardnadze. I think it will be a different civilization. And not only here within the present Union. It will be a virtually new civilization in general, on a global scale. I am certain the new world order will be firmly established. The world will become governable. This will be possible if we succeed in enhancing the prestige of the United Nations.

As for the Soviet Union, naturally there will be no return to the past. I think a single economic space, a single military and strategic space, a single democratic space will develop. I mean both those republics that will and will not be in the Union. For some regions the Union is an indispensable component of this progress. Therefore, we may speak of a single space over the entire territory of the Soviet Union.

Coordinated action in the international arena will also be retained, I am sure. This is quite sufficient for good cooperation. Whether it will be named a union or a commonwealth is not a matter of principle.

I believe, on September 5, 1991, the Congress of the USSR People's Deputies adopted fundamental documents which already serve as a good basis for enabling us to build jointly in a foreseeable future a new commonwealth, a new Union.

Now the development of sovereignty and independence of states, republics, is charged with emotion; there is to much euphoria, too much naïveté. But let time pass and we shall see that people think in a different way. They will realize that integration is vital. Integration is a necessity, a regularity of human development in present circumstances. This new tendency will become determinative. I believe, in the twenty-first century, as you have indicated, in 2001, we shall see a different world.

But what our country will be, whether we shall have socialism or capitalism or something else, is hard to say. We are again trying to use traditional, even dogmatic, ways to define and name that new society. This will be a synthesis of everything that human civilization has accumulated, of all progressive and positive experience. All republics, and our country as a whole, must take from capitalism all that is rational in it, such as the market economy. We have come to this very late. Where shall we obtain all this? Naturally, from developed countries themselves. They have great and unique experience. Take, for instance, the ownership of property. We were afraid of it and now we are convinced that this, together with many things, is central to human development.

The world will change. There will be fewer secrets of all sorts. Fewer secrets mean that countries will be able to exchange more freely the potential they have accumulated. There are tremendous intellectual potentials and achievements in science and technology. In fact, we are at the threshold of a new revolution in technology, one that knows no bounds, in a single space of knowledge and progress. I don't think this is all fantasy.

I Do Not Presage Elimination of the Center

B. Pyadyshev. What will happen to foreign policy?

E. Shevardnadze. I do not presage elimination of the center. It will be retained. Everyone is interested in it. Naturally it will deal more with coordination, the harmonization of efforts to solve major issues, including those in the realm of foreign policies.

Speaking about the role of the United Nations, when all republics become its members, must we lose our position in the Security Council? The role of the Security Council as a guarantor of stability in the world is growing. Mechanisms will be developed—you know my views on this—and the Union will necessarily preserve its position in the Security Council as a permanent member. Major problems, everything related to stability, will be dealt with by the Security Council. Republics will be interested in coordinating their efforts themselves and not in coordinating their activities through the Ministry of Foreign Affairs of the Union.

I believe we have to think seriously to ensure that external economic and political activities are coordinated by the center. I do not know whether this will be a ministry of foreign affairs, a committee, or something else. All the problems—economic and political—are so interrelated that it is difficult to say what is politics and what is economic. Therefore, I believe that the center's function—to coordinate these basic spheres of activity—will become increasingly prominent and indispensable for the republics.

B. Pyadyshev. The situation in our country is unique at present. We have neither a multiparty system, nor do we have a more-or-less influential party. Perhaps no normal country in the world is facing such a situation. The CPSU has disintegrated; other parties are still coming into being. And how can we imagine a political life without a party? What do you think are the ways of forming a multiparty system? And what are the prospects of your movement?

E. Shevardnadze. I believe that today we are going through a rather dangerous stage of evolution of the entire society. The fact that the CPSU is virtually not functioning now poses a challenge to fill this space. The CPSU—one can consider it good or bad, and in many cases it was actually bad—served as a guarantor of stability. The ongoing process of ending the party's rule is correct. Placing the CPSU activities, if any, within certain limits is a correct idea as well. However, I'm concerned about the lack of some strong political mechanisms which would guarantee stability.

We place our high hopes on the Democratic Reform Movement in this regard, and we do not discard the possibility of forming a party at this very moment. We have to make our choice. This new party is a must. By saying this I refer to electoral campaigns, elections of the President and other positions. The party is needed at a republican as well as a regional level, but it should operate only within the framework of the movement. The movement has to be preserved. This institutional structure allows us to cooperate with all the parties and democratic forces here and locally. We'll elaborate upon this theme at a congress.

B. Pyadyshev. Eduard Amvrosiyevich, don't you feel a kind of nostalgia for foreign policy activities and for the world diplomatic community, whose life was so closely connected with yours?

E. Shevardnadze. My present status—I'm talking about our movement and the Foreign Policy Association—allows me to maintain close contacts with all my colleagues. New people have entered the political scene. Active involvement in the movement and party activities will make it possible for me to establish contacts not only with diplomats, but also with newcomers representing political parties in various regions of the country. This is highly interesting work.

As for the nostalgia, I have no such feeling for the post or social status. That's not a problem for me.

I would like to further these contacts, these really unprecedented relations, which have been established. This is a wide circle of highly responsible and interesting people, many of them unique. Preserving these relations for establishing a new world order is what I actually dream about. So far, my mission has been a success.

I received numerous telephone calls during those tense days [of August]. I was at my office on Smolenskaya Square. I answered calls from Secretary Baker, German Foreign Minister Genscher, Prime Minister Major, French Foreign Minister Dumas, and many others. They all expressed support. George Shultz sent me a cable, anticipating acts of violence here. He informed me that I could expect a very high position at Stanford University with guarantees of residence and all other things. He showed touching consideration for me. Just a few years ago we were considered potential military opponents, but our current relations are unique.

Mr. Baker and his wife called me very late at night from Wyoming, speaking with me and my wife. I think much about the ways of preserving these relations for our children and for the coming generation.

B. Pyadyshev. At the Foreign Ministry on Smolenskaya Square a spontaneous movement has emerged to have you returned as foreign minister. What was your reaction to that?

E. Shevardnadze. I was deeply touched and moved by the attitude of the staff, of those whom I love and consider extremely talented.

I simply love this staff, and I've never been let down by any one of them. That's why I couldn't remain indifferent. Naturally, when the petition was received, I gave no clear-cut answer, although earlier I had stated that my return was out of the question. I told the delegation that I wasn't ready yet and that I had to think it all over. For me it would be a difficult move; that's why you should understand that I can't give any guarantees or promises.

I've reacted positively to the appointment of Boris Pankin to the post of the USSR Foreign Minister, because I've known him for a long time. But the present situation is complex, and he'll have a hard time facing problems. However, his potential, overall vision, his experience in the Soviet Union, governmental structures and diplomatic fields, enable him to be a good minister—if only the internal situation allows him to realize his plans and to work with the staff.

By the way, I feel that the assessment of Alexander Bessmertnkyh's work and the shameless attitude toward him are not justified. As for the grudges against him, as a minister, that's another matter. I can't touch upon it. I haven't found anything in his actions that wouldn't entitle him to work in the ministry. He acted courageously and refused to be a member of that committee, although his refusal could have a very negative personal impact on him. These are just my feelings. I have respect for both Boris Pankin and Bessmertnykh.

As for the staff members, I hold them in profound respect. For example, a totally inexperienced man comes in, and thanks to his staff, they manage to do a lot. Now they are not "visible" (due to the nature of the work) and are busy working out suggestions and ideas. And after that either the minister or the president, or someone else, will use the results of their work. We forget very often that the ideas and new thinking recognized all over the world are largely due to the efforts of this staff.

B. Pyadyshev. Eduard Amvrosiyevich, you were the "godfather" of *Mezhdunarodnaya Zhysn (International Affairs)* in its new form. At the very end of 1987 the Politbureau complied with the request of Andrei Gromyko (then the chairman of the USSR Supreme Soviet) and relieved him of his duties as the chief editor of *Mz* which he had fulfilled for three decades.

E. Shevardnadze. I keep a close eye on the journal. In my opinion, it has now achieved world standards. Its articles of in-depth thinking, originality, and analysis of problems typify a well-regarded journal. The journal has become one of the pilots of perestroika journalism in the intellectual pool we're swimming in. It may be considered a reference point in foreign policy and international affairs. Of late I know it is respected in foreign countries.

Considering the problems of the Union and its republics, republics and external policy, I would place these issues in the forefront. We must ensure that this process goes on smoothly. We should prevent competition between the Union's Ministry of Foreign Affairs (or any other body which may be established) and the republics, between the center and the sovereign constituent parts. It's very important to define the attitude toward those republics which would not form part of the new entity. We must not lose anything that linked us together in the best sense of the word. It's true that these are internal problems, but without solving them we cannot safely and constructively enter the international arena.

PART I

Perestroika: From 1985 to the Present

Introduction to Part I

As the new leadership headed by Mikhail Gorbachev came to power in the Soviet Union early in 1985, the nation's foreign policy was in a very difficult situation. The USSR was disproportionately burdened with involvement in an arms race and regional conflicts, its foreign policy lines crossing nearly all continents and oceans. Foreign affairs were consuming almost half of the national budget, their dynamics and orientation giving no promise of allocating more resources to peaceful development, to raising living standards, or to providing favorable and tranquil ambience.

Of course, some partial alterations could have been made in [Soviet] foreign policy. However, those would hardly have helped perestroika. The Gorbachev leadership opted for a radical change in the very concept of foreign policy thinking, and undertook forceful revision of traditional approaches to international affairs, taking specific and innovative steps which have substantially improved the USSR's international positions and added to its authority and prestige. New political thinking in the USSR foreign policy foundation offered quite a few ideas to indicate a clear-cut break with the policy postulates of all the preceding leaders of the Soviet Union. The heart of [this] new thinking was affirmation that human values stood supreme to the interests of classes, social movements, and groups. Advancement of this concept meant very much for all the Soviet society because it raised its hand against the "holy of holies" of the Marxist–Leninist ideology— the idea of class struggle being unavoidable and

3

eternal, with all aspirations and potential of the Soviet people and their allies being subjugated to it. There is every reason to state that a real turnabout has taken place in the outlook of the Soviet leadership and Soviet society. Some did not agree with nor accept the idea of primacy of human values. Nevertheless, the idea has been realized steadfastly and persistently through concrete effort and action in the international area.

New political thinking has yielded positive results. The Soviet Union has substantially improved its position in the world. It is party to no conflict, and no state is threatening the Soviet Union. Important progress has been made in the bilateral relations with the United States and other nations of the West.

—BORIS PYADYSHEV

What Is Our Society Today?

Alexander Bessmertnykh

I attached special importance to a thought which may have no direct relation to foreign policy, one concerning our economy. We still have no strategy for raising our economy to an up-to-date scientific and technological level. We must solve primarily our economic problems if perestroika is to go on. Yet we are still wandering in a maze of formulas, which are pretty old to boot. Take, for instance, the main functional echelons of our economy—say, the State Committee on Supplies. There were analogues to it in ancient Egypt. *Khozraschet* is the first, initial phase of medieval production, with the producer allowed to keep part of the output. This is not quite what we need. It

ALEXANDER BESSMERTNYKH was USSR Minister of Foreign Affairs from January to August 1991. Before this assignment he was Ambassador to the United States. This article was written in 1989 when Bessmertnykh held the office of first deputy Foreign Minister of the USSR.

alone would hardly be enough for us to attain a higher level of scientific and technological progress.

And so it seems to me that it would be very useful for us all to concern ourselves with these problems as much as possible. A recent all-Union opinion poll brought out the interesting fact that those polled on international problems were particularly keen on world economic relations. After that came disarmament and other problems. Nowadays you can't be a diplomat at all without taking an interest in economics. Speaking of the lever that could get our economy going, I'm sure we need a thoroughly thought-out concept of development. To make the economy work, we must fit everything in with a strictly calculated scientific concept. It's no exaggeration to say that science must play a historic role. But there is no concept, and nobody is really evolving it. We have excellent economic analysts. They pose questions, criticize the past, and reveal some information unknown to us before. But no one or hardly any one of them has produced anything real, except maybe for some isolated proposals. Yet we need an integral concept. To bring it into being, we must first know exactly what stage of development our society has reached. Indeed, what is this stage? And then, what is our society today?

Stupendous processes are taking place in the world economy. The two systems are moving in roughly one and the same direction, strange as it may seem. In the West, private property in its time-honored sense is disappearing under our very eyes. It's becoming cooperative, or rather corporative, since I am speaking of the West. Private property in its pure form as defined by Marxism is disappearing. The stock exchange is undergoing a transformation. Incidentally, the Americans keep a secret of this, but they are restructuring economic management through the stock exchange. They want to set up by means of an electronic stock exchange something of a guaranteed incomes distribution system. And this means creating a different society.

Generally speaking, the capitalist sphere encompasses economies and types of economic management developing in dissimilar ways. There is one type in the United States and an entirely different one in Japan, where an economy of a preset quality is emerging for the first time in history. And it's interesting to note that Western societies are analyzing themselves. Please note that ever since the seventies, nearly all Western studies of the United States have been withheld from the public. You will recall how many books there were before, such as structural or systems analyses. They used to disclose everything. Subsequently all that disappeared. It's because a struggle is on, an immense contest between Japan and the United States, except that the arena isn't trade. The tension field lies at a higher level. The economy is becoming global, and a battle is being fought to gain control of it.

We, too, should analyze ourselves. Why, we hardly know where we stand. We know it in simple State Planning Committee terms, that's all. Everything was clear until recently—we said ours was a society of developed socialism. This was like a passport. But now it's been taken away. As far as world socioeconomic development is concerned, we've become tramps having no papers.

To be sure, it's clear that ours is a socialist country building scientific socialism. But how far have we come? Could it be that on reaching a certain turning point, we accidentally struck out in a direction leading to a dead end? We are now talking of the need to return to the original source, but when did we abandon it? Was it in the 1917–1918 period, the twenties or the thirties? And then, would it be right to revert to the twenties even though the new economic policy is so attractive? After all, our productive forces have grown tremendously in spite of difficulties. Our country is a strong productive power. We were developing our productive forces but their further growth was checked by imperfect economic relations. This explains the "slippage." Its inherent cause is our bid to create a "pure" economic formation of the laboratory type. Yet there can be no such thing. Neither Lenin nor Marx ever spoke about it.

I think we should use the level attained by the productive forces and change the form of our economic management conceptually. Our economic system is now unreceptive to scientific and technological progress, which it doesn't see as a vital necessity. Yet it's imperative that the economy require progress like oxygen. That's the road to a boom. We cannot join directly in the world economy right now. Even if all international organizations were to open their doors and even windows to us, we would still be unable to get in. We are not prepared for that just yet. As it happens, the cogwheels of the world economy are turning and so are those of our economy, but trade is the only area where they interlock.

At a recent conference I heard the phrase "the socialist quality of commodities." I was amazed. We rightly say "the socialist economy" and "the capitalist economy." But what's socialist in it and what is universal? Can there be an industry whose output is "socialist" in quality and another whose products are "capitalist"? I suppose the difference between capitalist and socialist factors lies in the sphere of control over production and the sphere of distribution of the output. That is where the difference comes out. But what if our machine tools are inferior in quality to those made in the West, yet, they meet our standards? Can we flatter ourselves that they're all right because their "socialist" quality is high? If we do so we'll get completely mixed up and fall still farther behind.

We also hear phrases like "the socialist market" and "the capitalist market." Why not say simply "the market," meaning the system through which commodities must pass to take on a value? Because unless they take on a value we won't know their price. At this point we must ask ourselves whether we in the Soviet Union have money in its Marxian sense. Could what we have be paper symbols that don't reflect value? These are the questions we should begin with. We need to develop banking and finance which are the lifeblood of the economic organism.

Speaking of our relations with the international financial circles in broader terms, we're badly in need of a strategy for using credits. People in our country are now saying we must not get into debt. But we cannot advance our economy without investing more. In West and East alike, nearly everything begins with credits. Then comes a powerful up-to-date technology, powerful up-to-date production, and the credits are gradually repaid. But there's a danger. To repay your debts, you must achieve a major breakthrough in economic and technological development. This was done by Japan and by "four tiger cubs" in Asia. Turkey is doing it, too. We must study more carefully their experience of making effective use of credits.

But to return to the question of integration into the world economy. Our relations with it are very primitive at the moment. We supply raw materials and purchase goods of middling quality. Moreover, we're witnessing many strange things. We say we are going to establish up-to-date joint ventures with the West. We expect them to be geared to supplying the foreign market so as to earn us hard currency. This seems logical at first sight. But what do we need hard currency for? If there is a joint venture whose output meets world standards, why not sell its products on our starving market? I know that to repay the investment made by the Western partner, we must sell part of the output on the world market, but we should not ignore our home market, either. Yet some of our economists complicate things. They set up a company to supply the foreign market, sell the West first-class products meeting world standards, earn hard currency and, yes, buy products of middling quality. Do they really imagine that Soviet people are not mature enough to buy goods of high quality?

I believe the principal achievement of Soviet foreign policy is that in this period of perestroika we are doing our best to provide favorable external conditions for it. Indeed, should international tension persist, all talk about cutting military budgets, taking unilateral action, or scrapping missiles would be pointless.

From this we should move on to more concrete matters. For example, the abolition of intermediate- and shorter-range missiles is an unquestionable blessing from the point of view of our inner economic development. It is occasionally argued that destroying the missiles is a costly measure. Yes, it is, but I would not exaggerate. Every fifteen to seventeen years, missiles are scrapped anyway, and the budget provides for this. And so while we now spend money on scrapping missiles, we shall begin receiving a net revenue at a later stage, when the scrapping is over and done with. We'll stop spending money on the maintenance of missiles, which in itself is costly. We shall release production capacities used earlier for making these missiles, and so on.

There's another important thing. The fact that we have agreed to abolish certain missiles makes people in our military political sphere wonder whether they should give the go-ahead for anything that comes from designers and inventors. After all, the Americans now have three systems of ICBMs while we have about ten. This doesn't pay because it requires different technologies and different systems of personnel training.

The discontinuance of chemical weapons production is an even greater achievement in terms of profitable policy. The manufacture of chemical weapons does not cost too much money. But storage costs a lot, and besides, it is fraught with damage to the environment.

Lastly, conventional armaments are the costliest of all. We are also cutting expenditures on them.

There is a sphere which we generally do not see as having to do with the economy. I mean international crises and regional conflicts. We help our friends, which is understandable. They need it and ask us for military supplies, nor do we always sell them what they need but let them have it as a gift. It follows that the settlement of regional conflicts would also save resources for our economy.

The main thing is the overall situation—the easing of tensions, plus what I have already pointed out by saying that foreign policy dovetails with economic policy. We also try to help foreign trade. Our embassies supply interesting scientific and technological information and tell us what new discoveries of foreign technology we can use. We send a lot of information: analyses of the economic situation, suggestions concerning the choice of partners, economic surveys of the economies of the countries we do business with. This, too, is direct help from our diplomacy to our economy.

Having made a critical assessment of the forty-year history of our own involvement in the arms race, we have arrived at the conclusion that we took the liberty of surrendering to a predominantly military-strategic vision of world developments and real or spurious threats to the USSR and ways of countering them. The tension that arose in the world almost automatically meant for us at the time that we, like the West, set about forging additional weaponry. And this was repeated until stockpiles were packed high with needed and not always needed weapons, and we became heavily bogged down in the arms race.

Does this mean that our involvement in the arms race at all the postwar stages was equally unnecessary? Was it possible to avert it right from the start? I believe that there is a point in the postwar historical process prior to which we were forced to take part in the arms race for the sake of our security and the survival of socialism.

There was in effect no alternative. The USSR could not but set about the development of atomic weapons at a time when the U.S. atomic monopoly was threatening us with far-reaching military and political consequences. Soviet policy felt the pressure of this monopoly for several years. The appearance, in 1949, of this mass-destruction weaponry in the hands of the USSR was the first rude awakening for the United States, which limited its possibility for blackmail. It made considerable positive changes in the alignment of forces. The events that followed justified this step and ultimately—forty years later—have led to a workable possibility to close the nuclear circle, to fully eliminate nuclear weapons by the twenty-first century.

The decision of the Soviet Union to create and deploy modern strategic delivery vehicles—heavy bombers and intercontinental ballistic missiles (ICBMs)—was just as imperative for military and political strategy considerations as well. The TASS report of August 26, 1958, on the successful testing of a Soviet ICBM evidenced the appearance of a new quality in the Soviet defense potential. The same role was played by the development here in the 1960s of bombers capable of delivering a nuclear strike at U.S. territory.

The emerging vulnerability of American territory for a retaliatory Soviet strike was our second sobering warning to the hotheads in Washington, who, as is evidenced from recently disclosed archives of the late 1940s and early 1950s, were planning a preventive strike against the Soviet Union.

The appearance of new strategic systems in the Soviet armed forces still did not mean in and of itself that the task of ensuring our national security was accomplished, for the question was, what level should they be limited to? What amount could be considered sufficient? An absolute understanding of the belief that this level should be adequate to the American one was particularly manifest in the analysis of the outcome of the Caribbean crisis of 1962, which took place at a time when the United States enjoyed a considerable advantage in strategic offensive weapons. Hence there emerged the USSR's goal of attaining strategic parity which would guarantee it against chance and tragic misunderstanding.

Logically, our involvement in the arms race until strategic parity with the United States was attained was forced and, regrettably, inevitable. However, a question of signal importance arises here: How should it have behaved after the equilibrium was reached?

It can be assumed that the aftermath of the accomplishment of the historic task of creating a strategic balance with the United States in the early 1970s was not analyzed deeply enough from the standpoint of the necessary displacement of the accent on the political possibilities of ensuring national security and lessening world tensions.

The existence of strategic parity has made it senseless to continue the nuclear arms race. And, according to the truly creative conclusions which the Soviet leadership has now arrived at, a further spiraling of nuclear arms can lead to a situation where the safety value of parity will be undermined and at some point in the escalation it will no longer be able to function as a guarantor of strategic stability. For this reason the current task of deep cuts in strategic arms on a mutual basis becoming the key area of foreign policy activity which, while ensuring the USSR's national security, simultaneously promises a consider able saving of resources for an economy undergoing structural reform.

It will be easier to avoid the mesmerizing influence of the total increases of the current strategic arms levels if it is taken into consideration that underlying the sharp spiral in the strategic arms race initiated by the United States in the early 1960s was in essence improvisation and the absence of sufficiently grounded calculations. During the Caribbean crisis the strategic forces of the sides, particularly ICBMs and SLBMs, numbered in the dozens. Then the Kennedy Administration, which imparted the strongest impetus to the strategic arms race, made a decision to deploy 1,000 Minutemen ICBMs and 41 submarines carrying Polaris missiles.

Why 1,000 ICBMs? This question has long bothered me, because the documents, reminiscences, and monographs that have been published do not contain a convincing explanation of the calculations that led to this figure. Three years ago, during a conversation with a close Kennedy adviser who was in Moscow, I asked about the reasons for the decision. Now, after so many years had passed, and no longer feeling bound by security or professional considerations, he related that President Kennedy and Robert McNamara, who was the Defense Secretary at the time, took this as a ballpark figure, without preliminary extensive research at the Pentagon or in the scientific community. Considering that Kennedy had spoken a great deal about the United States lagging behind the USSR, the figure of 1,000 ICBMs looked almost ideal politically, from the standpoint of influencing the public, the former adviser said.

We, too, have progressed toward this figure in developing our strategic forces. There is a great lesson to be derived here. As Confucius said, we cognize wisdom along three paths: reflection, which is the most noble path; imitation, which is the easiest, and experience, which is the most difficult. Has not the easiest road tempted us at times in creating weapons?

Therefore, if our armed forces are to continue being a reliable guarantor of the security of the socialist state and simultaneously promote the country's economic stability and prosperity, we need to carry out a carefully verified analysis and, even better, a reassessment of the cycle "action—reaction—counteraction—action" in our relations with the United States in developing military hardware and determining the structure of armed forces. Strict economic substantiation of decisions in the sphere of arms R&D and production are absolutely imperative as well. (One of Washington's strategic tasks is to wear out the USSR economically, including by imposing upon it—with the aid of bluffs, misinformation and at times even demonstrations of any expensive "example" of military programs, which often lead to technical and strategic deadends). Evidently the time of gigantic figures and "ceilings" on military expenses is passing. Our perestroika is destined—and there is no other alternative—to lead the country onto the road of powerful and rapid development.

The U.S. sector of our foreign policy in comparison with others I call a paradox of the nuclear age. The paradox consists in the fact that most of our external problems have crossed the ocean. I would say that powerful transatlantic arcs of tension have arisen. But now we must find, especially in view of perestroika, a proper combination of our strategic interests, which make us cross oceans, with the everyday interests of our economy. To this end we must consolidate our relations with all countries, primarily neighbors. I think we should build up around the Soviet Union a dependable system of economic cooperation, friendship, and security. We will have to think over many things but I believe it's worthwhile.

One last question: How can the duration of the time-limit history allocated us for perestroika be predicted correctly? Do we have much or little time? The answer requires a detailed and careful weighing of the internal and external factors. For now, let us heed the parable from Francis Bacon's *New Atlantis*. I knew a wise man, it said, who used to say when he saw excessive haste: "Wait a little in order to finish faster."

Personal Security: The Top Priority

Yuri Ryzhov

If we are to talk about security on the whole, it should be structured according to the following hierarchy: security of the individual, security of society, and security of the state; state security is here because it will be able to ensure the first two tasks. In this country, the pyramid was turned upside down. It was important to protect the state and the structures in the state that administered it. The former was guarded by an enormous mass of troops and weaponry, and the latter, with the aid of the KGB. That, in effect, was our entire security.

The fear has been far from surmounted, and the word KGB still sends shivers down people's spines. Now people are beginning to

Academician YURI RYZHOV is People's Deputy of the USSR, chairman of the Scientific Committee of the USSR Supreme Soviet, and rector of the Moscow Aviation Institute.

allege that the army's image is breaking down in our consciousness and that our fine KGB officers are coming in for harsh criticism. It is not the KGB per se that is being lambasted but the fear associated with it. If we manage to overcome this fear and draw on democratic legal norms, then we will have a chance to become a civil state.

In the current conditions, the main threat to the country's national security is not external (from the United States and NATO), but internal—as a result of the political fragmentation of society, the exacerbation of national problems, and the sluggishness of the economic reforms.

It is for this reason that it is vitally imperative for us to lessen the military rivalry with the West in order to concentrate on our urgent domestic matters. The strategic arms that we have stockpiled will be sufficient for us to preserve until the beginning of the twenty-first century our status as a superpower and neutralize an external menace.

The optimal strategy of domestic reforms should combine a transition to market relations with sweeping conversion (not diversification) of the defense industry. Otherwise we will keep the most developed branches of our science and engineering outside the market framework, and having wasted the potential amassed in the defense industry, we will fail to spur on scientific advances in the civilian economy.

We should constantly raise before the American side the issue of joint or parallel measures to dismantle the material base of military confrontation and rechannel the resources released into purely civilian goals. Such an approach could include a coordinated reduction of the military budgets of the USSR and the United States, exchange of experience and plans for defense industry conversion, the establishment of joint ventures in a number of areas, joint study of technical matters pertaining to the retooling of production lines to production exclusively of civilian output, and ecological orientation of conversion.

Such a package would make it possible to approach, at least somewhat, a solution to a number of other problems in ensuring the nation's security.

For one thing, this is movement toward overcoming the USSR's isolation from the world market. This variant would open the way toward the development of normal trade ties. At the same time we would be able to avoid the typical mistake of concentrating on the development of our own production of obsolete everyday goods, which could not be turned out for several years, when the technology being used became hopelessly outmoded. That is, it would be possible to skip a generation of the pertinent technology by placing the emphasis on promising research and development that would enable us to assume a worthy place on the world market. This would also promote the country's economic security.

For another, the package would enable us to make a breakthrough to a new understanding of the USSR's information security. This approach will above all be conducive to a breakdown of the "domestic" COCOM and tear down the barriers for a transfusion of technology from the military sphere to the civilian one. This will also affect the external COCOM, promoting as it does our country's integration into the international information system.

Generally speaking, the main danger being posed to peace today is the excessive stockpiling of nuclear weapons. The probability of unsanctioned start-up of materiel, in particular, nuclear, is all the higher if, first, there is more materiel, and second, if much time has elapsed since it was produced. Therefore, the less weaponry there is in the world the newer and more qualitative it will be, provided the old weapons are destroyed, and the less probability there will be of a disaster occurring by chance.

Furthermore, the problem of the substantial number of nuclear power stations on the planet is an extremely acute one. They are potentially very dangerous nuclear bombs, especially if they are attended incompetently. We still do not realize the extent of this danger, hoping that the Chernobyl disaster was a chance occurrence. And then there are the highly powerful and concentrated chemical plants, which are no less dangerous than Chernobyl in terms of the consequences of the ecological or direct toxic action of people and entire areas. Like nuclear power stations, these plants are like Chernobyls scattered throughout the country. In the context of mounting international terrorism and domestic crime, they are doubly dangerous since they can be an object of blackmail or an attack. Today people threaten to blow up airplanes with bags if the course is not changed, and tomorrow some three persons may come to a nuclear power station or chemical plant and say: "We'll blow it up if. . ." What are we going to do then?

International cooperation, a sort of global monitoring, is no less important in this sphere than in the fight against the narcotics mafia.

We Are Living in a Wartime Economy

As a result of a distorted notion of security this country is being ruined in such proportions that even I, a person somehow associated with the defense industry, was astonished when I learned several figures during my work in the USSR Supreme Soviet. It has been officially stated that our military budget for 1990 is 70,900 million rubles. Through simple arithmetical computations I arrived at 300,000 million rubles. Several basic figures earlier published in the central press were sufficient for making estimations, just as it is possible to establish a function from its values on several points.

Among other things, the report that has appeared here and there about the cost of military property in the Baltic Military District applies to these figures.

Thus, according to my estimates, the Soviet military budget was close to 300,000 million rubles. For greater certainty, I culled 100,000 million and named the figure of 200,000 million in an article. And no one debated me.

After President Mikhail Gorbachev touched upon this issue in a speech in Sverdlovsk, I went over to him and thanked him. "What for?" he asked. "For your having supported me and assessed our military expenditures at 18 percent. This is much closer to my figure than to the one which was almost unanimously maintained by our parliament—70,900 million rubles," I replied. In the Supreme Soviet we called the attention of USSR Finance Minister V. Pavlov to the fact that he was vague regarding items very strangely called "other measures." For this year they comprise a whopping 33,000 million rubles. These expenditures increased by 11,000 million as compared to 1989. I asked the minister to decipher this figure, and he sent me a paper stamped "top secret," which I could not use at all. I asked him the same question when he was at the rostrum, and he immediately began listing what he had written on that paper. I asked him: "Is this paper therefore not classified, and can be used openly?" He replied, "yes," and promised to send an "open" text. However, he sent it with a list of the items, but without a single figure.

What does this bespeak? The fact that the parliament cannot see the entire budget item by item. That is, it has an opportunity to see something, but this is largely a fake. Therefore, executive power can hoodwink the legislative branch. And not only because it seeks to do so. I think that in many instances our executive power simply does not know the actual figures. Just as—I am absolutely certain of this— our military department does not known how many, say, Kalashnikov submachine guns or hand grenades there are in this country. Ownerless warehouses and freight carriages are being discovered where thousands of units of ammunition lie and are being stolen.

I realize, of course, that there are formidable social problems involved in reducing the army and arms production. What is to happen to the officers, how are we to convert enterprises of the military complex, where are we to find the money for conversion, etc.? But we should not lie either. The parliament does not dispose of truthful information. On one hand, the bodies of executive power can deceive all they want. On the other, given the chaotic state of accounting and the financial system, the executive arm does not have the real figures. All this is one of the prerequisites for considering what defense sufficiency actually is in the context of new political thinking. What are we going to do with these thousands of millions that are being spent god knows how? And not only with the thousands of millions but also with the enormous material resources which are going god knows where? According to some estimates, half of our industry works for the military sector. This is unthinkable! We are living not merely in a military economy but in a wartime economy where everything that the military demand—money, manpower, resources, material, etc.—is given to them. Everything that is limited in this country is procured in the civilian sector with great difficulty, or is out of reach altogether, but everything is unconditionally given to the military, even in peacetime.

It was in these conditions that our deputies—enthusiasts, including military officers, but not with high general ranks, and also economists and other experts, exhibited a desire to understand what defensive sufficiency is in the context of new political thinking—how much we need in the defense sphere, and what national security is after all. This past February we prepared a study; President Gorbachev supported it, saying that a working group of deputies had to be formed to elaborate this concept, an expert commission gathered, etc. We continued our work and prepared a fifteen page draft substantiating the need for and outlines of a comprehensive concept of national security. Two months later, an official order to establish a seventeen person working group of people's deputies headed by Ryzhkov was signed. In addition, we already had at our disposal several dozen experts—representatives of a wide range of institutions—people from the Ministry of Defence, the KGB, the Institute of the USA and Canada, from enterprises and institutes, and from other cities. We immediately encountered rather strong resistance to our work. Now, the KGB didn't send us an expert, now a representative from another city didn't come, and so on. It finally got to the point that, after forty days an order to halt the activities of the group was officially signed "as having completed its work" in connection with the fact that the President would now be considering improvements in the nation's security system.

Clearly, the group managed only to begin the complex yet necessary work. All the same, the effort was inaugurated. It was the beginning of the edifice of a concept of the nation's comprehensive security, for which a truly independent expert commission is necessary. A concept is needed because, for example, it is being proposed to the Supreme Soviet to consider the draft law on the State Security Committee. But without first defining what "security" is and without laying the foundation of legislation touching upon comprehensive security—economic, military-political, cultural, ecological, etc.—this is the same as building a house beginning with the roof. Are we again to create a state within a state?

Foreign Policy Dividends

I think any objective person will admit that the greatest progress in perestroika has been made in foreign policy. I fully applaud everything that has been done in the foreign policy sphere. However, foreign policy came under rather heavy fire at the 28th CPSU Congress. But, as we say, the caravan keeps on moving despite everything.

It is true that we buried the so-called Brezhnev Doctrine. President Gorbachev put it well at the Congress: "What, tanks again? Are we again going to teach others how to live?" Accusations are being leveled to the effect that we "lost" Eastern Europe, and Germany is uniting, while we lost 20 million people because of it. As far as Eastern Europe is concerned, let's examine the problem carefully. Did it protect us from a military threat? Of course not. Let's ask the question: For whom is it profitable to attack us now? As to territorial claims, conquering our vast state would spell catastrophe for any invader: maintenance of a poor country, establishment of an infrastructure, keeping huge masses of unsettled people obedient, responsibility for their fortunes. . .What other goals could prompt an invasion of us? Rich resources? It is much cheaper to buy them from a ruined country.

Generally speaking, I do not see any danger of a massed invasion of us on the part of anyone, especially considering our nuclear potential. Regional conflicts are a possibility. Even in Europe it is still unclear how everything will pan out. Everyone is swearing to one another that they do not have territorial claims. Nevertheless, we see that Hungary and Romania had national territorial claims against one another, and theoretically they can also emerge between Poland and Lithuania, and elsewhere. I think, however, that today's civilized world will not permit such conflicts and disputes to develop into a great catastrophe, at least in Europe. In other regions of the world such dangers exist; national conflicts can develop into political and state conflicts, wars, etc. Local aggressions perpetrated by totalitarian and militarist regimes are possible as well.

I repeat, we have sufficient weaponry, nuclear weapons above all, to enable us not to be afraid of this. And if we have a professional army, we will not have to suffer tragedies like the one in Afghanistan, or embarrassments like the Rust incident or the one involving his imitator in Batumi.

I am not discomfited in the least by the fact that something is being done incorrectly in foreign policy or that foreign policy information is being concealed from the public. Instead I feel that officialdom is conducting too few frank conversations with society both in the field of foreign policy and on the issue of the transition to a market economy. They should tell the public more understandably, but more concisely and truthfully, what possibilities there are for solving problems and what consequences they are fraught with, and calculate everything with the experts.

Specifically, with regard to the German issue and Eastern Europe, it should be stressed and explained that these countries were not our conquest. Our "conquest" is the fact that we nourished them and kept them obedient by force, and this if more than unprofitable for the people of a leader country. Soviet Russia found itself in a similar position with regard to many constituent republics in its attempts to stabilize the situation in them. The results were evident—self-attrition and a centrifugal explosion.

People should be told frankly what friendship with some of our "friends" has been costing us. Thus, Western economists estimate that today our aid to states which have not yet left our orbit costs us $15,000 million a year. This may be an exaggerated figure, but the fact that it runs into the thousands of millions is unquestionable. If we translate this into our currency, this is many tens of thousands of millions of rubles. The record has shown that our attempts to maintain totalitarian regimes in any regions of this rapidly changing world are unpromising.

This and much else that is related to it require unhypocritical public roundtable discussions at which alternative assessments are weighed without labels, slogans, and verbiage (with competent opponents being respected).

Party Affairs

Perhaps it is known that I'm not in the Party. I had thirty years in the CPSU, from the times of the first "thaw." Etymologically and conceptually, a "party" is but part of society, the part of existing views and stands which unite the adherents of these stands. But the interests of one part cannot be placed higher than those of society as a whole. Furthermore, a party can be considered a party when there are other political parties. If however, this party is the only one in the country, and it enjoys unlimited power to boot, this is merely a state structure, and not the best type of one. Moreover, it is one based on the feudal-hierarchical principle, i.e., according to the Orwellian model: there is an internal and external structure, an apparatus, and party masses.

At the beginning of the Khrushchev "thaw" the qualification according to which workers and farmers were accepted into the CPSU without restrictions and intellectuals were filtered and restricted, was done away with. The qualification's triumph reached its apogee during the years of stagnation. During the five-year plan of 1958–1962 intellectuals joined the Party on the wave of the emancipation that this "thaw" had brought. It was then that many people came into the Party not only for the sake of a primitively understood career, but to assert themselves in community affairs and attain freedom on the job. They came in the hope that they would be able to exert an influence on society. This hope did not justify itself. As early as the Khrushchev years an opposite process began that was rigid and irreversible in the foreseeable future.

The 20th CPSU Congress was conducive to impressive progress in society and in people's consciousness. I believed, and believe to this day, that no matter how we may feel about Khrushchev, he can be credited with at least three things: first, he largely told the truth about Stalinism; second, he raised the iron curtain a bit and enabled more people to compare lifestyles, although we continued living in destructive isolation; third, he started developing the housing construction industry. What motives were behind this comrade-in-arms of Stalin's in that period are not important.

Returning to the issue of the Party and my exit from it, let me put it this way: the Party should truly become a party, not an imperious state structure. But this was not desired by people who represented it at the 28th Congress or, rather, whom it permitted to represent it.

The 28th Congress demonstrated that hopes for sweeping democratic changes in the CPSU are unrealistic, and, jointly with the so-called Constituent Congress of the Communist Party of the Russian Federation, it showed that today a danger to the country's democratic development is emerging largely from the Party, or rather, from the military-ideological complex, which has explicitly revealed itself at these congresses, replacing as it has the military-industrial complex. Fearful of losing their omnipotence, the champions of this complex think neither about the fate of the country and society or the fortunes of their own children and grandchildren doomed to living in the postdisaster society. They are pushing the country toward a political, economic, and moral abyss; in effect, crossing the border of stability. The mentality of holding on to power at all cost and preserving their involvement in distributive functions continues to hold sway with these people. This applies not only to the older generation, but also to the middle and many members of the younger generation as well.

I think, therefore, that the present-day party structure as such does not have a political future, i.e., a future as a truly political Party, in the foreseeable time to come. Regrettably, I cannot claim the same about the prospects for restoration.

Is There Light at the End of the Tunnel?

Soviet society is not governable today; reasonable forces that could take charge of the situation have not taken shape yet in the country. The moment when this could have been done has largely been missed.

The question arises: What's in store for us? Making forecasts is a thankless, albeit necessary and most difficult affair. All the same, it we try and construct, if only for ourselves, scenarios of possible development, I feel that we will not arrive at the worst variant.

Let us suppose that tomorrow everything works out and we begin mapping out and implementing some areas of peaceful stabilization. At first glance, and at second glance, for that matter, our most critical problem is the low level of material life. It's not even the level, but the wretched quality of life. For, theoretically, we do have some measure of material boons, but the ways in which we obtain them in everyday life, the morality of these ways and mechanisms have such a destructive influence on the individual's mentality that society itself becomes immoral and degrading. And if economic recovery proceeds more or less successfully and is accompanied by a correct formation of national, state, and other structures, the officials who are to extricate the country from a catastrophe will, of course, have to concentrate on rapidly improving the material life of society. As soon as they began pulling themselves out of the dislocation of times of crisis—the 1930s and the postwar period—today's industrialized countries immediately geared their potential to parallel development of culture, education, and science, realizing that this would speed up and stabilize the countries' forward advance. Otherwise, everything would get bogged down again. If we, having barely begun to crawl out of the economic pit, fail to involve in parallel these spheres ensuring the spiritual and intellectual development of society, we will be witness to an irreversible loss of the prime components of civilization's potential. Upon realization of this loss we will pine for the cultural and spiritual level we possessed in the nineteenth and twentieth centuries. And then forces can appear (although this is debatable) that may try to revitalize the semblance of the past and the distortedly and demagogically interpreted might and influence of the country: "But we used to be a great country!" Generally speaking, at any stage, even today, opponents of change can play on this. They have not got to *Pamyat* Society yet, but under certain circumstances, like the ones described above, they can. This have been successfully drawn on in the past to effect upheavals in societies, even in such a fairly educated one as Germany of the early 1930s. This is not the only conceivable scenario, but it worries me, since it affects the destiny of spirituality and the intellect, without which no proper society can exist and without which there is always the threat of ideology and totalitarianism.

However, in purely economic terms as well, our peoples can still be turned against changes, against the market, for example. After all, for generations our society has been accustomed to dividing and distributing rather than to earning. Thus, as soon as someone has begun "getting rich" in cooperatives in accordance with the existing laws (they may be bad, but they are laws), our parliament, under the influence of sentiment, gathers and sits in session for three days and consigns intermediary cooperatives to anathema. The allegation is that they are becoming rich without producing anything. They forget about the fact that our thrice-lambasted ministries and departments are in effect intermediary, albeit inefficient structures, and today's complex society cannot do without such mediation.

Now, a few words about national-stage development. I believe the freewheeling disintegration of our multinational union could have been averted and a new community could have been built along a path similar to the one traversed by Western Europe after the war. In order to revitalize and further speed up economic development, countries with quite similar socioeconomic structures (parliamentary democracies) began improving economic ties. The Common Market and the European Economic Community appeared. This entailed some elements of political integration, such as the European Parliament, and now there is the issue of a European government. A fresh spiral of economic integration lies ahead. On this path, a political and economic community is being built and developed with all its inevitable complexities, without the national and political independence of the sovereign states comprising it being lost.

It is approximately along this path that we have begun moving, too. For example, let the republics assume full responsibility (political) from above, for their economical and internal affairs, which will inevitably require establishment of interrepublican ties and their lateral regulation. Then the center should engage in building a new community and the promotion of economic and then also political integration in delegating it such powers as the strategic security of the community, arbitration of disputes, etc. It should be kept in mind, of course, that the success of this path will largely be determined by the similarity of the sociopolitical systems of the sovereign republics involved in such a community and by the level of democracy. Regrettably, much time has been lost. The endeavor was launched without a concept, a model of nation-state structure, according to the well-known but debatable practice of jumping into the fray, taking it from there.

Today the Russian Federation, headed by Boris Yeltsin, is beginning to establish lateral ties. He went to Jurmala, Latvia, and gathered representatives of the three Baltic republics and offered them bilateral agreements. All, this of course, is fraught with frictions with the present-day central government. Nevertheless, what should have begun in 1986–1987 is beginning today. The problem is how to win time until the new economic and political mechanisms begin functioning. This requires a tactical maneuver which will make it possible to create a sense of stabilization, revive hopes, and consequently, lessen social tensions.

Obviously, the republics cannot do without external assistance. A breather could be obtained through a large commodity loan, a sort of new lend-lease. But it should be used in a concentrated fashion, for receiving a maximum effect on the consumer market. Attempts should not be made to cover all bases. The point at issue could be a limited product-mix of consumer goods, the cost of which would be six to ten times higher on our domestic market than in the West. This would also make it possible to receive funds for compensating the socially unprotected sections of the population, balance the budget, and proceed to a convertible ruble. These problems can hardly be solved in the immediate future through domestic resources alone. And delaying their solution is fraught with very serious domestic political consequences.

Whatever the case, the top priority is economic independence of the republics and regions, and then economic integration in an attempt to heighten economic efficiency. It is afterwards that all this will bring about phased political integration.

I would like to end on an optimistic note. The new foreign policy thinking and the successes scored by Soviet diplomacy in implementing it have given us a breather, a unique chance to revamp our society on the basis of political and economic democracy and universal values, and an opportunity to revive the morality and spirituality of future generations. Our road back to a civilized society will be unbelievably difficult and long. But we must take advantage of what is perhaps our last chance.

Defense Gets the Best, The Economy the Rest

Vladimir Rubanov

To define our country's vital interest, we need to know and establish the limits of political, economic, social, and moral behavior beyond which society and the state must not go if they are to avoid irreparable losses and unacceptable internal and external conditions of existence. The issue of national security becomes relevant in the context of political conflicts and economic hazards, increased social tensions, and a confrontation of interests and unexpected environmental and other effects of the scientific and technological revolution.

The Soviet Union is at a most complicated turning point. The need for a long-term strategy of "how to live" is occasionally as urgent as the tactical imperative of "how to survive." Hence the pressing social

VLADIMIR RUBANOV is deputy chairman of the RSFSR State Committee on National Security and Relations with the USSR Ministry of Defense and the KGB.

task of singling out of the boundless sea of crying problems those that involve vital national interests, ascertaining the source and nature of the threat to their solution, and concentrating the country's intellectual potential on working out political, legal and organizational guarantees of national security. At a time when the ship of state must put about if it is not to drift to national disaster, clarity about these things is indispensable.

We evidently require more radical steps if we want to bring our national security system into line with the realities of the process of renewing Soviet society. The discrepancy that is coming out between the country's foreign policy activity and its modest inner political efforts to remake national security mechanisms is fraught with our finding ourselves unable to meet our foreign policy commitments at home and with the formation of a gap between our policy and law, our words and deeds. This also poses the threat of limiting the international opportunities to solve its internal problems which our country has won by its open foreign policy.

What is National Security?

A new national security policy is a pressing exigency today. The difficulties of farming and implementing it are in the same class as those that make themselves felt in other sectors of perestroika. They are due to the tenacity of obsolete notions and false certainties, a stereotyped reaction to new developments, conservative organizational structures devised by the command system, the fact that their functions are out of keeping with the requirements and objectives of the country's development, and deformed social relations.

Almost since the rise of Soviet statehood, we have held that the country's vital interests were threatened solely from without. Fear of all things foreign—from secret services to the Western way of life—became part of the existence of several generations of Soviet people. Practically all difficulties and setbacks in building a new society were ascribed to the "baleful influence" and "birthmarks" of capitalism. Our thinking was dominated by a politically conflict-minded, militarized and repressive idea of national security ranging from "strengthening the positions of the world socialist system" to insisting on the superiority of the method of "socialist realism" in the spiritual progress of civilization.

Let us, however, ask ourselves some untraditional questions. Wasn't it our party and government structures, not enemy secret services that led the country to an economic crisis and the threat of political destabilization? Isn't it our political practices, not bourgeois propaganda, that are responsible to a considerable extent for discrediting our social ideals?

An unbiased attitude makes these questions rhetorical, even if maximum account is taken of all the unfavorable external factors in the evolution of Soviet society and state. It follows that national security is not only and not so much an external but an internal problem.

We may go farther in establishing the priority of external and internal factors for national security. This will lead us to the conclusion that the security of a country depends primarily on an efficient economy and on internal social and political stability. In the area of foreign relations, however, a state does not build a solid social system, lend a progressive character to social development and dynamism to its civil principles, attain might and acquire a capacity to defend its vital interests but merely demonstrates these qualities and achievements. This circumstances is aptly expressed by the well-know formula: "Foreign policy begins at home."

Departmental Illusions and Social Needs

The crisis shaking our country today is dangerous. But it is also purifying, for it is freeing rational social thought from the bondage of a deformed, irrational reality. After a long period during which social consciousness wandered in an imaginary world and in view of the shocks it is now experiencing as it gets to know both its "unpredictable past" and its present, which is not "pleasant in every respect," the shift to pragmatism and common sense is bound to contribute greatly to its intellectual recovery.

The loss of our social bearings with regard to the aims of our national security and the means of achieving them is due to the command system's ideologized concepts of the object of defense, the nature and sources of the threat to the normal development of society, and to the dependable functioning of society's political and economic systems. This expresses itself in the unwarranted identification of the interests of civil society with often selfish aspirations of the state (as represented by its power apparatus) as well as in substituting the activity of military and repressive bodies for the policy of ensuring national security and for activity to this end. This reduction of the problem of national security to ideological and theoretical dogma reflects and preserves the structural conservatism of the system of ensuring it and makes for the stagnation of concepts of the functioning of mechanisms defending vital national interests.

National security as a set of problems facing our nascent democratic structures is an entirely new problem. However, the substance of the political process, the level and forms of openness, the procedures of drafting and adopting decisions on national security, the organizational forms of participation in them by specialists and the public have become sufficiently unified in world practice. This experience can be drawn on as a starting point for a new approach to the problem. With regard to the subject and procedures of shaping national security policy and strategy, we must establish what methods tested through social practice we can use in democratizing our institutions and in identifying and defending vital national interests.

The internal solidity of a country's security system depends on the right definition of the interests of the leading forces of society and on achieving a balance between them and adequately reflecting the political and economic trends of government measures and the functions and structure of authority. To institute national security is to form and ensure the functioning of a political mechanism recording and eliminating contradictions in society between social values and strategic aspirations to their realization.

Safeguarding national security calls primarily for appropriate legislative, executive, and judicial activity in the sphere of vital interests of society and state. As for reducing security measures to secret or semisecret activity by specialized executive agencies of the state, it is wrong and may produce a political conflict. Vital national interests must be expressed publicly, with power structures fully representing them. Otherwise social illusions entertained by high-ranking officials and the selfish aims of government departments may be made out to be government priorities.

This circumstance poses the question of the subject of national security policy, the forms of framing and the means of implementing it, and of public control over government activity in this sphere. To provide a political framework for a national security system, it is necessary to formulate and answer these questions correctly.

The foregoing brings out a problem relating to the superstructure to the expression of social relations in the area of national security and its political principles by civil law. Of practical value is a security strategy; providing concepts of the material foundations of defining and defending vital interests. Hence the vast importance of establishing the connection between political and material factors in national security.

In accordance with the contemporary concept of international security, military means are seen as secondary in security policy while political and diplomatic means are put first. Yet diplomacy is effective only if it rests on a material basis in the form of a might state. What the latter's might should consist of is another matter.

The use of armed force holds no promise from the point of view of today's social consciousness and practical politics. Nowadays military might does not indicate that the interests of the state possessing it are reliably safeguarded but is rather material evidence of a threat to its existence and, indeed, to that of humanity. This does not make national security less dependent on might. But the character of might is undergoing a fundamental change in today's conditions. It therefore seems more correct to speak not of replacing military by diplomatic means but of adopting a new diplomacy based on nonmilitary means of defending vital national interests. In practice this calls for a diversification of the material means of ensuring national security and for a shift of the emphasis in the policy of defending vital national interests from military to economic might.

The lessening of the military threat to the Soviet Union is a universally recognized achievement of perestroika foreign policy. This is not to say, however, that the problem of our national security is becoming less relevant. It is still there. All that is changing is the object to vital national interests and the means of defending them. Both are losing their military security aspects as they assume the character of economic security.

In putting it on record in this connection that there is a stereotype—a militarized perception of a national security problem that has developed under the influence of both objective and subjective factors in the country's evolution—it is useful to give attention to the need to steadily destroy this stereotype by giving our political thinking an economic character. Such an ideological reorientation is prompted not only by a changed historical situation but by the very essence of concepts of universal progress, by the humanist quality of its dominant trends. The problem of using force as a means of influencing social relations admits of only one solution, the example of force.

However, we can hardly discount the fact that the tragic burden of the country's past hangs heavy on our consciousness. The Soviet people's concern about the state of our defenses is therefore perfectly understandable. Their oversensitiveness to all that bears on the problem of military might, with emotions prevailing over reason in assessing threats to the safe existence of the country, makes a new, rational approach to the issue of national security difficult. This reality must certainly be taken into consideration.

An unbiased analysis of the situation today shows that the threat of economic failure is an order of magnitude greater than that of military aggression against our country. Besides, we should remember that the peoples and governments of many countries devote increasing attention to the destiny of the world and the problem of averting war. As for the problem of economic survival, we are wrestling with it all alone, drawing on our internal potentialities.

Growing Security May Lead to Lessening It

The political thinking that has cropped up stubbornly refuses to appreciate the increased significance of economic security among the priorities and structure involved in defending vital interests of the Soviet Union. This contrasts above all with the boom in scientific research which helps the West in its current reorientation of national security strategies in a new historical context.

What is meant by economic security? The authors of *Problems of Economic Security in Foreign Literature,* a collection of papers brought out in 1988 by the USSR AS Institute of Scientific Information on the Social Sciences, make the following generalization: "Economic security should be defined as a state of the national economy that persists as long as the economic well-being of the nation and the stability of the domestic market are unaffected by the operation of external factors which means that negative influence from without is neutralized by compensative economic reserves of the country, enabling it to preserve economic, social, and political stability."

Giving national security theory and policy an economic character manifests itself in a new line of Western politology, the economic theory of a national security. A realization of the limitations of military methods and of the changed conditions of preserving European civilization has translated into stepping up the development of complex security models on the continent that integrate economic, social, and military factors.

An integral concept of national security system leads to the conclusion that there exists dialectical unity between its military and economic principles. This unity is contradictory and reinforcing one aspect of security does not necessarily make in all circumstances for reinforcing the other. Even if we were to cut military spending to between 5 and 8 percent of the national income, our economy would still be held down, in the opinion of academician Oleg Bogomolov, by an enormous burden that would doom society to a further lag. It emerges that there is a limit to the buildup of military security beyond which the economy is destabilized and national security is undermined as a result. According to this dialectic, growing security may lead to lessening it. This means that besides solving military and economic security problems, we must solve the equally difficult problem of keeping them commensurate. We can ensure national security only by establishing an optimum balance between the economic and military spheres and by removing the contradiction objectively existing between them. It is deplorable that this contradiction is still not perceived dialectically in our country and is becoming a conflict between army and society, provoking clashes between political forces and adding to social tensions.

But it is not even figures for military spending that are the main indicator of the impact of defense on the economy. The funding of military programs is also an industrial policy influencing the redistribution of resources in favor of definite social groups and regions. It is also a factor for the formation of what may be called intellectual zones, and spheres of application of the intellect for a particular technological orientation of production and a special pattern of exports and imports.

The Paris weekly *Témoignage Chrétien* (January 12–18, 1987) estimated that every additional billion dollars spent for military purposes led directly or indirectly to a $120 million increase in imports of strategic materials and in production of advanced technologies. At the same time, a similar increase in nonmilitary spending raised the demand for imports by only $89 million. Greater dependence in this respect indicated a weakening of national economic security.

Foreign research has revealed that the arms industry shows low productivity due to its structure, is more capital-intensive, and creates fewer jobs for the same amount of outlays than civilian industries. A civilian economy infected with the viruses of inefficiency and monopolized and overcentralized production, the development of contrasts between increasingly sophisticated armaments and the lagging level of the processes involved in their manufacture, a loosening of industrial unity due to the organizational nontransparency, and the secrecy of military programs are only some of the many consequences of the buildup of military power for national economic security.

This damage caused to national economies by the military-industrial complex puts in mind our own command economy, all the more since it is in fact a wartime economy. But doesn't the extent to which our economy is militarized correspond to the extent of its bondage to command methods and vice versa? Undoubtedly, there is a rather big problem here.

Notwithstanding so strong a militarization of our economy, no one is worried much, and besides, it is hoped that conversion will serve as an additional factor for economic growth. But it appears that the problem is far more complicated. If scientists and politicians overlook the phenomenon of militarization, it is not because the problem is insignificant but because our economic and political knowledge is inadequate.

The effects of militarizing the economy are widely taken into account by foreign experts in investigating the international situation of the United States and analyzing the reasons for the decline in American influence on world development. The American manufacturer R. Thomson has revealed the relationship between military and economic might by stating that America cannot afford to be both Sparta and Athens. It might lose its national economy in the name of national security.

We show no such concern about our economic security, I am sorry to say. Our political sentiments and more widespread interpretations and concepts of defense sufficiency geared it in the past and still gear it essentially to maintaining strategic parity. As for the problem of undermined economic possibilities, we treat it as a matter of second-ary importance.

I think we need a revision of the very philosophy of our military-economic thinking. The problem of the Soviet Union's survival now makes us begin our interpretation of defense sufficiency not with military sufficiency but with the economic residue which the military machine is built to defend. In the life of a country and in its coopera-tion with other countries there occur extraordinary periods that re-quire emergency measures, a switch of national priorities to the mili-tary sphere. But in normal, peacetime conditions the economy must certainly not be planned and developed as in wartime. This means that the strategy of defining and defending vital national interests must be aimed at achieving economic security. To put it figuratively, the computerization of schools must precede computerization in the army if we do not want to lose both our schools and our army.

The visible aspects of economic security is material prosperity, a stable home market, and competitive exports. But economic security also has an aspect driving a deeper insight into its essence. I mean the ability of the economic system to develop and adopt new progressive technologies and science-intensive products, expand the intellectual scope of work, and computerize society.

This is shown by the experience of progress in many countries and by their peoples' realization of their vital interests. In the National Security Strategy Report, submitted to Congress on March 20, 1990, President George Bush described the role of the scientific and tech-nological factor for national security as follows: "As industrial de-mocracies are steadily developing into a post-industrial era of super-computers, microelectronics and telecommunications the communist nations have stuck in stagnation, paralyzed by obsolete state dogmas which stifle innovations and labor productivity. . .The current infor-mation revolution has brought about a most serious challenge to the totalitarian regimes which lies in the fact that trying to keep to the old policy of banning information is leading to an invariable paralysis in the sphere of technology."

Such political documents, which are not intended "specially" for us, indicate the force that the United States banks on its relations with the Soviet Union. This force is considerably more effective in world politics today than military power. Nevertheless, our mass consciousness is still tuned in to guarding against the war danger, a vigilance shutting out everything else. This may be warranted historically and in terms of present-day reality and prompted by traditional wisdom. But by the world standard of vital interests—existence as a free and independent power preserving its main values and institutions and ensuring a healthy and growing economy—it is not in the military but the scientific and technological sectors of our economic development that these interests are in real danger.

What Force Is Threatening Us?

The general impression is that while our national security strategists were preparing to head off the war menace (their effort being accompanied by a weakening of the economy), and while we assessed our intellectual potential, our rivals in the arms race planned and accomplished a real breakthrough in science and technology.

Long-term U.S. intentions are of permanent interest to the Soviet Union. I hardly need to explain why. Ever since the mid-1970s Soviet and foreign analysts have pointed out an increasingly strong aspiration on the part of the U.S. ruling elite to use its scientific and technological power for the formation of new links in the system of international relations. Many Western theories of the "technotronic age" explicitly give the United States a leading role in the STR. In the world to come, it is expected to merely generate scientific ideas and offer complete scientific projects while other countries do the "dirty" job of producing metals, machinery, coal, and so on. This would make them dependent on America in science, technology, and the intellectual sphere generally.

One has only to compare the United State's strategic aims with the international situation of today to see that its aspirations are attainable to a high degree. Looking at the world while drawing a bead on it prevented us from realizing the gravity of the threat to our vital interests, which now manifests itself in our technological backwardness. Nor is COCOM the hitch. The experience of normalizing Soviet-American relations shows that this hurdle can be overcome. Yet the state of our science and technology is such that America's use of its technological superiority is becoming an effective means of achieving foreign policy ends.

The narrow-mindedness of prevailing notions of national security kept us from detecting the rise of new dimensions of it on time and from appraising them correctly. It is now obvious that the main threat to the security of the Soviet Union comes from the prospect of an irreversible lag in technology, from our ending up in the backyard of world economic and social progress and from a disintegration of our society.

The Soviet Union has long ago exceeded the limits of safe scientific and technological dependence on the West. Continued imports of advanced technologies paid for with credits and raw material exports, and accompanied by a brain drain, is tantamount to fast-approaching technological suicide.

In these circumstances, the country's scientific and technological security is a strategic factor in determining and defending our vital national interests. We must consider this factor in connection with the military and economic ones.

Lately we have interpreted foreign arms modernization programs as evidence of their aggressive designs regarding the Soviet Union. Of course, confrontation between military machines does not always follow political logic, for it is governed by its own inherent laws. Recent experience suggests that currently it is easier to come to terms with foreign politicians than with one's own military. This applies to both sides. But this is not the point, for we are not concerned at the moment with the military technological aspect of the problem but want to ascertain the political intentions of another country and the role which their implementation by military means is expected to play. Any careful analyst will see that the emphasis in the U.S. approach to strategic stability has lately been not so much on the quantity of armaments but on the pace of their modernization. This implies that pressure on the Soviet Union is not exerted directly, through arms, but through the pace at which these arms are improved technically and technologically. We are thus faced with indirect application of scientific and technological power in the form of military technology. This is shown by the completion of many military programs to the point of testing new weapons and new technologies, if without starting quantity production. It calls for a fundamentally new approach to the problem of national might, with the emphasis shifted from massive arms production to a military policy guaranteed by science and technology.

Information—the Major Component of Might

The present stage of the Scientific and Technological Resolution and the character of the productive forces embodying it are associated with information technology. This adds importance to information as a major national means and strategic commodity and brings to the fore the problem of developing computer and information technologies and raising the information culture of society.

Until recently, the approach to owning and using information resources was ideologized. This handicapped this country's political as well as economic, scientific, and technological advance. We have noted that this circumstance was taken into account in U.S. national security strategy. I do not think I need to give the reasons for our comment on foreign views of the state of affairs in this field. The fact that we lack an information culture and that this goes hand in hand with a "secrecy cult" is a commonplace among today's critics of our social reality. All this makes the problem of framing an information policy and ensuring the country's information security within this framework highly relevant.

Information security has external and internal aspects. Restrictions on information for security reasons should take account of both international realities and the internal requirements of state and society in their context. Even the toughest controls imposed by COCOM have so far been less negative for economic, scientific, and technological progress in our country than our "international COCOM." This has been pointed out repeatedly by various rostrums, including that of the First Congress of USSR People's Deputies.

Little has really changed since then. For the time being, the iron-clad wall of secrecy regulations resists successfully enough the political pressure of glasnost, economic circumstances, and the needs of science and technology. The mechanism of information arbitrariness that developed under the command system, and known as secrecy regulations, is making do with a mere face lift without undergoing any fundamental change. As a result, it is not that secrecy measures are prompted by information policy but that restrictions imposed by secrecy condition the information activities of subjects of politics, economics, and science. The country's information resources and intellectual potentialities remain shackled by deformed information security measures reproduced as ends in themselves. We do not put intellect and knowledge to economic uses on time and on the necessary scale, and so they fail to produce the material, social, and spiritual results they could—they are choked by a bureaucratic system disguised as a system "combating espionage." The situation is reminiscent of the case of the man who took offense and gouged his eye to make the son-in-law of his mother-in-law one-eyed because he disliked her.

I will refrain from asking who is to blame because I do not want to offer our ex officio "patriots" a pretext to accuse me of disloyalty to respected state structures. As for the question, What is to be done? It can be answered.

I consider that the Soviet side took a constructive step toward rationalizing the information security system by proclaiming at the London Information Forum in April–May 1989 the principle of all countries being equally open. Another such step is our aspiration to bring secrecy measures in the Soviet Union into line with international standards existing in the form of traditions and state-to-state agreements.

Information is both a result of scientific and technological progress and a condition for it. Knowledge acquired in the sphere of spiritual production is transformed into techniques, technologies, and articles of consumption. This makes society richer materially and attracts primarily those who are seeking to feed and clothe the country as early as possible. But an equally important aspect of the problem of computerizing society and mastering information technology and sophisticated techniques is to raise the nation's culture, to build up its intellectual potential. And this is something you can never buy anywhere at any price.

We Risk Losing Everything

Thus the intellectual and creative principle takes precedence in the material and spiritual tandem of factors for the saturation of society with information. This should predetermine the choice of national information security strategy.

In fact, this is the approach taken by a number of foreign students of the problem. Specifically, comparing the benefits of rigid regimes of protecting information with losses due to inevitable restrictions on information exchanges and research has produced an aphoristic formula saying that in the era of scientific and technological progress, it is much better to allow yourself to be robbed than to have to steal.

This formula is expressive of the simple idea that you can reproduce something borrowed but no amount of imitating can replace creative effort. Anyone who looks to others for inspiration is doomed to a permanent motor-paced race with doubtful prospects of finishing first. Such a practice does not foster scientific inquiries but leads to their degradation. What some dismiss as "immaterial" has an increasingly negative moral and psychological impact owing to the use of uncivilized methods of "borrowing" world scientific and technological achievements. This results in material losses sooner or later. After all, we do not know which costs more, whether lawfully obtaining information or going to the expense of "laundering" scientific and technological intelligence to avoid conflict over patents.

It is probably right to recall this circumstance now that the problem of intellectual property has passed from the sphere of an exotic political economy to that of legal practice (the USSR Supreme Soviet is going to adopt a relevant law). Having acted for too long on the "right" to what belonged to others without a right to what was ours, we seem to be in for moral and material discomfort.

In information security matters, we must consider not only material but intellectual factors in exchanges of know-how and technologies, weigh advantages and disadvantages with regard to both national and universal interests, and work for a more durable international information order.

The Means Should Correspond to the Ends

The problems of military, economic, scientific, technological, and information security of the country reveal the essential difference of their substance from what constitutes the object of the activities of government bodies and institutions performing intelligence, counterintelligence and other specific functions. Accordingly, it is advisable to separate national security strategy from measures providing specific (intelligence, counterintelligence, legal, and military technological) guarantees of it. This is very important because security today is considered to imply only what the armed forces and the KGB are engaged in.

Special measures for the defense of vital national interests do not quite solve the problem. This calls for the application of security guarantees adequate to the nature of social relations in need of protection. Economic security can be ensured primarily by economic ways and means. In any sector of national security, it is by adopting a set of measures that the greatest effect can be achieved. But at all events, the first line of defense of vital interests is formed by measures in keeping with the character of the given military, economic, scientific, and technological or intellectual conflict. They determine the character of all other guarantees and the methods of using them. There is no defending, say, the economy exclusively by counterintelligence and repressive measures.

This relationship between general and specific national security measures implies that vital national interests must be defined and their defense organized by government bodies exercising control in the sphere concerned. Using specific means of safeguarding national security as an end in itself produces little social effect, as national and foreign experience indicates. Nor should we overlook the damage which "Watergates" and "Irangates" are likely to cause to public interests. We cannot rule out the possibility of "gates" of our own. Certain signs of them can be detected in the Afghan and Iraqi "surprises."

We must not allow the means to determine the ends in defending vital national interests or the tasks involved. Indeed, in the absence of full-fledged mechanisms of political control in this sphere, it is in effect the secret services that form our notions of security. Yet a situation where the tail wags the dog is not only abnormal but dangerous.

The foregoing suggests that security policy should come first, security strategy second, and special security of guarantees third.

The right choice of priorities is of exceptional importance in evolving an overall national security strategy. I believe the requirements of economic security today should play a system-forming role in the set of measures for the defense of vital national interests.

National security strategies must be provided with special guarantees. It would be right to combine basic and guaranteeing measures in a single whole as state program. These may be, for instance, program envisaging intelligence guarantees of military security or counterintelligence guarantees of economic security.

Such an approach would allow the traditional functional branch pattern of control in the area of security to be renounced in favor of pattern following a special purpose program. This in turn would enable us to put under a "civilian" control structures dangerous to society and to make their special measures socially useful.

Such functional alterations in the organization of activities in the area of national security call for a fundamental restructuring.

State construction should apparently begin with devising means of political control and mechanisms of state control over the system of defining vital national interests and organizing their defense. It is for lack of such mechanisms that tensions between society, on the one hand, and the army, the KGB, and other national security structures persist. There is a growing threat of conflict between these entities and increasingly strong representative government bodies at all levels. Without new political mechanisms, no new security system encompassing the whole nation can be evolved, nor can the requisite reforms in the armed forces, the military-industrial complex, and the secret services be carried out.

World experience and the specifics of the evolution of our society and statehood suggest that the national security system can be effectively run and political control over measures safeguarding it exercised by means of such agencies as the Supreme Soviet Committee on Security, the Security Council under the head of state, and the Coordinating Committee on Crisis Situations under the head of government.

We also need guaranteeing structures such as a strategic research center and a common security data bank. The final component of the system of scientific and information guarantees in the area of national security should take the form of an "operation room" of the country's top leadership.

None but a deep-going legal and structural reform of our national security system can rid our society of the complex of past fears and build effective mechanisms to avert the real dangers threatening our country.

Humanity's Common Destiny

Anatoli Adamishin

These times are indeed highly interesting and fateful. What is taking place in the Soviet Union and in international affairs on the whole today is sparking a flurry of thoughts, hopes, doubts, and questions. Advancing to the forefront are dozens, hundreds of problems—not only practical ones, of course, but also theoretical and sometimes purely psychological ones. It is high time for mankind to display reason if it simply wants to survive, let alone develop normally.

I may be wrong, but deep down many people doubt whether we can speak at all in our world today—and we see its contradictions, and splits, and cruelty every day—of universal values, of overcoming egoism, and class, party, group, national, and other interests for their

ANATOLI ADAMISHIN is USSR ambassador to Italy. Before his departure to Rome, he was Deputy Minister of Foreign Affairs of the USSR.

sake. This question probably arises particularly often in people of my generation, which for decades was brought up on certain notions or, to put it more bluntly, stereotypes. How, for example, are we to accept unconditionally the primacy of universal values over class ones when we have heard for so many years that it is the struggle between classes that is the main driving force of society at all stages in its development, and so on and so forth?

The following consideration will perhaps help solve this didactic contradiction: Why must one absolutely negate the other? There is no pure substitution: there is a different correlation, a changed proportion of each factor. Obviously, the interests of people and their groups, parties and classes will clash within countries, and the interests of different countries will do so in the international arena. In any event, there will be plenty of this in our day.

However, there have arisen objective limits beyond which a clash of interest cannot extend if both or even all the opponents are not to be harmed. These limits have been created by the development of military technology, of the instruments of destruction, i.e., of the productive forces, in the final analysis. There is no escaping this objective reality. These limits have been set by the possibility, one which did not exist earlier, of physically destroying one another, and virtually the entire human race. Thus, people should impose intelligent limits on this struggle and find civilized ways and methods for it. Will they be able to do this? Past history, as well as many current phenomena, gave little grounds for an affirmative answer. But there have also been positive phenomena. One of them is the greater maturity of humanity. Will it prove sufficient to prevent a disaster? Only the future will provide a definite answer to this question. It should be underscored, however, that we people living today simply have no other choice than to bend every effort to guarantee the survival of humanity. It is in this context that Lenin's idea about the predominance of universal values over class values rings much truer today for us than at the start of the twentieth century, when it was formulated.

I personally have no doubt when speaking about people of our generation, we have raised to the absolute the range of concepts linked with the class struggle. The classics of Marxism singled out this element from the totality of the laws which govern the development of human society, for methodological purposes, to study its manifestations, on the one hand, and because it in fact plays a very important role, on the other. But not the only role. Class relations are far from the only relations among people. Today we are seeing this particularly clearly against the background of national enmity, tribalism, clannishness, religious divisions, and so on. In our time we found it very simple to measure absolutely everything against one tried-and-tested benchmark. The record, however, has shown that life is much deeper, richer, and more substantive than any theory, especially one that is understood simplistically. A classic example is the lengthy period of almost outright hostility between the USSR and China. How could class similarity allow bloody armed clashes? What about Vietnam and China? And the totally monstrous situation in Kampuchea under Pol Pot? One can, of course, allude to definitions and not consider particular states as being socialist. However, this, incidentally, reaffirms the need that a state possess much more attributes than we believed earlier for being socialist in the true sense.

Preservation of world civilization is justly linked with the possibility of resolving the formidable problems that have arisen at the end of the twentieth century. Two—the nuclear and the ecological problems—are usually singled out. Then there is a third, the world economy, above all, seen in terms of the yawning gap between the industrialized and the developing countries.

However, it would be correct to raise the issue of survival as follows: how not to allow differences between people to take the upper hand over their commonality; how not to permit political, economic, social, ideological, or other divergencies to become determinant today, when a threat to the Earth's existence has arisen.

This advances to the forefront the idea of the unity of the human race, an idea which once resounded very strongly in the humanistic tradition and which has sort of faded out over the past few decades. Meanwhile, our common affiliation to humanity should become the overriding prerequisite for any state policy and any ideology.

What is needed is a revitalization of the great humanistic ideas which are revered and professed in many countries, and, most of all, their implementation in practical policy. For each day we see that inner aspirations are one thing and practice is often quite another. This contradiction should be removed through joint efforts. In other words, state policy should be brought in line with the loftiest universal moral principles and values.

By and large, people have learned to live together, for example, on the level of the city, district, and country, although there are problems here, too and formidable ones at that. But evidently the process of realizing our main unity—universal unity—is moving too slowly. Selfish economic and political ambitions and pretensions are hampering the effort.

We may be different, but we are parts of one civilization, perhaps the only one, and we cannot live without one another. This world organism may be contradiction-ridden and complicated, but we are all bound by one destiny. Differences should not be a reason for a military confrontation; they should be prerequisites for exchange, comparison, and competition.

For centuries there has existed a gap between politics and morality. Few will venture to claim that it has been bridged today. But can one reconcile oneself to this in our age of global perils? Is not morality the instrument with which nature has endowed man to help him refrain from suicidal steps? There are probably laws of human behavior common to all times and peoples. They cannot be repealed, just as, according to the laws of physics, one cannot create a perpetual motion machine. Then isn't it high time to stop making a travesty of moral laws? Physicists, incidentally, have long realized the unity not only of the world but of the entire universe. It is now the politicians' turn.

The maturity of state policy consists precisely in its links with the conscience of man, or rather, with the conscience of the people. For all their necessity, the parliamentary or other mechanisms of democratic control over policy are not always safeguards against fateful mistakes. There have been sufficient allusions to national security to make these mechanisms captive to confrontational decisions. A false, selfish, and essentially immoral interpretation of national security can trigger off a catastrophe. Policy needs today more than ever before to draw on public forces and movements, on mass organizations and institutions which, in their activities, affirm universal norms of morality and universal values.

People's attention is focused on their differences to such an extent that the values that link them are often overshadowed. However, universal values are not an invented category. It includes quite real notions; namely, life, the continuation of the human race, the environment, world culture, scientific and technological advance, and the health of the individual and of humanity. Common values include the family, the dignity of the individual, mutual assistance and solidarity, and much else.

In addition to everything else, these are the most solid values. In the final analysis, it is simply profitable to be guided by the Ten Commandments. Common sense reaffirms this at each step of everyday life. It has to be made the guiding force in international affairs. The ancient Greeks built their temples according to the laws of harmony, and they have proved to be among the most solid structures in history. Consequently, beauty is also solidness, steadiness, security, if you will, and, even more, the "salvation of the world."

The diversity of nature does not run counter to its unity; quite the contrary, it corresponds to it. By the same token, pluralism is a norm and a natural state of world civilization. Take, for instance, such a phenomenon as the Non-Aligned Movement, within whose framework a very broad spectrum of political views is taken into account. The unity of humanity only stands to gain from mutual enrichment in international relations and from an interaction of different sociopolitical and cultural trends and the dialectical struggle among them.

This is what makes the imposition of uniformity in an essentially pluralistic world so unnatural. One of the uppermost features of new thinking is the unconditional recognition of the right to free choice and sharp repudiation of dictating one's writ in any form: in the form of export of revolution, in the form of conservative attempts to put the brakes on the course of historical development and guide it to suit oneself, and to restrict freedom of choice. In short, the slogan of the moment is to de-ideologize international relations.

In addition to the factors uniting the world, such a mighty one as the scientific and technological revolution has appeared in recent years. Right before our eyes (although, regrettably, this has not been seen by everyone who should have seen it) it is becoming increasingly global and all-encompassing. Science is becoming, or has already become, a decisive productive force. Futurologists claim that by dint of the universality of this process, that because it has embraced all spheres of human endeavour, it is unstoppable. We are experiencing certain difficulty in assimilating the discoveries that have already been made, and even more fantastic ones are being predicted.

As far as I can understand, the logic here is as follows: The scientific and technological revolution is emancipating people from their strict dependence on machines that is typical of the so-called industrial society. Manpower potential is at long last being given a free rein. The creative energy of the individual is becoming the most effective instrument for the growth of the productive forces, and his development and improvement is, as Karl Marx put it, turning into an end in itself. The scientific and technological revolution is liberating man for creativity, the human factor is being enhanced, and this in turn is leading to new discoveries and break throughs in science, technology, and production. The two sides of this process influence each other, this tandem making for solid, advance. The record of the leading industrialized countries has shown that the structure of industry is changing, that unskilled workers are being elbowed out, their number is decreasing in general and that of technicians and engineers is growing, and that the structure of society as a whole is reshaping. On the whole, the scientific and technological revolution is developing in such a way that specialization is giving way to universalism.

From all this stretches a whole series of threads to new political thinking. One of them is the following: Since technical advance requires universally prepared people, general human values and eternal truths are standing out in bolder relief; among them is the realization that truth, as one thinker wrote, cannot be national; it is always universal. Different nationalities, however, can be called upon to reveal particular aspects of truth. The main thing is that progress indeed seems to have begun towards not adapting man to the world but adapting the world to man, as John Bernal put it in the 1950s. More importantly, the USSR is not at all a passive observer of this advance. In the context of perestroika it has not merely become involved in it: our country is greatly speeding it up with its domestic and foreign policies. Affiliation to one civilization presupposes that all member-countries of the international community build their domestic life in accordance, if only in the major areas, with some common ideals, rules, if you will. Age-old human experience has elaborated certain standards—in the economy, in culture, and, as if synthesising all of them, in the sphere of human rights and freedoms. Conformity with them is considered compulsory.

It is true that that sphere was and continues to be considered more ideologized than any other. There are considerable differences in the attitudes of states to it as, incidentally, there are in approaches to other matters. There exist a host of coinciding views, of course. Upon closer examination there is perhaps no other field of international cooperation in which there are so many covenants, conventions, and other agreements as in human rights. They number over fifty to date. Some experts believe that here legislative activity has been finished altogether. Now it is a matter of applying the international agreements that have been elaborated upon and come into effect. Figuring prominent among them is the Universal Declaration of Human Rights, whose fortieth anniversary was first marked last December in the East as well in the West. Most UN member-countries have pledged to comply with the provisions of such fundamental documents as international human rights covenants. If other states, including the United States, of course, sign or ratify these covenants, a sort of integral rule-of-law humanitarian space will be created. It can play the role of counterweight to centrifugal ambitions, including those of an integrational nature.

If we view the development of human society as a consistent ascent, it is axiomatic that considerable progress was attained at the stage of the bourgeois formation in human rights, too. It could probably be expressed in two words—formal equality. Instead of dozens of criteria, such as estate and kinship, with which feudalism operated, there was one yardstick for assessing one's weight in society—money. The understanding was that in every other respect people were equal.

Without bourgeois law having spread nationwide, and having remained largely at the feudal level, we planned to reach essential equality after the October Revolution. We achieved a great deal in this unprecedented historical attempt to leap over all the steps. But there were also big losses, as we now see. One of them is a deep-seated negation of formal equality. It is succinctly expressed in the saying: "Not he is right who is really right but he who has more rights." Our Russian traditions at least most of them are highly baleful in this respect. "Full inequality before the court," wrote A. I. Herzen, "killed all respect for legality in him (the Russian). A Russian, no matter what rank he may be of, skirts or violates the law everywhere he can do so with impunity, and that is exactly how the government acts, too." Mistrust in the possibility of achieving justice spawned a persistent mistrust in the law and in jurisprudence in general. In building a rule-of-law state, it is useful to borrow some "formal" structures of bourgeois democracy. Some important questions we are now working or have been posed within its framework and have been handled in a unique way. They are the correlation between executive and legislative power, the independence of the judiciary, and safeguards of political pluralism. The mechanisms of bourgeois democracy were elaborated for many centuries, and they can certainly be used, given the corresponding transformation in our socialist society. Without this it will be more difficult for us to surmount deeply ingrained anti-law habits due to which the drafting of new laws is frankly proceeding in such a contradictory fashion. It would be naive to think that we are living in a vacuum, that others are not observing our sufferings. It has been quite rightly said that the image of a state is today judged above all by how it treats its citizens. We can in no way be indifferent to our international image. This is particularly true today, when we ourselves are calling for the creation of world law and order, for an end to power politics in favor of the power of politics.

Fortunately, in our current work to upgrade the political and legal structure we can draw on a strong humanistic democratic tradition. Today we can say that we are not prepared for democracy, alleging that the appropriate traditions do not exist. This is both true and false. We cannot forget such Russian pillars as Leo Tolstoy and Fyodor Dostoyevsky, and the whole of our literature, which championed morality so persistently. We cannot forget those who frequently proclaimed unsuccessfully that the development of the individual is the basis of social transformation. Lastly, we cannot forget the extremely valuable legacy of Lenin's ideas about the socialist state and legality and his struggle to lay the foundations of a rule-of-law state in this country. The indissoluble link between socialism and the development and affirmation of the supremacy of law was long comprehended and recognized in Russia. The following words, written eighty years ago, ring astonishingly true today: "Legally, the socialist system is only a rule-of-law system that has been implemented more consistently. Conversely, the implementation of a socialist system is only a rule-of-law system that has been implemented more consistently. Conversely, the implementation of a socialist system is possible only when all its institutions receive a rather precise legal formulation."

We simply need to know and remember our philosophers and political analysts, who are often better known (and quoted more frequently) in the West.

We shall now try to analyze the above "theoretical" structures on such a model as Soviet–American relations, which play so outstanding a role in the world situation as a whole. They are well suited to this because on one hand, striking changes have taken place in them over the past three or four years, and this means that an improvement in the world situation is realistic. On the other hand, there are evidently few people, even true advocates of cooperation between the USSR and the United States, who have not doubted how solid the current favorable changes are and whether they are a prelude to another eruption of confrontation as has often been the case in the past. Regrettably, the record of Soviet–American relations is not brilliant in this respect. And if Soviet–American cooperation fails, the rest of the world will not have things too easy.

The main thought which I want to bring home is my deep conviction that today there are serious objective prerequisites for the two states to establish long-term stable cooperation that is beneficial both for themselves and for the whole world—if, of course, we rise to the occasion ourselves and do not make mistakes.

What is this conviction based on?

First, the advance toward new relations between the USSR and the United States and toward a solid reconciliation between them is winning increasing support among the Soviet and American public at large, including young people and the creative intelligentsia. Tens of thousands of people on both sides have been involved in the practical implementation of Soviet–American ties. It is a very gratifying fact that the sides are adopting the most important decisions affecting their relations with due account for public and on the basis of considerations and conclusions of scientists, political analysts, and intellectuals. In other words, efforts to improve Soviet–American relations are becoming the common endeavour of millions of people.

The fact that international relations are increasingly becoming relations truly among peoples and not only among states is a sign of the times in general. But this is particularly important for Soviet–American relations. And the greater the chances that the positive changes in these relations can become long-term. Public influence is a powerful mainspring of further progress. One cannot but reckon with public sentiment. But these very changes have not emerged by themselves. They reflect the deep-going currents that have materialized and are a result of an analysis of present-day realities.

Second, today, when the overwhelming majority of nuclear charges on Earth is concentrated in Soviet and American arsenals, as is the bulk of other mass-destruction weapons, the need to ensure the survival of humanity is one of the prime components of the objective basis for Soviet–American cooperation. It may be argued that such a situation existed in the past, too. However, the realization of this imperative by the public at large as well as by politicians is a new and promising phenomenon. It is a realization which led to the first concrete actions such as the conclusion of the INF Treaty. There is reason to believe that both countries understand the importance of moving forward on the path they have embarked upon.

Third, Soviet–American cooperation is also being promoted by the fact that, for all our differences, we are parts of one common world civilization. There is no other one. Consequently, we bear the same responsibility for the preservation of civilization. Soviet–American relations have begun transcending the dangerous stereotype that our differences are virtually an automatic source of confrontation. The world is not to be dominated by any one country; it is not someone's backyard. A balance of interests needs to be sought. Attempts at hegemony boomerang against the pursuers of this policy. Soviet–American relations are now exhibiting a tendency to look for this balance of mutual interests. It is mirrored in the numerous agreements and accords that have been reached of late.

Fourth, few things underscore mutual dependence so much as global problems, problems which no country can solve single-handedly. We have already singled out one of them—the ecological problem. Incidentally, here, too, interesting things are happening which require a repudiation of former notions. A great deal of effort is being spent in the United States and some other Western countries so as not to give the Soviet Union advanced technology. Shouldn't consideration be given to the fact that obsolete technology can have ecological consequences that will also effect the supporters of the COCOM lists or the Jackson–Vanik amendments? And are not the economic problems that have amassed in the world while the USSR and the United States were engaged in a fruitless arms buildup, confronting each other, a time bomb? Isn't it high time to jointly explore solutions to these problems by cooperating, not competing, in the Third World? Recent agreements on settling regional conflicts indicate that this is possible.

There is still another reality in the nuclear-space age—the powerlessness of force. This is not a tribute to paradoxes in the spirit of Oscar Wilde but the result of a sober assessment of the record of history. Without enumerating the conflicts which have taken place in the world after the Second World War, let us ask ourselves whether they have yielded some palpable results, say, in changing the borders of states or in ensuring territorial aggrandizement. There have definitely been no changes of any scope. Even superior strength has not given the country unleashing hostilities the desired result, even when this superior force was beefed up with nuclear weapons. Therefore, the conclusion that the use of force is becoming senseless as an instrument of policy holds water. This is particularly evident on the example of the long and bloody Iran–Iraq war. Peaceful, political means have to be sought at the negotiating table.

This conclusion is also of enormous importance for Soviet–Amercian relations. They have been based too long on striving to outdo each other in military strength. The basic premise was that the more armed a state, the more reliable its security. The record has shown however, that the expensive arms race is yielding the opposite result. This was proven by American scientists on the example of their own country. At one time the United States was practically invulnerable militarily. However, the cold war, confrontation, and the arms race began. We will refrain from polemicizing on who was responsible. What is important is something else. Was the security of the United States strengthened by the appearance of intercontinental missiles, nuclear-capable submarines, and transcontinental bombers? The answer is unambiguous. This fully applies to the USSR, too, of course. Therefore, other paths have to be explored and, as has been formalized in joint Soviet–American documents, military superiority should not be sought.

Thus, it is in the national interests of the USSR and the United States not to disperse resources on confrontation but to concentrate them on problems of truly vital importance for security and well-being.

Soviet–American relations will most likely be put to more than one test. Illusions are inappropriate here. However, today there are definitely many more objective possibilities for hoping for success than in the past. I think this holds true for the sweeping changes taking place in the world as a whole. Force must give way to reason, to collective efforts to create reliable security based on peaceful coexistence as a universal principle, on the primacy of law and freedom of choice. This is an unbelievably difficult task, but it is not a fruitless dream either.

In summation, no matter how banal this metaphor may seem, the world is truly at a crossroads. There is a possibility to ensure it a better future. Broad intellectual and material potential is taking shape for the defense of civilization. Of course, there are still many dark, ignorant, and fanatic forces in the world. They still exert a great influence on the basest features of the human character, and it is easier to inspire a person to do evil than good. Regrettably, this is also shown by some events taking place in our own country.

What is important, however, is that the Soviet Union is gearing all its prestige, its policy, and its resources to peaceful development. A serious earnest of the success of the general undertaking is the innovativeness and initiative of Soviet policies and the renewal of foreign-policy approaches in major areas. It is wonderful to be living in these times of positive change.

Russia: The Earth's Heartland

Igor Malashenko

Geopolitical Alignment

Geopolitics, as the term suggest, is the politics of a country as determined by its geographical features.

Russia, as one of the founding fathers of geopolitics, H. Mackinder, held in his day, occupies a central position on the world's map
and lies in its key region, the Heartland, in a giant quadrangle bordering on the Caspian Sea and Lake Baikal in the south and the Arctic
seas in the north.

Relative though such realities are, this region does bring, as if in
focus, all lines of force of the great continent which constitutes the

IGOR MALASHENKO, a young scientist, was an employee of the International Department, Central Committee CPSU, until it ceased its activities.

greater part of the Earth's land surface and contains most of its man-power and economic resources. A classic postulate of geopolitics, as Mackinder formulated it, said: Those who control Eastern Europe dominate the Heartland; those who rule the Heartland dominate the World Island (that is, Eurasia); those who rule the World Island dominate the world. Zbigniew Brzezinski, dismissing the Heartland as an admittedly archaic notion, "straightens" this geopolitical syllogism: those who control Eurasia dominate the world.

The confrontation of the continental power which controls the heart of the Eurasia and the coalition opposing it is by no means confined, geopolitically, to a contest between East and West, social-ism and capitalism (or "totalitarianism" and "liberal democracy," in Western parlance), as it has quite often been made out over the last few decades, but is an element of genuinely global politics. Properly speaking, the very terms "East" and "West" also reflect in a way, if inadequately, the fact that it is not only ideological rivalry or even a clash of social-political systems but also a "deideologized" geopolitical confrontation.

Of course, genuinely global politics is a historically recent phe-nomenon. However, attempts at establishing control over the whole ecumenical world were made more than once in ancient times as well.

For centuries Russia was beating off the West's numerous attempts at establishing control over Eastern Europe, as through the expan-sionism of Lithuania, Poland, France, or Germany. There appeared to be only one way to assure the security of Russia and the key region belonging to it: it was by raising a well-defended geopolitical barrier around it, brick by brick, block by block. This task arose over and over again before various rulers, dynasties, and even political sys-tems. The creation of the Empire was a response to the geopolitical challenge of the West.

By the turn of the century, the imperial idea whose legitimacy had not been called into question for ages had ceased to serve as a raison d'être for polyethnic states; traditional empires began to crumble, and Russia seemed to have the same fate. However, the Revolution gave a fresh and powerful impulse to reinforcing the State, which possessed a machinery of violence of unprecedented proportions, and, what is particularly important, a new source of the legitimacy of power over vast territories of Eurasia.

Revolutionary ideology became an invisible, yet powerful force linking up the parts of the former empire, which disintegrating trends seemed bound to detach from each other. Whether necessary, the instrument used to preserve the unity of the State or to build it up was armed force, which seemed to be a quite lawful continuation of revolutionary violence. There emerged a new political body, a revolutionary empire actually based not on the discredited imperial idea and the nominal "democratic expression of the will" of the peoples in favor of a federation but a revolution which had welded together the power on the verge of disintegration, by iron, blood, and ideology.

The strength of the Soviet state was clearly underestimated by the Third Reich, whose strategists understood well that domination in the heart of Eurasia was the key to world supremacy. Nazi Germany's geopolitical challenge, monstrous by its scale and power, united the Soviet Union, (for which World War II was the struggle for survival), with the Western powers, who were also out to prevent the key geostrategic positions being seized by an avowedly aggressive State.

After the defeat of the Axis powers there was a sweeping realignment of forces, which grouped the Soviet Union's war-time allies with its recent opponents. The international order based on a balance of forces in Europe crumbled during the war, and a power vacuum arose on the European continent, in which the interests of the two mightiest powers, the Soviet Union and the United States, who became geopolitical rivals, were bound to clash. The USSR and the United States have become the main poles of the international system, and relations between them, the main axis of world politics.

The geopolitical division of Europe was kept up by a high level of military-political opposition which had "frozen" the development of traditional contradictions and problems on the continent, and supplemented by a separation due to ideological and social-political considerations. But while the "threat from the East" (or, at least, the belief in it) and the organically "Western" identity constituted a fairly solid base for the unity of the NATO countries, the nations of Eastern Europe for the most part found the Stalinist "socialism," imposed on them, obviously trying. In those circumstances, ideological opposition was largely no more than a "transformed" geopolitical confrontation.

What Moscow saw as the main threat to the nation's security was the prospect of a repetition of what happened in 1941; that is, yet another attempt by a hostile coalition to launch a massive invasion on the territory of the USSR and destroy it as a sovereign state. So it was the top priority of national security policy to avert that threat. One way to deter possible aspirants to domination in Eurasia was by making a "buffer zone" of the states of central and southeastern Europe, under direct military and political control of the USSR, and keeping mammoth ground forces, with their most efficient units advanced well to the West, on the line of contact with a potential enemy.

During the cold war, however, the Soviet Union's main opponent was a naval power which, considering the postwar alignment of force and the strengthened positions of the Soviet Union, could not count on establishing direct control over the heart of Eurasia. It was the founder of the American school of geopolitics, Admiral Alfred Mahan, who first warned that the center of Russia could not be broken and called for her to be "contained" by strong pressure on the flanks. As a matter of fact, this idea formed the basis of the United States postwar "grand strategy."

In the early postwar years, American strategists may have thought that the U. S. monopoly on atomic weapons and strategic delivery vehicles deprived the Heartland of its traditional defensibility and allowed Washington to hope for the acquisition of a global position of strength. However, with the Soviet Union developing a modern nuclear potential which made the mainland United States no longer invulnerable, there was no more ground left for any expectations about "breaking the center of Russia."

The mobility of the United States' power enabled it to put under its influence, in one form or another, a number of key areas on the periphery of Eurasia and to exert unrelenting pressure on the Soviet Union. The old geopolitical postulate revised from the positions of self-centered Americanism, now was that control over the continental edge of Eurasia (or the Rimland as it was called by Nicolas Spykman, another United States geopolitical theoretician) was the way to dominate the mainland as a whole, and eventually the world. The defeat in the Vietnam war and the collapse of such strongholds of American influence as the Shah's regime in Iran demonstrated, however, the futility of the supremacy-seeking ambitions even of such a superpower as the United States.

Postwar history has substantially corrected the straightforward theories about the ways to "world leadership": excessive strengthening of any power, however advantageous its geopolitical position may be, inevitably invites equal (or even superior) counteraction. The Soviet Union has learned this through its own experience when, driven by a desire to ensure its dependable security, not world leadership, it has augmented the size of the territories under its control so much and built up its armed forces to such an extent as to provoke a menacing consolidation of all its rivals.

By its scale and by the aims and priorities of the parties concerned, the cold war was the struggle of the United States and its allies to change the postwar geopolitical alignment in their favor, which was traditionally achieved through full-scale armed confrontations. The reason why there was no global armed confrontation in this case was because, first and foremost, the parties in the geopolitical opposition faced the danger of a nuclear conflict threatening total annihilation. The bipolar opposition generated incessant "small wars" on the world periphery, in the "gray zone" where clashes did not normally create a direct threat to the geopolitical equilibrium.

In an attempt to counter pressure on the flanks, the Soviet Union strove not only to keep all of its postwar gains but to increase its security and extend its sphere of influence. It could do so mostly in distant regions of little geopolitical importance. Yet control over them was, on one hand, extremely dear to achieve, and, on the other, practically of no use in resolving the key objective of ensuring national security. Besides, the traditional methods of military-political control over peripheral territories proved increasingly ineffective as time went on.

For instance, the attempt to solve the Afghan problem by armed force, far from adding to the security of the USSR, created a seat of instability across its southern border, while military aid to a number of Third World regimes turned out to be just an extra economic burden and damaged this country's political reputation.

The colossal Soviet military build-up on the territory of the Warsaw Pact countries did not prevent the social and political trends which ended Soviet political control. The weakening of the political positions of the USSR in Central Europe is accompanied by a reduction of its military presence in that region. In the meantime a united Germany sooner or later will succeed in translating its enormous economic strength into political influence, acquiring the status of a European superpower.

The opponents of the Soviet Union have enough ground for speaking of their success: the USSR has to relinquish its military-political control over Eastern Europe. It is no longer seeking to stop another center of force emerging on the European continent. Only a few rudiments have remained of its "sphere of influence" in the Third World. To cap it all, threatening seats of instability have arisen within its own national frontiers. In Washington's opinion, one of the objectives of the postwar United States strategy, which George Kennan once described as the "gradual mellowing of Soviet power," has been achieved. It is not surprising that, in the new circumstances, President Bush should have declared his intention of going beyond the framework of deterrence inasmuch as its objectives have been achieved. The point is, however, not just whether to concede the victory of the United States or the defeat of the Soviet Union, but to consider the significance of the present geopolitical shifts from the standpoint of national security.

The Post–Postwar Period

The end of the cold war has produced not only a feeling of relief in Soviet society over the winding up of the long drawn out confrontation but also fresh fears over our security and dissatisfaction with the results of years of efforts. Amid apprehensions over the erosion of this country's international positions, it is often asked whether we did the right thing by allowing Eastern Europe to slip out of Soviet control or by reducing our military potential there. Some are urging us to "remember 1941." Today the probability of war is drastically reduced by a new quality of political relations between practically all parties to the cold war. But however small the danger of a direct confrontation between the East (the Soviet Union, to be exact) and the West may be, it is still there, and, therefore, any change of the international order that means lessening the vulnerability of the Soviet armed forces means enhancing our national security.

The withdrawal of most (and, possibly all) Soviet forces from the territory of the Warsaw Pact countries will greatly reduce the danger arising from their forward deployment. Of course, this pullout must be accompanied by certain guarantees of the Soviet Union's security and by keeping a wide disengagement zone established along the perimeter of its Western frontier. This will not ward off any further attempts at exerting pressure on it but will conjure away the specter of yet another blitzkrieg.

There is, in point of fact, a dismantling of our system of military and political control that is going on over vast areas which have been traditionally considered crucial to this country's security. This in turn creates the possibility of transforming the cumbersome, vulnerable, and extremely expensive military machine, which is best suited— with all readjustments to meet the challenges of the day—for enacting the battles of World War II. It has to be replaced by truly modern armed forces, military and technologically upgraded and geared to resist not only the present war damage but also any future one.

I do not mean at all the possible danger of yet another armed invasion of this country's territory in order to "conquer the Heartland" or to "destroy socialism"; today that is a plot for a military-political fiction story. Wars can be brought on, however, not only by the action of an aggressor deliberately setting out to upset the status quo. The internationalization and escalation of conflicts on ethnic and religious grounds or an internal collapse in any country can lead to an armed conflict which nobody wished or foresaw. Therefore, the marked lessening of the threat which we feared so much and prepared to meet does not, unfortunately, mean the complete removal of the war danger.

There need be no fear that the withdrawal of Soviet troops from Afghanistan and Czechoslovakia, Mongolia, and Hungary, and the reduction of the armed forces and munitions production will diminish this country's security, the Soviet Union's colossal nuclear potential is a reliable shield capable of resisting attempts at obtaining domination in the heart of Eurasia by force of arms. Conversely, a further overextension of all forces and resources for the sake of maintaining military-political control over vast territories can deplete the nation's richest potential and undermine the source of its strength and security from within.

A heavy price had to be paid for the preservation of the "monolithic unity" of the huge geopolitical conglomerate. It was artificially isolated from the world economy, its scientific and technical level and living standards were low. The protracted crisis of the Soviet economy is a natural consequence not only of its antimarket character but also of its submission to geopolitics in its classical imperial interpretation.

Yet it is a nation's economic strength, its science and technology potential and the appeal of its model of social, political, and cultural development that increasingly become a guarantee of the maintenance and consolidation of its geopolitical positions and the basic parameters of its power. For instance, Germany and Japan, which sustained a crushing defeat in World War II, have, to judge by all accounts, realized the fatality of banking on armed force to achieve national ambitions. It is their reliance on the nonmilitary factors of strength that allowed them to secure international influence out of all proportion to their rather limited military potential—once the major yardstick of aggregate national power.

The Soviet Union's ability to influence its international environment and, in the long run, the strength of its geopolitical positions will depend in large measure on whether or not this country succeeds in embracing a basically new model of economic, social, and political development. For relative "demilitarization" and "economization" of international relations do not mean that geopolitical realignment is impossible. It cannot be achieved (at least, in the foreseeable future) by military means. The Soviet Union still holds the key geopolitical positions. If it grows so weak that a power vacuum appears in the middle of Eurasia, it will inevitably be filled by one or several contiguous powers greatly augmenting their specific weight and influence.

Why is it, then, that today, when many find the Soviet Union slipping downhill, Western leaders, above all those of the United States, far from trying to speed up this process, are speaking of their "support for perestroika" and do not go into raptures at all over the prospect of some republics leaving the USSR, let alone of it breaking up?

Successive American administration never tire of making the point that it is in the vital interest of the United States to "prevent any hostile power or group of powers from dominating Eurasian land mass." It should be added that any state aiming to achieve it—whatever its ideology or social-political system—would surely geopoliticians prefer, I think, to see the Heartland of Eurasia still controlled by the Soviet Union, worn down in the cold war and, in their opinion, growing weaker still, rather than face new "troublemakers" and, by the same token, a threat of succession of crises and conflicts.

What is happening today both because of the weakening of the Soviet Union and as a result of the emergence of new centers of power in Eurasia is an erosion of the postwar structure of bipolar confrontation, which is being replaced by a multipolar system of international relations built largely on a balance of forces (not only and not so much of military forces, in the present circumstances). If the system of the balance of forces that had taken shape on the European continent after the Napoleonic Wars was aimed at preventing anybody's supremacy in Europe (France's, first of all, in those days) in the present conditions it will have to ensure a balance in Eurasia as a whole. It means that the USSR is losing its status of a superpower and is becoming merely one of the power centers of Eurasis. In its turn, the United States, which retains its power in absolute parameters, will be increasingly operating as an external balance-wheel averting the rise of a pan-Eurasian center of power.

The geopolitical round, which was set going by the last gunshots of World War II, is over. Yet another realignment of forces is going on right before our eyes. A new geopolitical alignment will depend, first and foremost, on the outcome of the internal processes in the Soviet Union and on whether this country succeeds in stemming the tide of crisis and reviving the internal sources of its strength.

Beyond Geopolitics

Major shifts inside one of the principal centers of power may have far-reaching geopolitical consequences. For instance, the growing disintegrating trends and the prospect of a breakup of the Austro-Hungarian Empire—one of the basic elements of the balance of forces on the European continent—had become an important factor of destabilizing that system in advance of World War I. Still more far-reaching were the consequences of the resurgence of German nationalism and the ensuing refusal of the Kaiser and then Nazi Germany to follow "the rules" of the balance of forces and also banking on expansionism.

The energy essential for the geopolitical shifts we are witnessing today has taken decades to build up, but it is only the changes inside the Soviet Union that have made a transformation of the international order a reality. Of course, an appreciable effect was produced even by the opening foreign policy moves of the present Soviet leadership when our society had not in fact yet begun the perestroika process. But it was the internal development of the USSR that brought about changes which allow us to speak of the end of the cold war. That was particularly manifest in the events in Eastern Europe, stimulated precisely by the Soviet reform policy which has given the "green light" for the dismantling of Stalin's socialism and the acquisition of a new geopolitical status by this region.

The central political issue of perestroika is the problem of the legitimacy of power; that is, its "lawfulness" in the full sense of the term, not only and not so much in legal as in sociopolitical and historical respects. With our seven decades gone since the Revolution, one shouldn't be surprised at the gradual weakening of the role of revolutionary legacy as the source of the legitimacy of power and the cementing force in the polyethnic State. Remembering the historical fate of other revolutions, it is rather more surprising that this process should not have begun much earlier. The future of this polyethnic State also depends, to a certain extent, on the results of the search for a new framework of the legitimacy through democratic development.

The gradual dismantling of the structures of totalitarianism and the natural process of the extension and consolidation of democracy spotlight the imperial origin of the present federation in which disintegrating trends are gaining momentum. The idea of democracy and its political "materialization" can hardly by themselves serve as a sufficiently solid "backbone" for an updated federation. As one can see, for instance, from the record of Yugoslavia's democratic process after Tito, a stronger antidote is needed to neutralize nationalism.

It is an overall reform of the economy and progress towards economic integration, which it is quite likely to stimulate, and can set off centripetal trends. The present state of the Soviet economy is actually fueling the separatist trends: Just about every republic or region is dissatisfied with their place in the system of the division of labor and, still more so, with its share of the economic "pie." So long as the economic system ensured extensive growth, at least, with the political one blocking the outbreaks of nationalism and regionalism, that state of things was somehow tolerated. The crisis in the economy and political democratization made a recasting of that economic system imperative.

Not even the creation of a "normal" and effectively working economy will necessarily outweigh the disintegrating forces. What I mean is not only the pace of economic change which will take years to effect and will inevitably fall behind political change, but also the ability of economic leverage to contain separatist trends. Politics is by no means a wholly rational process based on a sober assessment of advantages and disadvantages, economic ones included, still less rational action prompted by national aspirations which an outside observer always finds totally irrational. Therefore, even the use of all economic leverage to preserve the federation at any cost (which, incidentally, will inevitably hold back the economic reform) may prove ineffective in deterring the republics from separating from the Union.

Does this mean that the disintegrating forces will inexorably build up and that all we can do is wait and see the genie of nationalism breaking free to destroy a centuries-old power, with unpredictable geopolitical consequences?

Another central question—from the standpoint of the Union's future and geopolitics—is one of the future of Russia, which has historically occupied the key region of Eurasia. It was largely for the sake of its security that an empire was built.

Geographic features would hardly have by themselves acquired such great importance for world politics if they had not been connected with ethnic factors. For "geography" in this context is taken to mean not just the geographic map but some real territory integral to the destinies of various peoples, or ethnoses, properly speaking. Ethnoses, in their turn, exist in the context of society and the State which pursues a certain policy. Therefore, the connection between geography and politics is indirect, rather than direct. For this reason, not only sociopolitical processes but, also ethnocultural ones inside a particular country can have far-reaching geopolitical consequences.

The crises and conflicts that are shaking this giant country of ours today are not only (and, perhaps, not so much) of a political and economic character but of an ethnocultural character as well. Russia is by no means an imperial state only, having mechanically united an incredibly multifarious conglomerate of lands. It is an ethnically and culturally unique country (a "superethnos," as Lev Gumilev called it), lying in Europe and Asia; that is, a Eurasian country in the true sense of the word, which was not only an instrument of expansionism but also a powerful center of attraction for numerous ehtnoses.[4]

But one can hardly deny Russia's appeal to those ethnoses of Eu-

rope and Asia which have formed an incredibly sophisticated organism over the centuries. If you take Western Europe as the starting
point, this is not a phenomenon of particular importance (for the
"true Europeans" have remained outside the field of attraction, anyway). However, Western Europe, having become the breeding
ground of two world wars because of its inability to cope with the
forces of nationalism, is only today groping its way to overall integration, and it is not so sure in doing that either, to judge by the fears
of German unification. Russia, on the other hand, so obviously inferior to the West in many parameters, succeeded in becoming what M.
Hefter described as a "nation of nations," "the Eurasia house."

Of course, Russian history is far from presenting a tinsel picture of
a voluntary union of peoples, many of whom have been incorporated
as a result of wars and conquests. Those territories of the former
empire, which have never become integral to the fabric of Russian
and irresistibly gravitate toward other superethnoses (not necessarily
Western, but, say, Muslim) are most likely to strive consistently for
secession. And however painful this process might be, the strength
and security of a reborn federation will hardly suffer in the end.

For centuries, the vast diversity of the various parts of Russia has
served not so much as a threat to her integrity as a condition for her
preservation as an ethnocultural system. Official Russification and
imperial depersonalization, even though provoking natural rejection
in the provinces, still did not create anything like a real danger to the
very survival of ethnoses and to their distinctive development. This
system must have become so complex and even unwieldy as to require to be altered and simplified at the turn of the century. The disintegration of the empire, with some "blocks" breaking away, would
quite likely have given rise to a more integral and compact entity
capable of evolution. What happened instead was an oversimplifica-
tion of the integral structure, the removal of the partitions which
separated the various ethnocultural elements, and the "straighten-
ing" of connections between them. It was like a giant steamroller
passing over the surface of this Eurasian country, leveling the distinctions between the various ethnoses and cultures.

For a time, the dismantling of the structure which had taken a
tremendous effort to keep up generated a vast amount of energy to
use outside national frontiers, as, for example, for establishing direct
military-political control of the State over vast new territories, and

advancing far to the West. But the same process of dismantling undermined the nation's major internal source of strength and viability and condemned it to stagnation.

Today, however, we have far less ground for pessimism that we had just a few years ago when this country floundered in the deadening grip of immobility. The hope for the better comes largely, strange though it might seem, from the same drive for independence and regionalism which in their extreme manifestation beget outbreaks of violence and militant separatism. The pressure of some regions, whether the national republics as such or the Russian Federation and its individual components, for secession and their pursuit of a form of autonomy spring largely not only from their economic interests (these are easy to see), but from intensified ethnocultural processes without which you cannot imagine the rebirth of Russia as a "nation of nations." And if Russia should still remain a symbiosis of various ethnoses and cultures, her rebirth will be a natural and powerful process, and we shall, beyond question, come to occupy a worthy place in Eurasia and, hence, in the world.

Russia and the empire have different lots in store for them. The cold war ended with the defeat of the empire. The defeat of the empire has been the starting point of the regeneration of Russia and a new geopolitical round.

PART II

"Pro" and "Con"

Introduction to Part II

For many years *International Affairs* magazine occupied an old mansion in a district that used to be called the German Village. It was the place where foreign merchants, artisans, teachers, and diplomats settled since the time of Czar Ivan the Terrible and, especially, Peter the Great. With the passage of time the district became Moscow's energetic commercial and political center where business was negotiated, deals struck, and contracts signed. Here the editorial board has launched a Guest Club of its own to hold meetings, talks, and discussions, and to generally seek concord. Politicians, businessmen, diplomats, artists, and plain men-of-the-street meet there every month. Ambassadors of the United States, Great Britain, and many other nations and prominent U.S. political scientists and members of the public have shared in our disputes.

A discussion in winter 1991 concentrated on some results, achievements, and failures of the "new thinking" policy of the recent past.

In the summer of 1990 our Guest Club hosted the first ever meeting of leaders of the country's new political parties. We found interesting a discussion young research workers of Moscow's leading centers of science held when they met in our Guest Club. They manifested a creative spirit and fresh approaches to problems of the USSR foreign political line. On another occasion, Moscovites of different professions, walks of life, and opinions were invited, almost randomly, to join a Guest Club discussion which ended with probing what they thought of the Soviet foreign policy.

—BORIS PYADYSHEV

Perestroika, Sixth Winter

Professor Yuri Gavrilov, D. Sc. (Hist.), head, chair of World Politics and International Relations, Academy of Social Sciences under the CPSU CC

Boris Kapustin, D. Ph., a professor at the Academy of Social Sciences

Yevgeni Kutovoi, D. Sc. (Hist.), chief adviser, Evaluations and Planning Directorate, USSR Ministry of Foreign Affairs

Igor Malashenko, Cand. Ph., senior reference, International Department, CPSU CC

Tatiana Matveyeva, Cand. Sc. (Hist.), assistant professor, Academy of Social Sciences

Boris Pugachev, D. Ph., a professor at the Academy of Social Sciences

Boris Pyadyshev, D. Sc. (Hist.), editor-in-chief, *International Affairs*

Igor Yanin, Cand. Sc. (Hist.), deputy head, Scientific Department, Academy of Social Sciences

Nikita Zagladin, D. Sc. (Hist.), a professor at the Academy of Social Sciences

B. Pyadyshev. Looking six years back, I can't help telling myself that it all started very long ago and that many things aren't going the way they were expected to at the time.

At the 27th CPSU Congress, or the last of the traditional party congresses, much was proclaimed and done by force of habit. If its records were to appear today, they would be resolutely voted down. And yet those were the days when the early shoots of the new came into sight as new political thinking took shape. Because ours is a highly dogmatized society, perestroika in foreign policy, too, proceeded as a clash between dogmas, a struggle to defeat long-standing stereotypes.

There is still a lot of controversy and rhetoric over what Mikhail Gorbachev said about the priority of universal values, which he first did at the meeting with participants in the Issyk Kul forum. Initially it turned out to be necessary to uphold that idea in the traditional manner, or dogmatically, by referring to Lenin, quoting sacred Marxist truths, and so on. Still, the idea is clear and indisputable: let us live as befits civilized people, let us stop what is a senseless war of attrition, let us cooperate with all countries. Nevertheless, some refuse to "forgo principles." They are worried about the disappearance of the class approach to world affairs.

Another idea of new political thinking, one that didn't immediately win recognition, concerns military strategic matters. It rejects as hopeless, unnecessary, and absurd any attempt to pursue a military policy calculated to build arsenals matching all those of the other blocs, to keep pace in military power not only with the United States as our chief adversary but with NATO as a whole.

Six years on, we realize that those ideas are sound and normal. They've become principles of our foreign policy in both theory and everyday practice and are already perceived in the main as normal. True, on being translated into deeds in the foreign policy sphere, especially in Eastern Europe, they were bound to produce results that aren't easy to accept. And whereas the first three or four years of perestroika saw Soviet foreign policy enjoy a "honeymoon," being exempt from criticism, lately Smolenskaya Square has tended to become a target for emotional, often scathing critical remarks.

Y. Gavrilov. I wish to add to what Boris Pyadyshev said, that six years ago it never occurred to even the boldest of us that the paradigms of our home and foreign policy concepts would be replaced so fast. Let us recall that before April 1985 we lived in a society "of which mankind's best mind dreamed." and was said to have "eliminated any objective basis for the rise of crises or social contradictions." Our ideology was essentially a Hegelian type of idealism, for the laws of dialectics and the struggle of opposites as the prime cause and bedrock of social progress were supposed to have been valid only at previous stages of history and to have had no relation to us since October 1917.

If we admitted in exceptional cases the rise of temporary and partial deviations here and there, we attributed them to the peculiarities of certain individuals and saw those people's death or the end of their tenure of office as a guarantee that no deviations or infringements of a similar nature would reoccur. Foreign policy held pride of place in the herd of our "sacred cows," for it always continued our home policy, developing it in breadth and depth, and was said to invariably provide optimum conditions for the realization of the interests of our working people and progressives throughout the world.

We always expressed and defended them in full, well knowing how to advance and how to lead others, so that the role of the rest was reduced to accepting our leadership and appreciating the wisdom and comprehensiveness of our proposals. In the circumstances, our awakening to the unity and interdependence of the world, if relative at first, and our renunciation of the dogma about the existence of two entirely separate worlds were a great moral, scientific, political, and human achievement.

I. Yanin. We've long known home and foreign policy to be interconnected. Foreign policy is a continuation of home policy, but how can it go well amid hunger and dislocation at home? We are offered food relief like paupers, which we actually are. And what are we to think of ourselves in connection with the Middle East, where we helped create an aggressive regime in Iraq, arming it to the teeth with the most up-to-date weapons? Who will answer for that?

These questions need to be put to leaders, to those responsible for general policy.

T. Matveyeva. Six years ago, it might have seemed rather strange to include humanitarian things in new political thinking alongside its military, political, and economic components. But this component proved vital and became inseparable from a comprehensive security system. Indeed, it enables new thinking to gain ground in world politics.

The task is to look primarily through man at all problems, at Afghanistan, disarmament, the economic crisis. This is indispensable for success. Humanitarian problems call for cooperation between scholars in East and West alike, for a search for politological consensus on these problems, if you will.

N. Zagladin. Who has changed more? We say that we changed policy and appealed to the world, making it change for its part. The implication is that both sides have changed. I believe this is wishful thinking. It's we who have changed. There's no particular perestroika under way in the West, except that it's revising its foreign policy and military political doctrines. It is our society that has been changing, becoming more open to the world, more acceptable to the other side as a partner in dialogue.

In carrying out perestroika, we've been eliminating factors which earlier prevented the West from joining in dialogue with us, from looking on us as a partner, and made it see us as a rival. What were those factors? I think they were something more than our ideology, our bid to back "revolutionary" forces all over the world, to act in a way injuring the interests of the other side. After all, the West followed the same rules of the game.

The reason must have been our command system and the foreign policy interests generated by its functioning. We had rigidly centralized economic planning. That centralized machine needed an international division of labor on some sort of mutually beneficial basis. But the logic of the command system's functioning is apparently such that the system can have no relations on an equal footing with countries where there is a free market. It can't coexist at all with the world market, which functions on the principle of free price formation, where there constantly appear new commodities not envisaged by our five-year plans, and so on.

There was only one way in which our society could meet its requirement for an international division of labor: by shaping in other countries a command system similar to ours and hence functioning on the same principles; that is, planning, coordination of plans, and so on. In other words, we really saw the whole thing as a question of who would win, of whether there would be centralization at a world level, with Moscow as its center, or a free market. The principles of economic activity were completely incompatible. The only possibility was to engage in natural trade, in a minimum of commodity exchange.

The fact that we opened ourselves to the world and entered the world market by accepting the principles of organizing a market economy removed the main cause of rivalry and confrontation. Had our ideas triumphed worldwide—assuming such a fantastic thing to be possible—this wouldn't have ensured lasting peace among nations. That's because a command system needs a center. As soon as a reasonably strong country took a road similar to the one chosen by us, it tried to become an independent center. China is a case in point.

The rivalry between the Soviet Union and China was, in effect, a struggle between two centers of the command system at a global level. The greater the number of strong countries making a choice comparable to ours, the more bitterly they would have fought among themselves and the less international stability there would have been.

B. Kapustin. I believe the new political thinking in 1985 and 1986 reflected a certain negative consensus, meaning primarily recognition by sufficiently influential political forces of what must not be. In the foreign policy sphere, that negative consensus was quite widespread and outspoken at the early stage, as I see it. If we don't want to get stuck in this early stage, which we must in principle go through both theoretically and in terms of our foreign policy, we must realize the utter insufficiency of this kind of consensus. We need a definite parallelogram of forces that would produce a vector of social development inside the country and in foreign policy.

Y. Kutovoi. I can't agree that new political thinking is "dogmatic" or imperfect as a factor influencing the policy of other countries. The past five and a half years have witnessed quite a few instances of real and tangible influence.

No new ideas can win minds overnight, for people prefer to judge the intentions of other countries' governments according to their deeds, all the more since in the past many foreign policy ideas and concepts were advanced for propaganda purposes.

It took us quite some time to convince Western leaders that our foreign policy based on new thinking was neither a tactical ploy nor a zigzag and that we hadn't proclaimed it for purely selfish ends.

I agree, however, that new thinking mustn't be allowed to become a rigid dogma. We must carry it forward now that we are moving on from cold war and confrontation to partnership and cooperation.

I. Malashenko. New thinking, within the contents of this discussion, is an ideology of liberal foreign policy activism. I don't believe it was accidental that everything began with new thinking. Ours was an extremely ideologized society, and the only way for us to change our behavior and foreign policy somehow was by also changing our ideology. Hence that attempt was made to appeal rather to ideological standards than to practical considerations.

I think that period is over and that this is well, because ideology in foreign policy is counterproductive. To use any ideology as a guide in foreign policy is to court very serious trouble. This is because foreign policy is basically a highly professional sphere of action in which you have to have a clear idea of what's going on, what objective laws and concrete considerations determine your partners' behavior on the international scene. It follows that by trying to start from abstractions, which is inevitable where ideology is involved, we are likely to come up in the end against formidable problems. Strictly speaking, we're already encountering them, and this situation may deteriorate at any moment.

T. Matveyeva. I see the strength and vitality of new political thinking in the fact that the decisive component of its worldview is its humanitarian approach. It regards the human dimension as part of the system of ensuring security along with the military, political, economic, and other components. What we describe as old thinking was burdened with ideologized paradigms and prevented politicians from assessing the twentieth-century world realistically, from seeing man as the main factor in it. That thinking reduced the possibility of appreciating the paramount importance of universal interests and subordinating the whole world political mechanism to them.

New thinking put that unnatural situation right by reviving the humanist ideas of ancient philosophers about every inhabitant of the earth being a dweller of a common home, about the common responsibility of all for the fortunes of civilization. It actually laid the groundwork for a new methodology of solving global problems and substantiated the idea of humanitarian cooperation in the process of evolving and molding a new world order.

Y. Gavrilov. I visited Beijing in 1960 with a Spartak junior soccer team. Every time our boys reached the halfway line, the Chinese referee would order a penalty kick. Nikolai Starostin and Pyotr Dementyev tried to protest but the Chinese reacted very calmly. "We aren't affiliated to FIFA," they said. "Its rules don't apply to us. We're playing according to our own rules." For years we imagined, or so I believe, that we could "play" in the world according to our rules.

But nothing came of it, nor could it have. There have to be common rules and common laws of world development. But this turned out to be very hard to grasp. We had to give up the conviction that we were unique and could set an example of development to the world.

B. Kapustin. Yuri Gavrilov said that new political thinking was being criticized, at least in our country, above all with references to our would-be uniqueness in the world community, to objective laws allegedly not applying to us, and so on.

I feel that new political thinking can be criticized from a different position by those who recognize that these laws also apply to us and know how they operate in a given civilization, culture, social group. To my mind, new political thinking, including the declarations we've heard from some of our leaders, isn't explicit enough on this point.

Y. Gavrilov. How are we to arrive at the realization that we aren't necessarily a beacon for the world? How to learn to live in a world where others have accomplished much more in many respects? I suppose this is something that also explains the criticism being levelled at Soviet foreign policy today. People bred to an ideology and psychology of uniqueness, of being entirely different from the rest of the world, find it difficult to rethink all that in favor of acknowledging that our country isn't the best part of the world.

B. Kapustin. The priority of universal values is a magnificent idea but it connotes an "anti." We proved unable to formulate these values in concrete terms as universal imperatives of world development. I would say that the universal, if carried beyond an abstraction, is the historic interests of the human race; that is, its interests at any given stage of development.

It's a set of universal imperatives. Any society which fails to meet them understandably finds itself on the sidelines of world development. Imperatives can't be reduced to abstract moral concepts, however much we may respect these concepts. After all, it wasn't accidental that Mikhail Gorbachev didn't speak about private property until last August in Odessa, was it? Surely we have an imperative in that form of multistructural world development, in that diversity of which private property is a very important element.

How could anyone who didn't see this imperative have talked about real foreign policy or about universal values? It's as clear as day that a pluralist political system is a further imperative of this kind. In our country, however, we are only just beginning to recognize the idea of a multiparty system. You will recall the furious resistance put up when it came to abolishing Article Six of the Constitution, including resistance from our top leadership held to be the exponent, ideologist, and vehicle of new political thinking.

In a word, the "universal" is still largely an abstraction or appeal actually meaning "anti." As for its constructive aspect, its substance, it plainly has yet to be worked out. This explains, I think, why it turned out to be extremely difficult to introduce the idea of universal values not only into our home policy, in which it practically failed to take root, but into foreign political affairs. Our foreign policy has really scored impressive successes that I have no intention of minimizing in the least. But the past five years have also been situations where it was very hard to put new political thinking into practice, with universal values as a priority.

There can be no doubt whatever that foreign policy has been and will remain an arena of struggle between definite forces. Of course, this struggle should go on in civilized forms, not as a fist fight. The forces forming the axis of world development are no longer what they used to be. They are entirely different now. We missed the mark whenever we tried to size up these forces by means of mirages and yardsticks of twenty or thirty years' standing. Anyway, there's a real struggle on.

I. Malashenko. Let us look at the problem of the Gulf crisis. Shall we use armed force to impose our idea of universal values on Iraq? Shall we support the Americans or condemn the use of any force in this situation and allow Saddam Hussein to swallow Kuwait? We have a whole array of alternatives here.

I wonder how we are to follow realistically universal values which aren't, in fact, accepted by most of humanity and which we vehemently rejected for decades. Did we do so for lack of comprehension or because the state of our society demanded it?

The result is a downright absurd situation where whole countries and peoples must periodically fully reject their former values. At present we apparently expect that the Iraq people will overcome their stupor sooner or later and say that they were wrong to reject universal values.

B. Pyadyshev. One result of our perestroika policy is that the issue of the "peaceful coexistence of countries with different social systems" is being struck off the agenda of world politics, or so it seems. This may sound like too bold a statement but I'll try to support it with facts.

Throughout the postwar decades, that formulation has been a necessary component of major bilateral and multilateral documents involving the East and the West. With politicians and political scientists, the understandable desire to find a universal formula for the preservation of peace was accompanied by painful quests, tactical maneuvering, and fortunate or not quite fortunate solutions. But we see as we look back that those constructions never carried much weight. Frequent references were made to Lenin, who was represented as the founding father of peaceful coexistence although he never uttered the phrase.

The slogan of peaceful coexistence occasionally won popularity, attracting politicians from both world camps. But euphoria would give way to disillusionment. Everyone in our country and elsewhere seemed to like the interpretation offered by Khrushchev. But it failed on being complemented by the promise to back national liberation movements in Asia, Africa, and Latin America or, in other words, to wage a discreet, backyard war against our Western partners, to whom we had made the call: "Let us live in harmony."

Everybody liked the clear-cut wording of the 1972 Soviet–U.S. Declaration, which said that in the nuclear era there was no alternative to peaceful coexistence. But this statement became a dead letter when we explained, in order to reassure our intransigent zealots of the purity of faith, that peaceful coexistence was a form of the class struggle. And we illustrated it in the seventies through activist operations in Africa, Central America, Southeast Asia, and, as the crowning folly, in Afghanistan.

In short, "peaceful coexistence" fared poorly in the contemporary world. It didn't work, nor could it have.

It's only now that opportunities for real, genuine peace are opening up. For the first time in postwar history, leaders of states similar in sociopolitical character or moving closer in this respect met in Paris. As far as the Soviet Union is concerned, this did not become possible until very recently. Emerging in our country are pluralism, a multiparty system, and, most importantly, a market economy. I therefore consider the key provision of the Paris Charter for a New Europe to be the following: "*Freedom and political pluralism* are necessary elements of our common goal-the development of a *market economy* (my italics.—B. P.) in the direction of stable economic growth, prosperity, social justice, greater employment, and effective utilization of economic resources."

In the new conditions, at a time when all-European areas with coinciding but also understandably diverse political, economic, and intellectual values are taking shape, there is no need for a policy of "peaceful coexistence." It has fulfilled its mission, at least passably, and should now retire into the textbooks of history.

The task is to live normally, not to coexist. Political life is coming to be determined by new, more realistic and reliable concepts and circumstances.

However, what I've said is true mainly of Europe. It is on this continent that new political thinking has been put to the test and has made appreciable progress.

I. Yanin. The Paris meeting may be described variously. We may "spell out" its deep meaning in the traditional way, constantly referring to new thinking and the dogmas of stagnation, which would certainly have made any such thing possible. Or we may interpret the meeting as a fine occasion for reflecting on our home and foreign policy. This would be very interesting, for the relationship between these two "policies" is only too curious.

In other words, we could describe the whole epic of our accomplishments on the international scene as "brilliant successes of our foreign policy coupled with a brilliant lack of home policy." Nor is this an affected paradox. Incidentally, I suppose all of us tried hard until recently to guess the source of the persistent criticism of all our foreign policy actions (obvious successes) that began shortly before the founding congress of the Communist Party of Russia. We wondered what grounds there were for it.

Impatient journalists asked questions about this at news conferences. The answer offered them was that we would by all means tell the press as soon as we ourselves got to know what was going on. But it's almost more revealing that annoyance at breakthroughs and gains by our diplomats and Mikhail Gorbachev is betrayed not only by CPR "neo-Bolsheviks" and other overvigilant defenders of the country but by perfectly reasonable people trying to think logically.

"We've scored some successes, all right," they argue, "and yet life is getting worse from day to day. Forty-five years after Victory, plans are being laid to introduce rationing. Our onetime enemies, who were defeated in the last war, are collecting food products for the Soviet Union, and Wehrmacht veterans are sending our war veterans Christmas parcels."

Our logical-minded citizens are told that the war menace has really been removed for the first time, the cold war has been solemnly buried, and the Soviet Union and United States have become friends. "That's all very well," they answer, "but with outside pressure and the war menace gone, our Union is falling apart and we've got refugees for the first time in conditions of peace."

All this is certainly depressing, especially since the successes in question are real or, in other words, their necessity doesn't have to be proved. Eduard Shevardnadze had reason to be worried when "rendering account" of his ministry's performance to the 28th CPSU Congress. After all, he was compelled to prove self-evident things.

Still, our public opinion can't understand why changes for the better on the "external front" are accompanied by a worsening situation at home. I think this is due to the existence of an enormous discrepancy between our home and foreign policy. "It's necessary to interlink things," whispered one of Tolstoy's literary characters hovering between life and death. He had found a clue to the mystery of life.

Y. Kutovoi. After proclaiming principles to which society responded calmly, we proceeded to practical political steps, particularly in the area of our military-industrial potential, but it emerged that we weren't mature enough to act on our political thinking. When we said that we had no "Brezhnev doctrine" applicable to East European countries, everybody agreed. But when, notwithstanding the turbulent processes that began unfolding there, we really refused to take any practical steps in, say, the GDR, there came a generally very serious reaction on various levels.

Such perfectly logical contradictions arise whenever theory clashes with practice. We must know how to resolve them. This is a requisite of the art of both political and diplomatic leadership.

B. Pugachev. It's obvious to everybody that the self-liquidation of the WTO as it now stands is a foregone conclusion. The only realistic alternative could be to transform the WTO into a political alliance guaranteeing general political configurations in Europe, primarily its eastern part, a smooth transition. Be that as it may, I feel that the fate of the WTO will be sealed within the next six months.

I also see few chances of NATO being preserved in a modified form. The overall trend of its coming reform is to shift the emphasis to the political aspects of the organization's activity and lend it a more European political slant, making it an instrument of all-European security. This effort is now being stepped up.

I consider the integration of the East and West of Europe a protracted process. The EC isn't prepared just yet to admit East European countries, although they want to join it and have in effect said so.

The integration process will evidently pass through several stages. What we can expect in the next five years is only the admission of individual East European countries to the EC as associated members. Hungary has already announced its intention to join the EC.

It seems to me that the West's political and economic efforts in relations with the Soviet Union are going to be shifted from the center, from Moscow, to the republican and subrepublican levels. East and West European countries are already intensifying their links with individual Soviet republics: Estonia, Latvia, Lithuania, the Ukraine, Byelorussia, Moldova, and Russia. We may expect a further intensification.

Reflecting on this from the theoretical point of view, I see one reason for it in the conservation of national relations with the totalitarian regimes of socialist countries at the level of the eighteenth century, in a kind of feudalization of these relations.

The breakup of totalitarian regimes moved Eastern Europe and the Soviet Union back to the nineteenth century, not forward to modern times. Everywhere we're witnessing the assertion of the idea of the nation-state, or what is basically a nineteenth-century idea. Western Europe will enter the twenty-first century as a single multinational political area. This is a fundamental change not only in thinking but in contemporary Western European politics. It amounts to a sort of a gap between Eastern and Western Europe. New political vision must perceive these realities in any contingency. I regard it as just a further utopian notion to imagine that building a new common European house will be easy and free from conflict.

N. Zagladin. To many of us, the process of change in the world came as a surprise. It didn't go as expected. We were used to viewing the world through the prism of Soviet–American rivalry and confrontation between the two military blocs. While we said abstractly that there were third countries, that there was a Third World having its interests, we saw that, nonetheless as something of secondary importance. We used to look at most conflicts and collisions in the Third World from the stand point of confrontation between the two blocs, trying above all to forecast the likely effect of a particular trend of development on the power balance between the two blocs.

That confrontation is a thing of the past now, and we can say that Soviet–American relations have been normalized while the third world is in turmoil—evidence that it has always had interests of its own. Confrontation between the blocs led to their deformation and made them adapt to it as a factor for global development. Now that this global factor is gone, the developed world is faced with the Third World.

This provides a basis for our interaction with the West.

I. Malahenko. Europe has been at the epicenter of change in recent years. I think the reason for this is clear enough. World War II destroyed the power balance that had existed in Europe for centuries. Europe was the center of the world order. And suddenly there appeared a vacuum that came to be filled by the Soviet Union and the United States. We shouldered a burden that was too heavy for us. We tried to freeze and maintain the status quo, and to that end we had to use an incredible proportion of our national resources. In other words, the conflict over Europe was probably inevitable although it was greatly aggravated by an ideological conflict. But there were also things that could have been avoided. For one thing, we could have avoided the dead-end concept of parity mentioned here by Boris Pyadyshev, meaning a bid to equal in power not only the United States but practically the rest of the world. We could also have refrained from attempts to build a Soviet sphere of influence in the Third World.

We overstrained ourselves. It was just inevitable. I think it's from this angle that we should consider first of all the changes which have occurred in Europe. Theoretically, even allowing for the obviously inevitable postwar partition of Europe, we could have tried to build our sphere of influence in Eastern Europe on less ideologized lines, to create a belt of neutral, friendly countries. But, of course, no such result would have been acceptable to the Soviet regime of the time.

Speaking of the unification of Germany, some ask who stands to gain from it and whether it could have been averted. It certainly could not because our postwar strategy provided not only for partitioning Europe but for trying to prevent the rise of a new power center in Europe. We lacked the means needed to follow that line.

B. Pugachev. I believe the very character of changes in Eastern Europe is markedly revolutionary. What has come about there is an enforced change of political leadership and social order, which have given way to an entirely new type of economy. I don't think the revolutions that are on in Eastern Europe can be squeezed into the doctrinal formula of a socialist or bourgeois revolution or a counter-revolution. Those are distinctive popular revolutions of an antitotalitarian nature structurally close—that is, close in form—to the revolutionary events of the seventies in Spain and Portugal. I suppose it was inevitable that these revolutions should assume an anticommunist character.

B. Pyadyshev. I'd like to add to what Boris Pugachev said here, that we are responsible for what happened in East European countries before and what is happening today. But we shouldn't take on the whole burden of responsibility. Part of the responsibility for disintegration falls on those countries themselves, on their leaderships. As far as I know, the socialist countries practically enjoyed freedom of political and economic action from the second half of the seventies onwards. Supervision on our part was purely symbolic. They did everything by themselves. This goes above all for Romania, where Ceausescu jealously kept everybody out of his affairs. But Hungary, Czechoslovakia, the GDR, Poland, and Bulgaria were largely alike. What has occurred in those countries is a product of the policy of their leaderships.

B. Pugachev. What can we expect in East European countries in the foreseeable future? I think the swift dismantling of totalitarian structures made the East European societies unstable. They find themselves in a state of transition. The political struggle there is bitter and will continue. We are in the presence of the formation of a new type of economy based on a real diversity of forms of property. We've seen no such thing so far. However, the actual experience of creating a market economy in Poland, Hungary, and Czechoslovakia shows, in my opinion, that building a mixed economy takes a long time and that half measures are apt to reduce the economy to painful stagnation. It is important for us to know this, especially now, for we are following the same model.

I believe the whole social structure of society will soon undergo a deep change. The share of wage labor in state enterprises will diminish sharply, a large stratum of private proprietors and a middle class will emerge, and we'll get whole groups of people working in private enterprises. With socially active, competitive groups gaining strength at one pole, marginal, noncompetitive ones will form at the other. This is socially dangerous and ultimately fraught with conflict.

Furthermore, I'm sure the next five to seven years will see in Eastern Europe new societies built on new social, economic, and political foundations and guided by a different set of values. The liberal democrats who've come to power there will evidently experience mounting pressure from national conservative forces. We can expect a rapid growth of nationalism in Eastern Europe, a resultant exacerbation of earlier conflicts between nation-states (Bulgaria and Yugoslavia, Hungary and Romania), the rise of new tensions. Unless the new German leadership succeeds in reassuring the Poles, in finding a modus vivendi, relations between the two states may become quite complicated.

Romania–Soviet Union—there's a certain aggravation of relations. Poland–Soviet Union—a whole number of population groups come out for the return of Polish lands. Interethnic conflicts are on the rise in multinational states (Czechoslovakia, Yugoslavia). Practically all contiguous East European countries may make a fundamentally new move by presenting us with territorial claims. It may well be that the general trend toward all-European cooperation will clash with a trend toward subregional confrontationism.

The ongoing political changes in Europe may yield a by-product in the form of various subregional political alliances: Balkan, Central European, North Baltic. Talks on this are going on at a brisk pace, mostly behind the scenes.

I consider that any counterreform leading to the restoration of a totalitarian system in the Soviet Union is bound to induce East European countries to set up a kind of sanitary cordon on our borders and revive projects of a "little entente." I find that very likely.

B. Pyadyshev. Boris Pugachev's analysis is very interesting but I can't help wondering if his approach isn't too cold and rational. Can we dismiss the spiritual, emotional element in speaking of East European countries? Don't we have many personal friends there, friends of Russia, who find themselves in a most trying plight? Aren't we the source of the original genes? Now that we're impressively analyzing the situation and distancing ourselves from everything, what about our souls?

B. Pugachev. The soul is an eternal theme going back to Dostoyevsky and earlier times. But politics is politics, and it has its guidelines. Personally I'm very sorry for many of our Communist fellow scholars. They are fine people wronged for no reason at all. They are principled, honest, highly competent. But politics is politics, and in it you have to pay a price for everything.

B. Pyadyshev. Too impassive and cold again. People must pay a price for mistakes—there's nothing to be done about it. But we can't turn away from people we've been linked with by so much that is good and honest.

Y. Kutovoi. People who arrive abroad from some of our scientific institutes often backbite not only former leaders, but many scholars and practitioners schooled by us. The Americans generally take their people back. We can't do as much for people who are really sympathetic to us and remain our friends in their heart of hearts although they can no longer say so openly because of the situation. Regrettably, we do not extend a helpful hand to them. This does not square with our general humanitarian principles.

B. Pyadyshev. We ought to agree that foreign policy is the most fruitful activity of state and government today. There's hardly any other component of the mighty mechanism of the Soviet state showing as much efficiency coupled with glasnost and openness as the Soviet Foreign Ministry. Yet we have far more powerful and numerous centers in Moscow that are, moreover, funded almost without restriction that are directly involved in foreign policy. I wish to mention especially the USSR Supreme Soviet and its committees concerned with international affairs. It's they who should provide general leadership and coordinate our foreign policy. But they don't do that as yet. Parliament is still moving too slowly and lacks adequate knowledge.

I. Yanin. To prove that we're pursuing the right foreign policy, Eduard Shevardnadze mentioned at the 28th CPSU Congress the vast amounts of money saved on armaments. This is good, of course, but I'm afraid the Foreign Ministry has never stated its view on the domestic situation, nor has it ever presented public opinion with a program for concerted efforts at home and abroad.

Let us turn to the discrepancy between home and foreign policy as an example. On one hand, we talk a lot about moving on to a market economy. The President recently signed the Main Lines of that transition. On the other hand, the day after the event, he made a trip abroad, where he signed a number of major credit agreements. It's gratifying that foreigners still grant us credits with Gorbachev as security, so to speak. But that also means that our foreign debt is growing in almost geometrical progression. To our deep regret, there is not a word in either the Main Lines or any other government document about how we're going to pay our external debts. There is not so much as an outline of the mechanism of repayment.

It follows that foreign economic policy and internal policy exist separately and independently of each other. It's literally a theater of the absurd. Or is Mikhail Gorbachev the only one who may think about that? Alas, the President's speeches invariably contain—formally or otherwise—two separate sections: "The International Situation of the USSR" (achievements and new thinking) and "Perestroika in the USSR." They couldn't be "married" in the Main Lines, nor is it clear if any attempt was made to do so.

I regard this as a sign of trouble, of the absence of a real policy, meaning not home or foreign policy but just policy. For some seventy years, we lived under virtual martial law and so had no need for such a policy: the leader would indicate the goal and give orders or issue decrees, setting the economy and society in motion. Where would policy have come in? But now that people are allowed to state their interests, we've discovered that our main shortage is the lack of policy.

What is that, come to think of it? A capacity to see interests, to understand them, to realize one's interests and their interconnections in forecasting them, to look at least one step ahead. After all, it is not for nothing that both the "left" and the "right" insist that "we" (meaning the central authority, Moscow, Gorbachev) are too late all the time. Nor is that going to change as long as we fail to make policy, following instead an ideology, decision, or course of action chosen at the outset.

B. Kapustin. Speaking of the state of affairs in Soviet foreign policy, it's important to ascertain what social force determined our foreign policy in the 1985–1986 period, what that force was like, end what its real social interests were.

How far was it equal to finding a place for itself in the new world; that is, both the global world, so to say, and our internal world? What were its social limitations? I believe new political thinking was conceived by the reform-minded section of our partyocracy. That had its merits and demerits. The point is that this section of the partyocracy has a capacity for perestroika, not revolution. On one hand, it adapts to new realities and new circumstances of life. But on the other, it is trying to tie, to strap also these new circumstances to it. What I mean is that it isn't at all free in this kind of historic movement dictated by the people's interests and by certain other lofty goals. And I feel that this dualism in social attitude has manifested itself in both home and foreign policy, if differently.

I think that in foreign policy that section was compelled to put greater emphasis on that side of the coin reflecting its need to adapt to new circumstances. Hence the considerably greater progress made by new thinking in foreign policy as against home policy.

T. Matveyeva. The people have joined in foreign policy. True, its diplomats still make no incursions into the Foreign Ministry. The militia keeps them out.

Nevertheless, we see foreign policy opening itself to the public. This is paving the way for social organizations to operate more efficiently, and they make many reasonable suggestions.

Recently there was a forum attended by twenty-five countries. It discussed problems of global morality. I'm grateful to Alexander Yakovlev, who put the ideas of global morality in world politics on a truly philosophical basis. Participants responded by offering remarks that were largely novel and original. The forum adopted an appeal for the establishment of an independent institute of global morality.

We seem unable to overcome the syndrome of looking for "enemies"—this time in our midst. You will recall that we urged everybody to learn to live democratically. There are world institutions we can learn from.

I must warn, however, that the opportunities for humanitarian cooperation are threatened. Many ideas may soon be buried. Why? Currency-free exchanges are practically being abolished, and contacts come up against hurdles that may be described as violations of human rights. If you entertain a foreigner at dinner you are likely to have to pay some kind of tax in hard currency to the Moscow City Soviet.

Y. Kutovoi. The Foreign Ministry traditionally played a secondary role in shaping our policy toward socialist countries, where so-called big politics was made on the level of party and state, with the relevant echelons of the party apparatus playing a decisive role in policy-making.

Looking three decades back, I can't think of a single ambassador assigned to an East European country by the Foreign Ministry. That practice was only revised in the last year.

I find it hard to agree with those who allege that our foreign policy service miscalculated in signing certain international treaties or that the Foreign Ministry ignored the opinion of other agencies, primarily the Defense Ministry, in drafting agreements on the withdrawal of Soviet troops from, say, Hungary, Czechoslovakia, or Poland.

Let me state explicitly and on the strength of my own experience that the drafting of all international treaties and agreements, including those on disarmament, the definition of the position of our country on problems constituting the subject of future international accords, and the agreeing of instructions for Soviet negotiators are a very intricate process. The preparation of relevant material, work on accords, and the agreeing of formulations are not a product of effort by the Union Foreign Ministry doing as it sees fit. The Ministry fulfills the will and decisions of the highest authorities, primarily our parliament. It cooperates most closely with the Ministries of Defense, the Fishing Industry, Merchant Marine, Finance and other ministries and departments. Representatives of these entities are included in delegations if necessary and often head them.

The talks on agreements concerning the withdrawal of Soviet forces from East European countries involved senior representatives of the Defense Ministry, who took part in the talks along with diplomats and agreed with partners on the texts of bilateral documents that were subsequently endorsed by the leaderships of the ministries concerned.

B. Pyadyshev. Our diplomacy has become something more than a paying branch of the economy. By doing away with external tension, it has relieved the country of the need to tell itself day and night that it must accept any sacrifices to be able to spend billions of rubles on missiles and tanks.

There is no such thing anymore, and billions of rubles have been switched from the military to the civilian sphere.

Nor is that all. Let us stop to think why Western countries so readily help the Soviet Union, which has pushed itself to the brink of economic disaster. Why is it that Germany, Italy, Spain, France, and other countries are sending us trainloads of grain, meat, butter? I've been in on some conversations between Eduard Shevardnadze and his foreign opposite numbers. The idea put forward discreetly yet clearly was that we would welcome prompt aid in solving our supply problems. The favorable response of foreign capitals has assumed such proportions that we are surprised at the extent of the humanitarian aid. Even Saudi Arabia is willing to grant us a $4 million credit.

Why is this? Not least of all, because our foreign policy and diplomacy have shown for foreign leaders and the foreign public the new, civilized essence of our aspirations. This alone entitles Soviet foreign policy to the highest rating.

First Approach to a Multiparty System in Diplomacy

Mikhail Astafyev, Secretary, Union of Constitutional Democrats (UCD); People's Deputy of the RSFSR

Georgi Deryagin, Chairman, Central Committee of Constitutional Democratic Party (CDP)

Leonid Dobrokhotov, Head of Sector, Ideological Department, CPSU CC, until the end of 1990; now counsellor at the USSR embassy in the USA

Pavel Kudyukin, Secretary, People's Front of Russia (PFR) Board Presidium Member, Social Democratic Party of Russia (SDPR)

Sergei Magaril, Board member, SDPR

Oleg Napolov, Leader, League of Young Liberal Democrats (LYLD)

Alexander Ogorodnikov, Chairman, Christian Democratic Union (CDU)

Valery Skurlatov, Secretary, People's Front of Russia (PFR)

Nikolai Travkin, Chairman, Democratic Party of Russia (DPR); People's Deputy of the USSR and the RSFSR

Vladimir Zhirinovsky, Chairman, Liberal Democratic Party (LDP)

Nikolai Travkin. Foreign policy remains a privilege belonging

not to the leadership of the state, that is, not to the USSR Supreme
Soviet, but to the political leadership, the Politbureau. Maybe the
Presidential Council discusses those problems to some extent. As for
the Supreme Soviet, it has so far examined no such questions.

So what kind of really new foreign policy do we need? I'm sure
that we need primarily the greatest openness in the economic sphere.
We must provide conditions ensuring that other countries, above all
developed ones, far from hesitating to invest in our economy, are
drawn to it, have an interest in investing capital, and promoting production. I wouldn't rule out even concessions as a form of economic
relations. After all, the world has long treated them as a normal thing.
It makes no difference to anybody what firm is operating in his country provided it supplies high-quality goods at reasonable prices. It is
only we who are obsessed by fear of it all, leading to a "selling off of
Russia." In short, I stand for maximizing openness on a mutually
beneficial economic basis. These can be no question of "selling off
Russia."

Speaking of the political sphere, I think we should advance more
boldly toward disarmament. Indeed, I wouldn't dismiss even the
possibility of declaring neutrality. If we did so, we would have sufficient money and other resources to introduce a market economy
more or less painlessly, without lowering the standard of living; that
is, at the expense of the military-industrial complex. We should go
further on this issue, right to the end, because nobody is threatening
us from without, nobody plans to attack us.

In general, we should renounce our imperial ambitions. Our country is no great power at all, seeing that our standard of life is fit for
paupers. And that standard is so low partly because we've been used
to putting too much money and resources in the military-industrial
complex. See what we have. Mikhail Gorbachev and George Bush
meet on a completely equal footing, and we can cut equal numbers of
missiles. But we and Americans aren't equal in standards of living,
are we? So let us decide what worries us most, whether unequal national arsenals or inequality in human rights. We need to convince
ourselves that nobody is threatening us. I, for one, would go to bed
with my mind at ease if we had one quarter as many tanks, missiles,
and so on, as now. But when I think that tomorrow I may have
nothing to eat, I can't sleep with my mind at ease. And this makes me
really fear for my family and the country.

Vladimir Zhirinovsky. To make our foreign policy as effective and profitable as possible, to make it a policy expressing the interests of the whole population, we need to radically restructure it as well as to reorganize the entire diplomatic service and the diplomatic apparatus itself. We must end as speedily as possible all that was negative in our foreign policy throughout the seventy-three years of the country's evolution since October 1917. It's hard to say what fact, what action undertaken by our foreign policy service in the past in European politics, in relations with American or the Third World, in trade and economic links, could really be given a top mark. This also applies to our prewar diplomacy. And what about the Finnish campaign? It's only now that we are told it was aggression by the Soviet Union. Yet the people were deceived into believing that we had been attacked by Finland. We were the loser in our policy toward China, a great country. One wonders what we were after.

N. Travkin. There is no doubt we must approach all relations with other countries from the standpoint of their usefulness to people, to ordinary inhabitants of our country. How can we render assistance to underdeveloped countries for political reasons (as we did so actively and proudly in earlier years) whereas our standard of living is far below that of some of them? We were willing to give away our last shirt just to keep people in those countries from spitting at the "communist ideas." I think that's wrong.

V. Zhirinovsky. Voluntarism pure and simple has pervaded Soviet foreign policy throughout the past seventy-three years. Is it really so difficult to realize what we stand to gain from, what meets our national interests economically, politically, and even ideologically? We were at the losing end on almost every point. We banked mainly on underdeveloped countries, on governments that wielded no influence and were overthrown afterward. We gave medals and awarded the stars of Hero of the Soviet Union to men who enjoyed no support in their own countries and had to step off the political scene.

Speaking of the profitability of our foreign policy, we can state explicitly that it has been completely unprofitable throughout the past seventy-three years. It devoured treasuries worth billions of rubles, huge amounts of national resources from the day Georgi Chicherin became People's Commissar. How can anyone fritter away a great power like that?

Alexander Ogorodnikov. Foreign policy constitutes the strong point of Gorbachev's activity but it could have been more fruitful had he renounced ideological and geopolitical ambitions. The Soviet government goes on backing the Najibullah regime even though that is contrary to Russia's interests, injures the prestige of the Soviet Union and keeps in power a government imposed with tanks. A step towards renouncing geopolitical ambitions could be taken by allowing a united Germany to join NATO, a move that would put Germany under the control of the Western community and help conclude a peace treaty with Japan.

Soviet foreign policy lacks system. On the one hand, it is gradually renouncing expansion. On the other hand, it refuses, for instance, to establish diplomatic relations with Israel although that would enable it to join the United States in arbitrating the Middle East conflict. Even a utilitarian approach compels the Soviet Union to take a more objective stand on Arab countries in connection with falling oil prices.

We have for centuries seen two main types of policy, messianic and liberal pragmatic, which placed their aims and the state above people. Christian Democrats reject in principle such a policy. The era of empires is over.

V. Zhirinovsky. We jettisoned international law right after the October Revolution. We refused to pay our debts, nor did we demand to the repaid what others owed us. Flouting international law and trying to establish a Soviet system of law, we embarked in foreign policy on the same voluntarist course as we had been steering in home policy. Our setbacks in foreign policy included many moral losses. Our diplomats were murdered or taken hostage. Those things happened not only in the twenties but in the recent period. We used to keep silent at first, and it wasn't until later that the country learned that somebody had been killed or kidnapped. There used to be no open, public reaction.

V. Zhirinovsky. In the event of our party taking part in government, we're going to insist that the office of Foreign Minister be entrusted to a member of the LDP. We say outright that we would like four departments—the Foreign Ministry, KGB, Ministry of the Interior, and Defense Ministry—to operate under the aegis of the LDP. All four are functioning at a loss and are to blame for the extremely critical state of which our country has been reduced.

V. Ivanov. It is obvious that the character of Soviet foreign policy is determined by the aggressiveness of the official Marxist–Leninist ideology with its ideas of a world revolution and proletarian dictatorship, an uncompromising class struggle, violence, terror, and so on. I think we must formally renounce Marxism–Leninism as the basis for foreign policy.

N. Travkin. The issue is not only the "ideology." Everything is even simpler than that. Is it surprising that the world was afraid of us? Just think: a huge part of the earth's dry land inhabited by hungry, furious people standing in line: And don't forget that they've got a powerful army and missiles galore. That is certainly frightening.

In the early years of perestroika, we took very serious positive steps in foreign policy by renouncing the priority of class values and recognizing universal ones. Hence our successes. But we must go further. What we've done isn't enough.

M. Astafyev. My colleagues from the People's Front of Russia and Liberal Democratic Party were so outspoken in describing past mistakes in foreign policy that I don't really feel like adding any further criticism. In principle I subscribe to their criticism. I might have put it differently but I think those mistakes are obvious to all. I won't elaborate on the subject.

I agree that the roots of all our mistakes lie in the one-party system and the primacy of ideology in foreign policy, meaning actions in Third World countries, confrontation with the West, the maintenance of whole countries and peoples, criminal squandering of our national resources, and so on.

And now for what my colleague Zhirinovsky said about sending armored divisions to free our prisoners of war.

V. Zhirinovsky. Not "armored divisions"—you're misquoting me.

M. Astafyev. Let us recall that the United States, too, couldn't for a pretty long time secure the release of its soldiers captured in Vietnam. And what about the problem of hostages? I think it exists all over the world. I don't believe we should solve such problems by resorting to the threat of outright invasion. It is a matter for diplomacy—that is, quiet diplomacy. An unquestionable duty of our foreign policy is to protect our citizens and their rights.

L. Dobrokhotov. All of us here ought to thank *International Affairs* for this first attempt at a dialogue between parties. The dialogue should become a tradition in the multiparty constitutional state to come. But it will be more useful if we show the cultural standard of mutual relations and tolerance which is basic to diplomacy and which we aspire to in foreign and home policy alike. This is why I'm against the tenor and terminology of the comments made by spokesmen for the LDP and RPF. Let us renounce insulting terms, which doesn't in the least imply limiting the right of those present here to offer any criticism or express any point of view.

As for the statement that the past seventy-three years have been an unbroken period of foreign policy mistakes, I see it as just an emotional exaggeration. In spite of very gross mistakes due to ideologization and the existence of one party that was totalitarian, like the political system as a whole, we also scored some successes in foreign policy. Incidentally, Russia's foreign policy has always been interesting and imaginative. But from what some participants in this discussion say, everything in our prerevolutionary foreign policy was just fine, including Russia's policy toward Central Asia and the Transcaucasus, while after 1917 it was bad throughout. Yet you have only to make a cursory study of history to see that Russian policy toward the outliving ethnic regions was far from ideal.

To be sure, Russia's foreign policy had much to be proud of, and we should recall and revert to some of its principles and approaches. Russia had an outstanding school of diplomacy based on excellent principles. We should bring all that back and put it in the service of our country. But it's hardly right to regard the whole of Russia's policy as faultless. Still, that overstatement as well as others notwithstanding, I believe that emerging in our discussion is the possibility of a certain consensus on foreign policy problems against the background of the nascent multiparty system. Personally I think the rise of a multiparty system in our country is going to enrich our foreign policy and enable it to steer clear in the future of the kind of mistakes mentioned here and other mistakes that could be added to the list.

A multiparty system will make it possible to put up opposition to foreign policy,to ensure that key decisions of the government and the country's leadership pass through a parliament representing the main parties, to freely criticize decisions and help rectify mistakes. This is very important, of course. But to bring it about, our political parties, the CPSU among them, must learn to cooperate. They must learn not only to criticize others but to lend an ear to criticism leveled at themselves, to listen to each other, to accept what is really acceptable in other parties' program even though it may wound their own self-esteem.

Although some of those present here show an emotional tendency to speak of nothing but mistakes, let us remember that over the past five years our foreign policy has been undergoing a radical change. After all, even the West recognizes that Soviet foreign policy, which reflects transformations under way in the country, is the motor of the positive changes taking place in the world. Credit for the breakthrough that has come about in international relations isn't due to us alone, of course, but to our international partners as well. We've adopted the ideas of new thinking advanced in the late forties and carried forward in the Russell–Einstein "Manifest." We are deideologizing our foreign policy although we have yet to complete the process. A lot has been or is being done to put our foreign policy right but there's a lot more to do.

I don't agree that we must repent all the time. We repented by admitting that sending troops to Hungary, Czechoslovakia, and Afghanistan was a mistake. But repentance isn't all that is needed. The Americans have still not repented for their aggression either against Vietnam or against other countries and peoples. The important thing, they tell us, is not repentance but what we are now doing in practice to show that we're giving up the determinate class policy we pursued for decades. It is primarily in deeds that we must show that we are changing. As a matter of fact, we are changing.

Pavel Kudyukin. I would like to point out that our foreign policy has been substantially renewed since 1985, and so I think it would be unfair and wrong to say it has achieved nothing. This is confirmed by the Reagan administration's reversal of its attitude to the Soviet Union, by the change from treating our country as the "evil empire" in the early eighties to signing concrete agreements on arms cuts after 1985. That couldn't have come without our perestroika. Had the approach been the same as before perestroika, such results could hardly have been achieved.

And now I wish to take exception to what my colleague from the CPSU, Leonid Dobrokhotov, said here. Indeed, a declared renunciation of class politics is the basis on which our foreign policy has scored some results and possibly even successes. But judging by the evidence, this renunciation is only on record in our foreign policy. As for home policy, it is hard to say that the ideological position of the ruling party is equally explicit.

An Outline of Multiparty Diplomacy

V. Zhirinovsky. As soon as the Liberal Democratic Party was founded, we wrote into the foreign policy section of its program what we were going to seek in the foreign policy sphere in the event of the electorate giving us a mandate to participate in government. We declare for a precise definition of the country's strategic priorities and interests. We must decide once and for all what we need to make it an everlasting policy and not a policy for ten, fifty, or sixty years. Our country must be clear about its goals and national interests. It may change its name—what was Russia is the Soviet Union now, and tomorrow there may be some other name—but the goals and interests remain. The United States, Britain, Japan, all other countries have national interests. I mean real national interests and goals.

If we want to remain forever a great state, we must become once and for all a component of a united Europe, one of the leading countries of the world, and remove all ideological obstacles to this. We are part of the West while the East lies beyond the Urals, in the same region where Mongolia, Vietnam, and other countries lie. Some of those countries are ahead of us on many parameters, I regret to say.

The artificial classing of Moscow as belonging to the East took place in 1917. But now we must again become part of the Western world, to which we've historically belonged at all times. Our goals in this respect are open, and we state them straightforwardly, without concealing anything or using Aesopian language. We say that Moscow must become part of the West and one of the leading countries of the world. Those countries are the United States, Britain, France, Italy, Germany, Japan, and Canada. We are strong enough economically and enjoy sufficient prestige to be one of seven or eight leading countries of the world. Nor should our joining this group of countries be hindered by the kind of obstacles we used to raise ourselves, scaring everybody still through our "Red policy."

S. Magaril. We're going over from extremely negative opinions about the results achieved by foreign policy in the past and the trend of its restructuring since 1985 to a more balanced and sober view that I see as more correct. According to this view, our foreign policy has already undergone or continues undergoing very noticeable and substantial changes, but I would hesitate to describe them as a radical transformation. The point is that this policy is still dual, being essentially a reflection of the dual policy which the CPSU as a whole has been pursuing and which makes itself felt in everything.

Take the Soviet Constitution, for one. The article on the leading role of the CPSU has been abolished in favor of a multiparty system. That's a big step forward. On the other hand, the CPSU still lays claim to a privileged position in society and actually holds it. This duality also finds a reflection in foreign policy. There are changes and a new approach but at the same time activities serving the interests of one party are continuing.

V. Zhirinovsky. Our party is going to seek substantial changes in the country's foreign policy in favor of going over from East–West to North–South relations. The outside world effected that change long ago, and we know it. I'm speaking of our foreign policy, of the need for us to thoroughly revise its objectives and to switch to North–South relations. As regards East–West relations, our party is of the opinion that there are not and cannot be any contradictions over this. Those relations should extend eastward from Moscow, for Moscow is part of the West.

Shifting the emphasis to the North–South direction of relations is necessary because the South is the seat of dangers that threaten us today or may threaten tomorrow. At the same time, it's there, all the way to the Indian Ocean, that our priority interests lie. We need such a revision of foreign policy also because North–South relations are more economical and profitable.

P. Kudyukin. While supporting our LDP colleague's idea about reorienting foreign policy to North–South relations, I wish to note that, to our great regret, we in this country are in the South rather than in the North. Let us look at things realistically. It can be a question not only of partnership with the West but of some forms of mutual aid involving Third World countries. The experience of the more advanced of those countries may be more useful to us than Western experience. I mean primarily the newly industrialized countries. Besides, the West is in no hurry to revise its attitude to us, and we can see that. It hails perestroika but is in no hurry to cooperate, to help advance our economy. And then, it has no interest in our inconvertible currency, nor is it certain of the return of its capital.

O. Napolov. I agree that the most painful problems come and are going to come to us from the south, including Afghanistan, where stability still hasn't been restored. We must stop backing the Najibullah regime, for that would immediately normalize the situation there as well as our relations with Iran, Pakistan, Saudi Arabia, the Muslim world as a whole. We wouldn't have to keep the Turkestan and Transcaucasian military districts. Such a move mould release resources worth tens of billions of rubles.

I. Dobrokhotov. I would like to note that the Najibullah regime differs greatly from all its predecessors. It is evolving. Recently Najibullah said that if elections were held under the auspices of the UN and if the PDPA were defeated, he would cede power to others.

V. Ivanov. It's obvious that our country must stop financing fraternal totalitarian regimes, Communist parties, and bandits' organizations abroad. We need this as a means of stabilizing the international situation, establishing confidence and making real progress on the road to peace.

S. Magaril. Our cooperation priorities are in need of a substantial revision. While desisting from its ideologization, we must raise the role of our economic interests. For what we witnessed until recently was based, in effect, on nothing but ideology. I mean our imposing and supporting a state sector, our giganticism in building production plants abroad, and so on, all of which ultimately translated into both economic and political losses for us.

A problem of importance to us is to train our work force in developed countries of the West. The low efficiency of labor in industry and agriculture is a drag on the economic reform. Why not consider setting up a mechanism of training our work force in the West, if only on short-term contracts? On coming back, our people would not only disseminate new knowledge but champion radical changes.

A. Ogorodnikov. It's a very important fact that we speak more and more often on interest as we leave ideology on one side.

The Christian Democratic Union is of the opinion that policy should rest on values and proceed from the fundamental concept of Christian democracy: the absolute value of the individual and people's responsibility to each other. It's on these foundations that our national interests must be built.

The paramount task would be disarmament under international control, a reduction in armed forces, conversion and an end to trade in arms by reciprocal agreement with the main military powers of the world.

Fruitful cooperation and active participation in the international division of labor and integration should become the chief objective of Russian foreign policy. There are certain priorities to which Christian policy is particularly sensitive. I mean steps to combat hunger, epidemics, and drug addiction and aid to disabled and aged people. We realize our responsibility to the outside world and are convinced of the necessity for an international control mechanism to deal with environmental problems.

We favor the creation of a new Europe, a Europe of union and freedom. And we consider that the European Council sets us an example of unification and cooperation in the form of an assembly of nations grouped in a community based on the rule of law, pluralist democracy, and a marketplace economy. We stress that peace, freedom, and security can only be preserved by adopting balanced disarmament measures and respecting frontiers. Foreign policy should help carry on exchanges and a dialogue between cultures, should open our great heritage to the world. Let us recall Alexander Solzhenitsyn's words: "To lead such a country, one has to have a national line and be constantly aware of all the 1,100 years of its history..." The conclusion is self-evident.

And now for borrowing experience. It is clear that we must borrow the experience of the newly industrialized countries and that of China's successful foreign policy moves to open the country and create economic zones. To my way of thinking, these zones are the most important thing for our sick economy although we aren't yet working on the problem. We should begin by creating a free economic zone in the country's northwest, which comprises the Kaliningrad and Leningrad regions and could include the Novgorod and Pskov regions. The People's Front of Russia favors setting up free economic zones in the Far East that could serve as an important extra source of products for Siberia and the Urals and would make it possible to put both regions back on their feet.

But at the moment the idea of such zones is only being discussed in general terms. We need serious concrete research, in particular by the Foreign Ministry. The only way to solve our problems is to harness foreign technologies on a comprehensive basis and a large scale.

M. Astafyev. Establishing constructive links with the large Russian diaspora could become a new component of our foreign policy. This, too, calls for some form of repentance. A hand proffered to our compatriots who find themselves abroad could become a new factor in addition to general disarmament and economic ties that would contribute in a measure to progress in our domestic affairs. It would help invest our compatriots' money in economic reforms. Look at other countries. The Chinese, Poles, Armenians maintain extensive ties with their compatriots living in the United States and elsewhere. It seems to me that this factor could also prove its worth in Russia.

G. Deryagin. To cure our ailing economy, we must revise our every foreign political and economic activity. Take arms sales as an example. Generally speaking there is nothing wrong about the phenomenon. Arms are like any other commodity in demand. If we don't offer them for sale they'll be bought in some other country. But may I ask why do we supply arms practically free to regimes fighting against their own people or posing a threat to other peoples? The only reason can be our geopolitical aspirations, which is inadmissible.

I welcome without qualification the idea of forging extensive links with our diaspora: Russians, Armenians, Ukrainians, Jews. This is a most promising thing if only we define our interests correctly and take proper account of others' interests.

M. Astafyev. We are for removing ideology from foreign policy and introducing moral principles in this policy. Unfortunately, many of our foreign policy activities may be described as amoral in the general sense of the word: a vague line toward China, support for Cuba, the PDRK, and Vietnam and their maintenance at our expense. Such a policy doesn't do us much credit. Besides, it's a drain on our economy.

S. Magaril. Yes, our foreign policy must be moral. Using double standards in it is inadmissible. The past five years have undoubtedly seen serious progress on this. Still, let me add that while criticizing, say, violations of human rights in Israel or South Africa, we shut our eyes to the Ceausescu dictatorship and remain reticent about the problems of the PDRK, South Korea, China, and Cuba. We should draw a clear-cut line between noninterference in the affairs of other countries and opposition to a policy violating human rights. Our approach to this problem must be principled and uniform in regard to South Africa and North Korea alike.

It's very important for us to renounce all messianists at home or abroad. We're often told that "our people have opted for socialism." But the people should have the opportunity to make their choice in every election, all the more since we have yet to offer a definition of socialism. We were told that our country had built a developed socialist society but it turned out that Sweden, Switzerland, and Austria had built socialist societies of their own. And while those societies aren't called "developed socialism," they assure people a comfortable life.

V. Skurlatov. A comparison of the strategy of the Foreign Ministry and the policy of our party, the People's Front of Russia, leads me to the conclusion that they coincide roughly 80 percent, for we consider that Soviet foreign policy has really begun to take account of present world realities and that the international activity of our state is fairly successful. We could therefore assist our foreign policy through our links with allies; that is, the Tories in Britain, the Republicans in the United States, the LDP in Japan, the Free Democrats in West Germany, and other neoconservatives in the West.

V. Skurlatov. But there's no business we can do with developing countries. As for the West, we must further our relations with it. We have a strong advantage in this respect. Ours is the world's cheapest labor power but at the same time it's skilled enough. In view of the tremendous discrepancy between advanced Western technology and very cheap labor, we can provide ourselves with up-to-date products at very low cost. We are an excellent partner for developed countries and a competitor to developing countries. This is why we should pursue a foreign policy assuring us effective partnership with developed, rich countries and favorable conditions for competing with the newly industrialized nations and developing countries.

As we accept the main lines of the country's foreign policy and the Foreign Ministry's activity, our party, the PFR, is willing to assist the Ministry not only through its international links but through parliamentary activity and in other forms inside the country.

G. Deryagin. Here at home we are up against a new problem, the breakup of our state. It is surprising that in the case of, say, Lithuania, the Supreme Soviet, rather than doing its utmost to evolve a new concept of relations and trying to keep that republic, virtually did nothing while the leadership resorted to the old device of taking emergency steps.

V. Zhirinovsky. The problem of secession is not as simple as the Lithuanians imagine, not to mention others. The Tatars, for instance, have had to give away billions of tons of oil and gas, with Lithuania and other republics at the receiving end. It's all been supplied free. And now those republics are stepping out. So the Tatars ask: "What are we left with? We gave it all to them as to our brothers but not they're saying 'farewell' to us, leaving us out in the cold." This is a problem like any other. The Tatars are unlikely to let it go at that.

The possible breakup of our federation would create a further serious problem. We have at our disposal roughly 50 percent of all the nuclear weapons stockpiled in the world. That's about 25,000 nuclear warheads scattered all over the country. Think what would happen if the Baltic, Transcaucasian, and Central Asian republics were to secede from the Union. Where would we move those warheads? And what would be their new role? This is a further circumstance demanding the preservation of the federation's territorial integrity.

V. Skurlatov. We can't just look on as the Union falls apart. We must do something. Going on all over the world today are integrational, not disintegrational processes. I believe the creation of a wideranging free economic zone in the northwest of the country, which I've already spoken about, could block to a degree the Baltic republics' separatist aspirations.

S. Magaril. I wish to join this issue with colleagues concerned about the disintegration of our state. I think every people should have a real right to secede from the Soviet Union, and we can't condemn an aspiration to do so. We are used to a bipolar world but now the world is becoming multipolar, with every country upholding its interests and making its demands, whereas we aren't used to that sort of thing.

V. Zhirinovsky. Could you tell us whether your party recognizes the right of every people or republic to secede?

S. Magaril. Any people or republic wanting to secede must have the right to do so. The only thing that can save and preserve our federation is a new and strong integrating factor of an economic nature. Our peoples are tired of living in poverty within the Union. They want to try and solve their problems in conditions of freedom and independence. I think secession is possible and will lead to a new integration at a higher level.

P. Kudyukin. It is perfectly obvious that the rise and development of a multiparty system in our country will necessitate a serious reorganization, deideologization and depolitization of the diplomatic service. But I believe a distinction should be made between foreign policy and the diplomatic service. Politics are politics precisely because they can't be completely deideologized or depoliticized. The Foreign Minister is likely to belong to some party in any circumstances. And depending on the model we adopt, our ambassadors, too, will be members of some parties.

Not so the staffs of embassies and the Foreign Ministry. They should be made up of what may be called non professional politicians but professional diplomats. Unlike the LDP, we aren't going to insist that the Foreign Ministry or other ministries should function under the aegis of our party. We consider such claims unjustified. Cooperation? Yes. Participation? Without any doubt.

V. Zhirinovsky. It's essential to deideologize and depoliticize the staffs of the Foreign Ministry and other departments also because otherwise a new party that came to power would be dominated by the old apparatus, with all that this implies. It is therefore necessary that members of various parties should become deputy ministers at the Foreign Ministry or other ministries and join in restructuring these agencies.

Our diplomats abroad feel slighted. They live and work behind bars, as it were, hardly every venturing beyond them. They feel bound hand and foot by our secret services and party committees, and so their main concern is to stay quietly abroad for as long as they're allowed to and then to return home. That's all.

I wish to dwell especially on our diplomacy's personnel policy. It has been fallacious throughout the past seventy-three years. First we had "Red' ambassadors, and then foreign policy came to a pass where, under Khrushchev, a collective farm chairman could be appointed ambassador.

G. Deryagin. The Foreign Ministry must be not only depoliticized and deideologized but freed from the dominating influence of the KGB.

A further point is that we are badly short of information, including foreign political information. Hence it's necessary that the Foreign Ministry regularly supply all political forces with information received from abroad through its channels. We must train leaders meeting high professional standards and conversant with the situation at home and abroad in case they come to power or enter the government. They can't start from scratch, can they? They should be able to tackle their tasks as professionals.

The Foreign Ministry should set up a department for relations with political parties and the public. It should regularly brief spokesman for the most diverse political trends and parties.

P. Kudyukin. It's important to note, I think, that the Soviet Union accedes with the Foreign Ministry's aid to numerous international agreements, declarations, statements, and legal acts; yet its internal legislation, ranging from the Constitution to any set of regulations, grossly flouts those international acts with the result that the signatures put by us to them virtually lose all value. I'm of the opinion that since the Foreign Ministry respects and, moreover, expresses the country's interests, it must take the initiative of ensuring that internal legislation is brought into line with international norms. Without this our signatures to those acts are meaningless and merely discredit our country.

Let me give you an example of how our consular service functions. We invited foreign parties to our founding congress, complying with all the customary formalities. But when they applied to our embassies for visas, they were refused on the grounds that the embassies knew nothing about the matter. In West Germany, for one, a visa was refused to Weiskirchen, and SPD member of the Bundestag well known for his statements and activity in support of friendship and cooperation with the Soviet Union. In the end he did get a visa but not until after he had received an invitation from the Moscow mission of the Ebert Fund, so that he could arrive only on the eve of the last day of congress. His Danish colleague got no visa at all.

I believe the visa problem can be solved even now by granting parties the same right as the CPSU enjoys. But if this is impossible for now, let the Consular Directorate of the Foreign Ministry entrust one of its officers with handling the parties' foreign relations.

I can't understand why our embassies still invite none of the leading members of new Soviet political parties to deliver lectures, join in discussions, and meet our diplomats and the foreign public. After all, that would help transform our embassies from the forbidding institutions they are into centers for contact between our public and the most diverse political forces abroad. This could be done right now, and it would not require much effort.

M. Astafyev. I support that idea although it may encounter some difficulties at first, including purely financial ones. Meanwhile the Foreign Ministry's press center could make it a rule to invite various parties to its briefings. We will soon be making statements on various events, and so our state and the ruling Communist Party have a stake in those statements being balanced. This will be possible only if there is no discrimination and if the CPSU doesn't ignore the new parties.

L. Dobrokhotov. That's a very reasonable suggestion. I think every registered party has a right to unhampered international contacts. I suppose we could borrow foreign experience of how various ruling or opposition parties can influence foreign policy.

In including the multiparty system in its sphere of activity, the Foreign Ministry should apparently bear it in mind that when a new government takes over it replaces senior officers of the Foreign Ministry with members of the victorious party or parties. As for the lower echelons of the Ministry, they remain the same under all parties and continue carrying out the government's program. That's how all democratic countries proceed, nor can we think up anything different.

V. Zhirinovsky. Our chief goal now that we're ridding ourselves of a negative legacy is neither to make new mistakes nor to repeat old ones. We simply have no time left. Historians allow us little time for any further shilly-shallying. This is why the LDP is against the calls for political persecution that we hear from some parties. Previously that was done by the Communists, who are accused of having destroyed 66 million people, so are we to expect those who come next to persecute the Communists? They number 20 million and from 60 to 70 million if counted with their families. Sixty million before and 60 million now. Some people abroad would gloat over it if we started destroying each other.

At present we must attract all the healthy forces of our society like a magnet in order to unite them. We are definitely against persecution. I'm making this point because recently a group of Social Democrats—just think—called for the persecution of Communists. If we did anything like that, it would throw us right back to a new GULAG. It would simply mean switching the roles. Yet the main condition for success is consolidation under a pluralist system.

It may well be that not all of the new parties' leaders will stay on top as new people enter the scene. At all events, the ideas uniting members of democratic, social democratic, liberal democratic, constitutional democratic, and other parties and movements are becoming a real and inseparable feature of the Soviet political landscape. To disregard this would mean prejudicing both home and foreign policy.

May 1988

The Soviet Union in an Interdependent World

Aleksei Zagorsky, Aleksandr Medvedev and *Aleksandr Pikayev,* Institute of World Economy and International Relations of the USSR Academy of Sciences
Konstantin Pleshakov and *Alla Solovyova,* Institute of the United States and Canada of the USSR Academy of Sciences
Sergei Lunev, Viktor Nemchinov and *Sergei Shilovtsev,* Institute of Oriental Studies of the USSR Academy of Sciences
Nikolai Kapralov, Institute for Far Eastern Studies of the USSR Academy of Sciences
Vadim Udalov, Research Coordination Center, USSR Foreign Ministry

New World Realities

K. Pleshakov. History has proven that there is no mistake more dangerous given the changeability of the world, than assessing these changes through the prism of yesterday's principles. The most complex thing is not merely taking note of the changes but altering one's manner of thinking accordingly by scuttling outmoded dogmas and stereotypes. This constitutes, in my opinion, the essence of new thinking.

111

The latter should be understood not as a ready-made concept but as a method for creating the concept of an interdependent and integral world. This is on the theoretical plane. Practically, it should be comprehended as a method of leading the world away from confrontation and toward real cooperation.

One may logically query: What are the stands of the Soviet Union in this integral and interdependent world? They are unquestionably well-grounded, but they are not optimal. The same applies to the United States. I'll venture to say that only a few countries have managed to adapt fully to present-day realities.

The world today is prepared objectively for the concept of interdependence and integrality—in the economy, science, and technology, and in military strategy. But it is not ready psychologically. Herein lies a great danger. We are coming up against the problems of perceiving one another. Much is being said today about the "image of the enemy." Meanwhile we continue to underestimate the importance of perception problems. Without a high sociopsychological level an adequate perception of the world is impossible. It is risky business to grope about in the darkness of one's prejudices, having a poor idea of the foreign policy priorities of one's partners.

A. Solovyova. After World War II, the so-called bipolar model of the world took shape in the foreign policy mentality of states. It boiled down to the existence of two opposing hostile systems: the camp of capitalist countries headed by the United States and the camp of socialist states led by the USSR. This model was in effect proclaimed by the U.S. ruling elite to "contain" and "roll back" socialism through the joint efforts of imperialism, on one hand, and to consolidate its own dominating position within the capitalist system, on the other.

In the 1960s, the vision of the world as a bipolar structure clearly began to develop chasms. There were a number of reasons for this: first, the correlation of forces within the capitalist camp had changed, the allies demanding that their role in world development be revised, and the unevenness of the economic growth of individual states had led to the formation of new centers of power; second, the development of Soviet science and technology had brought forward a number of promising areas of Soviet–American cooperation, and other spheres of coinciding interests had appeared; and third, a number of nonaligned states that had been formally excluded from the bipolar structure of the world had energetically emerged in the world arena.

All this led to the emergence of a multipolar model of the world, whose overriding feature was close interdependence of and interaction between states on the international scene. Even then this multipolarity was manifest not only in the formation of new centers of power on the level of individual countries, but also in the emergence of new regions as poles: States of the rapidly developing Asia and Pacific region, linked with one another by growing centripetal tendencies, entered the mainstream of world economics and politics.

In the 1980s, the Republican administration in the United States has resorted to a sort of artificial rebirth of the bipolar structure of the world in the form of an ideologized confrontation between the United States and the USSR on a new level. tf failed, however, to take due account of the ties of interdependence among states that had taken shape by then. The incongruity between this model and the actual state of affairs in the world led to a rather rapid (within a few years), departure from its basic principles and to a return to the concept of multipolarity.

The approach to the surrounding world as a bipolar structure gives dominance in the bloc to only one state, while conferring on it greater commitments in comparison with the other countries. The multipolar model, on the other hand, reduces the rights of the leader, while increasing its allies' independence and their contribution to world developments. The former variant thus conditions the presence of one "pacesetter" in each of the opposing camps; the latter forces each state to take into account the factor not only of the influence of the opposite social system but also that of the allies, of economic, scientific and technological, raw-material or other forms of dependence on them, on surrounding states, etc.

What is more, the bipolar world concept predetermines a sharply ideologized capitalist-socialist confrontation, which is based chiefly on power politics. Multipolarity, on the other hand, presupposes more pragmatic foreign policy,which is being increasingly shaped by considerations of national gain and which is ensured by the broadest possible spectrum of foreign policy instruments and the proportional use of military force, economic levers, diplomacy, and propaganda.

I think that for the USSR the existence of many centers of power is, by and large, a positive factor, since it makes it possible to utilize more fully multilateral cooperation for domestic development, thereby enhancing the USSR's involvement in global development and consolidating its position in the world community.

A. Zagorsky. I would like to call into question the very tenet that multipolarity in international relations is a phenomenon that will come to us in the immediate future. I feel that if viewed through the prism of power factors, present-day international relations are developing on the basis of a confrontation between socioeconomic systems. The rivalry between the systems—between imperialism and socialism, or any hypothetical third system—inevitably poses the problem of a leader, which assumes the brunt of this struggle.

Regional problems are quite another matter. Here, of course, the problem of diversity in the correlation of forces and the influence of individual centers can be singled out. But this phenomenon is hardly anything new. After the collapse of the colonial system we can see in each region its own specific system of the balance of the different levels and quality of the centers and the different numbers of strong countries that influence these relations. And I have yet to see new centers of power either on the global or the regional level.

K. Pleshakov. Upon closer examination, we find two poles, two poles of military might which will play the determining role in the decades to come. As to the centers of power, there will tentatively be five of them, not counting regional ones: the USSR, the United States, Western Europe, Japan, and China. But I feel that, even in the foreseeable future, Japan will not play the role of a third equal partner with the USSR or the United States. Economically perhaps, Japan's role will be decisive within the next twenty years, but militarily the situation will evidently remain the same as it is today. So it is apparently premature to speak of a sunset of the bipolar world. Only in the very long term will the world perhaps cease to be bipolar.

V. Nemchinov. I agree that there may be many power centers, but there are only two poles. However, to the five existing power centers one could in the future probably add Indonesia, Brazil, and the four Southeast Asian countries, which are playing an important role in the world even today. Perhaps in the future the countries of the Association of South East Asian Nations will be able to aspire to still another power center, one different from Indonesia, in a multipower world.

It is incorrect to believe that positions of strength and weakness in a multipolar world are becoming senseless. Today, when many power centers are appearing, the concept of head-on confrontation is receding to the background, but it is not becoming more senseless. Simply, the vectors of strength and the vectors of weakness are changing and increasing in number. I would propose the following metaphor for analyzing the emerging political situation: a host of swinging pendulums, where potential energy is amassed and kinetic energy declines, and, conversely, noncoinciding trajectories of swinging pendulums in a multipolar world.

A. Solovyova. But this will not necessarily be a model of pendulums swinging in different directions. The existing power centers do not have to possess the same policies at all, although this does not presuppose the involvement of states in conflicts.

A. Pikayev. I believe that international relations have never been singularly bipolar. They have always been more or less multipolar. The only sphere where bipolarity stands out in particularly bold relief is that of strategic nuclear weapons. There are two clear-cut poles here—the USSR and the United States. Here, too, there are a host of differing views as to the transition to a multipolar model.

Is a multipolar model in the sphere of nuclear arms possible at all, for that matter? Is it desirable? As far as the first question is concerned, no changes can be expected until the end of the century, since if we examine the nuclear programs of other states, Britain will have between 500 and 900 strategic nuclear warheads by the end of the century, and France will have about 1,000. As far as China is concerned, it is hard to say, but I think that its possibilities will be no less than France's. All told, this is about 3,000 warheads, while the USSR and the United States, even if agreement of a 50 percent reduction is reached, will possess 6,000 strategic warheads each plus warheads on sea-based cruise missiles. The poles will thus be kept intact, but the bipolar structure will be eroded. This will create difficulties at the Soviet–American talks on further reductions in strategic arms. In the early 1980s the problem of the nuclear forces of third countries was one of the chief stumbling blocks at the talks. But now a decision has been taken to disregard these forces since they are incalculably small in comparison to what the USSR and the United States have. However, the situation will change by the mid-1990s. These forces will have to be taken into account somehow.

Here the three other nuclear powers have the following choice. They can continue their current foreign policies, and the latter are really unconstructive, as these powers have objected to their nuclear potentials being taken into account, although they have promised to join the talks when the USSR and the United State substantially reduce their stockpiles. If this trend in their policies persists, I feel the nuclear powers will be impelled to inaugurate a new spiral of the arms race. Or these three powers, mindful of the danger of such a course for their own interests, will in fact join the nuclear disarmament talks, in which I am certain they have an objective vested interest, since nuclear weapons have yet to yield them political dividends.

The Prestige and Might of the State

A. Zagorsky. The answer here is quite unequivocal. The historical record of many countries has shown that the military factor alone cannot ensure a strong political potential and influence. The international influence of Japan, for example, is hardly based on military might.

It would be just as erroneous to say that the military factor alone buttresses the prestige the Soviet Union enjoys in world affairs. Even though this factor has played a major role, the USSR's political role in international relations, including its efforts to present military conflicts, has been no less instrumental to its prestige. Of course, the possibility to defend itself and to fulfill its commitments to its allies is the factor which ensures trust. But there has been an instance in our practice when the priority of the military factor, i.e., the stress on the military-political aspects of international relations, led to directly opposite results. The Far East is one specific example. What with the limited political contacts and the marginal role the region plays in the economy of the USSR and other socialist countries, we are visualized there primarily in military terms.

K. Pleshakov. What is the criterion of a nation's might—military strength or the economy? Two layers have to be understood here. One is the long term. Here one can draw on the record of history, which attests that military might will not survive without the economy. The first thing that comes to mind is the rivalry between Spain and England in the sixteenth and seventeenth centuries. Because England had advanced more economically it undermined Spain's might as a world power, even though they were approximately equal militarily. Military strength does not last long without economic might.

Today the role of economic factors of strength in world relations is enhancing.

As far as the second layer—the short term—is concerned, unfortunately, military power here plays a much more prominent role than the economy, because even if regional centers of power consolidate in the person of, say, the "four dragons," ten nuclear bombs of some Islamic state will nonetheless outweigh them. And if economically weak states acquire nuclear weapons, they will begin to wield more clout than the new industrialized countries. For this reason I would be against elevating economic factors to an absolute.

N. Kapralov. I cannot fully agree with the premise that military might alone plays a dominating role in the short- and medium-term perspective. Apart from military might, economic influence is of enormous importance as well. Take, for example, Singapore, which has neither natural resources nor a work force. But its rapid economic development has been revealing.

A. Medvedev. Of course, the military component is very important in present-day international relations. But other aspects—economic, political, and humanitarian—are becoming increasingly significant. It is hard to say at times which component plays a greater role. It is common knowledge that the modern world economy is characterized by greater economic, financial, political, ecological, scientific and technological, and informational interdependence of states. The deepening involvement of each country in the international division of labor is, in fact, an imperative, irrespective of the country's size and its economic and military potential.

The Soviet Union is no exception in this sense either. The sweeping measures being taken in the country are aimed precisely at enhancing the role of the economy both in tackling our domestic problems and in attaining our goals in the world arena. The point at issue is laying the material foundation for maintaining world stability and building a system of international economic security as one of the components of the comprehensive system of international security.

It must be stated, however, that the current model of Soviet involvement in international economic relations is still not in line with the goals the country is committed to on the whole and with the USSR's political weight as a leading world power. The following facts will illustrate this point. The USSR's share in world economic contacts is marginal. We account for approximately four percent of world trade, despite the fact that the USSR produces a third of the world's industrial output. And even this small fraction has been attained through fuel and other types of raw materials. The Soviet Union's share in the most promising forms of world economic cooperation is extremely low.

A. Solovyova. What do you see to be the solution?

A. Medvedev. Radical reform of the economic mechanism as a whole, the foreign economic sphere included, will make the USSR's foreign policy strategy and the cardinal changes in the country's position in the world economic system a success. The overriding tasks of this reorganization is to establish an entirely new system of managing the USSR's activity on the world economic scene, activity which will be based on economic elements of management. One of the prime elements in my opinion is the gradual introduction of the convertible Soviet ruble, which will enable Soviet enterprises to align domestic performance with world market tendencies and scientific and technological progress.

I would like to stress two more elements which I believe are important from the standpoint of the USSR's integration into the world economy. It is imperative to reassess our attitude to international economic organizations which in one way or another take part in regulating ties in the world economy as a whole. Today we have set the task of establishing closer contacts with the General Agreement on Tariffs and Trade. I think that the establishment of relations with the International Monetary Fund, the International Bank for Reconstruction and Development, and the Bank for International Settlements in Basel is on the agenda. This will have a political as well as economic effect.

S. Shilovtsev. In this connection we should touch upon the problem of the oil factor which was expected to somehow improve our economy. The attitude that oil was a magic wand was compatible with an administrative approach to running the economy. In that situation there was no need to think about the correlation between labor inputs and consumption, as there was no need for genuine self-accounting which does away with the established links in the administrative system. Suffice it to reallocate resources and channel them to a particular project. However, today oil has become a less significant factor. This has happened not only because of the drop in oil prices: there were much more important circumstances. In the 1980s industrialized countries began to establish totally new systems of production (reindustrialization). They are based on microelectronics, biotechnology, new materials, unconventional sources of energy. The restructuring carried out on the basis of the latest technologies makes it more difficult to get accustomed to the changing situation on the world market. The administrative system in the economy and the restructuring are incompatible. If we resort to the method of patching up the holes in the economy there will be no chance to modernize the economic mechanism as a whole.

N. Kapralov. As far as the USSR's integration into international economic ties is concerned, I would like to dwell on one point. It is common knowledge that the Soviet Union is ten to fifteen years ahead of Japan in fundamental research. Japan, on the other hand, is outstripping the Soviet Union in concrete application of research findings. In the USSR eighteen months is the shortest period between R&D and introduction; in Japan three months is the longest. But I feel that if we continue to purchase technology and orient ourselves toward exporting finished output, we will program our lag behind the leading capitalist countries for many years to come. What we can and should do now is to develop the priority areas of new technology, set up joint ventures, and draw on the experience of the leading countries.

The New Thinking: Combating Political Stagnation

S. Lunev. I feel the new political thinking should mean that the military factor, the factor of military might, should play a lesser and lesser role in international relations. This applies not only to the major powers in today's world. The burden of military expenditures is not weighing upon the economy of the Soviet Union alone. It is also a heavy onus for the economies of the developing countries, many of which are being strangled by foreign debts.

It seems to me that until recently the Soviet Union placed inordinate emphasis on military might. This line was continued even after strategic parity had been achieved. Today, however, we have managed, thanks to the new political thinking, to take a real step forward toward weapons reductions. The turn to the new thinking in foreign policy is also telling on our country's greatly enhanced efforts toward settling regional conflicts.

V. Nemchinov. It would be worthwhile in this connection to examine the model of international relations as we saw it in the past and as it is today. The main thing in the old model of international relations was the factor of policy, and within the framework of this policy there were two levels. The first is the diplomatic level, and the second military-strategic. The factor of military power was the prevailing one at the level of diplomatic relations. I feel that here was the area where the old thinking ran aground, for the emphasis was placed on an inflexible, confrontational course.

How do I view the new mode of thinking? What gives a country prestige today? Certainly not a rigid diplomatic line that is buttressed by military might.

I would like to set forth an analytic model, a "matrix" of present-day international relations. I would portray the structure of international relations as a layer cake, where politics is merely the filling. Over politics lies the propaganda layer of international relations. Directly over it is the ideological layer. Still higher is the layer of moral and ethical problems, topped by the philosophical and conceptual layer of the system of international relations.

When we talk about the new thinking, we are referring above all to the breakthrough from the diplomatic level of relations to those of morality and ethics and of philosophical concepts. Contrary to the tradition of policy established through diplomatic channels, we have now come to appeal to the broad strata of public opinion, to take into account the vital interests of the public at large. We have reached the moral level of political problems and here we have made a decisive breakthrough and won the sincere support for our new course. For this to happen, we had to change a great deal, both in our military-strategic concepts and in traditional diplomacy. When diplomats realized that the problem of survival today is a global and urgent one, our moral choice gave us our current prestige worldwide.

Under the level of policy lay the military-strategic level, and below that the technological and technical levels of international relations. Lastly, the base of the model of international relations is comprised by economic ties, of which make up the foundation of foreign policy.

If all the horizontal layers are divided into vertical blocks we will have a sphere of short-term analysis of international relations (from one day to four months), a zone of medium-term analysis (from four months to four or five years), and a sphere of long-term analysis (from a five- to fifteen-year perspective). Such is a general matrix for a comprehensive analysis of international relations.

Spain suffered a military defeat under King Philip II, at the time of the Armada, I think, because the structure of the public consciousness in Spain was not as dynamic as it was in England. Spain remained a closed country in many respects, while England was rapidly advancing internally and becoming open for trade with other countries. This comparison may seem far-fetched, but I would say that risks must be taken if domestic political problems are to be resolved, the consciousness liberated, and initiative developed within the country. This is what will enable us to forge ahead with our foreign economic ties as well. The measures which are being taken today, such as granting major Soviet enterprises the right to deal internationally at their discretion and the right to competitiveness—these factors will propel our economy in the right direction. Entrusting everything to the apparatus, to officials who were not interested in taking risks, produced negative results.

S. Lunev. I believe the new thinking will be able to bring out its potential in full only if it is embraced by other countries, too. It cannot be a one-way street. And here we are observing the appearance of new obstacles as well as fresh opportunities.

The divergences among the imperialist powers involve methods, not goals. Western European countries advocate more energetic "social reform" methods, while the United States relies above all on military strength. Shifts in the use of these methods hinge chiefly on changes at the global level. Now that international tensions are lessening, even the Republican administration in the United States is utilizing "social reform" methods much more extensively.

However, the West is coordinating actions in the military-political sphere to a much greater extent at present. NATO's new military strategy presupposes a shift in the epicenter of East-West confrontation from Europe to other continents, increased military might on the territories of emergent states, and multifaceted interference in the countries of the East. The developments in the Persian Gulf are graphic evidence of the new doctrine in action.

N. Kapralov. I would define the old and new thinking as follows: In policy and diplomacy the old mode was an attempt to outdo one's partner and dictate one's writ, while the new political thinking is

equality and mutual respect. In the military–political, military–strategic and security spheres the old thinking was the ensuring of one's
security without taking account of the changes that one's actions
might have for neighboring countries. The new political thinking is
ensuring one's security without jeopardizing the security of others.
In the economy, the old political thinking was an attempt to asset
oneself at all costs as the leader at the regional or global level. The
new political thinking takes into consideration the economic interests
of partners; it is the international division of labor and by implication, the ensuring of economic security. Lastly, there is the moral,
ethical, philosophical, and ideological level. The old political thinking was a division of universal moral norms and political norms. The
new thinking is a unity of these norms.

V. Nemchinov. In addition to what has been said, I would define
the new thinking as a set of approaches expressing the primacy of
universal, socially active interests which repudiate the philosophy of
military–political rivalry and demarcation. Rejecting the logic of fear,
the new thinking is a counterbalance to the American philosophy of
pragmatism and the political concept of "zero playing." Under this
concept each action of the USSR's must be brought to naught by the
appropriate action on the part of the United States. According to this
faulty logic each American gain was a loss for the USSR and vice
versa. I call this "kitchen logic." In world politics it quickly betrays
its limitations. For example, in order to nullify our actions, they have
to be reacted to with at least equal force, or better still, with a bit of
overkill. And a negative political balance appears. When such pre-
emptive steps or retaliatory actions amass, we have an exacerbated
international situation, a sliding toward the dangerous brink of
confrontation.

A. Pikayev. I want to talk about a dogma that long played a very
negative role both in our propaganda efforts and possibly our foreign
policy. It is the dogma of secrecy. The following example will illustrate my point. To confirm the tenet that the Soviet Union is engaged
in research on its own SDI program and is already close to emplacing
something in outer space, and that SDI is supposedly needed for
catching up to the Soviet Union, the Pentagon publication **Soviet Military Power** carried a photograph of the Soviet destroyer *Sovremenny*
with commentary to the effect that a laser cannon is mounted on it.
The point most likely at issue is a laser guidance system which, inci-

dentally, is installed in American weapons systems. But we failed to say anything about this ourselves, and the American version about the laser cannon continues to spread around the globe, buttressing the arguments in favor of SDI.

There are other facts, however. This applies above all to the memorandum on the INF Treaty. The Americans did not want to issue it for consideration of their own. The Soviet Union was the first to put out this memorandum right after the treaty was signed. So here we moved ahead of the Americans in the sphere of glasnost.

Furthermore, glasnost is very important for our own security as well. For example, we learned from the memorandum that the Americans had long deceived Western public opinion by contending that they had only 108 Pershing-2 missiles in West Germany. The memorandum showed that there were more than 108.

On-site inspection is another important question. For a long time we used to call it legalized espionage. Before we attained strategic parity this evidently was objectively the case. But now we have agreed to this, thus debunking the long-standing contention of the American administration that the Soviet Union is a closed society. And now, at the talks on chemical weapons at the Conference on Disarmament in Geneva we have agreed to the most radical control measures, while the Americans have backtracked, claiming that they are against control at private enterprises. In other words, everybody is seeing that it's the United States, not the USSR, that is against openness.

A. Medvedev. The implementation of our new economic course requires aside from all else, definitive repudiation of some dogmas which took shape behind the "iron curtain" and later germinated feverishly and still continue to develop. I will single out the most important ones for our domestic economic practices, and external economic policy. Are low and unstable rates of economic growth and foreign-trade turnover a sign of economic crisis? What is the capitalist of the final quarter of the twentieth century like? How are the functions of the owner, entrepreneur, and manager in the present-day capitalist economy divided? What are the place, role, and organizational and management principles of the transnational corporations, on one hand, and small-scale business on the other? How is the position of state-monopoly regulation in the domestic economies of the capitalist countries and in the world economy changing? What is the correlation between cooperation, competition, and contradictions among the capitalist countries? In this country the accent is being placed on contradictions. You open a newspaper or a magazine and everywhere you read: "acute contradictions on the verge of trade wars," and the like. But the other side of the phenomenon is not covered. Another question: How do international economic organizations function and how important are they for regulating the world economy? The General Agreement on Trade and Tariffs, the International Monetary Fund, the International Bank for Reconstruction and Development, and the like are of particular interest to us. And another thing: What are the functions of the joint-stock form of property in the modern world and how do working people take part in production management under capitalism? This list of questions could go on and on. And as the USSR becomes more involved in world affairs and the integration of the world economy, many dogmas will wither away and it is preferable that this be promoted in every way.

V. Udalov. I would merely like to point out that the USSR Foreign Ministry has been energetically revamping its activities, and the efforts to utilize more productively the possibilities which science has to offer are an important part of this reorganization. The old thinking and policies which were based on it were detrimentally monolithic and inflexible and had pretensions to absolute truth. In the final analysis, this was evidently obtained from a lack of interest in other viewpoints. Such viewpoints are born in discussion. And discussion is debate, it is a property of science. Hence the natural link: Attention to science is dictated by the very essence of the new political thinking. Policy is made by people. It is all the more important to draw on different viewpoints, and these viewpoints can be given to us by science.

The Research Coordination Center has been set up at the USSR Foreign Ministry recently. It is headed by V. V. Shustov, a member of the Collegium of the Foreign Ministry. It is our job to help the Ministry sections and departments utilize what science has to offer and to keep our diplomats who work in specific areas from closing themselves off in their own little practical worlds. Our goal is to establish regular feedback, from us to the scholars. We are in favor of vigorous cooperation between the academic community and Foreign Ministry staff members. This is important both for the scholars, because they will in effect be involved in the shaping of foreign policy, and for the diplomats.

The Research Coordination Center has already begun functioning. It is still small. But then this is not fortuitous, as we do not want to create unwieldy structures. The first steps have provided useful. Conferences and meetings are being held at the Foreign Ministry and at research institutes not only in Moscow but in the different republics. We place particular hopes on establishing cooperation with young scholars. I think that today's discussion will be a good impetus for further work in this sphere.

International Affairs. The leitmotif of almost all the statements has been a critical posing and analysis of problems dealing directly with foreign policy. This is a good sign. Although, to be frank, one cannot help noticing that the critical fervor at times outweighed another prime element—problem analysis per se and constructive. well-considered alternatives. Negation is also a method of thinking, but it can be accepted solely as the most initial basis for developing a debate, as a bridgehead for attacking established stereotypes and ossified dogmas. It is important not only to name particular dogmas but also to investigate the reasons which spawned them and the conditions which enabled them to go on existing. The vitality of stereotypes and dogmas lies not only, and perhaps not so much, in the conservatism of their exponents, but in the fact that they have come to be accepted as mathematical axioms that are taken on faith. Furthermore, doubting these axioms was almost tantamount to apostasy. Dogmas were placed higher than reality, and reality was made to fit dogmas.

The Party lay bare our mistakes in domestic policy and resolutely deplored styles and approaches which were grounded on fidelity to dogmas and stereotypes. And they are no less dangerous in the international sphere, for that matter. The decisive break with the outmoded way of thinking has been vital to our policy in the international arena. Calm realism has breathed fresh energy into our policy and enhanced its potential. It has also helped Soviet foreign policy reach new heights, which long seemed inaccessible. All this is manifest in the well-considered and balanced set of practical measures and proposals which the USSR has advanced.

The atmosphere in world politics is changing.

International Affairs *Guest Club*

Muscovites on Soviet Foreign Policy

Mikhail Belousov, tool maker, Automobile and Tractor Electrical Equipment Plant

Anataly Katalymov, assistant professor of chemical technology and automated designing, Moscow Institute of Chemical Machine-Building

Olga Kokshaiskaya, historian, staff member of the Decembrists Museum

Alexander Kraiko, People's Deputy of the USSR head of department, Central Institute of Aircraft Engine-Building

Vitaly Krikov, "Afghan" veteran, installer of radio equipment, Punch Card Machine Plant

Rear-Admiral *Vitaly Losikov*, chief, political department, Chief Navy Staff

Alexander Nikonov, head, Ecological and Industrial Safety Laboratory, Algoritm; deputy chairman, Council Bureau, USSR Ecological Union

Victor Olenev-Hirschfeld, coordinator, People-to-People Diplomacy Independent Inter-Institute Group for International Studies

Vladimir Sokolov, pensioner, former senior investigator of cases of special importance, USSR Ministry of the Interior

Timur Esadze, student, Dramatic Art Section, Studio School under the Moscow Academic Art Theatre

New Thinking, Ghosts of the Past, and Perestroika

A. Katalymov. A consensus over interests is something the whole world needs. It is anachronistic today to defend "class interests" in the international arena. It's downright dangerous. What we must bear in mind is things benefiting humanity. We stand to gain where humanity benefits from a reasonable foreign policy on our part. Nobody can now secure advantages by himself alone, neither a small nor a large nation. The ecological problem is the most striking case in point.

V. Olenev-Hirschfeld. I agree. but let us see just the same who we are. They call our country a superpower. Very well, let us accept the term—why shouldn't we? After all, it is true objectively, nor am I speaking of our military strength. Our country is a great world power, a continent comprising hundreds of peoples and influencing the lives of its neighbors.

The only point is to interpret this "superpower" status of ours correctly. We are doing so already, it seems. Our country isn't a formidable monolithic colossus that has only to stretch itself for the world to be shaken by upheavals. On the contrary, it is a great pacifying and stabilizing force. This is so objectively, and it's the view we should take ourselves. It puts all conflicts, all regional collisions, in a entirely different light.

What is, from the point of view of our interests, the Soviet–Albanian conflict, which has lasted so unnaturally long? In the past we did a lot for Albania, and it found its feet. But what happened afterward? There occurred events which made us psychologically unacceptable to the Albanians, and on top of this the discord was made worse by perfectly incomprehensible grievances and ambitions. Great powers have neither ambitions nor grievances, for those are the weaknesses of small countries.

Let me express a general opinion. For a superpower, to be the first to speak openly of its mistakes, to apologize, and so on, is to take a fine, dignified stand that is also to its advantage, if you will. A superpower cannot lose face by doing so (a small state dreads just that), but can, on the contrary, acquire a human face and even make political capital.

Nowadays it is profitable to be kind and humane. At home and abroad, and in every sense. This is an objective reality which all leaders would do well to appreciate, for some of them still imagine that new thinking is a cunning stratagem of Gorbachev's. The time is over when Frederick II could say: "Take the territory you like. Afterward you can find a hundred lawyers who will prove that the seizure was legitimate." Everything has changed, and the process of change is objective. And so the less cynical you now are, the better for yourself and the world. The inference with regard to us is: What is good for the world and humanity is good for the Soviet Union. Conversely, what objectively benefits the Soviet Union benefits civilization. This is the gist of the idea of interdependence provided that you see in it a working concept and not a slogan.

I think the notion of sufficient defense should be seen from the same point of view. Far from being a weakness or a concession, it is an objective conclusion prompted by an analysis of the development of the modern warfare means, of our ever democratizing and humanizing world, and of properly understood superpower pride. This is, incidentally, what guided me in 1983–1985 when I was developing my conception of sufficient defense, a fact immediately noted by the *Detente* magazine and *The Guardian* and *The Observer* newspapers. At the time this idea was, unfortunately, viewed here as heretic, but time flies fast. . . .

T. Esadze. For me, the problem of new thinking is primarily a human problem. I'm a playwright, and this means that I'm a politician in a sense because politicians, too, must work with people, at least theoretically must know them. Nobody will therefore deny, I suppose, that people are central to diplomacy and foreign policy. They are both the subject and the object of politics. Indeed, what's the purpose of politics? What makes is profitable? It is the welfare of people and society as a whole.

But let there be no misktake: I don't at all want to invoke the concept of the "human factor." Incidentally, it's a coinage of the new period, the period of perestroika, but genetically it belongs in our past. The phrase is absurd, false, and ultimately harmful. Why? Let us realize at long last that man neither can nor must be a factor. He is a goal. The economy, diplomacy, ideology are all factors. The blame for this misconception of the essence of man must evidently be put on ideology, especially its notorious propositions about "class content" and "class values."

It's clearly time we reappraised this slogan-like concept. For ten years, it made us look continuously for enemies in our society, for those who were "right" in class terms and those who were "wrong" and hence guilty. We tried to distinguish between the "pure" and the "impure," that is, were engaged in a permanent civil war. As it happens, war—any war—invariably cripples people spiritually, deforms the accepted set of values and psychology, distorts the sense of morality, and occasionally even kills it. Isn't this the reason for our current troubles? Why, we are still fighting against ourselves.

We also have to "thank" past rounds of that war for many things. Their results are well known: depeasantization, the destruction of millions of peasants and intellectuals, a disastrous decline in cultural standards. And here's another paradox. We talked for decades about "class values" and the hegemony of the proletariat, but what good, specifically, did that scanning of slogans do to the proletariat? Now that we know all our troubles, this question sounds rhetorical. But I think we still haven't quite renounced this approach (which classifies people as botany and biology classifies plants and animals). Yet what we need first and foremost is democracy and humanism.

The thesis about "class values" has an amazingly bizarre record in our country. Let us recall that Marx didn't evolve his doctrine of classes for its own sake but because he had been investigating a specific philosophical and social problem—that of man's total alienation from the products of his labor, from production and society and politics, from other people. A class vision of the world in the Marxian sense is needed primarily as a means of ending that alienation. But what did we do? Having mesmerized ourselves by insisting on the primacy of "class values" (even without comprehending them properly—isn't this why we now find it hard to define what class values we are defending on the international scene?), we not only failed to solve the problem of alienation but aggravated it to a monstrous degree. It looks as if we have yet to realize that the situation in our country is analogous: while admitting that man was alienated from power, production, and property for decades, we affirm just the same that we "live under socialism" and we must merely "restore its human image."

I think this universal alienation, which makes people drop out of the social context, stop feeling responsible for the political situation in the country, and blame their troubles on others, is the chief trouble affecting our society and the chief obstacle to perestroika.

V. Krikov. I would like to go further on that point. Yes, we now talk a lot about the primacy of universal over class values, of new thinking, democracy, and other useful things. All that is correct. But I fear that we may start praising and overpraising ourselves all over again and slide back into the old rut.

We mustn't fear the truth nor a sober outlook on life. I am all for Gorbachev, for perestroika, but I was better off before, under Brezhnev. Do you see what I mean? Here's a simple example. In the past, I could buy baby food without difficulty before nine a.m. But now it is sold from half past six, and you get nothing if you come at seven. Why is this? Somebody in our country has forgotten to buy milk cartons from the West. But why must my child smart for that? And what can I do as an individual to ensure that the guilty bureaucrat is fired? Nothing.

This prompts me to ask a question about our electoral system. I agree that the earlier Supreme Soviet was no good—it was a body of supers, a mass meeting. But how am I to go about toppling a bureaucrat who is minister now? Theoretically, I can bring him down through my MP by asking him to make inquiries with the bureaucrat in question, and then to have him black-balled. But I will no longer have that kind of connection or will only have it for a short time and rather by chance. Indeed, I haven't elected an MP, have I? It's a member of the Congress of People's Deputies that I elected. Yet previously we elected people directly to the Supreme Soviet. Does this imply that the earlier system was better? I'm saying all this because we don't seem to have a precise idea of how to democratize the country. We are still afraid of something and so take up a step back.

O. Kokshaiskaya. I don't quite understand why we call new thinking "political." I believe we should desist at long last from a "political" approach—we've politicized and ideologized everything, beyond all measure as it is. Why not cultivate elementary economic thinking, for instance? It's what we lack more than anything else. Why not calculate how much a human life is worth—say, mine? What we now have is just a distorted set of values: we make tanks to defend our people, yet children born to these people are poisoned by the nearest chemical plant. But parents cannot take offence because that plant has provided them with housing.

Since we don't seem to be able to tell good from bad, let us see what can benefit us. If we figure out everything we'll discover that museums mustn't be starved of funds or the country will "lose" its citizens, that it doesn't pay to keep people made diplomats by way of "penalizing" them (they may do harm), that it's better for society to have healthy and cheerful members, who can spend their leisure time pleasantly, take a walk in the woods, smell flowers—in short, can live a normal, comfortable life, which is still something unfamiliar to us, I'm sorry to say.

A. Nikonov. It is really high time we updated the concept of national security. The Ecological Union in which I'm deputy chairman already has international ties. They have shown us many things, such as the fact that serious people abroad have long ago stopped seeing our country as a war menace—they now look on it as a source of ecological danger. That is quite understandable, I suppose, because our industries lacking cleanup facilities "present" emissions not only to us but to our neighbors across the frontier and those farther away. There is the Baltic Sea, for one, whose state is worrying the Scandinavians and the rest of the continent. It is something to think about.

We must realize that what is required for the solution of the ecological problem isn't appeals or declarations coming from various platforms, not yet sounding the alarm but above all comprehensive, painstaking, intelligent efforts in our own country. We must show no mercy to bureaucrats active in the economy because we and the world are paying too dearly for their activity. In fact, they are undermining our security. I'm sure our effort for cleanliness in our house and around it will be fully appreciated by all.

Many countries are willing to cooperate with us in both ecological education and specific areas of nature conservation. Joint research and production complexes could be a promising form of such cooperation. The problem of universal security might be solved as a result of joint efforts to eliminate the threat to the environment. After all, environmental security is part of national security.

V. Krikov. I keep wondering what sort of country and society we have. This is a question asked by many today but I haven't yet heard a clear answer from anybody. Many phrases are used nowadays, such as "command system," "state socialism," "barracks," and even "military-feudal socialism." What seems to be lacking is "capitalist socialism." In history, it's a juggling of words that makes you dizzy. But see what Reagan did. To be able to give the Somozistas money (just money!), he had to squabble with Congress for a long time; that is, he had to ask his parliament's permission. By contrast, Brezhnev moved troops into Afghanistan without asking anybody's permission. He sprung a big surprise on all, civilians and us servicemen alike. And that war lasted longer than the Great Patriotic War.

I wonder which variety of socialism made that move possible. Who is to blame? Our system?

V. Sokolov. You shouldn't talk like that. Our socialism is a very good system except that we should do everything properly and fairly. Had Brezhnev and his entourage been real, honest Communists and not just party members, nothing happened. You must simply be honest. Where does the system come in? Had there been honesty and a Leninist concept of party principle in the leadership, it would never have come to one or two men deciding whether or not to move troops in, whether or not to send off our boys to get killed. You have to be honest, that's the point.

V. Krikov. I will tell you about my experience to illustrate what you said about honesty. I served in an airborne unit. In 1984, I found myself in Afghanistan. It's important to say how.

Nobody even hinted that we would be sent to Afghanistan. On the contrary, we were told that we were going to do regimental training. A commission from airborne troop headquarters ordered the dismantling of all our powder jet systems used for landing military equipment. The order seemed strange but we were told we wouldn't need the systems any longer because we were going to Lake Sevan and wouldn't be airdropped there but landed in the usual way. We believed that because it came from very high up.

About lunchtime our regiment was informed that it would be alerted at 4.00 hours and so we had better get ready, do our shopping, and so on. Once again there was not a hint. The only thing that put us on our guard was sniper rifles. The regiment had none but this time they were delivered and immediate training of "sharpshooters" was ordered. Finally we were alerted and drove to the airfield. Officers told us there to fill out "killed in action" forms, that is, cards giving our home addresses, our parents' names, and everything else in case we "died by accident while training" as we were told. We boarded a plane at 6.00 hours and stayed on board for six hours, or until 12.00, when we took off. Some time during the flight a pilot came out. "Is this your first flight to those parts, boys?" he asked. "What parts?" we asked. He was surprised. "Don't you know?" he replied. "We're flying to Kabul." That was when our company commander said yes, we were on our way to Kabul. We were surprised because the only weapons we had were tommy guns.

How did we take the news? We felt kind of elated at first, as if it were a game. We certainly had no inkling of what was coming. Finally the plane landed at an airfield and we got off, saying to ourselves it was probably a stopover, which we believed all the more since we were surrounded by Soviet soldiers. "Where are we?" we asked. "This is Kabul international airport," they replied. Two hours later, the airfield came under shell fire. That was how it all started. We finally realized that we had been cheated by the talk about "training."

In Afghanistan we trained for two months on mountainous terrain. Our first combat operation came in the fourth month of our stay there. Those operations are described variously now but there is little truth in what we hear or read. It wasn't only we who beat the enemy, but the other way around, too, and a sound thrashing it was. Just imagine a boy of eighteen who fired his tommy gun a couple of times before taking the oath. He was faced with an enemy who had been fighting for five to eight years and had handled his weapon from childhood, with his own people and his native mountains around him. Many of our boys were killed. I think this is just the time to ask: What did they die for? But who can we ask? Not Brezhnev, because he rests in a place of honor, on Red Square. It follows that there's nobody we can ask, or am I wrong?

M. Belousov. We must certainly help the Afghan revolution, but how? This is one question. And here's another: Who benefitted through all that?

O. Kokshaiskaya. You said "revolution." I'm a historian and yet I can't understand what kind of revolution it was. Afghanistan is a peasant country with a feudal system. Does that mean that the revolution was bourgeois? Or socialist? What was it?

V. Olenev-Hirschfeld. It's disgraceful. Indeed, we've been neighbors for a thousand years but we never got around to finding out who the neighbor was next door. We are "lazy and uninquisitive," as Pushkin put it. To come to the point, the whole business of sending troops is evidence of the absence of any scientific analysis of the situation. I suppose part of the blame must be put on diplomats and the Embassy but the heaviest responsibility falls on those who acted without consulting experts. They should learn thoroughly, at least, the lesson of the Afghan war.

Generally speaking, we are deficient in sound geopolitical thinking. What I mean is a capacity to analyze our international situation calmly and with due regard to every option. The result was Afghanistan. Why, we always prepare for a war that is over. We feared that this neighbor of ours would become a bridgehead for Western aggression against us. But that was a myth. Afghanistan is primarily a security area for three great Asian powers: the Soviet Union, China, and India. Had there been no Soviet–Chinese confrontation, neither would we have had the Afghan war.

Now do we have the slightest reason to speak of a "Chinese danger"? It's equally absurd to fear for our borders with Iran, Turkey, or the Balkans. Our military strategic situation is just splendid right now. There is talk of a "Western front." That's serious, all right. But let us realize that underlying it is the so-called German question. Hence the conclusions to be drawn.

The important thing, however, is to put an end to the costliest and most provocative foolishness of this century, Soviet–American rivalry. This is the chief bastion of old thinking that has yet to be taken. Let us realize this and tell the Americans that objectively we are not enemies and that there are no objective reasons for rivalry. Unless we realize this we'll change from two superpowers to two superfools, for good.

One of the working mottos of our Civic Diplomacy group is: "Open your eyes and get to the root." It means that now is the time to shake off ideological torpor and see things in their right perspective.

Foreign Policy, Diplomacy and Glasnost

M. Belousov. "See things in their right perspective." But I who only follow our foreign policy on the basis of press reports find that very difficult. Occasionally I'm simply baffled. For instance, I cannot understand our concept of foreign trade. It looks as if we're carrying it on as we are "used" to doing. We seem to feel that we must by all means resist America, export caviar and oil, and buy our coffee from Brazil. But why from Brazil? Why can't we buy coffee in Ethiopia? It might cost us less. Does anybody ever consider the options? You can find no competition of alternatives in the press. How is a foreign policy decision normally drafted in our country? What are my chances of keeping track of its drafting?

In preparing for today's discussion, I did some reading on our foreign policy. All comments praise it for its predictability. But to be frank, I see is as full of unexpected things. I learned from Mikhail Gorbachev's UN address that we were going to cut our army by half a milion men. Is that a good idea? It's excellent! The trouble is, however, that the news was first heard by the Americans and as for me, a Soviet citizen, it came to me literally from overseas. The same address said that we were willing to declare a one hundred-year moratorium on the servicing of debts owed to us by developing countries or even to cancel them altogether. That's a noble step, of course. Still, I don't know who owes us money and how much. And so I have no idea of how much I would have to sacrifice.

We have many expenses brooking no delay. It might therefore have been right to consult public opinion and submit the matter to the coming session of the new Supreme Soviet—in short, to carefully calculate everything. This is a time of glasnost, isn't it?

V. Olenev-Hirschfeld. Just think: we have millions of "ambassadors," our compatriots living in different countries since different periods. Why should we "write them off"? They embody a very important human link between our country and the outside world. Besides, let us remember that the diaspora from the historical homeland is a more serious problem for the Soviet Union, a union of numerous peoples, than for any other country. There are millions of Ukrainians, Armenians, Azerbaijanis, Tajiks, Jews, and others living abroad. Encouraging the activity of the diaspora would benefit us both externally—in terms of, say, foreign trade—and internally. One indication of this is the Armenian phenomenon, the Armenians' attachment to their historical homeland. And what if we look into this phenomenon in terms of promoting joint ventures? Isn't this a powerful economic lever? I'm certain Armenian businessmen from the West and the Arab East could revive Soviet Armenia's foreign economic ties more successfully than our lazy trade mission officials. Ties, joint projects, and funds could help effectively in rebuilding the cities destroyed by the earthquake. That would be merely a small part of the many things that could be done. In short, our countrymen abroad are a treasure, especially if not counted by million, as we used to do in the past, but down to the individual man or woman as required by the spirit of new thinking. As the poet put it: "The people are incomplete without me."

Let us realize at last that our country is the first unique integration of peoples in the twentieth century. But they are represented as a union, that is, in the dame way as Britain, France, Italy, Poland, and other countries which are nationally homogeneous in principle. Why not mobilize our tremendous diplomatic reserves in the form of missions of the Soviet Unions peoples? This would be all the more logical because their explicit aspiration for self-expression and self-assertion are urging us to do so. It seems to me, therefore, that we should be represented abroad in a twofold form, that is, as a federation (through republican consulates, funds, cultural and trading centers, and so on). Nor should this be seen as an innovation. It's rather an idea carried through to its logical end. Indeed, it is this logic that underlies our government system, or the very concept behind our Supreme Soviet, to be exact, meaning the Soviet of the Union and the Soviet of Nationalities. Perestroika, far from abolishing this logic, is carrying it forward, especially since decentralization is the watchword of democratization, if you will. So let us be logical and consistent.

A. Kraiko. I fully agree with Victor Olenev, who says that we have a huge informal "diplomatic corps" abroad made up of our compatriots and that it's unwise to ignore it. Why not help those of our citizens living abroad who wish to retain their Soviet citizenship? Why not give them due credit for it? Retained Soviet citizenship creates problems in some cases, as we all know. In developing countries, all job restrictions hit primarily foreign nationals—they are the last to be hired and the first to be fired.

Here's another example. During U.S. presidential elections, a special commission arrived in Japan to enable American wives of Japanese to vote. The gesture is probably unimportant as far as the elections are concerned. What is important is the idea that a great democratic power has no stepchildren. Incidentally, when the electoral law was being drafted I wrote to the Commission for Proposed Legislation to suggest that a similar practice be introduced in our country. As for our citizens in Ethiopia who are refused employment at our own Embassy, I think it's scandal.

V. Losikov. The fact that I serve in the Soviet navy, has understandably put its mark on my contacts with Soviet missions abroad. I disagree with Victor Olenev, who suggested that each of our republics should be represented separately abroad. I think what makes us strong, as in the case of a ship's crew, is unity of mind and will. Otherwise we could dilute everything. Our joint efforts are particularly necessary abroad.

When the world was marking the thirtieth anniversary of victory over Nazi Germany we paid a friendly visit to Boston, in the United States. U.S. ships reciprocated by arriving in Leningrad. We spent five days in Boston. Well, our whole Embassy headed by Anatoli Dobrynin installed itself on board ship, or so it seemed. We worked together in harmony, the Embassy helped us greatly, and I think we helped it in accomplishing a common task, effacing the "enemy image."

Everything would have been all right except for an annoying circumstance. Our ship, that is, about one thousand men, was America's guest for five days, and there were very interesting meetings. But our press confined itself to reporting dryly: "Soviet ships visited Boston, USA..." It follows that while we talk a lot about "people-to-people diplomacy," our people hardly know anything about its real actions.

How did the American press cover the event? It carried ample comments on everything from a description of our ship to details of the biography of, say, a Soviet sailor. One of our men had only to taste American ice cream and put up his thumb, saying "OK," for a reporter to take his photograph then and there, supply it with a caption and publish it in his paper. What's wrong with that? It was both publicity and simple fact showing the perfectly human image of Soviet people. But why can't we do that sort of thing? Why is there no "parity" in information? I think we may put the blame on our Embassy. It should cooperate with the press more actively, on more modern lines, I suppose.

O. Kokshaiskaya. It was said here that occasionaly the ambassador stays in his office until as late as eight p.m. Yes, he does, but then he is paid for it, and let us agree that he isn't paid so very poorly, at least in comparison with me, for one. However, money is beside the point because if our money were a real currency and not just banknotes I could save enough to make a trip abroad so as to undergo treatment in the same hospital or spend my vacation in the same holiday hotel as our ambassador. I cannot afford that because ambassadors stand on a different rung of the social ladder and are therefore spoken to, treated as patients, and catered for in a manner differing from what I am entitled to. That's how it is, you see. So let us not delude ourselves on this point, either. Ambassadors belong by every formal standard to precisely the elite typical and indicative of our society.

That they cannot be blamed for being members of the elite is a different matter, of course. And so I think we should try and find out how come we have social groups differing in standards of comfort. What am I in comparison with, say, an ambassador? Something of a serf who must live where she's registered and seek medical aid where she's registered. And so I lie in one place seek medical aid in another, and order spectacles in a third.

V. Sokolov. You know, our ambassadors aren't paid so very well, and besides, pay isn't the point. As the ambassador is merely a mirror of the country he represents, we must look at the problem more broadly. I mean the responsibility of those holding positions of responsibility. They must answer for the fruits of their activity, primarily in material terms. Why keep that "iron curtain" inside the country, between leaders and the people? If a leader's wife were to stand in a queue and then tell him about her impressions he would stop to think.

Maybe that's no way out. But I know by experience that nothing adds to social tension in the country as much as an awareness that there is a leading elite whose members always have everything, no matter what.

T. Esadze. Let us return to glasnost, however. There is no question that it must be complete, without any exceptions, particularly in the diplomatic sphere. We know nothing about newly-appointed ambassadors except their names reported by the press. Yet this post should go to people well known to the public. Maybe the new Supreme Soviet should hold hearings on such appointments, as the U.S. Senate does. I know that the Foreign Ministry now selects chauffeurs, cooks, and technical personnel generally for embassies by competitive examination. That's a good idea but why not extend the practice to prospective ambassadors? If it were done we would have competent diplomats abroad who had proved in competition with opponents that they were fit for precisely that kind of job.

Now for glasnost once again. It was described here as a new "epoch" in our history. Yet the word is as old as the concept itself, which gained currency as far back as the last century. Dal's Russian dictionary defines "glasnost" as an "announcement." But this isn't enough. We need something more than a spelling out of our own diplomacy to ourselves. After all, this is still an "epoch" of democratization and new thinking, which require that every citizen be in a position to influence policy, to shape or criticize it. And so I ask: What is the relationship between glasnost and freedom of speech as written into our constitution? Freedom of speech is a fundamental concept going deeper than the narrow concept of glasnost. If follows that what we need are guarantees of precisely free speech.

A. Kraiko. Yes, our diplomacy is still shackled by relics of old thinking. One of them is the practice of "penalizing" officials by appointing them ambassadors—I mean people who've botched their job in, say, agriculture, are no longer backed by a highly-placed patron, and so on. We ought to respect our own foreign policy and hence our diplomacy. Also, we should respect the country chosen as a place of "exile" for an official made ambassador.

For nine years running, our ambassadors in Afghanistan were former party functionaries whose worldview and very behavior had shaped up when they were Party committee secretaries. We all know the result.

A. Katalymov. I wish to touch specially on that last point. We "consumers" of our foreign policy, so to speak, still come across attempts to uphold some solution supposed to be the only correct one, and across the lack of any competition in evaluating past solutions, let alone in proposing a solution. This explains why people often feel that they are merely part of a mass of plastic material that can be molded at will. And it annoys them, you know. After the signing of the INF Treaty, everybody said it was a triumph of reason, a "breakthrough," and so on. But, if so, what are we to make NATO's "zero option" so scathingly criticized in the past? And what are we to think of Rejkjavik? Why, we were told that the "package" could in no circumstances be "unpacked" but when it "unpacked" after all, the same people argued that this was the only correct solution. Wasn't that a striking recurrence of a past practice?

Generally speaking, our politicians, political scientists, and public should stop to think very seriously about why we cannot advance to a goal in a straight line, making but few adjustments. Why do we advance as through a corridor, lurching from wall to wall and bumping our heads against them? Isn't this a matter of an effective policy which is being discussed so widely today?

Where Reserves of New Thinking Lie

T. Esadze. We've come to a topic intriguing us all. We really need to emancipate and transform people. And to this end we need not only glasnost but something greater than that, namely, alternatives. Not only at the level of personal opinion, which I hope will now be represented in the Supreme Soviet, but at political level. We don't have to invent anything because there exists a universal, general democratic value such as political pluralism and a multiparty system. Why should we be afraid of it?

V. Losikov. Each of us interprets pluralism in his own way. Yet the principles of new thinking apply to both foreign and home policy. And so the more tolerant we are of each other's opinion and the more democratically we proceed at home, the easier it will be for us to bring about a democratization of international relations. We admittedly influence them most of all by our home policy. Why not draw on past experience in this matter?

Let us recall Lenin's approach. At the Seventh All-Russian Conference of the RSDLP(B), a large group of delegates objected to nominating Kamenev for the election to the Central Committee. Lenin took the floor and said that Kamenev expressed the sentiments of a definite section of the people and therefore it was important to have an exponent of those sentiments on the CC. And he added:

"Our arguing with Comrade Kamenev yields but positive results. Comrade Kamenev's presence is very important, for the debates I am waging with him are very valuable. When you persuade him, after overcoming some difficulties, you realize that by so doing you overcome the difficulties that spring up among the masses."

That was how the country's leaders argued in the past. Lenin taught an excellent lesson which is still highly relevant. It's this culture of argument that we should carry forward. There is a severe shortage of it.

A. Kraiko. Since we've now come to recognize the wholesome effect of pluralist opinion, I think we ought to take the next step by providing real forms for expressing this diversity. Let us admit that out entire press is in fact a state press either by definition or by virtue of being semiofficial on a "compulsorily voluntary" basis. This is particularly obvious whenever our press comments on international politics.

There is another tangle of problems that is worrying me. I mean conversion. We are now cutting our armed forces, our military production, program and expenditures. That's fine. But unless there is a precise concept of conversion we may incur serious loss. Why so? Because should we deprive many of our research centers, such as those concerned with aircraft, of military contracts, demand for their research would plummet. This is because our industry has no competitors and objectively needs no innovations whatever, being a monopolist. It isn't accidental that we virtually impose scientific and technological achievements on industry. In short, we run a perfectly real risk of incurring considerable economic, technological, intellectual, and moral loss.

Incidentally, the Votkinsk missile plant is going to make prams. But has anybody calculated their cost?

Joint science-intensive ventures could be one solution in the circumstances. We could, for instance, cooperate with West Germany or Japan in manufacturing airliners that would compete even with Boeings. Why not? The Germans or Japanese would supply electronic equipment and technology and we, designs, aerodynamic know-how, and so on. That would earn us money, stimulate our science, and help solve our social problems. My idea is simple: Disarmament requires an economic, competent approach and a precise conversion program.

T. Esadze. Our whole economy is in need of competence. The inconceivable paradox of our society is that we have a noneconomic economy. Noneconomic! It is still dominated by commands, slogans, and instructions. Let us somebody higher up suggests promoting joint ventures. There comes—from those who are eager to report execution—a spate of joint ventures ranging from firms selling liquor or renting cars of foreign cars make to foreigners to leasing our natural resources and parts of our territory for the construction of chemical giants. As a result a useful and important idea is distorted.

If you ask what we need such joint ventures for the answer you get is: "We need them to secure hard currency and new technology." "But what do we need hard currency for?" "Don't you see? We need it to buy up-to-date equipment." The trouble is, however, that we cannot bring world progress in science and technology to our country bit by bit as we bring cucumbers from a neighbors' vegetable garden. Yet the situation with regard to introducing new technologies is just like that—it couldn't be worse. Everybody is fed up with talking about Western machinery rotting in the rain or production lines churning out nothing but rejects. Yet there is nothing surprising about the phenomenon because it's natural and logical with us.

The reason is that to master advanced technology, we need an entirely different production culture, a streamlined enterprise infrastructure, a new, civilized kind of worker, special economic areas where this whole new technological and economic civilization of ours could develop. As for confining ourselves to a particular, widely advertised joint venture, it is not just pointless but harmful. This could land us in the vicious circle of earning and squandering hard currency and reduce us to an existence fit for an underdeveloped and dependent country. The inference is that just as we need a conversion program, so we need—possibly to a greater extent—a streamlined, unorthodox concept of joint ventures.

V. Krikov. I wish to ask our People's Deputy a question. Alexander Nikolayevich, you've just given us a good idea of conversion and the opportunities which a wise policy of reducing armed forces could provide. But shouldn't we go even further? Look—we've pulled out of Afghanistan although the war is still on there and the situation around the country is as complicated as ever. Besides, everything is taking place close to our frontiers. Not so in Eastern Europe because there is no war there, and come to think of it, neither is the situation likely to lead to a recurrence of 1941. Carrying forward the logic of Afghanistan, wouldn't it be right and useful—allowing for all alternative trends of development west of our borders—to withdraw our troops from the East European countries where they are still stationed?

A. Kraiko. I stand in principle for our pulling out. I think it is the ideal both we and our allies are seeking. but don't let us forget that there is a third party, the West and NATO. It's therefore necessary to carefully explore the situation from every point of view, including that of reciprocity on the part of the North Atlantic bloc. My general feeling, however, is that developments will gradually take a course desirable for everybody. The process is on already, isn't it?

A. Nikonov. We seem to be hypnotized by one goal. If we are fighting for disarmament it gradually becomes an end in itself. Growing in the back of our minds is the conviction that the abolition of arms will lead to a nonviolent world. But violence will always find some weapon. I think it's more important to create a mechanism blocking violence, something of a behavioral stereotype for states.

We often find in nature analogues of concepts current in man's world: love, morality, religion, war, aggression. Zoopsychologist Konrad Lorentz writes in his book *On Aggression* that beasts, like the lion, capable of killing a member of their own species at one blow, never do so. If two lions are fighting for a female the weaker lion may lie down and stop the fight that way. His rival, heated by the duel, may claw at himself with rage but will never "raise a paw" against his prostrate adversary. By contrast, doves—that symbol of gentleness and peace—often peck each other to death. This should give us food for thought.

Right now we humans are in a position thanks to our intellect to wipe out entire nations and, indeed, all humanity at one blow. I think awareness of our might must curb our aggressive intentions, taking the place of the "ban" on killing one's kin, which is the rule with certain animals. In short, we must develop a new, nonviolent consciousness by rallying our reason.

O. Kokshaiskaya. The problem of state-to-state or rather international intercourse is overburdened in our country with all sorts of artificial difficulties, with a kind of dreary ideological prejudice. Right now we talk a lot about mutual confidence, the "enemy image," and so forth. Yet the problem is very simple. That foolish self-isolation, shutting ourselves off from everybody, primarily from ourselves, was self-imposed, and had every one of us been free to travel abroad and mix, just as tourists, with Americans, for example, I'm sure many problems wouldn't be there at all. In any case, neither professional nor "people's" diplomats would have to prove that we have no horns and know how to use a spoon or fork like anybody else.

V. Krikov. Quite true. We've already said a lot about self-respect, respect of our country, and so on. But we need to do something—what are we waiting for? I've long wanted to respect myself, my country Russia, to take pride in it. But look around you. We are in the editorial offices of the journal, in one of Moscow's oldest neighborhoods. There are numerous monuments to the past around us, such as we should be proud of because they belong in the category of spiritual values which everybody is now freely talking about, and we here can even feel them with our hands. But look at the state of nearby churches. I'm sure no European nation would have tolerated such a thing. Yet we aren't worse than others, are we? The nearest church—it dates from the eighteenth century—in a storehouse of the Ministry of Culture. Just think: a cultural institution set up a storehouse in a church, of all places!

They say there's no money to restore the church. So give those crumbling buildings back to their original owner, the Church. The public would help it by both contributing funds and joining in restoration work. Personally I'm willing to work without pay, to carry bricks, so as not to see that insulting decay any longer. Otherwise nothing will be left but fine talk.

V. Sokolov. I disagree with our historian here. She said everybody was friendly and over there strangers were sympathetic and responsive to each other. Maybe, but where? In a lounge or on a hike? Probably. But besides them there is the state with its interests and principles which have to be defended. Or take another example, the Second International during World War I. Everybody seemed to be at one with everybody else but when the war broke out everyone rushed to the defense of his state. It's the same now. And so the conclusion I draw is that a strong, powerful state is the chief factor for our security and we must therefore defend its interests and principles.

Why, some now go almost as far as to say we have no enemies any longer. Oh, yes, we do have them, now as before, and always will. Let us open our frontiers, we are told. I cannot agree with that, either, because we could lose everything that way. I wonder why we keep tacking?

We certainly need interchanges, meetings, people-to-people diplomacy and all that. But everything has a limit. We must do things properly and not rush from one extreme to another, as we often do.

O. Kokshaiskaya. So where would you say our chief enemy is?

V. Sokolov. I have no doubt about that—he's at home. Irrespective of in our own society itself. Everybody here has been speaking about spiritual values—it's a fashionable topic. What I would say as a professional, if you will, is that we now need just elementary honesty. See what I mean? Honesty with regard to our history. Let the archives be opened for us to study the records. Because we are guessing what Stalin thought of this or that. Speaking of the honesty of our leaders, we need to know everything about them—how much they earn, where exactly they prefer to do their shopping. In short, we need honesty toward ourselves. We must tolerate no shortage of the truth. There's a shortage of sausages for the moment—well, we can wait. We are used to it. But if somebody lies to us or conceals something it will be the end because he will forfeit our confidence for good.

O. Kokshaiskaya. Let me give you a last example. At the museum I often have to help children as a guide or in some other way. What amazes and distresses me is that when I ask a junior pupil a question he takes his time over answering it. He stops to think, trying to guess what kind of answer would suit me best. And then he answers me, doing so "correctly," of course that is, as he "should," as he has been "taught" to.

It's children who do that. Yet we are talking of new thinking. The problem is that our lives were robbed of independent opinion, of free, independent thinking. Indeed, we had come to be afraid of these words. The episode I've told you reveals our whole system without our having to read articles by publicists.

This makes us ponder on the destiny of new thinking. Our children may learn its correct slogans by heart, may repeat certain words, may scan them, but where would new thinking come in? There wouldn't be any at all.

And so I believe the important thing now is to educate people, to remold them, if I may say so. They should be induced to respect themselves, their ideas, convictions and actions, should be educated as citizens. That would make new thinking really new. You cannot just tell people to switch from old to new thinking.

PART III

What Security Do We Need?

Introduction to Part III

Until not long ago, USSR foreign policy excited the envy of other lines of perestroika, being practically exempt from criticism. It was a zone invaded once in a while by brawny men who would deliver one or two saber thrusts and pull back shortly after. But the situation is changing now. The salvos have become more rapid and better aimed. Well, this was only to be expected. Over the past years, foreign policy has really done much for the country. But the safe conduct issued to it is not permanent.

It is important to see clearly in to the character of the doubts in question. I can understand those whom the reduction of missiles to junk and the discharge of half million troops have prompted to sound the alarm because we may be undermining our national security. After all, the country must be like an impregnable fortress, and generally speaking, power is respected in today's changing world. However, it is time we knew how much power we needed. There is no answer yet. But when academic experts make a serious attempt to ascertain "how much defense is sufficient" some people resent it. In recent years, the idea of "reasonable defense sufficiency" has been tampered with so badly that having more weapons may be seen as the most reasonable answer.

Criticism is leveled above all at the foreign policy aspect of perestroika, being provoked by bitter impressions of developments in Eastern Europe. Indeed, what we lived with for more than four decades fell apart almost overnight. The trouble is not that the "empire" is disintegrating but that the theory and practice to which the ruling parties had adhered in imitating us turned out to be helpless. This is certainly disheartening. But it would be very wrong to blame everything on a miscalculated foreign policy even though part of the blame must be put on it.

The concern I have mentioned is justified and comprehensible. But there is also a group of other motives. What we have is a bid to curb or slow down some lines of internal perestroika, primarily the processes of democratizing society and ridding it of worthless ideological dogmas, by raising a panic over developments in the foreign policy sphere. An effort is being made to chain foreign policy to a conservative home policy. Openness to the outside world and integration into the community of civilized nations apparently affect the interests of those who prefer to live and rule surrounded by a thriving military-industrial complex, with civil rights and freedoms at home, such as freedom of information, of press and others, falling short of European standards.

All this calls for scrutiny. Fair criticism helps while biased criticism fetters people's activity and imagination and tells on the general course of perestroika.

—BORIS PYADYSHEV

We Need a National Security Concept

Boris Pyadyshev

As time passes every event, slogan, and plan finds its proper place and assessment.

This fully applies to the program of a nuclear-free world advanced by the Soviet leadership on January 15, 1986. In a broader sense, it applies to the Soviet comprehensive concept of national security which is still at the stage of elaboration.

Viewed after the past few years this program no longer evokes joy or deserves superlatives because, conceived at the beginning of perestroika, it bears the cumbersome inertia of the claim to speak on behalf of, and for the entire humankind. Once can also perceive the naïveté of the striving to elaborate stage-by-stage and year-by-year deliver-

BORIS D. PYADYSHEV, is USSR Ambassador Extraordinary and Plenipotentiary member of Collegium of the Ministry of Foreign Affairs, as well as editor in chief of *Mezhdunarodnaya Zhizn* magazine.

ance of the world from nuclear, chemical, and other mass-destruction weapons by the year 2000.

While making these unavoidable remarks we have to pay tribute to the program.

Let us begin with facts. Striking as it may seem, the present situation in the field of arms limitation accurately coincides with the ideas advanced for the first stage of the program. Namely, it was expected that within five to eight years the Soviet Union and the United States would cut by half their strategic nuclear weapons, scrap their medium-range missiles, and thereby give impetus to processes of reduction of conventional weapons and armed forces.

Well, there are no longer any medium-range or short range missiles. On November 19, 1990, Paris saw the signing of the vital Treaty on Conventional Armed Forces in Europe which puts drastic limits on the armaments levels of states, thus paving the way from overabundance in weaponry to the sufficiency of weapons for the defense of any country on the continent.

Actually, as far as its political aspects are concerned, the treaty on cutting by half the strategic offensive weapons of the USSR and the United States is ready for signing. What remains to be done is to come to accord on some inessential matters and bring to an end the technical finalizing of the text. So, hopefully, when President George Bush visits Moscow, that instrument will be signed. Important accords have been reached on a new generation of measures to consolidate confidence and security in Europe.

The initial disarmament measures were passed quite smoothly and not because they involved issues of lesser importance. Far form it: These are large-scale and drastic measures. However, this is just the first approach to the cardinal problem since we witness so far only reductions of weapons which are in overabundance. Besides, it is only the stockpiles of the two superpowers that are being shaken down, and the difficulties that arose were only those which emerged within the framework of Soviet–American relations.

It will be a rather different matter with the second stage of the program, when all the other nuclear powers are expected to pitch in. A common denominator will be much more difficult to find. Will France agree? And what about Britain and China? This is a big question. So far, they were not too eager to scrap their missiles.

Now it seems appropriate to look at the prospects for the program of a nuclear-free world. As we see it the ideal end is the mutual renunciation of nuclear weapons, the discontinuation of their testing, the total destruction of stockpiles, and safeguards guaranteeing that they would not be made anywhere in the world. That is the principle that was and remains. However, today it is also clear that this ideal is being pushed beyond the projected timetable.

Moreover, I would venture to say that a totally nuclear-free world in the foreseeable future is hardly possible and is even fraught with risks.

Why is it not possible? Because of the stand taken by nuclear states other than the USSR. And because of the determination of such states as Israel, Iraq, Pakistan, and others to join the nuclear club on whose threshold they already are.

Now the one and only way to prevent this from happening is by consolidating the Treaty on the Non-Proliferation of Nuclear Weapons. In 1990 it was acceded to by two more states and now its parties number 141. This makes the Treaty the most universal instrument by the number of the participants in an accord in the field of arms limitation. And yet, the nonproliferation problem may have some surprising twists and turns in our own country. As has been asked abroad, is it improbable that the Soviet Union will disintegrate into several independent states which will "inherit" Soviet nuclear weapons. There would emerge a new zone of instability and acute conflicts which, quite probably, might lead to the use of nuclear weapons, provided they are readily at hand. This prospect is rather a headache for politicians.

Further on, I shall explain why a nuclear-free world is risky in a sense. Given even the most excellent relations between states, they need a guaranteed reserve of security within the international community. We need, if it comes to it, a big, but civilized "stick" to protect our common order against dangerous escapades of adventuristic regimes. To be on the safe side we have to have a certain amount of superweapons, which may remain in the possession of some leading powers. A UN nuclear force may be set up for this purpose. It is hardly possible to do without such a force in the coming era, which is already pregnant with a lot of regional conflicts and crises.

Of course, the nuclear arsenal to guarantee security should be as small as possible. It should not include destabilizing weapons systems which could be used to make a preventive strike.

Taking all this into account, is it not high time to start talks with the West on the problems of minimal nuclear containment? So far, in staunchily upholding the idea of a totally nuclear-free world we have been sidetracking the issue.

The foundation has now been laid for a conceptual breakthrough in the issues involving our national security. For decades before that Rubicon, the philosphy of the Soviet Union military-political leadership was never above the idea that military might was the main instrument to ensure security, while political means were pushed far to sidelines. Moreover, it was believed that the military might must be impressive enough to retaliate not only against the United States but against the entire bloc of NATO as well, and all thinkable adversaries, wherever they might be. And it should be said that we have almost attained a strategic parity with the rest of the world. But the price we had to pay was terrible: the country could no longer stand the overstrain of the arms race.

The program for a nuclear-free world made tentative approaches to the elaboration of a new national security concept. There began a gradual transfer of effort from predominantly military ways and means of attaining that goal to a combination of military and political means, with the steadily growing role of the latter. The candid dialogue with the West allowed us to draw a vital new conclusion that the USSR and the United States, and other NATO countries, are no longer adversaries and are ready from now on to base their relations on principles of partnership and cooperation.

Naturally, it will take some time before the mechanisms of ensuring security by political means, both at the regional and global levels, are created and become operative. During that period military means are called upon to back security. They can play their part in a situation when efforts to reduce the military threat go hand in hand with consistent practical implementation of the principle of reasonable defense sufficiency.

We are now left alone, without the Warsaw Bloc or allies. Our domestic affairs are going from bad to worse. Hence the question: How in these conditions can we make plans in the military field? As before, by taking into account only how many missiles and nuclear warheads the Pentagon has? I think that would be wrong. We ourselves must accurately and soberly decide on what is the minimum of weapons which would guarantee that any aggression against the Soviet Union would bring irreparable damage to its initiators. Besides, our efforts should ensure that there would be no potential aggressor among major powers, and that we should consolidate open and normal relations with them.

If we manage to define the quantitative and qualitative volumes of weapons proceeding from the principle of reasonable defense sufficiency, would it not be sensible for us to lower our stockpile levels in the course of our own military effort rather than in the process of protracted and painful international talks? This would be a reasonable step toward answering our national interests. Incidentally, the pioneer in this field was France, who already in the sixties began to define its military needs without looking over its shoulder into the strategic plans of other states and simply following a simple logic of having just enouth nuclear and other weapons to scare away anyone form the attempt to encroach on its security. Once we criticized France for the fact that it avoided international talks on disarmament, that it successfully and consistently pursued the policy of independent and unilateral measures in the military field, reaping quite a few benefits from that line.

It is not all that important whether the program for a nuclear-free world will follow the phases mapped out five years ago. The crucial thing is that these initiatives of Moscow have played a historical role by providing a good impetus to the disarmament processes. It seems that in the present-day situation it is more reliable to proceed from one accord to another without making them interdependent. The really important thing is to maintain the pace in limiting armaments. Some people lament that in foreign policy the coachman drives horses too hard. This can be said only by the people who are in no hurry to arrive anywhere. Naturally, sober-minded people will not rush head over heels in matters of national security. However, it would be wrong to slow down the pace in arms limitation, in ridding the arsenals of unnectessary burdensome wight and flabby muscle. That would be contrary to our military and political interests and our domestic situation, which has suffered too much under the war machine.

How Much Defense Is Sufficient?

Alexei Arbatov

The idea that political means of safeguarding security, that is, primarily diplomacy and treaties, should be preferred to military means was proclaimed at top political levels.

In practice, however, strategic plans and armament programs are still often regarded as something immutable and independent of external circumstances. These program are a strong obstacle to the efforts of diplomats seeking compromise and therefore set very tangible limits to the range of attainable accords.

It is perfectly logical that military institutions take the most active part in deciding on the line to be followed in talks since the object of the latter is what these agencies are responsible for. But is feedback

ALEXEI ARBATOV, D. Sc. (Hist.), is head of the Department of Political and Military Studies at the Institute of World Economics and International Relations of the USSR Academy of Sciences.

effective enough? How great is the contribution of our politicians, diplomats, scientists, and disarmament experts to the shaping of strategy, the specification of military plans, decision-making on new weapons systems, the assessment of defense requirements? Who can vouch and on what grounds, in the light of past experience (such as that of unrestrained tank buildup in postwar years), that all the provisions of our long-range military program and our strategic and operational concepts are really indispensable to our security?

Our defense potential and our plans for improving it are not a "thing in itself" existing outside political time and space. On the contrary, they are the most important factor in disarmament talks and in general political relations between the Soviet Union and other powers. This implies that people, agencies, and research centers directly responsible for these talks and relations are in duty bound to contribute their share to the framing of our military policy. Otherwise they will be doomed (*ex post facto*) to clear the "mess" resulting from decisions they had nothing to do with.

Direct inclusion of the above considerations is likely to substantially widen the scope of feasible accords and eliminate collisions between our foreign policy plans and military measures. This is entirely in keeping with the new philosophy of security, with the orientation to political means of safeguarding it, to the renunciation of military power as a foundation of relations with the world around us.

Military Strategic Realities

Anyone who has concerned himself at all with strategic problems knows that the military requirements of a country (in terms of troops and armaments and their types and characteristics) cannot be directly deduced from the strength and resources of likely opponents. To specify these requirements, it is also necessary to ascertain in what manner the other side is capable of using its armed forces. Thereupon the country can decide what tasks its army and navy must fulfill accordingly. This is the only way to define its requirements as to the quantity, quality, and deployment of armed forces and armaments.

Official documents adopted by the Soviet Union and the WTO in recent years as well as statements by political and military leaders contain key provisions offering a starting point for a revision of military doctrine and strategy. I refer, first of all, to the fact that victory in a world nuclear war is recognized as impossible (because the damage it would cause could not be reduced to an acceptable level) as is the waging of a limited and protracted nuclear war. Victory would also be out of the question in a large-scale conventional war in Europe because of the disastrous consequences which even conventional hostilities would have for the population, economy, and environment of the continent and in view of the practically inevitable nuclear escalation of such a conflict.

Apart from the foreign political and moral aspects of the problem, this leads even from the purely military point of view to the fundamental conclusion that it is necessary to regard the prevention of nuclear and conventional war as the chief task of the armed forces, pledge no-first-use of either nuclear or conventional weapons and revise strategy, operational plans and military capability on the principles of defense.

We can infer from the foregoing some further and more specific amendments to the strategy of defensive sufficiency without forgetting, of course, that generalizations of this nature are relative and inevitably open to question:

–Until such time as all nuclear weapons are eliminated under relevant agreements, the combat task of offensive and defensive strategic forces will be not to limit damage in the event of nuclear war (which is impossible in any circumstances) nor to defeat the aggressor's armed forces, but to deliver a crushing blow against its life centers.

–The task of armed forces and conventional armaments is not to conduct offensive strategic operations in the main European and Asian theaters of war but to engage in defensive operations in order to frustrate offensive operations by the enemy.

–A protracted conventional war is impossible, and the task of the armed forces is to prevent the enemy from winning the upper hand in intensive short-term combat operations and from resorting to nuclear escalation with impunity.

–A war on two fronts simultaneously (that is, against the United Stated and its allies and against China) is very unlikely in the foreseeable future.

–No future use of limited Soviet forces in international conflicts or in internal conflicts in developing countries shall be envisaged.

Such analogies, though artificial, may be described in simplified terms as a transition from the strategy of two and a half wars to a strategy of one war, or rather of the ability to stave it off on the basis of a reliable defense potential.

I can list another three general principles. First, the emphasis must be shifted from extensive to intensive means of ensuring defense. Second, the buildup of possible enemies' military potential is not only an objective reality for our planning but a process directly influenced by our measures. Our activity is likely to lead to an intensification and extension of their program or, on the contrary, to these being slowed and wound down. Third, disarmament talks offer ample additional opportunities to strengthen our security at lower cost.

Colonel General Vladimir Lobov told *Moscow News* in commenting on the announced unilateral reduction in the Soviet military potential that from now on the task of safeguarding the security of the country and its allies would have to be fulfilled by smaller forces. This approach is acceptable with the important proviso that the safeguarding of security as the most general goal does not explicitly answer the question of what armed forces are needed for this. The answer can vary depending on differences in the appraisal of political, economic, and strategic realities, on the goals the country sets itself in a possible war, on its doctrine, strategy, and concrete operational plans.

In line with the new approach to security, we must recognize that more missiles, aircraft, tanks, and other weapons do not necessarily strengthen the country's defenses. If these weapons and other resources are built up with a view to accomplishing unrealistic tasks, if too large production affects quality and maintenance of equipment, the living conditions of servicemen and reasonable objectives, this may affect the defense potential. Limited strategic objectives and operational plans with smaller but efficient and well-supplied armed forces to match would be a much stronger guarantee of reliable defense.

Thus what we mean by reasonable or defensive sufficiency is not simply a reduction in troops and armaments but a thorough revision of strategy, operational plans, and armed forces, in part by reducing them, revising modernization program and redeploying forces, primarily with the aim of greatly stengthening the country's defenses on a long-term basis.

Strategic Offensive and Defensive Weapons

Strategic nuclear forces and conventional armed forces differ fundamentally in tasks, the pattern of financing and requirements from the point of view of keeping up an acceptable military balance. Hence there can be no standard approach to assessing their sufficiency or cutting the costs involved.

The greater part of spending on strategic armaments is necessitated, with rare exceptions, by their development and testing and by investments in production capacities. This spending depends to a relatively lesser degree on the amount of serial production (that is, the number of produced models) and the maintenance costs of deployed forces. This is why expenditures for strategic offensive forces (SOFs) depend chiefly on the diversity of new systems put into service in place of or in addition to existing ones and not on the quantity of delivery vehicles or warheads.

It should be noted that Soviet and U.S. SOF delivery vehicles and warhead totals plainly tend to become stabilized (with the number of delivery vehicles even going down), and this is irrespective of the course of talks on their reduction. The arms race in this sphere generally consists in replacing old by new and more effective weapons systems that are also costlier and are therefore manufactured in smaller quantities.

Consequently, the principle of sufficiency in this area demands a justified and consistent decision on not only how many delivery vehicles and warheads we need altogether but, more important, on how many and what new systems we need to introduce so as to counter the American ones. Our answers to these questions will be decisive for establishing how far we can cut economic costs in this sphere. A mere reduction in the total number of SOFs is unlikely to produce a large saving if in spite of lower numerical limits set to delivery vehicles and warheads the renewal of systems by introducing new generations goes on as intensively as before, if in somewhat smaller series.

The task of our strategic offensive weapons is defined by the new military doctrine as preventing a U.S. nuclear attack, through the possibility of surviving a U.S. first strike and causing the enemy unacceptable losses by retaliation. A convincing capability for a devastating response is what constitutes our defensive potential and a guarantee of our security until nuclear weapons are destroyed completely and everywhere under international agreements.

The strategic and military-technological reality now is the following: It is impossible to reduce one's damage in a nuclear war by hitting the aggressor's strategic forces. Indeed, it implies delivering a first strike; that is, assuming the role of aggressor and responsibility for a holocaust. This is unacceptable either politically (in the light of our commitment to no-first-use of nuclear weapons) or technically (since from 30 to 70 percent of U.S. weapons, such as those carried by submarines and bombers, are invulnerable to attack).

The idea of striking back at U.S. SOFs is evidently strategic nonsense, too. Why should the United States leave part of its forces as targets after it has delivered a first strike? In terms of reasonable sufficiency, targets suitable fore retaliation are the aggressor's economic facilities. A mere 400 nuclear warheads of the megaton class could destroy up to 70 percent of the U.S. industrial potential. This number of warheads hardly exceeds 10 to 15 percent of the Soviet Union's present strategic forces. Defense will be ensured if this many of them survive any attack and reach their targets. All further weapons and operations involving the use of SOFs would be doubtful in any respect and evidently unnecessary in terms of sufficiency.

Our current military programs therefore raise certain questions from the point of view of the declared principle of reasonable sufficiency. To judge by the information published in foreign sources, we have responded to each SOF system deployed by the United States at this stage in the arms race with two new systems of our own simultaneously.

Aren't quantity-oriented mechanisms typical of other echelons of the command system at work here? Are such "asymmetric" responses inevitable? They suit those Americans who advocate wearing out the Soviet Union economically, encouraging them to carry on talks from "positions of strength." This is all the more so because countermeasures in the ration of 2:1 will be even harder for us to adopt in the event of signing a treaty on reduction in SOFs and on a drastic lowering of strategic force levels and sublevels. We could probably effect a serious reduction in economic expenditures without undermining our security while strengthening and not weakening our negotiating positions if we followed a ration of 1:1 or, better till, 1:2, with the emphasis on the qualitative aspect of new strategic systems and on the high efficiency of their command-control-communication and early warning systems.

The strategic task of the MX ICBM system and the new Trident 2

SLBM is admittedly to hit Soviet silo-based missiles. It follows that to maintain our capability for adequate retaliation, we could envisage as a countermeasure against both systems one new system (instead of the present two systems) of land-based mobile ICBMs with either a single-warhead or MIRV missile, depending on the system's combat tasks and targets. Mobility in this case is the principal means of assuring the survival of deployed missiles, which is essential for our capability for retaliation. However, our second strike would not be aimed at the numerous protected targets of the aggressor's strategic forces, such as launch silos, for these would have fired their missiles in delivering a first strike. It is more likely that retaliation would be directed against the enemy's few main unprotected administrative and industrial centers. This, it seems, should be taken into consideration, first of all, when deciding on the type of ICBM for mobile land-based deployment.

To reinforce land-based missile forces, it would apparently be enough for us to have one new long-range submarine missile system capable of hitting targets from near the Soviet coast, hence making it unnecessary to venture on to the high seas through enemy antisubmarine barriers. In the light of the expected lowering of SOF ceilings by treaty, parallel construction of two new types of submarines seems all the more questionable (the nuclear-powered missile submarine is the costliest single SOF system).

Furthermore, increasingly experts in the United States recognize that the B-1B bomber ($280 billion per item) is an ill-advised and unreliable system. And even stronger doubts are relevant to our analogous aircraft, TU 160, called Blackjack in the West. The U.S. bomber is intended to penetrate deep into our large-scale air defense system. But the United States practically lacks such a system, for it dismantled almost completely the one it had in the sixties. To support our ICBMs and would be quite enough to have on type of bomber carrying ALCMs (based on, say, TU-95s or new wide-bodied high-capacity aircraft) and capable of hitting targets over a long distance without entering deep into U.S. air space. Finally, would it not be enough to have one type (instead of two) of sea-based cruise missiles?

In accordance with the principle of reasonable sufficiency, we could apparently save large resources by desisting from the manufacture of certain weapon systems. By way of taking reciprocal steps at the START talks, it is possible, of course, to take even more radical decisions.

With regard to strategic defensive weapons, it is time to reconsider at long last our apparently very costly air defenses echeloned in depth. According to foreign sources, our air defense system comprises 8,600 anti-aircraft missile launching sites and 2,300 interceptor fighters. The United States has 290 fighters (including the National Guard forces) but no antiaircraft missiles.

Now what is wrong with that since defense strategy implies putting the emphasis on defense? The point is that while this is true of conventional armed forces and weapons, in the sphere of nuclear arms hopes of direct military technological defense are a costly and counterproductive illusion, as the experience of the last forty years has shown very well. The only defense against nuclear weapons in view of their fundamental difference from conventional arms is to prevent their use by maintaining a dependable capability for retaliation and ultimately to get rid of them by means of accords. Mikhail Gorbachev has repeatedly stressed that there neither is nor can be any defence against nuclear weapons and that it is high time "to recognize that there is no roof on earth or in space under which one could take shelter from a nuclear thunderstorm should it breakout."

It is evidently not only the peace-loving foreign public, the Palme Commission or the Delhi Six that these words apply to. Surely statements by the head of our state and our Defense Council are a strategic guidance for all the military agencies concerned.

The country's system of air defense against strategic weapons is doubtful for at least three reasons. First, it could hardly intercept all U.S. airborne strategic weapons, especially with the deployment of cruise missiles on heavy bombers, that is, many thousands of "Rusts" carrying 200-kiloton warheads. After all, to intercept 60, 70, or 80 percent of them would not mean more than intercepting none. The 20 or even 10 percent of heavy bombers and cruise missiles that could break through, carrying 400 to 800 nuclear warheads with a yield ranging form 200 kilotons to nine megatons, would be able just the same to inflict disastrous, unsustainable damage. It is like a bridge reaching to the middle or spanning two-thirds of a river: no matter how wide, solid, or fine, no matter how expensive, it would be as useless as if it had not been there at all. Nor is that all.

Second, radars, the launch sites of air defense missiles, and the airfields of interceptors are in themselves entirely vulnerable to ballistic missiles. Incidentally, the United States actually plans in the event of war a "precursor" strike with sea-based missiles to open "corridors" for its bombers in air defense zones.

Third, land and sea-based ballistic missiles (some 8,000 warheads in all) could, if necessary, hit practically all targets by themselves, without the aid of heavy bombers. The chief reason now given for preserving and renewing them in the United States (B-1B, Stealth) is that the Soviet Union will have to spend many times more on modernizing its air defenses, which means that this is seen as one of the most advantageous lines of economically exhausting the Soviet Union.

A far more modest air defense system is certainly necessary for an early warning of attack, controlling air space in peacetime and safeguarding the country against possible terrorists. Certain events have suggested that this is something to work on. We also need an air defense system at a tactical nonnuclear level to shield troops from air strikes. As for the doctrine of averting nuclear war, military-technological and strategic realities demand admitting explicitly and without qualification that the concepts of "repulsing missile space attack" and "destroying the armed forces and military potential of the enemy" are hopelessly out-dated. They are a typical instance of projecting prenuclear military thinking into the solution of the historically unprecedented problem of security in the nuclear and space age, which calls for fundamentally new approaches.

It would be useful to think once again whether it is advisable to maintain the modernize the ABM complex around Moscow. The 100 antimissiles allowed under the ABM Treaty are clearly insufficient for defense against a dedicated strike by major U.S., British, and French forces. Defense against strikes by terrorists or by other nuclear powers as well as against unauthorized and accidental missile launches necessitates cover, if only a "thin layer" of it, for the whole territory of the country, and this is something the Moscow ABM complex cannot provide in any circumstances. The defense of Moscow hardly justifies the expenditures it entails, since foreign ballistic missiles would still hold hostage Leningrad, Kiev, Tbilisi, Sverdlovsk, Novosibirsk, and other cities, not to mention the fact that for terrorists, ballistic missiles are the most inconvenient system of delivering nuclear weapons and the hardest to acquire.

The possibility of nuclear arms and missile technology spreading to Third World countries, including their purchase by unstable and adventurist regimes, cannot be ruled out and will remain a serious threat in the foreseeable future. Even so, military-technological solutions are likely to prove rather counterproductive. What is needed are political measures, a common policy by many responsible powers, and international organizations. Since we hope that in our relations with the mightiest power, the United States, security can be safeguarded by political means, it should be all the easier to devise effective political means of doing away with less grandiose military threats. It is important that the interests of the whole civilized world coincide fully on this point.

Preventing a "decapitating" strike against the military and political leadership-a threat coming from the United States and third nuclear powers and not from terrorists—would probably cost less if we diverted at least part of the resources saved to raising the survivability, efficiency, and quality of our underground and air command and communications systems. Needless to say, Soviet–U.S. agreements must guarantee the inviolability of the ABM Treaty and the prevention of an arms race in space.

Conventional Armaments

In the area of armed forces and conventional armaments as distinct from SOFs, substantial cuts could be made in spending by lowering quantitative levels and reducing the series of weapons and combat equipment put out. As in the case of strategic forces, a great saving could be produced by building fewer types and modifications of systems while accentuating the qualitative aspect. This is particularly important because the greater part of military expenditures goes to conventional armed forces. The United States, for one, spends roughly 15 percent of its military budget on strategic forces and over 60 percent, on its conventional forces. True, personnel, whose share in conventional armed forces is much greater, costs considerably more in the United States than in the Soviet Union. But our conventional armed forces have a larger personnel than that of the United States, and we produce many more types and modifications of weapons systems than that country, doing it, moreover, in larger series and replacing combat equipment of new models more frequently than the United States.

We declare officially that a protracted large-scale conventional war with NATO in Europe is impossible and unacceptable. This presumably applies also to the United States and Japan in the Far East and in still greater measure, to China, a great Asian socialist power. In line with our new doctrine and strategy, we could apparently disband without detriment to our defenses all divisions whose combat readiness is low, scrap the enormous stockpiles of obsolete arms and equipment, and abolish the unwieldy system of mobilizing industry for war with due regard to the realities of the quick pace and super-technologization of modern warfare. The new doctrine calls for a more compact, more combat-ready and well paid army having the latest equipment.

As a protracted conventional war on two fronts is highly improbable, it is hardly right to keep major forces on a permanent basis for independent large-scale military operations in Europe, Asia, and the Far East. We could, for instance, effect through demobilization radical cuts in the number of divisions deployed along the frontier with China and in the Far East.

Generally speaking, the surest way to dissipate our resources and wear ourselves out economically is to build a sort of Chinese Wall (in the form of major forces) along all the greatly extended boundaries of the socialist community. The other way of safeguarding security, that is, the intensive way, is apparently to set up a rear infrastructure, including facilities for storing arms, supplies, and equipment plus proper ground and air communications (needed also for economic development, by the way), that would make it possible to quickly redeploy major forces to any threatened area.

How many divisions would be enough for defense, with the NATO forces unchanged? On the main front, in Central Europe, the West permanently keeps about 30 divisions whose number could be increased to some 50 in the event of mobilization. Throughout the European zone NATO has about 100 divisions. To close the 800-kilometer Central European front, from 20 to 30 divisions are needed. Defense echeloned in depth (including the troops stationed in the European part of Soviet territory, some of which are intended to close the southern and northern flanks) could evidently be ensured with the aid of 50 to 60 divisions. This is organizationally roughly one-third of the forces now deployed on the extensive principle.

Comparison by divisions is quite approximate of course, for there are divisions and divisions. But we can fully rely on our military agencies in that an appropriate reorganization of our divisions, armies, and groups of armies would guarantee reliable defense with smaller forces. Such defense would also make it possible to counterattack, deliver flanking strikes, and meet engagements at tactical levels in order to expel the invading enemy from our territory.

This approach could be applied also to air forces in view of their high mobility and multipurpose character. Air force defense strategy obviously calls for stronger emphasis on reliable air defense of one's own ground troops, powerful air support for them, and the attainment of superiority in one's air space, coupled with a reduction in resources for offensive operations against targets in the deep enemy rear and airfields.

Special mention should be made of naval forces, in view of the high cost and complexity of modern surface ships and submarines and of the time it takes to build them. Logically, defense sufficiency in the case of these forces implies restricting their combat tasks to defending the Soviet coast against strikes from the sea by carrier task forces and amphibious landings of the West as well as to defending strategic submarines with long-range missiles in coastal seas against antisubmarine enemy forces.

Such functions as interdicting Atlantic and Pacific communications are hardly consonant with a defensive strategy, especially where ground troops and air forces dependably ensure defense in the main continental theaters.

An even more doubtful mission is that of searching for and destroying the strategic sumbarines of the United States, Britain, and France on the high seas, which are dominated by the hostile navy. As the range of modern SLBMs of the Trident 1 and Trident 2 type enables them to be launched from the coast of Uruguay and New Guinea, to chase strategic missile carriers there would be as absurd as sowing selected seeds in the Kara Kum desert. It would divert resources from important tasks to unattainable goals.

Defense against sea-based strategic and nuclear cruise missiles (as well as against ICBMs and heavy bombers) should be ensured by means of a capability for preventing nuclear aggression; i.e., for delivering a devastating retaliatory strike, and not through the ineffective and costly hunt for submarines.

The extension of naval confrontation with the United States in distant seas, in conflict areas involving developing countries—the Mediterranean, the Indian Ocean, and South China Sea, the South Atlantic—is for objective geostrategic reasons the most disadvantageous sphere of rivalry for us, an extremely costly area having no direct bearing on the security of the Soviet Union or its main allies. Even if we had a navy three times as large as that of the United States (something unthinkable for economic reasons), the West would still retain its superiority in this field. Unlike our country, the United States has free access to the oceans of the world. Its fleets are in a position to rapidly reinforce each other and are supported by a vast network of bases on foreign soil. The United States has allies possessing impressive naval forces, and does not have to bear a burden comparable to ours in supporting defense on continental theaters.

Why enter into rivalry on a hostile field since all conditions at our own are favorable to us? The other side is superior to us in large surface ships (7.6 times over), aircraft carriers and naval aircraft and amphibious forces. We are superior to it in multipurpose submarines with antiship missiles and torpedoes (1.2 times over), land-based missile-carrying naval aircraft, small ships, and boats for coastal operations (1.6 times over). Trying to break this asymmetry would get us nowhere. It would be better for us to place it in the service of our strategy. We are capable of sinking all NATO aircraft carriers operating off our coast (this is admitted by impartial experts in Washington). As for exposing surface targets worth many millions to attack by carrier aircraft and cruise missiles in faraway seas and oceans, there is no point in that at all.

Hence it would be useful to seriously revise plans for the construction of a large surface fleet, including aircraft carriers, nuclear-powered cruisers, and landing ships. The forces we have are plainly sufficient for defending our coastline and protecting our sea-based strategic forces equipped with long-range missiles in coastal seas. Henceforward we ought to concentrate on building multipurpose submarines in smaller numbers and in smaller variety but with higher qualitative indices and armed with antiship missiles and torpedoes, plus, if necessary, long-range sea-based nuclear cruise missiles. Land-based naval missile-carrying aircraft would within the range of escort fighters give powerful support to submarines and surface ships carrying out strictly defensive operations.

Military Production

Conventional armed forces-ground troops, air and naval forces-as well as strategic nuclear forces are faced with the pressing task of going over from extensive (quantity) to intensive military program, and putting the emphasis on quality. The point at issue is not only quantitative levels but modernization program swallowing the lion's share of appropriations. Our party has called for a radical change in the expenditure mechanism typical of the arms industry and construction bureaus which turn out diverse weapons systems duplicating each other and continuously develop new modifications of these systems that are introduced (in more and more new, large series) although they only raise effectiveness by a negligible margin.

According to foreign sources, Soviet ground troops today deploy three types of tanks and three types of combat vehicles and armored carriers simultaneously (against one of each in the United States); nonstrategic air and naval forces, seven models of fighters, strike planes, and bombers (against three in the United States); naval forces, five different classes of warships and three multipurpose submarines (against four and one, respectively, in the United States). The same sources claim (while ours are silent) that from 1977 to 1986 the Soviet Union produced twice as many fighters and submarines as the United States, three times as many tanks and combat helicopters and nine times as many artillery pieces and antiaircraft missiles. It was only in the construction of large warships that the United States found itself ahead of us (by 10 percent). As far as nuclear weapons are concerned, the USSR produced four times as many ballistic missiles and thirteen times as many heavy and medium bombers.

These data cannot be taken at face value. But if they reflect the actual state of affairs at least to some degree, then perestroika in this field should include a whole set of measures, such as broader discussion on key program from the standpoint of defense sufficiency and stricter selection of them on the principle of comparing cost ad effectiveness. There is also the need to end unnecessary duplication and introduce healthy competition between construction bureaus and in industry, limit output series and effect renewal at longer intervals while taking bigger leaps in quality. Lastly, it is essential to encourage saving and capital productivity, fix realistic prices on skilled labor, raw materials, and other resources and impose financial penalties for exceeding deadlines of expenditures and time limits.

Defense needs a sort of self-accounting like other fields. Security is invaluable to us but in the final analysis, whatever the military budget, it expresses itself in perfectly definite expenditures of labor and material resources. It is vitally important to us in every respect that these enormous investments should really produce the maximum by safeguarding the security of the Soviet people, who are engaged in perestroika.

With the accute deficit of information on our armed forces and military budget, it is very difficult to estimate the likely economic effect of the proposals I have set out. However, tentative calculations indicate that their implementation in the next five-year plan period could reduce our defense spending by 40 to 50 percent, which would not weaken but strengthen the country's defense, to say nothing of other security aspects, both economic and political.

It is occasionally said that the military has "no stake" in cutting armaments or military expenditures or in extending military glasnost. It is hard to accept this view. There is no reason whatever to deny that in this area as in other sphere of our society and state there are sincere supporters of perestroika just as there are staunch opponents and those who hold forth about perestroika yet would like to reduce it to cosmetic adjustments.

While processes typical of society as a whole are going on also in the military field, the latter has its peculiarities. Due to their profession and duty, military men are responsible for the military aspect of security. The other aspects of security and a more comprehensive approach to it are the prerogative of other people and bodies, both governmental and nongovernmental. We need not fear alternative points of view. The task of perestroika is to assure every approach and every opinion adequate participation on the basis of democratization and glasnost, of broad and constructive debates—as distinct from the decisions made behind closed doors in the past—in the people's cause of keeping the defense potential at a level of reasonable sufficiency.

April 1990

From Mr. "No" to Mr. "Yes"

Letter to the Editors by the People's Deputy of the USSR Captain Eduard Gams

Recently, various newspapers have carried explanations in response to the concern expressed by apparently quite a few readers with reference to the terms of the treaty between the USSR and the United States on the Elimination of Their Intermediate-Range and Shorter-Range Missiles [known also as the INF Treaty].

I suppose we will have to return to this subject more than once, if only because the arguments marshaled every time in reply to readers do not sound convincing enough and, far from reassuring them, add to their misgivings.

The problem is not so simple as it seems at first sight. Practically every argument can and obviously should be refuted by citing evidence to the contrary. The totality of counterarguments is apt to mar to a notable extent the idyllic picture painted by various analysts.

Look, for instance, at the difference in the number of Soviet and American missiles to be eliminated (1,752 and 859, respectively). It is particularly distressing in the light of the number of warheads, which are rarely mentioned at all.

There is no denying that we turned out to have more intermediate- and shorter-range missiles than the Americans. So what? We needed more because we had to take account of the nuclear forces of France and Britain. For many years, the Soviet side saw inclusion of West European nuclear forces in the tally as a requisite for any agreement on intermediate-range nuclear weapons. Was it reasonable to re- nounce this principle in order to sign the treaty we now have? Andrei Gromyko wisely pointed out that the nationality of missiles to be dropped on our cities made no difference whatever to our people. Since then, the military plans of Paris and London have undergone no change inspiring us with optimism.

Here is what l'Humanité wrote about French nuclear ambitions: "In 1985, the French nuclear forces were capable of destroying from 25 to 34 million Soviet people and 16 to 25 percent of the Soviet indus- trial potential. By 1990, Soviet casualties resulting from a French nuclear strike might range between 48 and 55 million and destruction of the industrial potential, between 25 and 40 percent. By 1995, Paris plans to have nuclear forces capable of killing 81 million Soviet peo- ple and razing two-thirds of the Soviet industrial potential to the ground."

Yet we accepted Reagan's "zero option" in Europe. Wasn't the step too daring? If it was a manifestation of new thinking, which is in- voked at present in reasoning with doubters, I prefer old thinking, to be frank. In the past, we had at least missiles to rely on. And now? Are we to pin our hopes on the fact that the Americans and French are humans like anybody else, that Armand Hammer is our big friend or that Margaret Thatcher is a woman, after all, even though there is something very stern about her? Some of our leaders seem to have adopted the political philosphy of Leopold the Cat [a famous charac- ter of TV cartoon series-Ed.], whose wisdom does not go beyond the formula, "Boys, let us be nice to each other."

I recall what I have read about the early days of the Great Patriotic War, when many of our men and officers, lulled by ill-advised propa- ganda, earnestly expected that German soldiers would show prole- tarian solidarity and that this would immediately put an end to the war. Elements of this kind of "worldview" are also taking hold of the thinking of many of our contemporaries, and this not without help from the media.

It may be a comfort to know that stationed somewhere beyond the

Urals are one or two hundred intercontinental missiles which compensate for the Eurostrategic systems being scrapped. They form a component of strategic parity between the Soviet Union and the United States, and their reorientation in practice would amount to our losing this parity. This is not a purely hypothetical possibility as I see it but also a perfectly "physical" one, whose negative impact we will soon feel at the political and diplomatic level and ultimately at the military level, as well. The issue will become still more acute in the event of a Soviet–U.S. accord on a 50 percent cut in SOWs, which would at the very least double the "value" of our every missile left.

There is another argument against unequal commitments under the INF Treaty, one that is probably even more important as a matter of principle.

Long-standing political wisdom advises against creating a precedent. By accepting, if with the best intentions, a treaty imposing greater obligations upon us than upon the other side, we will have created a most undesirable precedent.

Some write that in years past, Soviet diplomacy got a bad name in the world as Mr. "No" by refusing to make any concessions whatever even where a compromise could have been reached. I wish we didn't now go to the other extreme by becoming a Mr. "Yes" who is obliging enough not only to compromise but to go still further. Our acceptance of Reagan's formula of eliminating Euromissiles seems to have been interpreted to our disadvantage abroad. There is a real threat of our opponents considerably toughening position at subsequent political and military talks, of their making additional demands unthinkable in a different set of circumstances. Indications of such an evolution are in evidence already. The signing of the INF Treaty was followed in Japan by a clear uptrend in the campaign for the "return of the Northern territories," as Tokyo calls the Soviet Union's Kurile Islands. The Japanese side seems to be hoping in earnest that the Soviet leadership will display "new thinking" on this issue as well.

The assertion that the difference in reductions was programmed by the initial missile imbalance between the two countries is untenable. Arithmetically, we must scrap twice as many missiles as the Americans. But there is also a thing like higher mathematics. Nobody has ever proved that politics must follow the four rules of arithmetic.

At any rate, it is obvious that our diplomats at Geneva should in any circumstances have sought a formula of agreement imposing completely equal obligations on the two sides (meaning their totality) and hence doing no harm to our international prestige. If the framework of the Geneva talks on intermediate- and shorter-range missiles was too narrow to allow such a formula to be adopted, they should have been widened by extending the talks to further spheres, by switching to the practice of package agreements—in short, everything possible should have been done to ensure that ultimately the two sides assumed equal obligations.

Opportunities for this were not lacking. There is, for example, the enormous discrepancy in power between the two countries' surface fleets. Why not put this problem on the agenda of the talks so as to offset the issue of our superiority in Euromissiles? To be sure, Washington is unlikely to relish such an approach but why should we worry about that? We must defend our interests. Indeed, see what is going on: while we are scrapping our missiles, their aircraft carriers keep on hanging around all seas as if nothing had changed. In choosing areas and a framework for talks, aren't we taking our cue from that "good man," Uncle Sam? When he is unwilling to discuss an issue he blocks the talks. Naval forces and the notorious SDI are cases in point. The result is that we only discuss with the Americans what they are ready to discuss and that we only do so within a framework acceptable to them. Yet it is not without malicious intent that the West decides on parameters for its talks with the East.

Who benefits from the fact that talks on military matters are conducted chiefly on a bilateral (Soviet–American) and not a bloc-to-bloc basis? One does not have to be very clever to realize that this is in the interest of the West, for it leaves out the military power of Britain, France, West Germany, Japan, and other countries in the imperialist camp, which remain, nonetheless, members of an integral anti-Soviet, antisocialist club. It would certainly be preferable for the Soviet Union, which has no such strong allies, to carry on talks at the level of the military coalitions because this would allow real (or absolute) military parity to be achieved instead of a parity artificially deduced from Soviet–U.S. parity as a whole.

Our military parity with the United States is depreciated by completely uncontrolled superiority over us in the sum total of imperialist armaments. Meanwhile the West pretends to regard this state of affairs as the only possible one. It thwarts all our attempts to shift the military dialogue onto a coalition-to-coalition basis. Hence the fifteen-year-long beating of the air at the Vienna talks on troop and arms reductions in Central Europe. Hence also the more than tepid reaction registered at first to the proposal for a European forum on military detente, the WTO initiative pronounced in Warsaw. All signs are that our opponents have no intention of renouncing the bilateral Soviet-U.S. dialogue, which they seem to like and whose progress tends to lead to a further relative weakening of the military coalition of socialist countries in the face of the West's military alliance. Having agreed to this bilateral formula when the power balance came down to the Soviet–American military or rather missile balance, we risk getting into serious trouble that subsequently may become still worse. This is why we must revise priorities and feed a new algorithm into the program for military dialogue with the West before it is too late. This would be genuine new thinking, unlike the semblance of it created by the INF Treaty.

This treaty, a typical product of the given political situation, is essentialy tantamount to a major diplomatic setback for us, one fraught with foreign political consequences. By upsetting the principle of equality, it impairs the prospect of further disarmament talks and works objectively against the policy of lowering military confrontation levels and providing greater world security.

Conclusions regarding certain particulars also breed doubts. I am sure many Soviet people cannot understand the reason for the haste shown by our side in setting out to implement the provisions of the treaty on a practically unilateral basis. We began withdrawing our missiles from the GDR and Czechoslovakia even before the treaty was ratified; that is, before it came into force. The Americans began to eliminate their missiles on September 8, 1988, but we had blown up as many as seventy missiles already on August 26. Also in August, we proceeded to eliminate SS-20 intermediate-range missiles, while the 56th Field Artillery Command equipped with Pershing-2 IRBMs held exercises in the FRG.

Why must we hurry so? Did a bid to score a propaganda point (to show that we were "ahead of everybody else" on this as well) prove stronger than elementary self-respect? What is this irresistible urge to report victories?

I am convinced that the time frame for the destruction of the first batch of missiles should have been the same for the two powers. It would be hard to think of a more forceful symbol emphasizing the equality of the contracting parties and their mutual respect. That we had more missiles of this type than the other side was immaterial. Afterward we could have blown up a hundred missiles a day if we chose to.

As for inspection, the issue is less simple than analysts would have it. It was no accident that the problem of control almost became a stumbling block at the eleventh hour, during treaty ratification hearings in the U.S. Senate. *Za rubezhom* published a report by an American journalist about a visit to U.S. missile bases in some states by Soviet inspectors. The brief account is noteworthy for what is a rare absence of euphoria nowadays in dealing with the issue of compliance with the INF Treaty. The writer pointed out that even at a base subject to inspection, by far not all facilities were allowed to be inspected and that the inspectors were admitted to eighteen depots and kept out of another eighteen of the same type. He quoted the American colonel responsible for secrecy as saying that he would not allow anybody to see what he was not intended to.

Of course, we can scornfully dismiss the bourgeois journalist's report as discordant to the chorus of praise.

Still, if we take sober stock of things, we must admit that inspection cannot guarantee compliance with treaty provisions (any inspectors' team can be fooled by keeping it out of "eighteen depots" because they are "off limits"). The only guarantee is reciprocal goodwill. We can say with a fair degree of certainty that right now goodwill exists. But nobody can guarantee that it will still be there tomorrow. Nor does anybody know how the whole thing will work out in the end.

I wonder whether the near future will not see us start restoring in all haste the missilery we are now scrapping. This is quite an interesting question, all the more since there was a precedent in our recent history. The only difference at the time was that Khrushchev had everything but missiles scrapped whereas this once it is missiles that turn out to be "unwanted." I shudder to think what will happen if a further spiral of history (there will yet be many of them) faces us with the need for a new round of arms modernization. We must realize quite clearly that such turnarounds are more disastrous to us than to the West. The United States would hardly suffer much from a new spurt in the arms race, and as for American business, it would be delighted. Besides, the West fully uses the possibilities of sharing out the military burden among partners.

For our overtaxed economy and our state as a whole, which is bound hand and foot by unsolved social problems, the task of modernizing weapons, which we might have to accomplish in order not to find ourselves defenseless in the face of powerful enemies, could prove ruinous, especially after the "brilliant" disarmament we are now carrying out. The West is in effect playing a winning game. Even while disarming in part on terms favorable to it (remember that is prefers bilateral talks to talks between the two coalitions), it retains a capacity for a possible new spurt in the military contest. As regards us, we risk being duped because we are destroying what we have in the area of defense and also because we lack a comparable potential to counter a new spurt by the West should it come. Our military potentialities are diminishing in view of our current policy of adopting intensive methods of management and curbing command methods of leadership.

I would like to deal at some length with the history of the SS-23 missile. Eduard Shevardnadze says that we showed goodwill by agreeing to destroy this missile under the INF Treaty, although the treaty does not cover it. But the Americans, ignoring our noble gesture, decided to deploy in Europe missiles analogous with the ones we are destroying in accordance with the treaty.

Now, if matters stand as Shevardnadze puts it, why did we have to include in the treaty a missile not covered by it? What kind of "goodwill" is that? I doubt whether any other country would demonstrate its goodwill in the same way. The Americans are unlikely to go back on their plan to deploy new systems with a range of up to 500 kilometers. There is no law to stop them. And this means that we may have to deploy something similar but not SS-23s. The hints of our possible withdrawal from the INF Treaty over these systems cannot be serious because the Soviet Union never violates treaties, as everybody knows.

Incidentally, the assertion that our country was prompted by "goodwill" in eliminating SS-23s of its own accord does not seem very credible. There is some evidence that the explanation is far more prosaic. When the draft treaty was under discussion, the Americans insisted on SS-23 being included on the grounds that it had a rated range of 500 kilometers or more. We probably tried to prove that they were wrong but nothing came of it. The new missile complex that was to have been substituted for obsolete mobile systems (with a range of up to 300 kilometers) came to be covered by reductions while old missiles were left to rot quietly on site. Besides, it seems certain that the lower range limit of the missiles included in the INF Treaty was not chosen accidentally but with due regard to the potential of Soviet missiles, primarily SS-23. There is hardly any reason to doubt that had this missile had a rated range of, say, 450 and not 500 kilometers, the lower range limit would also have been brought down to this level under the treaty.

The foregoing suggests that the problem of SS-23s should have been settled while the INF Treaty was in its drafting phase. The line of the Soviet side at the time must have been prompted in large measure, if not chiefly, by a desire to sign at all costs, a treaty seen as a very important political victory for our new leadership, and the Soviet Union therefore showed an inclination for a certain flexibility in settling disputed issues, even at the cost of injuring some of its legitimate interests. Now that the treaty is in force, there are those who apparently regret the "goodwill" shown by us in those days. But it is too late.

To prove that the treaty is so indispensable to the Soviet Union as to justify unilateral concessions, reference is made to the extraordinary nature of the threat to our security posed by the deployment of Pershing-2s in West Germany, from where they could have reached Moscow in ten minutes. This development is said to have greatly heightened the risk of an armed clash (meaning also an unsanctioned one) and disastrously shortened the time left for the adoption of any political decisions. Quite right. Pershing-2s fired from West Germany could have reached our country three times faster than Minutemen flying in from North Dakota. The danger of any conflict automatically assuming a total character would have increased accordingly. But then it would have threatened the two sides in equal measure. Our missiles could have hit most NATO capitals in a matter of five to ten minutes. The in-flight time for Soviet missiles aimed directly at American territory was reduced by moving part of our missile-carrying submarines to forward areas. All this guaranteed maintenance of a rough "balance of terror" at the new level reached by the military balance with the deployment of Euromissiles.

It follows that we did not have much more reason for apprehension than the West. Hence there was no reason, either, for us to accept terms providing for great sacrifices on our part.

The above is by no means an ex post facto statement. It is precisely today, when far more important disarmament accords are in the making, that we must weigh the pros and cons once again and submit our disarmament strategy for exhaustive public discussion.

The one-sided glasnost prevailing in our country at the moment and aptly described by Mikhail Gorbachev at the 19th Party Conference as degenerating into the supremacy of various "groups" in the media virtually makes it impossible to ensure unbiased discussion of a number of disputed aspects of our home and foreign policy, with the INF Treaty unquestionably one of them. It is clear to me that in our country in general and in its Armed Forces in particular there are people, including competent specialists, who take a critical view of the treaty as it now stands. Yet not one of them was given a chance either before or after the signing of the treaty to state his opinion in public. As in earlier times, healthy and fruitful debate and comparison of differing points of view were replaced by sweet-voiced, harmful hallelujahs and perfunctory unanimity. In the United States, meanwhile, discussion on the treaty and the outlook for Soviet–American talks generally is going on continuously, bringing out dozens and hundreds of viewpoints which provide the American administration soil for optimum foreign policy decisions.

My arguments may be completely wrong but I had to state them. I am by no means the only one to have misgivings. And this is why we need a serious debate and not a further campaign of hollow propaganda.

Readers' Views

The letter to *International Affairs* by the USSR People's Deputy Captain E. Gams evoked a lively discussion. Below are two responses to the letter which reflect different views on military-political problems.

We Shall Strive Toward Full Understanding

I had a mixed feeling on reading USSR People's Deputy Captain Eduard Gams' angry article. And that not even just because of the author's specific stand on the INF Treaty, that first sprout of common sense after years of senseless discussions, but because of the type of thinking fearful of innovation. It is fearful, I think, not on account of hidebound conservatism but, rather, because of having no habit of analyzing things by proceeding from precise information.

Eduard Gams rightfully protests against "hollow propaganda" with which we were and still are forced to make do. The point is just what we must regard as such "hollow propaganda."

Why must we hurry so? Eduard Gams asks. To my mind, however, our foreign policy does suffer from being sluggish and contradictory. We lose momentum and initiative over and over again, bargaining for concessions and insisting on arithmetical parity, only to yield ground in the long run instead of undertaking a series of full-scale unilateral measures, not just to lessen the developed world's mistrust of us, but to shatter the very foundations of that mistrust. For, as a matter of fact, Europe would no longer go to war and so the scale of European confrontation does not count for much. Now, the argument that this continent has more than once been the breeding ground of conflicts in the past is no more relevant than the fear of European plague epidemics on the grounds that they used to wipe out up to one third of the population.

That is why my conviction is that we should have long ago, and without any talks, cut down unilaterally both the medium-range missiles and tens of thousands of obsolete tanks; the only thing these contained was our trustworthiness, to say nothing of the Soviet people's well-being through senseless expenditures on the upkeep of these weapons. For the same reason we should have given up tactical nuclear weapons where we have a twelve-fold edge [sic] which can be compared only to our thirty-fold edge [sic] in air-defense interceptors. For the fact is that the confrontation is between the United States and the USSR, and that our tactical missiles do not reach the Unites States.

Still, we have "to take account of the nuclear forces of France and Britain," Eduard Gams objects. Yet what escapes him, it seems to me, is the essence of their nuclear concept. The estimates of the percentage of the USSR that the French nuclear forces are capable of "wiping off the face of the earth" should be left on the "bookkeepers" conscience. If there is any country for which any conventional, let alone nuclear conflict would be suicidal, it is France, with her nuclear power plants, and, incidentally, Britain as well. Therefore, the most reasonable thing, to my mind, would be to recognize that the nuclear arsenals of these two countries are no more than guarantors of their stable position in the world where there are still too many unstable and unreasonable rulers and, indeed, whole societies. And that is why there is no point in discussing those arsenals at all.

There could be a by no means trivial approach to the problem of chemical weapons. Why couldn't the USSR declare that it is willing to turn over unilaterally to NATO all of its stock of chemical weapons which worry the West? Let NATO decide for itself what to do with them: destroy or store up (without the right to re-sell them, of course). At the same time, the USSR would declare its consent to an inspection of chemical production (certainly, without attempts at industrial spying). The logic is simple: let the dear (and wealthy) NATO countries bear the cost of saving themselves from our chemical weapons. We, on our part, would have been glad to get rid of them even yesterday, but we have no means to spare for their destruction.

The West can react to it in two ways: one, by accepting our offer and so letting us save billions we need so badly by eliminating the arms which in no way add to our security; another, by declining it and so putting themselves in an awkward predicament and forcing their leaders to explain to their peoples what cannot be explained.

In any event, we would gain an honest and unprecedented asset of confidence and open a wide breach in the wall of mistrust. Eduard Gams, while mentioning the forthcoming halving of strategic offensive arms, writes that the "weight" of each remaining missile will then double, at least. But that is true only as long as you take a confrontational view of the historical process. With a different approach, we will see that the weight of each of our unilaterally scrapped missiles will increase a hundred-fold because it will provide conclusive evidence for even the most incredulous that we have no ulterior motives, but earnestly want to get integrated in the world community as a partner in wide-ranging cooperation.

There are many more things we can speak about. We can say it is illogical to compare the importance that the surface navies of the United States and the USSR have for their national interests. Or that it is just on account of the onerous legacy Mr. "No" has left behind that we must as soon as possible become—not a Mr. "Yes," but a partner saying: "Let us decide together!" But the main trouble is that we have lived in an information vacuum during almost the whole of our recent history, and nature abhors a vacuum, of course, so this vacuum has been filled with myths and "hollow propaganda."

The only thing that demolishes a myth is sure knowledge. Should the People's Deputy, Eduard Gams, and, indeed, all of us, have had an opportunity of unrestricted exchange of information, opinion, and visits with the rest of the world since childhood, we would realize that the developed outside world has neither the need, nor the desire to resolve its problems by force of arms just to get a dugout or even a flat with a six-square-mile kitchen and a ration in place of a cottage and a supermarket. Our self-isolation has not been conducive to our proper appreciation of common values. The world, however, is inevitably changing, in some ways, alas, for the worse, getting covered with oil slicks, for instance, and in some ways for the better, washing itself clean of mistrust and lies.

So let us seek full clarity. It is to be hoped that People's Deputy Eduard Gams will get down to considering, among other issues, when, at long last, will an account of the budget of the USSR (and not of defense spending only, by the way) consist not of a few lines and figures, but something like those one and a half thousand pages (!) that make up the U.S. budget, and which are open to any American (and, indeed, in principle, Soviet) citizen? Perhaps, Eduard Gams will likewise pause to wonder whether it is logical to expect parity in disarmament while there is none in information on armaments, military program and plans? It is not until we get such parity and access to all information required that we can really talk business.

Sergei Brezkun, Civil Engineer, Arzamas

Express–Disarmament

Let me note straight away that I support the Captain's arguments. Like him, I have my doubts (or feel "concerned," as the current phrase is) about the fairness of the terms under which the Soviet American INF Treaty has been signed, and, above all, about the need to include the SS-23 missiles in it. By their tactical and technical characteristics these missiles did not fall within the terms of that treaty at all. Our "goodwill" thus shown cannot be considered a foreign policy asset.

The SS-23 missile complex was, due to its mission and tactical and technical characteristics, an essential element in the balance of forces between NATO and the Warsaw Pact, and, by design, it was superior to comparable Western samples.

Under the treaty we have no right anymore to have missiles with an equivalent of the SS-23 range. There will be no such missiles in the Warsaw Treaty Organization at all. (In fact, the very survival of this organization is open to question.) But what about NATO and other countries? As none of the NATO countries, except the United States, have signed the treaty, they are not bound by such a commitment. The conclusion of the treaty, as experience shows, has in no way affected the interest of other armies and nations of the world in missiles of the SS-23 type. West Germany and France engage in large-scale development of missiles with a range of up to 500 kilometers. Israel has already tested a Jericho-2 missile and, besides, has missiles with a range of 1,300 kilometers. Libya and Brazil are developing 600-kilometer missiles. Iran is making 800-kilometer and 200-kilometer missiles, while Iraq is cooperating with Libya and Brazil in creating a missile with a range of 300 kilometers. Egypt has joined forces with Argentina in developing a missile system named Condor-2. Pakistan has tried out two types of missiles, with a range of 80 kilometers and 300 kilometers while India has test-fired an Agni missile, with a range of 2,500 kilometers. South Korea has upgraded the American Nike Hercules missile. West Germany and France also have to be listed as missile-producing countries (RK Technecke, RK Gades). The CIA expects at least fifteen countries to be producing ballistic missiles by the year 2000.

I can see that as nothing short of a detraction from the fighting capacity of our missile units, and, accordingly, our armed forces. The concept of "strong, up-to-date" is relative, not absolute. Its "relativity" is established by comparing the combat potentials of the opposing coalitions' armed forces. What should be considered is the armed forces of the sides in their totality and not their individual components, that is, not troop types or service arms (as was regrettably done in drafting the INF Treaty). There should be no artificial exclusion of any country, or any interested agency of a country, from negotiating teams.

I agree that Soviet foreign policy has, indeed, a great record of achievement to its credit in the past four years. This policy is, beyond doubt, in the forefront of our reform effort. Yet there is a point we cannot forget about. I know from my own experience, not from hearsay, that it cost this country a sustained and inordinate exertion to reach parity with the West in defense capability. In this way, our country has built up powerful and modern armed forces and has come to be recognized all over the world as a superpower. Our economy is nothing to boast about. And now, as a result of the policy which has weakened our armed forces, some of those across the Atlantic are already writing us off as a "superpower." The weak are the underdogs, of course.

I am not calling, on that account, for militarization, for guns before butter. The army certainly has to reform itself in answer to the call of the times. But it is my conviction that the nation must have strong and modern armed forces. But here is a paradox: while the restructuring of the economy, that is, a constructive effort, has not justified our hopes (for the time being, at least at any rate), "express disarmament," as a destructive effort, has surpassed all expectations.

Col. Anatoli Svobodin,
Cand. Sc. (Tech.),
Moscow

PART IV

Reality As It Is

Introduction to Part IV

The years of perestroika saw a breakthrough in the area of political ways and means that ensure the USSR national security in every direction of world politics. Soviet diplomacy has been active in shaping a new model of world order to be based on states' interaction in political, military, humanitarian, economic, environmental, and other fields.

The experience of the past years has demonstrated that the Soviet-proposed concept of a common European house is timely and important in practical ways. That idea was in accord with views of the new Europe's "architecture" that other participant states of the European process had regarding a "European confederation," "European world order," "European Security Council," and others.

The USSR has commenced constructively oriented activity in the Asia and Pacific region and on other continents. The Kremlin's approaches to the Third World problems underwent radical changes to help settle protracted regional conflicts.

Soviet–American relations occupy a special place among the world's problems. The growing confidence of the two superpowers in each other has had a powerful and positive impact on the overall situation in the world.

The first signal that warned of the dangers of euphoria was

sounded in February 1991, with the postponement of the Soviet and U.S. presidents' meeting, originally scheduled for that date. It prompted a more sober and realistic assessment of the nature and potentialities of Soviet–American cooperation, and of the hurdles in its way.

The world has entered a postconfrontational period; meanwhile the material foundation of confrontation remains intact in the shape of the mighty military industry and vested interests of different strata of U.S. society. A part of U.S. political and military-industrial quarters are deliberately trying to apply brakes to the Soviet–U.S. dialogue. Indeed, they are not happy with an agreement on arms limitation, particularly the plans of the Kremlin and the White House to cut their strategic stockpiles. I must say in full justice that there is no lack of similar sentiment in certain quarters of the Soviet society. Some people believe that the summits have produced little of practical value, above all in the sphere of economic cooperation. They say also that, instead, the Soviet foreign policy has found itself under U.S. influence, especially in the dramatic issue of the war in the Gulf. The Soviet military-industrial complex and army leadership also have their own opinions, none very enthusiastic, in regard to a deeper interaction with the United States in the political and disarmament areas.

So the question now is, how strong is the alliance of such sentiment on both shores of the ocean, and can it block further improvement of Soviet–U.S. relations? One would like to believe that people of both nations have had a chance to understand and assess advantages of cooperation versus confrontation. It is not that easy to wipe out the solid capital that has been built up after the first Soviet–U.S. Summit in 1985 in Geneva. President Bush wants good relations with the Kremlin. They are as important to President Gorbachev.

Finally, continued progress in Soviet–U.S. relations serves the interests of many other countries. The times of a bipolar world are indeed ending. Nevertheless, the two superpowers' interaction still remains a decisive factor in many contemporary problems. Therefore, whenever Soviet–U.S. relations are shaky, the rest of the world trembles.

The situation is reminiscent of the one in summer 1979, after the SALT-2 Treaty was signed in Vienna. The two nations had come to Vienna on the high crest of détente. As I remember it, President

Jimmy Carter embraced and kissed Leonid Brezhnev: an effort of many years had culminated in success, and one could show one's feelings.

However, the treaty was torpedoed in the U.S. Congress, détente was thrown back, and right-wing politicians came to the forefront of U.S. politics. Moscow responded to the blow in its own manner, the outcome being the Afghan invasion by Soviet troops, and the cold war raging on as before.

The similarity is too obscure, and God forbid that the present slowdown of Soviet–U.S. relations should bring about a reversal of the kind that took place some ten years before. But we must keep that in mind. And we must also have a clear understanding that time has changed, and that there is too much interest everywhere to allow a time-out, still less to face a turnabout in the relations between the USSR and the United States.

—BORIS PYADYSHEV

February 1991

The UN Mirrors the Whole World

Andrei Kolosovsky

In those warm September days, tourists and New Yorkers walking past the park near the UN building were somewhat surprised to see a huge equestrian statue with the rider, Saint George, breaking up Pershing-2 and SS-20 missiles with his cross-shaped weapon. Workmen are busy raising it. Press reports did not say whether that gift to the intentional organization came from the Soviet government or the sculptor, Zurab Tsereteli. There is no point in arguing over the artistic quality of the statue, over whether the image of the cross suits Muslims, Buddhists, or adherents of other religions or whether the "conversion" represented by Tsereteli is of the kind that all who have been fighting for nuclear disarmament had wanted to bring

---

ANDREI KOLOSOVSKY is Deputy Minister of Foreign Affairs of the Russian Federation.

about. But this is incontestably a rare case of a symbol displayed in time.

From the very beginning of the 45th Session of the UN General Assembly, the participants, who included many heads of state and government, were unanimous in stating for the first time that the cold war was over and that the threat of global confrontation had receded, with the two most heavily armed powers moving on from permanent opposition to partnership. In addition to improved Soviet–American relations, they mentioned the unification of Germany as evidence of the transition of the world to a new stage of development. Speakers pointed out that during the previous session few people could have expected such far-reaching changes in Europe. Nevertheless, goodwill, uncommon diplomatic solutions, and above all, the determination of the German people and their leaders to overcome the legacy of World War II had made it possible. It was also stressed that the transformations affected in Europe would have been impossible but for the changes initiated in 1985 by the Soviet Union, whose new political thinking, coupled with democratization processes inside the country, was a major factor for changes in the world.

The unification of Germany was not the only development that enabled Europe to set an example of positive changes in the world. The East European countries' amazing liberation from totalitarianism, the deepening integration under way in Western Europe, progress toward disarmament in Europe, the successful evolution of the all-European process, all show that a new model of international relations is taking shape and winning approval on the continent. The importance of developments in Europe was accentuated by the fact that during the same General Assembly session, the foreign ministers of the CSCE countries met for the first time on American soil, at the other edge of Manhattan. But while that proximity to the General Assembly hall aroused a certain jealousy, this did not overshadow the appreciation of what was going on in Europe. Nor did it prevent many non-European delegates, primarily from Asia, pondering whether that experience could be used elsewhere.

Another indication of positive world trends in addition to Europe was the headway made toward settling many regional conflicts. First to be mentioned was Namibia, with delegates giving credit for its winning independence both to those directly involved in the process and largely to the UN and its Secretary-General. Delegates also spoke of the democratic settlement of the conflict in Nicaragua and voiced hope that further advances would be made in settling the conflict in Cambodia and normalizing the situation in Western Sahara.

Opinions concerning changes in the world and their likely long-term effects varied considerably. But by far most of them were positive. And it was indicative that spokesmen for practically all groups of nations and Third World trends recognized, if not with equal confidence, that these changes would benefit all. The only discordant note was sounded by the Cuban delegate, who claimed that the détente which had set in was not of the kind developing countries had been fighting for, that it was undemocratic and would not benefit the Third World. People usually look forward to changes but beware of them when they come.

Still, it would be wrong to describe the mood expressed by the world community at the session as entirely optimistic. While there are many stable and prosperous states, it is generally realized that the planet is going through the most significant transformation since the end of World War II. Major changes also took place before, one of them being the rise of dozens of independent states in what had been colonial empires. But the postwar world remained bipolar. Everybody knew that its bipolarity hampered the development of even those who were on the free side of the area divided by the "iron curtain" or were not directly involved in confrontation. All countries were seeking an end to confrontation. But while this is now coming about, it is only natural that any deep-going change, whatever the prospects offered by it, should give rise to many problems demanding immediate solution in terms of practical policy.

The old, bipolar framework is being removed, nor can it be left, for it is hopelessly rusty. But what is going to take its place as a factor for world stability? Is the new world order in the making durable enough?

The old world was built not only on military, political, and economic confrontation but above all on the antithesis between two sets of values, which was so bitter that virtually all countries had to make their choice, at least outwardly. One of these sets has broken down, but what next? Are we to look forward to a worldwide triumph of the other set or is the world about to be torn apart by an orgy of ideological, ethnic and religious discord? "Deideologization of international or state-to-state relations," and "universal values" are rather general and loose terms that played a useful role when we began to abandon our so-called class approach to world politics, an approach actually motivated by the interests of a totalitarian great power. Assuming that world politics is really deideologized, is it to be based on an unprincipled drive for profit in the interest of one country or regime? How many more Saddam Husseins or Pol Pots can that produce? And what common criterion of universal values is there? People and their aspirations have much in common. But where it is a question of concepts of human rights and the political organization of society, the world is still nowhere near universal standards. The values which we agree so haltingly and inconsistently to regard as binding on us within the framework of the all-European process are Western values after all, or values evolved over the centuries by the Christian world and Western Europe with a tremendous contribution from North America. They include world experience and are greatly varied in form and tolerant of other values. This is not to say, however, that the Western system of concepts of the organization of public life is acceptable to all nations, especially now that to reject this ideology does not mean, as it did in the past, coming almost automatically within the range of the other, still less acceptable ideology.

The earlier confrontational system was not limited to deep defense in Europe but was global. It led to cultivating clients, winking at attempts to acquire nuclear, chemical, or other powerful weapons, offering preferential terms for overt or covert trade in arms. The system of bloc-to-bloc confrontation is being dismantled, and Europe is disarming on an unprecedented scale, removing the most dangerous malignant tumor affecting it. But what about the metastases scattered all over the world and now ignored? Some elements of a European mechanism of maintaining peace and stability have been or are being devised. On the other hand, there are still no regional or global mechanisms capable of maintaining them in other regions, where stability (if any) was preserved primarily through a precarious balance of influence between the two antagonistic power centers. The biggest unknown factor of everybody's concern is the Soviet Union's possible future and the effect of whatever happens to it on the regional and global structures.

Indeed, Europe itself shows that the solution of old problems does not exempt it from the emergence of new ones. For years the chief concern of theorists and politicians was to end or prevent conflicts between the western and eastern parts of the continent, conflicts which threatened its very existence for decades, or so it seemed. This threat has now been removed, let us hope for ever. Europe owes this in part to the efforts of the architects and negotiators of a common European home but primarily to the peoples of its eastern part, who resolved to cast off the shackles of totalitarianism. The result is that the East ceased to be its former self. What has been achieved at talks is very important for curbing the Soviet military machine and providing certain safeguards. After all, the decision on drastic cuts in Soviet forces in Central Europe was not really made in Vienna but in the capitals of East European countries, which refused to have them on their soil any longer.

The foregoing does not imply, however, that Europe is rid of problems and has a perfectly clear vision of its future. Many of the conflicts that broke out within the two blocs before were halted in the name of fighting the "chief enemy." The West has an intricate system of settling various conflicts. Even if NATO structures are loosened, the alliance will still have its mechanisms of coordinating interests or creating new ones. In the east of Europe, however, contradictions are sharper and have been neglected more than in the west. Besides, all that is left by now are bilateral contacts and residual meetings between signatories to the Warsaw Treaty and forums called to settle their conflicting situations. Add the acuteness of internal problems the often swift growth of national awareness, the difficulties of overcoming the political, economic, legal, and sociopsychological legacy of totalitarianism, which often turn out to be greater than expected at first. A further question that does not appear to be entirely theoretical is the extent to which each West European country is immune to antidemocratic and nationalist trends at a time when tension in the area of resistance to totalitarianism is down. Nor is it quite clear how Europe is to advance to unity given the marked difference in development levels and degree of integration between its various parts.

The chief problem worrying everyone is undoubtedly the likely future of the Soviet Union and the impact which developments here may have on regional and world structures. Fear of the specter of hunger and chaos in one-sixth of the globe, a region abounding in nuclear weapons and reactors, is apparently strong. This explains why analysis of the preferable road for advancing the Soviet Union as a whole or part by part to a democratic, open society with a real market economy is replaced to a considerable extent by a largely mechanical superimposition of the unprecedented processes going on in our country on traditional patterns of public law and the model of doing business with us that evolved over the decades.

The future world order is bound to be influenced just as seriously by further trends in the Third World. Many recognize that with the danger of a Soviet–U.S. nuclear conflict over, the greatest global danger is posed by the developing countries' unsolved social and economic problems and the urgency of finding ways and means of helping them, to create the most effective progress, lending them the greatest possible flexibility in reacting to new problems, and assuring them conditions of life fit for human beings.

These are only some of the questions arising now that the end of the cold war and the beginning of hopes of building a qualitatively new, peaceful and durable world order have been put on record at the General Assembly session in New York, in festive Berlin, and at the Paris CSCE summit. Coupled with lingering regional conflicts, unsolved disarmament and "traditional" economic, legal, and social problems as well as those of environmental protection, the fight against drug trafficking, terrorism, and other problems that are relatively new to international forums, they may be expected to determine in large measure the world's political agenda for the years ahead.

Anyone who compares it with the formal agenda of the latest GA session or with those of future sessions will discover few coinciding items. This is understandable, seeing that the agenda of the GA session held ten years ago does not differ much from today's—a reflection of one of the organization's serious shortcomings.

There is often little connection between a session's agenda and the issues it concentrates on. While the developments in the Gulf were put on the agenda just in case, so to speak, and were not discussed formally, they became the centerpiece of the meeting.

It would have been unpardonably unrealistic to expect the new world order based on adherence to the UN Charter principles and the faith in a free and democratic society to come about overnight in a miraculous way through a general accord. Iraq's annexation of Kuwait and its stubborn refusal to comply with the resolution of the Security Council and the will of the international community caused deep concern. The point at issue is not only the tragedy that has befallen the Kuwaiti people, the increased tension in an area as important for the world economy as the Gulf, or the threat of a big war with unforeseeable consequences. Iraq's aggression is seen as a tough test for the capacity of the world with its instruments, such as the UN, to react adequately. It is primarily a test for the positive processes that are unfolding in the world and offers what virtually everyone regards as vast, indeed unique, opportunities to solve many problems.

When the Gulf crisis broke out there was no certainty about whether the world could preserve those positive trends and hence use the opportunities afforded by them. While this perception was common, it is hard to understand, on looking at the matter more calmly, how the invasion of Kuwait, unquestionably a flagrant violation of international law threatening a major war in the region, can affect the core and chief motor of positive world trends; the renunciation of the cold war and the end of global Soviet–U.S. confrontation.

This must be due partly to the inertia of international political thinking, which had been used to interact between Soviet–U.S. confrontation and any major regional crisis. Lying deeper down—almost in the subconscious—were doubts about how far the Soviet Union had overcome the genetic code of its earlier policy. The Gulf crisis resulting from Iraq's aggression (a country with whom we are bound by a treaty of friendship and who for many years had been one of our closest partners in the Arab world and a major recipient of Soviet armaments) put our new political thinking and the depth of changes in our foreign policy to a really exacting test. This is no place for analyzing the various shades of the Soviet reaction to the crisis or the bends of the Soviet line in the new situation. But it is beyond doubt that there were signs of a certain vacillation and, moreover, contradictory trends that came out alternately. The lack of clarity about the Soviet position and, more importantly, about whether it is an organic part of its policy or a result of pressure and compelling circumstances, is still there, I believe—although in the Security Council the Soviet Union has adhered, if not from the outset, to a common line in favor of condemning the aggressor and building up pressure against him.

The unease over the events in the Gulf is also due to their undermining the hope that changes in East–West relations imply a more tranquil future for the world and not just for the countries involved in confrontation. Leaders of both blocs had repeatedly called on the world to help normalize relations between them, arguing that this would produce positive results at a global level. The case of Iraq put these hopes and is still putting them to a severe trial, and they can apparently survive only if joint efforts, with Soviet–U.S. cooperation playing the chief role, help ensure that Saddam Hussein is not rewarded for aggression, that the eventual use of force does not prove disastrous to the region, and that the change in the regional power balance to be ultimately brought about by Arabs and non-Arabs does not have a destabilizing or too painful an impact on individual Arab countries. It is also important that in the postcrisis period the standards applied by the anti-Saddam coalition should extend to other situations of vital importance to the Arab world and other groups of developing countries. In any set of circumstances, the outcome of the events in the Gulf must not have any serious effect on the trend of East–West relations—provided that the list of priorities is drawn up correctly. But it is only on the above complex conditions that the new model of a world order being formed jointly by the East and West can be expected to have a chance to spread to other regions and that no dangerous estrangement will develop between North and South over political problems and the issue of maintaining international security.

Iraq's actions were also an acid test for the UN, primarily its Security Council. For the first time in years, the latter had to concern itself with what the organization's founders had visualized as its business, namely, stopping aggression and eliminating its effects. The SC demonstrated its efficiency, if not without difficulty, by not only adopting a number of resolutions but by devising an implementation mechanism in the form of sanctions, a control committee responsible for the enforcement of these sanctions, and so on. This carries great risks, however, for failure to implement the resolutions would show the world that in really complicated situations, with the parties to a conflict disinclined to come to terms, the SC can only pass resolutions without achieving the necessary result by ending aggression and settling the conflict. Throughout the Gulf crisis, the "Big Five" were the driving force in the SC, as the founders of the UN had intended them to be. It was not always easy for them to preserve unity but they nearly always did. The reaction of the other SC members and, for that matter, of the organization as a whole, to the role of the five powers and the nature of their actions was not uniform.

They realize that without cooperation between the permanent members of the Council, who have the right of veto, that body can hardly be expected to function efficiently. On the other hand, there is growing protest against what many see as imposing the will of the five great powers on all other UN members. The situation around Iraq did not engender very strong contradictions, and all UN members showed a fair degree of unanimity. There is a feeling, however, that concerted action by the Five in a different context may meet with strong resistance. Much will depend on how the Five cooperate and how individual permanent members of the SC proceed. Advance consultations with the nonpermanent members and constant evidence of respect for them can largely solve the problem of unity. And it is known that the Five are only just learning to operate in the new conditions, with the result that there are many imperfections in their work.

The Kuwaiti crisis revived debates over the possibility and technicalities of the use of force by or on behalf of the UN which had died down years before. Under discussion now are the legal, political, military-technological, and financial aspects of the problem. It is very complicated but the important thing is that the fear of using force due to decades of confrontation is clearly being overcome. It would be unpardonably idealistic to imagine that a new world order based primarily on adherence to the principles of the UN and on belief in a freely, democratically organized society can be established as if by magic overnight, everybody agreeing with everybody else. That order will inspire confidence in its solidity only if everyone knows that encroaching on it is fraught with serious consequences. And it will be much better for East–West and North–South relations if a real threat of such consequences emanates from the UN as a world center, not from one country or a group of countries.

All countries have been wondering both severally and collectively about the causes of the events in the Gulf. Quite a few opinions are expressed, and each of them is probably correct, at least to a degree. It is said that the Iraqi leader is an irrational man, that he finds it necessary for inner political reasons to maintain a state of expansion, that his action is a trial balloon preceding a march on Israel, and so on. Worthy of special note is the general proposition that Iraq is in effect a product of the cold war and regional rivalries between big powers. Putting their bid for influence above other considerations, the Soviet Union as well as Western countries and China had courted the Iraqi regime, arming it and helping it create the military monster they are now faced with. It is particularly distressing that not only the Soviet Union but nearly all other countries shut their eyes to the totalitarian character of the Iraqi regime, to the complete lack of democracy in Iraq, where human rights are violated widely and systematically. Nor did that attitude seem to be influenced by alarm signals coming from there: Draconian laws against all dissent, the suppression of the Kurds' uprising by using even chemical weapons, the recent shooting of British correspondents. There was no adequate reaction to those signals. With regard to Iraq, even the most zealous champions of human rights used a double standard. What subsequently happened in the Gulf is a lesson to all. It showed anew that any totalitarian regime is aggressive by nature and that a well-armed totalitarian regime is extremely dangerous for its neighbors and the world.

It is odd that man's consciousness should be so forgetful and selective. After all, Europe had taught terrible lessons making clear that the phenomenon was universal and not just European. It is now important to draw the right conclusion and realize that the case of Iraq has relevance to all regions, not to the Third World alone. This experience tells us once again that war and a threat to security are least likely on the part of countries having a truly democratic, open and free social system. National stability is an important factor for security. But while this is indisputable, we must not forget that for those who have experienced totalitarian rule, it is generally more important how irrevocably they have moved away from totalitarianism. (Iraq was a very stable country in its own way.) This is true above all of the transitional period, when there is a particularly great danger that stability actually means a pause in the advance to freedom. A key requisite for the irreversibility of this advance is to allow citizens freedom of economic activity. This is the only effective way to really destroy the material foundations of totalitarianism.

Now the connection between democracy and peace, freedom, openness, and security, while perfectly obvious, is neither simple nor direct. We know of countries which are reputedly democratic yet show an enviable "national consensus" in building up armaments and getting involved in conflict after conflict with their neighbors. It is fair to ask how applicable democratic criteria are to countries adhering to a different kind of law, at least for the time being. In their case it is apparently important to ascertain how far their "way of life" is consonant with the nature of society and whether they resort to repression to maintain it. The dilemma of using or not using force when democratic and undemocratic states come into contact is not easy to resolve. There is always a danger that the desire to defend or establish democracy somewhere may unjustifiably lower the threshold of using force. All this suggests that the best guarantee of tranquility and security is cooperation between two democratic countries. It is really unthinkable that the Iraqi Kuwaiti dispute over money, oil, and ports would have assumed such a character had both countries been committed to democratic principals.

The events in the Gulf also showed that any tendency toward regional hegemonism prompting major regional states to acquire large quantities of more and more up-to-date weapons not only poses a grave danger to this or that area but may seriously undermine international security, destabilize the situation in the world, and deal severe blows to the world economy. Those events indicate that the concept of defense sufficiency should not be a privilege of Europe but should extend to other regions. This is particularly true now that confrontation between the two blocs has eased and Europe is working to lower the level of military confrontation. It is hardly reasonable to expect major arms importers to show wisdom by renouncing deliveries. The time has come to recognize that arms deliveries cannot be regarded as distributing political honeycakes or doing good business. On passing the necessary minimum limit, arms concentration begins to follow its own laws. The more important of these laws are that arms must be steadily built up qualitatively and quantitatively and that sooner or later a situation arises when guns begin shooting. Besides, arms buildup generally leads to serious changes in the political balance in various countries or whole regions. Deliveries of arms as well as of technologies making it possible to manufacture them, must therefore be carefully regulated at national and international levels. This is increasingly realized also at the UN, whose 45th GA Session devoted a great deal of attention to the problem.

The Gulf crisis showed for its part that regional conflicts tend to become almost the only source of war danger and of powerful destabilizing waves that sweep across to the world. It is they that make it impossible to move on in the military-political sphere to a new period of comprehensive peaceful evolution. In the new context of lack of confrontation, these conflicts revealed the interlocking and indivisibility of today's world, if from a somewhat different angle, but just as clearly.

There is no doubt that progress has been made toward settling many conflicts although it is less than what could be achieved if the inertia of earlier approaches and stereotypes were fully overcome. The most pressing problem for our country is Afghanistan. The point is that currently our continuing involvement in this conflict— one of the ugliest outgrowths of an earlier confrontational, imperial foreign policy—looks like a strange anachronism, to say the least. There is also the fact that Afghanistan still involves our country, which has been reduced to a state of ruin, in enormous expenditures in money and, in kind, compels us to go on supplying the military-industrial complex with resources on a scale incommensurate with our present possibilities and on lines running counter to the trend toward cutting armed forces and conventional armaments. There is no denying the complexity of the Afghan problem but it can certainly be solved soon enough, provided that no further recourse is had to armed force, even on the present scale, nor is there any further standing pat on the idea of introducing into a pattern of settlement— designed to open a new, peaceful chapter in Afghan history—the power structures and centers associated with the most trying periods of that history.

Progress in settling other conflicts and the shadow cast by the events in the Gulf reemphasized the imperative need to end the dangerously smoldering Arab–Israeli conflict. In the new international situation, it is not subsiding but tends to flare up time and again, which shows that practically every regional conflict is distinctive no matter how East–West confrontation may aggravate it. Obviously, the problem will be hard to solve in the old way, especially in view of the burden of earlier attitudes, the resolutions which the General Assembly passed for decades, some of which were far from objective, and so on. To avoid a tragic denouement, all parties to the conflict should try to take a fresh look at the situation, proceeding not so much from historical claims or grievances but from a desire to take account of both one's own and others' interests and to work out a sound formula for settlement.

The state of the world economy, or rather the increasingly grim economic situation in many developing countries compounded by a population explosion, disease and hunger, should be classed along with the need to end East–West confrontation, the Kuwaiti crisis, and regional conflicts among the priorities claiming the attention of the world community. The alienation of the poor South from positive world trends and the threat of a social explosion there involving ethnic and religious factors is a truly painful problem worrying the world. There is evidence, however, that common sense is gradually gaining ground in this sphere as well. There are signs of a more pragmatic approach on the part of nearly all countries, of their realizing that economic problems cannot be solved by serving ultimatums on "rich" countries or restructuring established international economic relations and that countries where the situation is tical need not only aid but, above all, economic reform. With East–West confrontation at a low point, contradictions between North and South have become more visible. But also visible is a desire to prevent one kind of confrontation being replaced by another, avoid rhetoric, and search in common for a way out of current difficulties.

Growing in the Third World, if not very fast, is an awareness that economic and social problems can be reliably solved only be developing a free market economy and building a democratic society.

In close connection with economic and social problems, speakers at the latest UN General Assembly session voiced much greater concern than before about mounting nationalism in various regions of the globe and the danger it presents not only to the stability of frontiers and international relations but to human life and rights. They pointed out, however, that a distinction must be made between extremism and aggressive insistence on one's national exclusiveness and the natural growth of national consciousness, which is also in evidence in small groups. Those who look deeper into the problem, approaching it calmly, note that humanity is passing through a qualitatively new stage in the evolution of the concepts of sovereignty and nation-state. Integrational processes, standardization of human rights, and the increasing interdependence of the world are effacing in a measure the kind of national boundaries habitually conceived in the case of earlier states. As a result, some of the problems, especially problems at macrolevel such as those of the environment or some aspects of the economy, are now solved on a more general level going beyond individual nation-states. At the same time, a liberalization of the idea of national frontiers has enabled small ethnic and autonomous formations to seek international contacts with greater resolve and to uphold their distinctive rights. An example of this is furnished by Western Europe. The West European community is advancing to a situation where it will be represented in foreign policy by old states severally and at the same time as a single subject of international intercourse. Along with this, German states Flanders, Quebec, and other components of various countries are becoming more and more active primarily in the foreign economic sphere and to a degree in foreign policy. These realities suggest that however alarming the processes going on in the Soviet Union today may be for the outside world, they are of the same nature as the radical changes under way in Europe and to a lesser extent in other parts of the world. They are ultimately indicative of a transition from the earlier kind of stability, kept up primarily from a position of strength, to a new, organic stability in conditions of freedom.

Adaptation to the new trends will require effort on the part of regional and world structures, including the UN. The increased activity and independence of the Ukraine and Belorussia at the GA session and the visible presence of spokesmen for the RSFSR and other republics as members of the Soviet delegation are some of the early signs of this process. There is growing emphasis on the need to adapt the UN to the new conditions and the new world, to its requirements and composition. Everything is being scrutinized: the composition and powers of UN agencies, the established procedure of their functioning, the role and powers of the Secretary General and the Secretariat, the principles of funding the organization's activities. There is also much talk about what the UN will be like now that Soviet–U.S. confrontation is over, that the United States takes a renewed interest in the UN, and that the Soviet Union and the United States tend to cooperate in the organization.

Time will answer all these questions. People generally look forward to changes but are frightened when these come. There is reason to hope that changes in the nineties will really be for the better despite the problems they will create.

Ecology and Politics

Eduard Shevardnadze

Strictly speaking, I could have left out the conjunction "and." Unfortunately for all, natural scientists are no longer the only ones to take an interest in the environment. At present the latter also gets close attention from politicians, and therefore ecology and politics do not have to be separated from or linked to each other in words. Their interpenetration is so complete that even terms like "environmental diplomacy" or "environmental policy" do not seem very new.

What a pity that neither do they seem very old. Whereas the problem of environmental protection has troubled our public opinion for decades, it was only a relatively short time ago that politicians admitted its existence and began giving it increased attention. As far as I am concerned, this came when, in April 1986, the Foreign Ministry was literally flooded with inquiries, representations, and notes from the foreign policy departments of neighboring countries. On that day,

EDUARD SHEVARDNADZE was Minister of Foreign Affairs from 1985 to January 1991.

about a dozen and a half ambassadors asked for an immediate meeting at the Ministry, saying that they had urgent instructions from their governments to seek an explanation for the appearance of radioactive elements in the atmosphere, soil, and water on their national territories.

It was the day when the Chernobyl accident occurred. We had still not uttered that name nor revealed the proportions of the disaster to ourselves and the world but it already indicated that, from then on, no ecological calamity could be treated any longer as affecting solely the national territory involved. It showed that the limits of catastrophes due to a conflict between technosphere and biosphere are highly conventional in today's world while transboundary international resistance to the environmental disintegration of the planet, a danger as terrible as that of nuclear war, is an absolute necessity.

The danger has been existing for some time but it was not until a comparatively short time ago, at least in our country, that it came to be perceived as an ecological imperative of survival posing numerous problems.

In our country, many things relating to nature conservancy may be described as taking place for the first time.

For instance, we have begun, if belatedly in many cases and not necessarily of our own free will, to declassify the sad truth about ecological disasters as destructive as the one that has hit the Aral Sea. There is little in this to rejoice over but it is certainly easier to protect the truth when you know the facts.

For the first time ever, we have proclaimed that to protect the environment means protecting man.

For the first time ever, we have declared that the state must guarantee the protection of nature and man, in particular by adopting a long-term environmental protection program for the country as a whole and for all Union and autonomous republics, enacting relevant legislation and improving the structure and functioning of ecological agencies.

For the first time ever, we have set out to establish by law procedures for rigorous estimates by experts and to take account of public opinion in deciding on the construction of new production facilities.

For the first time ever, we have raised to the level of economic policy the demand for closer attention to the need to carry out programs for rational nature management, for saving energy and resources, and to stop treating nature as an object of reckless exploitation.

For the first time ever, we have recognized the need to solve these problems together with the world community, in close international environmental cooperation.

We have pointed out more than once that we were very late in awakening to the dramatic implications of environmental problems. Let us call a spade a spade by saying that while the people sounded the alarm long ago, the inborn deafness of the powers that be constantly prevented them from hearing it. On top of that, the philosophy of time-servers — *après moi le déluge* — plus the mechanism of unquestioning execution of orders invariably doomed all fears and warnings to indifference. Every reasonable argument was rejected by invoking "overriding national interests." Wasteful utilization of unique natural resources, for instance, was "justified" by referring to defense requirements. The war menace was considered to outweigh all others. Some did not realize until recently that it is hardly wise to classify and list threats according to gravity; that a nuclear conflict and an environmental disaster present an equal threat to life as the main universal value; that between these two global problems there is a real connection which expresses itself in, among other things, disarmament being the only major source of means for environmental protection.

However, our misconceived notion of the threat to peace, humanity, and ourselves that we have already overcome is not the only point. In unfolding industrialization when our material and financial resources were limited, seeking to accomplish it in a short time and by extensive methods under the slogan of "overtaking and surpassing" the West, we were inclined to ignore the need for environmental protection. Why, it had been impressed on our minds since childhood that our immense country had inexhaustible resources and that we could not wait for the favors of nature. What was instilled in us was not only ecological carelessness but a tendency to treat our country as a huge industrial building site. We were urged to build and master everything ahead of schedule without stopping to think of the consequences. Well, these have now caught up with us.

New political thinking paved the way for a thorough review of our approach to nature conservancy. The USSR Supreme Soviet adopted a decision "On Urgent Measures to Improve the Environmental Situation in the Country." The drafting of a long-term state program for environmental protection and rational utilization of natural resources has entered its final stage. We will have to enact a nature conservancy law, the first in the country's history, before long. We have approved and are drafting special-purpose programs by regions and entities. Thus the state is shaping a new environmental policy.

Even so, we have yet to make a real beginning. Overall, the state of the environment in the Soviet Union is unfavorable; in some areas (whose number is growing) it is becoming a disaster. In 103 cities, which account for 18 percent of the country's population, the level of atmospheric pollution is ten or more times higher than maximum admissible concentration. Areas where the ecological situation is critical are seventeen times larger as a total than those of reservations and preserves. The state of two-thirds of the country's water resources is at variance with environmental health standards. Every year "ecological" diseases rob us of up to 10 billion rubles. There is evidence of declining natural fertility and soil degradation owing to erosion, salinization, and technological overuse. Every three to five years see the complete extinction of one mammal species. The damage caused to nature entails economic losses ranging from 25 to 30 billion rubles a year.

Thus the situation points unmistakably to a drift toward catastrophe. There is no stopping this trend through local palliatives. What is needed is a complete, thorough reorganization of this activity all over the country. We must primarily bring about a radical change in the character of production activity from the point of view of its impact on the environment. Even before drawing up specific economic plans, to say nothing of implementing them, we must take account of the ecological capacity of the various areas for the installation of economic complexes, correlate the possibilities of the ecosystems of individual regions with economic plans and take the results into consideration in demographic, regional, and national policy.

In terms of atmospheric pollution background, our country may be divided into three regions: the European territory of the Union, Central Asia and Kazakhstan, Siberia, and the Far East. In the European part of the country, where pollution is at its worst, combating it calls for joint efforts by all the republics and regions situated here and for close cooperation between them and their Western neighbors.

Environmental problems can apparently be settled much faster if cooperation encompasses whole geographic regions linked together primarily by a common natural environment on which the economic activity of the countries concerned or of certain of their regions has put a heavy burden.

It is in this direction that the Baltic countries are now developing cooperation. Preparations for the conference on protecting the unique natural environment of the Arctic proposed by Finland are in full swing.

Worthy of special note is the idea of setting up national reservations on both sides of the frontiers separating neighbors. In the Soviet–Polish border area, it is being put into effect in the Belovezha Forest. And it is close to materialization at the other end of the country, where we have come to terms with the Americans on opening an international natural and ethnographic park in the Bering Strait area in 1991. Finland has proposed setting up a joint reservation in border areas of our two countries. Its proposal can be put into practice in cooperation with the Karelian Autonomous Republic, the Baltic republics, and adjacent regions.

To be sure, all the problems of bilateral environmental cooperation, to say nothing of regional cooperation, cannot be solved just by creating border area reserves. These are only one component of cooperation, which offers ample opportunities for the participation of our republics, territories, and regions.

A further consideration is that to save the environment in countries and regions, it is necessary to make bold, occasionally unpleasant and often tough decisions. To carve territories forming part of a single ecosystem into pieces and raise barriers on the principle "I know what is best for me" could block solution of the problem of joining forces.

We must not forget that, largely through our own fault, seats of global ecological calamities have arisen on our soil that also affect the peoples of other countries. Chernobyl is not the only case in point: look at the Aral Sea.

Practically in the lifetime of just one generation, that sea has lost two-thirds of its water. About three million hectares of its bottom is bare now, and every year winds blow away hundreds of millions of tons of sand and dust. The quality of river water has greatly deteriorated. Soil fertility is declining. In other words, the situation has virtually gotten out of hand. Yet the Aral area is home to nearly four million people, whose very existence is now affected. Experts estimate that not less than 30 to 35 billion rubles would have to be spent on regenerating the sea. It is clear that the local authorities cannot cope with this task either financially or otherwise and that it must therefore be tackled by all.

The whole set of environmental protection measures in the Soviet Union will require about 130 billion rubles, or four times as much as is invested currently. No such amount can be put up at once but joining efforts at all levels would lead to multiplying investments. The priority task is to work for the steadfast implementation and buildup of urgent as well as current and long-range conservation measures. Preference should be given to the territorial principle of planning conservation and rational management.

It is essential to acquaint the whole country with useful local initiatives especially experience gained in developing a new mechanism for nature management. We must generalize the results of an experiment being carried out in dozens of cities and industrial centers of various regions of our country with a view to evolving a methodology and establishing practical parameters for charging a price for nature management and setting up conservation funds.

Environmental revival and the molding of an up-to-date attitude to nature objectively have a most important role to play in strengthening, stabilizing, and renewing society, in improving its moral health. We all need to get schooling in democracy and tolerance as speedily as possible. I am confident that ecology will be one of the main disciplines listed in our graduation certificates.

The point of departure is the statement that the current ecological crisis dramatically reflects the interdependence and interconnection of today's world. This in turn calls for a *coordinated international environmental policy*. The only way to stave off tragedy and provide environmental security is to carry on such a policy by joint efforts. Hence the urgent need for consolidation, this time at a global level. A global environmental policy can be evolved through collective efforts even though its framing poses difficult problems, some of which affect national sovereignty.

As in other spheres of international security, the starting point must be the primacy of international law, which gives priority to universal values. The UN should unquestionably play a central role.

According to the decision "On the Main Lines of Soviet Home and Foreign Policy" adopted by the First Congress of People's Deputies, the security of the country, including the environmental component, must be ensured primarily by political means and by leaning on the prestige and possibilities of the UN for support.

This is the line which the multilateral dialogue on the environment is following at the UN. We consider it one of the major achievements of the 44th Session of the UN General Assembly that it approved by consensus all ecological resolutions, primarily the one on preparations for the 1992 UN Conference on the Environment and Development.

The planned conference requires careful preparations, for the effectiveness and proper trend of conservation efforts at the world level will depend on the decisions it adopts. We note with satisfaction that these decisions were outlined at the first (Nairobi) meeting of the Preparatory Committee of the Conference, which is to sit in Brazil from June 1 to 12, 1992. Particular importance attaches to the Committee's recommendation for holding the Conference at the level of heads of state and government, as proposed by the Soviet Union.

What results do we expect the conference to produce?

I think one of them could be the approval of a code of principles of ecological ethics.

Such a document adopted by heads of state or government would introduce new ethical principles into international relations suggested by the ecological imperative. It would attest to the resolve of the world community to build its life in the twenty-first century according to new rules.

Another important result could be a program setting out a planetary strategy for international environmental cooperation and indicating the sources of funding the measures envisaged by the program. We would like the drafting of international conventions on protecting the earth's climate and preserving biodiversity to be completed by the opening date of the conference. No one can make an accurate forecast today of the likely economic and social impact which a several-hundred-kilometer northward shift in climatic belts would have on present and future generations. Still, some scientists regard this as very likely given a mere 1.5 to 4.5°C global warming. At a time when nature daily loses up to one hundred biological species, there is no need to enlarge on the seriousness of the danger of exhausting the earth's genetic resources. To curb negative trends due to the phenomena noted above, humanity needs global agreements.

Lastly, there is a need for sound recommendations for the promotion of ecological education and an improved system of international bodies working on environmental problems.

The UN Environment Program (UNEP) holds a special place in this system. Our cooperation with UNEP, an activity backed by a growing voluntary financial contribution yields concrete results. This is exemplified by the agreement signed in January 1990 between the Soviet Union and UNEP on cooperation in planning measures to overcome the unfavorable environmental situation in the Aral area.

A further provision of principle has to do with working out an international legal regime for the conservation of unique natural zones of planetary significance. This applies primarily to Antarctica. We are at one with many scientists and public figures who are concerned about the exploitation of that continents's natural resources. The Soviet Union, being committed to reasonable self-limitation in the name of universal values, is ready to join in the effort to transform Antarctica into a global reservation and a universal natural laboratory. Moves to this end should understandably be based on the Treaty on Antarctica, which has formalized the creation of the first nuclear-free zone in the world and the first territory on the planet that is completely open to international scientific research.

Now is the time for all of us to put our heads together in order to find solutions to the problems of the Danube, Black Sea, and Mediterranean. There is no geographic shortcut to the solution of any one of them. Take the Danube–Black Sea link as an example. The Danube discharges up to three-quarters of all pollutants into the sea. What is more, the upper level of the hydrogen sulphide layer of Black Sea water has risen from a depth of 200 meters to 75 meters from the surface, which is fraught with this layer "spilling over" into the Marmara, Aegean, and Mediterranean seas. In light of this reality, there appears to be no justification for Bulgaria, Romania, Turkey, and the Soviet Union being the only signatories to agreements on the Black Sea since there are other Danubian countries. Nor do attempts to solve the problem of conserving the Mediterranean without Black Sea countries hold any promise. There is an obvious need for new solutions, and collective work on them should be started without delay.

Humanity must give attention to an environmental legacy like the rain forests and large forested areas in general, those lungs of the planet, as well as to coral reefs and other unique natural entities, such as Lake Baikal. The time has come to translate attention into action aimed at, among other things, making up for self-limitation in utilizing forests, unique freshwater resources, and so on.

Speaking of Lake Baikal, I wish to point out that a Baikal International Environmental Research Center is being set up in Listvyanka, a settlement in Irkutsk Region. Scientists from the Soviet Union, the United States, Britain, Germany, China, Canada, Sweden, and elsewhere have joined efforts to explore the largest freshwater lake in the world. The results of their research are bound to be of great theoretical and practical value to many countries.

There are some other interesting ideas of furthering mutually beneficial international environmental cooperation on Soviet soil. They include our proposal to Germany for joint research on general problems of the Volga and Rhine ecosystems; the establishment on the basis of the Repetek State Reservation, Kara Kum Desert, of an international center for research into problems of desertification; the working out of an international project for the exploration and improvement of the environmental situation in areas contaminated in the wake of the Chernobyl accident. In terms of international cooperation, the potentialities of the Polar Region, Siberia, the Far East, and other unique natural zones of international significance are far from exhausted.

An international mechanism of technological cooperation in environmental protection should become part of the system of measures to improve the ecological situation in the world. I mean technologies making it possible to prevent the rise of new sources of pollution and to minimize the harmful impact of existing industries on nature. Distinctions in the socioeconomic growth levels of various countries predetermine an uneven distribution of the technological potential in the world. Most technologies whose application would help reduce or even prevent environmental pollution are concentrated in developed countries. Yet it is perfectly clear that no country can be clean as an exception and that the problem of saving nature leaves no room for national or commercial egoism.

It follows that there has to be a system of international exchanges of ecologically clean technologies, one that would effectively guarantee all countries access to them on the principle of most-favored nation.

We are willing to share such technologies. At the First Conference of the Parties to the Vienna Convention and the Montreal Protocol on Substances Destroying the Ozone Layer (London, June 1990), the Soviet Union reaffirmed its readiness to make its ozone-safe technologies available free of charge.

Our technological cooperation with Norway and Finland is growing and gaining experience. The Soviet–Finnish Declaration provides for "the development of nature conservation technologies and their exchange as a common obligation of all states."

Of course, technological cooperation in environmental protection has its problems, which diplomats as well as officials of environmental protection and other agencies will have to solve.

In the West, by far, most technological investigations and projects are in the hands of private business. We can hardly expect private firms to offer gratuitously innovations in which they have invested large sums. This poses the problems of copyright, licensing, and financial compensation, which are anything but simple.

There are also problems engendered by developing countries' fears of slowing down their overall economic growth by allocating funds for the introduction of conservation technologies. In the course of discussions on international technological cooperation, developing countries emphasize the connection between conservation measures and the allocation of funds in addition to those supplied by various countries and international financial institutions.

The essence of our position on the range of problems involved in the transfer of conservation technologies is that the Soviet Union is agreeable to the most extensive technological cooperation on the principles of equality aimed at achieving real results in the preservation of the biosphere of the planet. We are also ready to allow inspection on our territory so as to remove all suspicions of misusing technology.

We have proposed drawing up an international register of the more ecologically dangerous enterprises whose retooling should be carried out as a priority task with credits out of an international fund.

An acute problem is that of inducing the business world to join more actively in the discussion and solution of problems of environmental cooperation, an activity which can only be based on a balance of interests. Incidentally, this is confirmed by the experience of drafting a convention on the prohibition of chemical weapons and, in the ecological sphere, by the experience of drafting new accords and implementing existing ones. The effort to avert the likely disastrous effects of a global climatic change is an example.

In recent years Toronto, Hamburg, the Hague, Tokyo, Nordwijk (the Netherlands) have hosted a series of major international conferences of scientists, noted politicians, and statesmen on integrational efforts in this sphere. Prominent among proposals for preventing a drastic warming is the idea of reducing emissions of carbon dioxide, which come mainly from power plants. The more radical proposals call for a 20 to 30 percent cut in emissions of CO_2 by the years 2000–2005, to be brought about by saving energy, switching to gas, and other alternative energy source. However, the international community has yet to reach a consensus on reducing or at least stabilizing those emissions. This is primarily because most countries find it very difficult to switch abruptly to technologies making it possible to cut releases of CO_2, for this would entail considerable expenditures.

The conference of experts on global changes called in April 1990 in Washington on U.S. president George Bush's initiative failed to arrive at explicit conclusions regarding the evolution of the earth's climate.

Agreement at international level upon actions that may be necessitated by likely climatic changes constitutes a formidable task. It has been assigned to the Intergovernmental Group of Experts on Climatic Changes set up by the WMO and UNEP in 1988 and comprising over forty countries, among them the Soviet Union. The group is to prepare a scientifically sound report on the state of the problem, with recommendations for a response to changes. Its findings will be submitted to the Second World Climatic Conference and the 45th Session of the UN General Assembly and will serve as the basis for an international convention on climatic changes.

One of the major causes of climatic changes is the thinning of the ozone layer protecting the earth's biosphere. The tropospheric ozone destroyed under the impact of chlorofluorocarbons is estimated to account for roughly 20 percent of the greenhouse effect. Steps are being taken to solve the problem by preserving and restoring the ozone layer. On January 1, 1989, the Montreal Protocol (adopted in 1987) came into force; it binds the participating states to freeze and subsequently to reduce production of ozone-destroying substances. The Conference of the Parties to the Montreal Protocol reached an explicit conclusion about the need to toughen the schedule set by the protocol and added a decision on ending by the year 2000 production of all chlorocarbons covered by the protocol.

The international mechanism of environmental monitoring and control is to play an important role among new forms of international environmental cooperation.

Openness and transparency, which should enable partners to satisfy themselves of each other's conscientious compliance with commitments, are indispensable components of international environmental cooperation. With the publication of a detailed report on the national ecological situation making an in-depth and impartial analysis of the troubles and dangers we are beset by, it is all the more urgent that we should overcome our long-standing syndrome of secretiveness. Is it normal, for instance, that roughly 10 percent of Soviet territory is still closed to visitors? I do not think so. We must cut the number of closed areas and reduce them to reasonable proportions, which would help our country join in extensive international environmental cooperation.

We think ecological confidence-building measures could begin with the opening of national reservations. We attach great importance to the preservation of undeveloped ecosystems and the creation of new reservations and other reserved areas, for they can become models of the real nature as well as of open, unhampered international cooperation between environmentalists.

Civilized, ecologically correct international interaction between countries serves man. The right to a healthy environment is a human right and the rockbed of ecological ethics. It should include the right of the individual or groups to participate in shaping environmental policy. All the roots of environmental protection of contemporary "big politics" lie in the mass environmental movement. We owe it to this movement, which sprang up in the sixties, that today, at the beginning of the nineties, humanity realizes the need to solve environmental problems. We need to set up specialized state-to-state political structures to this end, and appreciate the importance of establishing strict international ecological law and order and new ecological ethics.

Operating in practically all countries today are powerful nongovernmental associations championing environmental protection. The Greens in Scandinavian countries, Germany, the Netherlands, Belgium, Denmark, Switzerland, and Britain are particularly active. At the European Parliament last year, representatives of twenty-four different European ecological parties resolved to form a Green group in order to pursue a common policy. There are numerous ecology groups and organizations in the United States, Canada, and Australia. The Green movement in Eastern Europe is gaining ground.

Recent years have been marked by the rapid growth in number of ecological organizations in the Soviet Union.

More and more vigorously, these organizations establish direct contacts with foreign partners; they fit in ever more harmoniously with international environmental cooperation. For the first time ever, delegates from Soviet and American nongovernmental ecological organizations took part in the 12th Session of the mixed Soviet–U.S. commission for environmental cooperation. The Soviet Union was represented by the Socio-Ecological League, and the United States, by the Sierra Club, Audubon Society, Greenpeace, World Wildlife Fund, Legacy International, Friends of the Earth, and other entities. An understanding was reached on concrete cooperation projects. The session released a joint statement recognizing the advisability of bringing nongovernmental organizations of both countries in to work under the 1972 agreement on environmental cooperation on a permanent basis.

I am certain that the ten principles of the international Green movement will become part of the ecological ethical code. These principles are as follows: ecological wisdom, democracy from below, personal and social responsibility, nonviolence, decentralization, local economic growth as the basis for man's business activity, respect for pluralist opinions and concepts, collective action, global responsibility, encouragement of an individual vision of the future.

Curbing military activity today is a task imposed not only by the need to reduce the war menace but by the interests of environmental protection.

The focal tissue in this respect is nuclear disarmament and a complete ban on nuclear tests. We reaffirm the Soviet Unions' readiness to end all nuclear weapons testing at any moment and for all time, provided that the United States does likewise.

Another task of major ecological significance is that of winding down and ultimately banning production of fissionable materials for arms manufacture. I believe the suspension of their production in the United States today and our program for closing down all Soviet plutonium weapon reactors by the end of this century are a direct invitation to cooperation in developing appropriate environmental protection technologies and planning the requisite measures.

The destruction of chemical weapons that is to start under Soviet–U.S. accords and in the context of talks on a multilateral convention to ban them makes it a matter brooking no delay to evolve ecologically safe ways and means of accomplishing this task. Such cooperation is gaining in relevance as large-scale cuts are made in armed forces and conventional armaments, primarily in Europe.

It is not only a question of directly switching funds from the military to the civilian sphere or of adapting the defense industry to the manufacture of nature-conserving equipment. There is also the need to make rational use of all that we have today and that was only used in the military sphere until recently.

For instance, the Soviet defense industry has appreciable experience of developing automated information systems. Data made public indicate that a standard component of such a system can comprise several thousand measuring modules and control both an area of up to 10,000 square kilometers and the environmental situation with regard to as many as up to a hundred pollutants. Specialists also consider it feasible to develop in a short time up-to-date flying ecological laboratories on the basis of strategic bombers. Converted heavy bombers can prove useful in combating forest fires.

Russian scientist, Vladimir Vernadsky called for the entire biosphere of humanity to be transformed into a noosphere. Reason as a threefold embodiment of scientific knowledge, the humanist principle, and universal ethics is becoming a driving force in the search for a new and more effective approach to the environmental imperative. To consistently use it in practice is to guarantee success in solving the numerous ecopolitical problems which daily and forcefully remind us all of how much more has yet to be done.

I trust that we will do it or at least begin doing it.

Reappraisal of USSR Third World Policy

Andrei Kolosov

Over the years of perestroika, official foreign policy orientations have developed into the realization that in economics, politics, and law there are universal achievements of civilization which ensure freedom and development and that, guided by them, we can harmonize the interests of our nation with the interests of others. The difficult words that we do not consider the United States our enemy were pronounced at long last. A lowering of the level of military rivalry has become a reality. During the European process the proclaimed commitment to the common values of civilization has begun to materialize. People on both sides of what used to be called the "iron curtain" now breathe easier, they have begun to rid themselves of a fear of war, to come to know one another better, and to cooperate.

ANDREI KOLOSOV is a political analyst.

Real progress has just begun, but it is already obvious that living like this is easier and freer, that much less energy can be spent on weaponry and the struggle against the enemy, and much more on development.

This does not mean that today or tomorrow everything will be peaches and cream. There will still be conflicts of interests. At the first stage problems that were latent for a long time will surface. However, such a turbulent period, unlike the previous one, has prospects; there is progress from senselessly stubborn military rivalry and whipping up of tensions to a pragmatic search for a "balance of interests," to positive cooperation.

The correctness of this course is not obvious to everyone. Some evidently view it as a betrayal of the principles in which elements of Marxism–Leninism in the Stalinist understanding, of imperial monarchism and blind patriotism, are united under the common denominator of a reluctance for change.

However, few people who espouse these views can explain intelligently where the material and cultural needs of our impoverished society clash with American interests to such a degree as to consider the United States the enemy and, sacrificing a great deal, bear the burden of confrontation with that country and its allies. Few can explain how the interests of our people are served by the foisting of our will or our model on other peoples, and what Soviet people have received for decades of such policies. It is just as difficult to show how, without fundamentally changing our foreign policy, we could hope to become a respectable part of the modern world on a par with others and use its achievements and overcome our growing lag behind the industrialized, and in very many parameters, behind what are not the most industrialized, states. One cannot seriously continue to believe that today a country can be great only by stockpiling destructive weapons, not to mention that the economy, which does not measure up to advanced standards, will not be able sooner or later to produce modern weapons.

The people who are against the repudiation of confrontation and expansionism, and against the removal of barriers between the outside world and us, are guided not by the interests of the people of the country but by a desire to preserve the preperestroika situation, the preperestroika political system and power structure. The division of the world into warring camps is a direct continuation of internal camps. Conversely, recognition of pluralism, and the liberation of society from the oppression of the state are indivisible from a renewal of foreign policy, from the repudiation of confrontation and secretiveness. The influence here is mutual. Insufficient resolve and consistency in altering foreign policy is simultaneously a sign of insufficient boldness of internal reforms and a continuing dangerous reserve of opponents of any reforms at all.

Foreign policy should be brought in line with the new principles on a comprehensive basis. It cannot be selective since it is called upon to promote the country's renewal in the interests of the people, and does not serve anymore what we call the administer-by-command system. In the 1970s we were going through a period of relative normalization of relations with the West which went down in history as detente. It was not a product of the changes within our country; it was, in effect, of a time-serving nature and was doomed the moment the logic of changes in foreign policy began impelling us to work changes domestically. For all its innovativeness, the course for detente in foreign policy was not consistent or full, either. Essentially, it affected only political, trade, and economic relations with the United States and the other Western countries and, in part, control over existing armaments, virtually without affecting military development and policies in the Third World. These areas in the foreign policy context became the levers that enabled the system to very easily break down the seemingly irreversible achievements of detente, which began demanding true openness and democratization in society.

The depth of the current changes in foreign policy has, of course, greatly overshadowed what was done in the period of detente. But they are palpable once again above all in relations with the West in the political and economic areas, in the sphere of arms reductions and limitations, and in tolerance toward the changes in Eastern Europe. There were added the desire for broader people-to-people contacts and cooperation on a wide range of global problems and, what is of no small importance, a readiness to assume commitments in human rights. However, fulfillment of these commitments such as, say, the course of the discussion on the Law on the Press, is proceeding with great difficulty.

Military development and plans are still in the shadows. Even though it is linked much more now than in the past with disarmament agreements, virtually no safeguards against the unexpected appearance of new versions of the SS-20 or the Krasnoyarsk radar station have been created yet.

As to the policy in the Third World, it was believed that peaceful coexistence could not apply to this part of the globe, that it was there that the antagonistic contest between the two systems was being decided, that it was there that the center of the military rivalry with the United States was located. The focal point of policy in the Third World was the desire to put as many countries as possible under our control and do as much damage as possible to the other side's interests. On the other side, this was veiled by the philosphy of solidarity with progressive regimes and support for social transformations, although in reality the ideological motives and, all the more so, a real assessment of the nature of the regime and its policy vis-à-vis its people did not have substantial meaning. Brazen anticommunism and anti-Sovietism, if the situation fitted into the scheme of anti-Americanism, was forgiven. A typical example was the then widespread assessment of the Iranian revolution, which essentially boiled down to the fact that, all its specifics notwithstanding, it accorded with our interests as being strikingly anti-American.

The "Vietnamese syndrome" that the United States went through only whetted appetites. As a result, we waged an outright war in Afghanistan, we were deeply enmeshed in several acute regional conflicts (and we encouraged socialist developing countries to take part in them), and we promoted the creation of regimes in different parts of the world that tried, under the banner of anti-imperialism, to implement in their own conditions, the administer-by-command model and therefore counted on us in everything. The specifics of these regimes, the militarist bent typical of our domestic and foreign policy, and the backwardness of the Soviet civilian economy that was strongly manifest even then made for the fact that military cooperation and arms deliveries were the heart of our relations with developing states "friendly" to us. Their militarization only pushed them even farther into participation in conflicts and into authoritarian rule and worsened the situation in their economy that was rapidly falling apart as it was, as a result of the application of our scheme. The "allies" demanded more and more resources, became more deeply involved in conflicts, and increasingly strengthened in everyone's eyes the association between Soviet policy and instability, authoritarianism, and economic failures. Other developing states, above all the most economically prosperous ones, cooperation with whom could have yielded us real benefits, came to have a stronger distrust in the Soviet Union and a reluctance to have anything to do with it, and even openly protested against its adventures in the Third World.

After 1985, the reassessment of our Third World policy did not begin right away. It took several years to set about the withdrawal of troops from Afghanistan and even more time to admit that the Afghanistan war was a mistake. Clearly, this decision was a difficult one and required great political courage; nevertheless, this was obviously the most urgent foreign policy problem. Soviet people continued to die in Afghanistan, and our participation in the war there remained the chief impediment to normalization of relations with the rest of the world. Our turn toward settling other regional conflicts and reducing our involvement in developments in different parts of the Third World also began very gradually. Dialogue on this topic was launched with the United States, we began energetically using multilateral mechanisms, the United Nations above all, in the search for solutions to conflict situations, and we started urging our partners in the Third World to work for peaceful settlements of problems and to attain reconciliation within their countries.

The successes scored on this path are obvious: with UN participation, the framework for the withdrawal of troops from Afghanistan was devised, the process of provision of independence to Namibia drew to a close, the war between Iran and Iraq has been ended, progress toward a peaceful settlement in Central America has begun, and the outlines of a normalization of the situation in Cambodia and the Western Sahara are starting to take shape.

At the same time, many Third World countries' attitudes toward the Soviet Union have changed drastically; we have begun winning trust even among those which did not want to have anything to do with us at all. Many of these states are promising and quite solvent counterparts for developing trade and economic relations.

The changes in our foreign policy philosophy and in the nature of our actions in the Third World, and the development of extensive relations with different countries from this region have enabled us to take a fresh approach to many global problems on a multilateral basis as well. Our confrontational approach to the West and desire to involve the Third World in it and divide the latter into countries that were "ours" and "not ours" largely impeded a possibility for the UN and the other organizations to solve international economic and many other problems. The removal of tensions and the realization that today's problems require cooperation from everyone who is prepared to tackle them have made it possible to normalize the situation there somewhat, and to begin exploring ways out of politicized dead ends and proceed toward pragmatic compromise solutions based on our practical interests, not ideological ambitions.

Nevertheless, the changes in our relations with the Third World are less impressive than those in our relations with our former "enemy"-the West. Some of the most odious manifestations of the old policy have been eliminated, the elements that created the most difficulties for us in our relations with the United States and other Western and developing states not oriented to us have been removed, and attempts have been made to lessen the economic burden of our involvement in Third World affairs. However, a detailed assessment of the former policy is still at development stage, and the tenet on the repudiation of confrontation has not been brought to the logical conclusion that the system of priorities and the nature of the ties that have taken shape in the epoch of the support of the "anti-imperialist struggle" in the Third World should be reassessed. The latest of our official statements and the noticeable evolution in the positions of countries close to us inspire hope that there will be faster progress toward a new policy in the Third World. For these changes to become more profound it is important that the old infrastructure be discarded, above all in the military sphere, which ensured and generated a confrontation policy.

All our partners in Eastern Europe, this region that is truly important for us, have been replaced over these years. There is nothing wrong with this. Without such revolutionary breakthroughs, a new nonconfrontational period cannot be ushered in, the splitting up of the world cannot be overcome, and its advanced achievements cannot be drawn on. As to the Third World, virtually all our partners are in place. They continue to receive our political support and military and economic assistance, albeit perhaps to a slightly lesser extent. In most cases they are not the initiators of the settlement of conflicts into which they have been drawn. They are brought with great difficulty to stands which open at least somewhat the door to a settlement. More often than not these countries are in a catastrophic economic state and cannot ensure the elementary needs of their populations. More often they are far removed from democracy and respect for human rights, and many of them are waging war with part of their own people.

This continuing state of affairs is harmful. Wars continue in Afghanistan, Angola, Ethiopia, and, to a certain extent, Central America. The situation is explosive in Cambodia, Mozambique, and elsewhere. We or our closest allies have been drawn into all of them in one form or another. People are dying in all of them. Our weapons are being used in all of them in one form or another. All of them are potentially fraught with a drastic worsening of the regional and overall international situation, a worsening that is capable of throwing the world far back. The arms race continues, also not without our participation, in Southern Asia, the Near and Middle East, Northern Africa, and the Caribbean Basin. Reports are still coming in of the appearance, now in one point, now in another, of new Soviet weapons; weapons that are likely more destructive and modern than those in other countries of this region.

The paradox is that we took an active part in the attempts to settle the situation in all these regions and, moreover, scored certain but almost always limited success. Of course, we cannot settle conflicts, some of which are rather difficult, unilaterally or only together with the Americans. On the other hand, all these wars would have been nearly impossible if we had not supplied the weapons and resources for them, if we had honestly told the forces waging them that we would not be supporting them anymore. However, in order to do this, we need to scuttle our former categories of victory or defeat, we need to carry out the same revolutionary turnabout as in Europe, and overcome internally the confrontational logic of rivalry with the United States, most of which spawned or perpetuated these conflicts. Thus far, this is not taking place, or it is taking place very slowly. The most vivid and difficult example for us is Afghanistan. Our troops left Afghan territory; Soviet people have stopped dying there. This is an enormous and indisputable achievement. This does not mean, however, that we have left the war, that we have rid ourselves of its moral, political, and material burdens. The war in Afghanistan continues, and at times even more actively than during the period of our military presence there. Afghanis continue to die, and there is still a hotbed of tensions in direct proximity to our borders, at a most im-

portant point of Asia. Afghanistan continues to be a country that
cannot ensure its development, or even feed its people, for that matter. Aside from arms deliveries, we are still shouldering the burden of
extensive economic aid to Afghanistan, and not the aid that ensures
independent development, since the war in effect rules out construction, but daily supplies of food and other essentials that are not in
great supply in our country. Differing expenditure figures are named,
but, regrettably, not in our press or in our official statements. Nor are
our deputies taking a real interest in this. As far as weapons per se are
concerned, Western sources are quoting between $250 and $400 million a month. It is not hard to calculate how much this has cost since
the troop withdrawal.

Of course, the conflict in Afghanistan and around it is a highly
complicated problem where the inertia of hatred and irreconcilability
is enormous. Many participants, above all a motley kaleidoscope of
intra-Afghan forces, are involved there. It is difficult to settle this
conflict, no matter how much we want to do so. It would be incorrect to maintain that throughout these years the Americans were consistent in their attempts to extinguish this fire. Their line exhibited a
vacillation between a desire to truly settle this conflict and a desire to
preserve it as a burdensome thorn for the Soviet Union. Pakistan's
line is even more contradictory. On the other hand, it would be
wrong to assert that the Americans are not giving, nor have ever
given a chance for settlement. The United States is not interested in
Afghanistan turning into another Iran, and is definitively declaring in
favor of Afghanistan's not being hostile to the Soviet Union and of
its legitimate interests being taken into consideration in a settlement.
With all that it should not be forgotten that the mujaheddin are difficult interlocutors even for those who are supporting them.

The situation is also complicated by the fact that the mujaheddin
are also more inclined to a settlement through force in hopes of winning a military victory over the Najibullah government. Nevertheless, our main task in Afghanistan should have been not only the
troop withdrawal, but also efforts for solutions that would promote
the establishment of such a structure against which the Afghan people would not fight and which would normalize political life in the
country, when the struggle would not be waged by force of arms.
There is no guarantee that this goal would have been reached, but the
aspiration to it should be dictated by a sense of responsibility for the

many years of armed intervention and by a sincere desire to put an end to the war and truly halt the interference in the affairs of another country. Otherwise, this is not a sweeping reexamination of the view of this conflict, and of all conflicts in general, but merely a change in the means of politics and no direct involvement of troops.

It is only today, when the strong-arm line is increasingly showing its futility, when at least a stalemated outcome of the war there has become even more obvious, that slow progress to other positions, aimed at settling the conflict, has begun. We understand that the path to normalization of the situation is through a somewhat transitional, neutral state, not reconciliation with one of the belligerents remaining in power.

The same approach, in principle, not in detail, holds true for the other conflict situations in which we were involved most of all and which were linked above all with internal contradictions and struggle. In principle it should be obvious to everyone that we have no intentions of continuing to preserve a situation where such wars are waged with our weapons and our resources. The only aid we can render is to promote a rapid settlement formula that would enable the people to determine freely, with safeguards, and, preferrably, under international control, what form of administration and what government it prefers. Only in this way will talk of freedom of choice have real meaning, rather than serve as a veil for preserving the status quo. There can be different concrete schemes of action here—from preserving the government in power and simply holding fair elections, as in Nicaragua, to UN representatives' more or less fully replacing the state structures, as seems to be taking shape in the Cambodian case. If this variant does not suit the government in power, there can be only one alternative—the cessation of our military, economic, and other aid, and of political support in the international arena. We cannot force an end of the war, but we certainly should not fuel it.

Such an approach will not only yield us big political and economic dividends but also accord with norms of universal morality and solidarity. It cannot be seriously believed that, from the moral standpoint, it is more important to observe and extend commitments made to certain governments in earlier times, when the entire logic of a vision of the world was different, than to try and end the destruction of people and rid one's ruined country of additional burdens and prompt other countries to develop independently. What solidarity can we be talking about when in practice it develops above all into military aid to countries whose peoples are literally starving not as a result of natural calamities but largely as a result of war and political ambitions? True human solidarity is being manifested at this time by the other world, one which, despite political antipathies, helps with foodstuffs and other things required for people's survival. We, however, "helped" to such an extent that, even without new deliveries of weapons, so many of them had been stockpiled that hostilities can still be actively carried on. This, incidentally, is taking place in many areas where both sides are fighting, ultimately, with our, essentially unpaid-for, weapons, which demonstrates once again the absurdities and immorality of such policy.

Military cooperation is the main element of the structure of relations with the Third World countries closest to us who are used to imitate us in basing their foreign and home policies on force. It is practically impossible to obtain our official data on arms deliveries, all the more so with regard to individual countries. It is also impossible to learn how much resources are being spent on all this. The claim that arms deliveries yield us enormous hard-currency profits seems, at this juncture, nothing more than a myth. Of course, individual transactions are profitable, but they have long been cancelled out by all sorts of debts and gratuitous deliveries. The theme of arms deliveries is becoming increasingly acute in our talk about the Third World. It is becoming a self-sufficing factor of our policies, one which prevents us from maneuvring freely.

Arms deliveries, which are uncontrolled and not linked with the strategy of new political thinking, to countries where the situation is relatively calm, are dangerous, too. More often than not, our weapons are being stockpiled on a large scale that often tips the regional balance of power. Some of our steps to beef up the military potential in the Third World, including those that might, even indirectly, help the appearance of potentialities in the nuclear, chemical, and missile spheres, will sooner or later inevitably complicate the global disarmament situation as well. Talk about any "strategic alliances" and defense needs can hardly be convincing in this case.

Evidently, we will have certain interests in the Third World linked with our security. However, they are extremely limited. The specifics of our geographical location and economic development level, and the nature of economic ties, do not make it possible to talk seriously about our having vital interests in the developing world which need to be protected with the aid of weapons. We do not consider such interests to be the senseless race to establish our influence far beyond our borders, a race dictated only by the logic of preserving confrontation. Nor will we forget that even the most massive weapons deliveries do not guarantee stable influence at all, as was shown by the example of Egypt and other countries.

While remaining a nuclear power, we probably need certain military installations abroad to maintain communications with the submarine fleet and to carry out electronic surveillance. However, we need to weigh well, not only with participation of the military department, the scope in which this is necessary, and if it is necessary, then to see whether it would be cheaper to meet these needs through the development of space-based facilities. The tenet of the need for the virtual omnipresence of our Navy and, by implication, bridgeheads for supplying it evokes still greater doubts. It would not be bad if the military clearly explained how and what vital interests of our country it protects in oceans far from our shores. If it turns out that its presence there is expedient, after all, then it is worthwhile to weigh our possibilities and decide whether we can supply it there on a commercial basis. Incidentally, although the United States and other Western countries have interests in the Third World that are objectively somewhat different from ours, our restraint will inevitably lead to a substantial scaling down of military presence abroad, above all by dint of financial considerations. Demands for this are persistently being made in the West.

Evidently we are not prepared, like Czechoslovakia, to end weapons exports in principle. Economically, it is expedient not to stop this entirely; but they should be delivered on a completely different basis. For one thing, firm restrictions should be introduced that are linked with the undesirability of deliveries to explosive areas and of deliveries that would violate the principle of reasonable sufficiency at the regional level which change the balance of power there or introduce qualitatively new weaponry there. Such restrictions could be introduced on both a unilateral and a coordinated basis. In principle, the West is prepared for talks on this theme, if we do not attempt to make arbitrary exceptions for ourselves. For another, arms deliveries should be made on a purely commercial basis, one that would take account not only of current solvency but also of the prospects for economic development. We simply have no other option in our current state.

Economic expediency, not ideological and political preferences, should become the determinant for developing economic ties with the Third World as well. This will be ultimately profitable not only for us but also for the countries with which we cooperate. Other kinds of economic interaction corrupt more often than not. It is not fortuitous that virtually no country that counted above all on cooperation with us has been able to establish a mechanism of stable development, even though it has put up some major facilities and scored certain successes in individual areas. In our integral and interdependent world it is preferable for such a big and potentially rich country as ours not to fully stop rendering gratuitous aid. This is not only a moral obligation but also a certain contribution to the future, to its development and stability. However, the volume, nature and direction of this aid should be discussed publicly and promote what our country can do without detriment to its own development. In any event, the procedure for using it should be strictly controlled, including through multilateral mechanisms, and it should be aimed above all at the development of the economies of Third World countries, and, in extreme instances, at aid to the population directly. Otherwise this is both a waste of our resources and a disservice to the peoples of the developing countries. Our experience, and that of the West, too, for that matter, has amassed much proof of this.

Our approach to global, above all economic, problems and a discussion of them on a multilateral level should change accordingly, as well. We should be guided not by considerations of "unification of forces in the struggle against imperialism" and not by abstract slogans of solidarity, but by calculations of expedience based on the objective laws governing the economy, and by our interests. Considering our "intermediate" position between the industrialized and developing worlds, our interests in different matters can coincide with the different groups of countries.

Such a turnabout in relations with so many states will evoke a host of questions. What about our friends and our moral commitments to them? What about the entire "three worlds" concept and the West's role in the developing countries? What should our criteria in assessing Third World governments be?

Of course, every state and every people have moral commitments.

However, one should regard moral commitments above all to peoples, not governments or regimes. If we are talking about internationalism, we need to clearly visualize what internationalism the point at issue is-the internationalism of authoritarian regimes, the internationalism of the administer-by-command system which existed in the past and which has not died yet, or universal internationalism? If we are talking about the latter, free development and wellbeing of our people and other peoples should be our main concern. We cannot force regimes to leave, but we can honestly talk about changes in our policy, in our political morality. And if it is truly new, it cannot ignore such a criterion as democracy in assessing the situations in the Third World. Societies in the developing countries are different, and they cannot be made democratic overnight. But tolerance has its limits here as well. We must make it clear that our sympathies lie on the side of compliance with democratic norms and human rights as they are understood in international documents. Neither should we be afraid of insisting on international control, nor of determining our attitude to any regime depending on the results of such control.

It is important to depart once and for all from dividing the world into camps. There should be criteria of universal morality and human rights, a criterion of our national interests, and a criterion of the need to pragmatically tackle the development needs facing humanity. With whom we will be solving these or other problems depends on how close a country is to these criteria, not on whether this country is a member of our camp or another camp. An analysis, including a critical one, of the U.S. policies in the Third World is a separate subject. Unlike the earlier practice, we should determine our line not by the rule of contraries but by our interests realistically understood and openly discussed. Should they clash with U.S. interests we shall have to seek solutions jointly. In any other case U.S. actions should be of no concern to us.

The term "Third World" has come from the times when there was a split into two hostile worlds. Today, when we are trying to overcome the split of the world into two hostile camps, the term "Third World" loses its former meaning, although, of course, there is still some commonality in the developing countries, which is linked with historical roots and economic and political development levels. However, all of us are moving more and more rapidly to an integral world in which contradictions and problems will remain but which will be able to be solved only through concerted efforts. The quicker the legacy of confrontation is surmounted in the Third World, too, the quicker we will all move forward.

We and Afghanistan

Boris Pyadyshev

The war in Afghanistan has entered its twelfth winter, a winter of anxiety as well as of hope that the long-running disaster will come to an end.

I recently visited Kabul.

The sky is blue and sunny there these winter days and the limpid mountain air is full of permanent tension. The atmosphere in the presidential palace, to which I made my way in a car, zigzagging as in a slalom race between tanks, armored personnel carriers, and patrols, was calm and steady. Only occasionally did something like the sound of a blast or the roar of aircraft intrude from beyond the carefully curtained windows.

The president, who was wearing a semimilitary khaki shirt, greeted me in Eastern fashion by putting his arms around my shoul-

BORIS PYADYSHEV, USSR Ambassador Extraordinary and Plenipotentiary, is a Collegium member of the USSR Ministry of Foreign Affairs and editor in chief of *International Affairs*.

ders and touching my cheek twice with his. And then he said in Russian: "Welcome, Boris Dmitrievich." (The first meeting lasted for over three hours.)

It was my second visit to the palace. I first found myself there in the king's days, in the spring of 1973, when I accompanied our then president on his official visit to Kabul. I sat near the edge of a massive, richly inlaid table. Nikolai Podgorny and King Zahir Shah sat in the middle, with cabinet ministers and other officials flanking them on the left and right. The talks went swimmingly, nor could relations between our countries have been better.

But the flywheel of events, whose logic and trend threatened to involve us in Afghanistan's internal affairs, had begun to turn. However, that involvement was not entirely inevitable. There was a chance to keep out provided that we foresaw the impending changes and the morass that they could land us in.

An antiroyal coup was to have taken place precisely during the Soviet president's stay in Kabul. Of course, plans for it were made beforehand, without any knowledge of the time of the visit. The coup had to be put off, and the king was overthrown a few months later. Daoud took over but he was not fated to rule long. The April Revolution, accomplished a few years after, made us direct parties to internal processes in a country which is our neighbor, sure enough, but is an independent, sovereign state nonetheless. This circumstance must have been dismissed as immaterial by the ideologues of misconceived internationalism, which once in a while was transformed in the minds and deeds of our onetime leaders into something closely resembling export of revolution.

How the Decision to Withdraw Was Made

"Where shall we begin?" Najibullah asked.

"Could we begin from the beginning? From the day that the possibility of withdrawing our troops first came up between the Moscow and Kabul leaderships?"

"All right. We arrived in Moscow in October 1985. You had a new political situation in your country, perestroika. In charge of the talks were Mikhail Gorbachev on the Soviet side and Babrak Karmal on the Afghan side. I didn't belong to the top leadership at the time and found myself three or four seats away from the middle of the table.

At a certain moment, Mikhail Gorbachev said: 'We must think together about withdrawing the Soviet force from Afghanistan.' The response of the Afghan side to that suggestion was mainly negative. Karmal's darkish face darkened still more. 'If you were to pull out now,' he said, 'next time you would have to move in a million troops.' He put it just like that."

The president raised to his lips a quaintly worked square cup with green tea and took a sip.

"I didn't say anything right away, didn't voice my opinion. But when, during the interval, we came out of the conference hall I told my colleagues that Karmal was wrong and that his statement shouldn't be taken for the position of the whole Afghan leadership."

Sitting at the negotiating table was a man who was watching closely to see the reaction of our Afghan friends, to guess from the look on their faces and from their gestures what was going on in their minds. He noticed that Najib (that was the president's name at the time) was perhaps the only one to acquiesce in the proposed step. It was obvious that Najib himself felt that a settlement would be impossible for as long there were foreign troops on Afghan soil.

"I reasoned this way," the president reminisced, speaking of that dramatic day. "After the April 1985 Plenum, the new Soviet leadership initiated a great policy of renewal. But who could believe in the Soviet Union's sincerity as long as its troops were in Afghanistan? The Soviet Union and Afghanistan could fight the war for a long time because they had a sufficient potential for that, but what for? After all, nearly the whole world was against the war, and the UN General Assembly voted against us year after year. Everybody was saying that Afghanistan was occupied. More importantly, the Afghan people were sympathetic to the counterrevolution whatever we might say. A real revolutionary can fight to the last cartridge but he must think about the people first and foremost."

In the spring of 1986, Najib was elected general secretary of the PDPA CC and then president of the Republic. From then on, he was in a position to work to ensure that the policy of national reconciliation conceived by him became state policy. This policy was something more than a turning point in the destiny of Afghanistan. Its wisdom and humane character had an echo in Central America, Cambodia, Africa, and wherever else regional conflicts were still raging.

Easier said than done. Among the Afghan leaders of the time, far from everybody found the policy of national reconciliation acceptable. The president showed me the minutes of a meeting of the top leadership. Many speakers were sceptical. They wondered how the country could hold its ground without Soviet troops. Some asked their opinion to be put on record so as to be able to say "I warned you" in the event of failure.

In those days, Najibullah said that the important thing was to have a clear vision of the ultimate goal no matter how dim it looked at the moment. He spoke of the need to be prepared for the worst outcome. There had always been victories and reverses in history. The People's Party of Iran (Tudeh) had been routed three times but it lived on. Nor was the PDPA secure from defeat. But with Afghanistan still there, the party would revive. The LCST (limited contingent of Soviet troops) must be withdrawn no matter what. There would be no progress unless this was done.

All of that was logical.

Najibullah proceeded step by step in convincing his colleagues of the advantages of the policy of national reconciliation. They were getting used to the idea of withdrawal, but that was as far as it went, for no date had yet been proposed for the evacuation of the LCST.

This was done at a meeting between the Soviet and Afghan leaderships in Moscow in December 1986.

Majibullah said: "It was my first visit in my new capacity. I told the Soviet comrades about the policy of national reconciliation, about its gains and the difficulties it encountered. I spoke frankly, in particular about the attitude to the idea of Soviet withdrawal.

"Mikhail Gorbachev said on that occasion that the Soviet force would pull out of Afghan territory within eighteen months to two years."

Talks were launched in Geneva with a view to producing a package of agreements on Afghan settlement. Mikhail Gorbachev and President Najibullah agreed to meet on April 7, 1988, in Tashkent, to come to terms on their fundamental position on the issue of signing accords in Geneva.

Najibullah flew to Tashkent, having a mandate from the PDPA CC Political Bureau meeting held the day before to endorse the proposed accords. At the eleventh hour, however, word came that not all members of the Afghan delegation to Geneva were in favor of the accords.

This created a further dramatic situation. The president rang up the delegation from Tashkent to discuss the matter. The discussion bore scant fruit, for developments were evoking too emotional a response at the Geneva end of the line. A tense night passed. There came another conversation. Passions subsided somewhat, and predictably, it was common sense and realistic appreciation of the need for international accords that won the upper hand.

East Is East

Don't let us dismiss offhand the wise British poet Rudyard Kipling's observation: "East is East, and West is West, and never the twain shall meet."

People in our country and elsewhere say, mostly for effect, that that is all a thing of the past. But it is not, for East is still East. And it is as hard to understand and adapt to as in Kipling's days.

In December 1979, we moved troops into a country that is our neighbor geographically but was several light-years away in terms of way of life, tradition, and elementary development level. We invaded others' lives without knowing them, having no idea of how divided that state was because of the many tribes inhabiting it, because of distinctions in religious convictions, of hostility between the two wings of the PDPA.

"When I was a boy of seven," Najibullah told me, "I went to a distant village to see my old aunt. Before greeting me by touching my hand, she wrapped her hand in the hem of her veil. The Koran forbids Afghan women to touch men, even relatives under age. This is unchanged. Nothing can alter those laws and customs."

Prior to December 1979, there were only eight garrisons in Afghanistan's thirty provinces. The troops had to stay in barracks, and even the bazaar was off limits. The unexpected appearance of a soldier at the threshold of a house was invariably taken for sign of something out of the ordinary.

And then came the LCST. The country reacted very sharply. The opposition forces had been less than 30,000 strong until then and were armed with primitive weapons, including British bore guns, and Kalashnikov automatic rifles of Chinese make. But their strength grew fast to between 270,000 and 280,000 men equipped with up-to-date arms.

President Najibullah confirmed that the Taraki and Amin leaderships had repeatedly asked Moscow to send troops against the opposition forces. Could they have done without help? The president is sure they could have, had the Afghan leadership of the time not hung on so grimly to ideological dogma that led to disaster. Those leaders had proceeded from the fallacious assumption that all backward countries, Afghanistan included, had reached the stage of national democratic revolution irrespective of objective conditions.

"I think we are only just approaching that stage. Theoretical mistakes entailed a chain of practical ones, and the process of power monopolizing by the PDPA set in. A struggle began literally against all. In the end we found ourselves all alone as a weak party torn by factional squabbling and by a process of isolation from the people. Hence the requests for aid. As a result, the PDPA and the Soviet army came to be opposed to the people and the Afghan national movement.

"Our troubles snowballed. We lost confidence in ourselves and forgot how to act on our own. Not one of our armed units went into action without Soviet support. The Afghan army didn't exist as an efficient force. Neither we nor you saw to making it efficient."

Much of what happened in that period smacks of a theater of the absurd. To begin with, consider the irresponsibility and conceit of our leader of the time, who decided to move troops into Afghanistan on the advice of three or four courtiers from his immediate entourage.

The president spoke reproachfully of many Afghans in positions of authority who throughout those years preferred to hide behind the backs of Soviet advisers. The damage done was enormous. Many Afghans, including members of the leadership, left everything in the hands of Soviet representatives to concentrate on factional activity and a struggle for power. "The Soviet comrades," they said, "are going to build communism in Afghanistan, and we are going to live under it."

"Was that a parody of common sense?" the president asked.

"No, because that was exactly how they reasoned and acted."

That reproach can be just as rightfully addressed to us. Besides the several thousand military advisers, we have sent to Afghanistan a host of other people. There was a large group of party workers. Mentioned among them was one who had been dismissed from a high-ranking position in a neighboring Soviet Central Asian republic and was well-versed in the corrupt practices of its former leadership. At the Kabul Polytechnical there was even a Soviet adviser on water-plumbing. They marched in crowds from one ministerial office to another getting into each other's way and "snarling at each other like a pack of dogs," as one of our former ambassadors to Kabul put it, unable to keep his temper down.

Today the president recalls that with a humorous touch, but the humor seems to have a bitter edge to it.

"The Council of Ministers gathers for a session," he reminisces. "We sit down around the table. Each minister has brought a Soviet adviser with him. As the conference goes on the debate gets higher and the advisers move closer to the table, while the Afghans move away, and finally the Soviets are left to quarrel among themselves."

It was the advisers who often wrote the texts of high-placed Afghan officials' interviews and newspaper articles. You can imagine how Najibullah himself—a brilliant orator, a man of great refinement, I would say, a poet of political debate—must have winced at those stodgy writings.

The Test

On May 15, 1988, the Geneva accords came into force, and half the LCST pulled out of Afghanistan in three months. Another six months later, not one of our soldiers was left on Afghan soil.

That was when many Afghans found themselves face to face with a brutal reality, the need to choose between life and death. It would be life if they succeeded in overcoming complacency and reliance on others' military strength, in forgetting their quarrels and building an efficient army. And it would be death if they failed.

In either case the ultimate responsibility would fall on President Najibullah.

He knew that after February 15, the Kabul government would have to confront the opposition all alone, being at a military disadvantage. The more than 100,000-strong 40th Army had left. The defenses of the republic lay bared. The opposition's armed forces had overwhelming numerical superiority in the early days. There was no such thing as a real government army. What many tried to foresee was not whether the Najibullah government would fall but how many weeks or days it would last. The president was told, in particular by some of his associates, that he had signed his death sentence by signing the Geneva accords.

"Just before the Soviet pullout began," the president said, "Eduard Shevardnadze and Vladimir Kryuchkov called at my house. It was a warm meeting which my wife Fatana and our three daughters needed badly. My interlocutors suggested delicately that my wife and daughters should leave for a safe place in the Soviet Union while fighting went on and live there until the worst was over."

Fatana's answer was firm. "We won't leave home for any other place but will stay together right here. I will get a tommy gun and shoot if necessary. We're going to win together or die together."

(That proud and courageous young woman is of royal blood. She is descended from King Amanullah Khan of Afghanistan, who in 1921 concluded a treaty with the RSFSR. One thing more: one of her paternal relatives, Gailani, heads the Alliance of Three, an opposition group fighting the government under President Najibullah.)

The worst did not happen. The Najibullah government did not fall. Indeed, it is gaining in vitality. Najibullah refuted many forecasts and political appraisals. Those who misread the evidence are still wondering what helps today's regime retain its structure and hold its territory.

The president's courage and wisdom won people's hearts. While factional passions flare up now and then in the Afghan leadership, there is not more unity in it than ever before. The efficiency and patriotism of the army have been glowing in fighting, at Jalalabad, Khost, and Kabul.

The difficulties are enormous. Now, as in the past, the Soviet Union is the main supplier of shells, bombs, and other items of ammunition. They are delivered along an only land route, the Khairaton-Kabul Highway, and by air. There is no other solution for the time being. The other side is amply supplied with arms by the United States, Pakistan, Saudi Arabia, and Egypt. Arms convoys keep on arriving from Iran and China.

"The Geneva agreements," Najibullah said, "could have helped in bringing about an early end to bloodshed had all governments shown an equal sense of responsibility for compliance with their commitments on the principle 'treaties must be fulfilled,' and had they respected their own signatures to the documents concerned." He had said so once again in a message sent to Mikhail Gorbachev and George Bush during their December meeting. President Najibullah voiced disquiet at the manifest intention of the other side to bury the Geneva agreements. He believes that this disquiet should be shared by the guarantor states as well as by the UN. Military confrontation in Afghanistan after the Soviet withdrawal had not eased as expected. On the contrary, the escalation of extremist military operations as a result of efforts by some foreign countries had risen to a higher level. There was an increase in the number of foreign advisers and mercenaries fighting on the extremists' side. Foreign advisers were trying to paralyze what was a growing objective trend toward reconciliation. Extremists linked with foreign secret services and the drug barons delivered rocket strikes against cities from launchers operated by foreign mercenaries.

These are all incontrovertible facts. But there is also the fact that the Republic of Afghanistan has demonstrated in practice its ability to defend its independence, sovereignty, and territorial integrity. The policy of national reconciliation bears fruit. The president spoke about the activity of Foreign Minister Wakil and the efforts of Afghan diplomacy generally, about expanding useful contacts with the outside world. The program for an Afghan settlement meets with increasing response.

The president listed the key provisions of the comprehensive plan put forward recently to call a halt to the killing of Afghans by Afghans.

"We are in favor of peace talks between all the political forces of the country without exception, of convening an all-Afghanistan peace conference that would adopt a decision on setting up a governing council and on a six-month cease-fire. The council would proceed to form a broad-based coalition government and appoint a commission to draft a new constitution and regulations on the holding of a general election to be approved by the *Loya Jirga*. The leadership of the republic is agreeable to the elections being monitored by an international commission if necessary. It also declares for an international conference on Afghanistan involving all the sides concerned and for proclaiming Afghanistan a neutral, nonaligned, and demilitarized state. This plan not only meets the interests of Afghanistan but takes account of the interests of all the countries having a relation to the Afghan problem.

Some leaders claim—according to what the foreign minister of a neighbor of Afghanistan, for one, has told me—that an international conference cannot be called because the leaders of opposition alignments refuse to negotiate with the Kabul government.

"Is that true?" I asked the president. "Do spokesmen for the opposition really refuse to discuss anything with you, to maintain contacts at least privately if not publicly?"

The answer I got was detailed. The president named many members of the Peshawar Seven, the field commanders with whom a dialogue has been going on, often of a fairly positive nature. Two-thirds of the field commanders refuse to fight the government whereas earlier all of them fought it. The Soviet withdrawal gave rise to a predictable phenomenon. It generated in the opposition camp, once held together by the struggle against an alien force, such sharp contradictions that nothing is likely to help eliminate them.

What about the ex-king of Afghanistan, Zahir Shah?

On November 30, 1989, Eduard Shevardnadze met with him in Rome. Kabul perceived the meeting as an indication that the ex-king might play a positive role in putting an end to bloodshed in the country by helping bring about a dialogue between all the political forces of the country, the PDPA included, in the interest of forming a genuine coalition government on a broad basis.

Leader of the Afghans

Najibullah is by no means of humble origin. He is a member of the Pathan tribe which has traditionally exercised power in Paktia, an Afghan province bordering on Pakistan. Many of his ancestors played an important part in Afghan politics. Najibullah has inherited national pride and patriotism from his father, who served as consul in Peshawar and maintained contacts with Pathan tribal chiefs on the king's instructions. Recalling his past, the president mentioned compatriots who, like him, had been concerned about the fate of Afghanistan, the poorest country in the region, with the overwhelming majority of its population living in poverty. Their roads parted afterward.

Ahmad Shah Masood, once a schoolmate of Najibullah's at Kabul's Habibiya Lyceum, saw the future of his country in a society resting on stronger Islamic foundations. It is from this position that he is now carrying on an armed struggle against the government as leader of the opposition's largest military grouping.

Gulbuddin Hekmatyar, a graduate of Kabul University like Najibullah, has gone still further. He has carried the fundamentalist dogmas of Islam to fanatical extremes. Blindly uncompromising, he makes his Islamic Party of Afghanistan fight not only Kabul but other opposition groups, seen by him as not loyal enough to Islam. Bloody skirmishes with Masood's Islamic Society of Afghanistan occur time and again, with hundreds of rank and file mojaheddin and field commanders losing their lives in them.

Najibullah proposes to these and other opposition leaders interaction and cooperation within a broad-based coalition. He points out that power could be shared after all because the PDPA lays no claim to monopoly rule. The paramount taks is to end bloodshed and establish peace on Afghan soil.

Najibullah is the Afghans' leader. Why do the enemies of Kabul insist on his relinquishing his post? Why do they say this is the only way to advance to a compromise? Because they are fearful of the president's political prestige, of his personal leverage. Their reasoning is that Najibullah's departure from the scene would greatly weaken the whole structure of renewal. There is no political figure of national stature to take his place.

The president's political qualities are matched by his personality, traits which cannot but appeal to people. Before he was elected to his present post, he lived with his family in a small three-room apartment. He knows and respects the customs of tribes and peoples and looks on Afghan tradition and culture with pride. And he is versed in the Koran.

Najibullah may be said to perceive as broadly as befits a reformer not only Afghan problems but developments in other countries, in the Soviet Union, in Eastern Europe.

"The Soviet Union's new political thinking," he said, "is a real revolution of our times. It should be admitted that capitalism is ahead of socialism in many respects. We all used to advance slogans and theorize instead of coming up with initiatives. You can't feed people on slogans. That's the truth. The party, no matter how strong, can't accomplish anything without the people. It should really be the guiding and leading force but instead it often becomes a bureaucratic force.

"The situation in some countries was like a boiling cauldron with the lid on. If Mikhail Gorbachev hadn't launched perestroika, a terrible explosion would have been inevitable. When the idea of new political thinking was put forward, not everybody realized that Afghanistan was an important component of that process. We who hailed the perestroika approach were often described as almost traitors. But now everybody sees that perestroika has opened up new prospects for many countries, with Afghanistan as one of them."

Najibullah is prompted by the people's aspirations. I would even say that he proceeds like an Afghan nationalist although some would object to the term because it has long had a negative connotation. Yet originally a "nationalist" was one who championed the cause of his nation, doing so not blindly or fanatically but in a way to serve his people's interests. Surely this applies to the president.

Not long ago, President Najibullah and Eduard Shevardnadze had a telephone conversation that was amazing in content. With fighting going on in many parts of Afghanistan, the president unfolded a whole program for the peaceful rehabilitation of his country's economy and for more extensive Afghan–Soviet economic relations on a mutually beneficial basis, not in the form of aid from the Soviet Union.

The president said that the threat of a collapse in Afghanistan was over and the time had come to end the stupor in economic ties. For instance, Afghanistan could resume deliveries of natural gas or the working of heavy spar at Herat, not far from the Soviet border. The two countries could discuss building a meat-packing plant whose output would go to the Soviet Union.

Eduard Shevardnadze voiced approval for all these suggestions. The interlocutors agreed to entrust the agencies concerned with making plans.

"Since then," the president said, "the Afghan Council of Ministers has formulated a sizable package of proposals. We've discussed them with the Soviet ambassador. Most of them are worth being put into effect. But the main thing is to safeguard the normal operation of facilities. In any case, it's important to take a first step showing that our relations are moving to a new plane, that of reciprocity.

"That would mean a lot to us Afghans. I believe it would also be welcomed by Soviet people. After all, we realize that you are compelled to help Afghanistan at a time when you have lots of problems of your own. You distribute, say, sugar on coupons yet tens of thousands of tons of it are stored in Khayraton to be delivered to Afghanistan. We would like to reciprocate Soviet generosity, if only to some little extent."

I asked Najibullah what further efforts could be made to secure the release of our prisoners of war.

"We've been using all channels, including diplomatic ones," the president replied. "Nor do we decline the good offices which other countries and international organizations can offer us. On several occasions already, we've released from jail people sentenced by courts. We did so hoping for reciprocity. Here is the latest case. When the deputy chairman of the Europarliament's Commission for Human Rights was on visit here, we turned over to him three men we had pardoned.

"We made that goodwill gesture unilaterally and are willing to continue our efforts in all directions so as to bring about the release of Soviet prisoners of war. I also use my personal contacts, in particular confidential talks. I can tell you that this has already produced some concrete results.

"It is fair to ask: How far is the other side willing to cooperate? How willing is it to be reasonable, to take a reasonable approach? Do you know why I say 'reasonable approach'? Because one day they demanded 40,000 prisoners in exchange for the Soviet prisoners of war. Yet on taking stock, so to speak, we established that we had 2,404 prisoners, or 2,500, to use a round figure. In short, we aren't indifferent to the sentiments of the families of the Soviet prisoners of war still in the military opposition's hands. We will do all in our power."

President Najibullah can already be entered in the annals of history as the first Afghan leader under whom foreign troops withdrew from his country by the terms of international accords, without bloodshed and with everybody drawing a sigh of relief.

Alien soldiers, even if asked to help, can never be a source of joy when they appear near your house. Still less do foreign troops fit in with the atmosphere of a country like Afghanistan, where all that is alien is rejected by both past history—a long succession of liberation wars—and present-day reality, which barely stands out from medieval history and a past resting on Islamic principles and traditions.

So how about our further policy toward that country? I would say that if we want our foreign policy of perestroika to really serve our national interests, it must relieve us as much as possible of ideologized military commitments to foreign countries far and near, commitments that put a heavy burden on Russia.

But Afghanistan is a special case. The bonds linking us with it are too strong for us to shove the Afghan burden off without more ado. Heavy as it may be, we have no moral right, dear compatriots, to refuse the Afghan people further support.

The day I flew into Kabul, eighteen rockets were fired at the city. And the day I left as we passengers stood waiting not far from the plane we were to board, a rocket dug into the mountain overlooking the airport. The plane sped along the runway, took off and veered to the left, away from the mountain ahead. All the way to our border in the north, we saw nothing below but mountain ridges, snow-covered peaks, lifeless rocks. That is what the typical Afghan landscape is like.

Forty-Eight Hours of Risk

Boris Chaplin

On December 1, 1989, I returned home from work at 10:30 p.m., and about half an hour later the telephone rang. It was the secretariat of the USSR Ministry of Foreign Affairs informing me that terrorists in Ordzhonikidze had seized children and wanted to use them as hostages, and were demanding an airplane to take them abroad. Inasmuch as the incident affected other countries, the Foreign Ministry would have to be involved. The minister asked me personally to handle this matter; i.e., set up a headquarters and enter into contact with other organizations.

At 11:30 p.m. I arrived at the Foreign Ministry, and it can be said that at this moment an emergency team began functioning. Aside from me, it included Victor Zelenov, chief of the Consular Adminis-

---

BORIS CHAPLIN is USSR Deputy Minister of Foreign Affairs.

tration, Igor Ivanov, first deputy chief of the General Secretariat; and two other ministry officials.

First of all, we contacted the central headquarters of the KGB, which was carrying out the operation to save the children. In Moscow, the KGB's efforts were headed by its chairman, Vladimir Kryuchkov, first deputy chairman Filipp Bobkov, and deputy chairman Geni Ageyev. From time to time I was in contact with the chairman, and was constantly in touch with Ageyev. In Ordzhonikidze, the operation was headed by another KGB deputy chairman, Vitali Ponomaryov, who had urgently flown there.

Ageyev briefed us on what had happened. Thirty children between the ages of ten and twelve were on an excursion. At the end of their walking tour a bus pulled up. Some men stated that they were from the organization which had a patronage agreement with the school and had come to take them back. The children together with their teacher, Natalia Yefimova, got on the bus. When the doors closed it became clear that these "nice guys" were up to something fishy. The children were told to sit quietly. Weapons appeared.

The bus entered the city's central square and stopped opposite the Regional Party Committee building. The terrorists began demanding a radio. When they received it they demanded two million dollars. Then an airplane—one big enough to accommodate a bus.

The bandits threatened to blow up the bus if their demands were not met. They in fact had several cans of petrol, and they poured out some of it inside the bus. The perpetrators also demanded that one of the men they had once been in prison with, and also Tamara Fotaki, the wife of the head of the band, thirty-eight-year-old Pavel Yakshiyants, be delivered to them. This demand was passed on to the local department of the Internal Affairs Ministry and to Moscow.

The Soviet government adopted a decision to do everything possible and impossible to save the children. The order was given to get the money. This was not easy to do at night, of course. The idea even arose that since the money was to be turned over in sacks, perhaps a smaller amount could be given. It was rejected, however.

I want to reiterate the fact that one task faced all the participants of the operation from the outset: under no circumstances should steps be taken that could threaten the children's lives. Previous experiences, including negative ones, of dealing with hijackers were taken into account.

A joint headquarters was set up which included representatives of the Foreign Ministry, the KGB, and the Ministry of Civil Aviation. The latter was represented by the minister Alexander Volkov. Vladimir Kryuchkov constantly reported to Mikhail Gorbachev on the course of the operation, which was codenamed "Grom" (Thunder).

The perpetrators declared that they wanted to fly to Pakistan. For this reason we wanted to study precisely such a variant as this. None of us at the time could count on getting the children away from the terrorists. We proceeded on the worst assumption—that they would be taken away as hostages.

Meanwhile, Tamara Fotaki and the criminal whom the bandits had demanded were delivered to Ordzhonikidze. However, he refused to have anything to do with them, saying, "I haven't sunk that low." The head of the band, Yakshiyants, told him, "Let's say, we have failed to reach an understanding, you and me."

The terrorists repeated that they wanted to go to Tashkent and from there to Pakistan. These were dramatic hours. During the night a column of vehicles proceeded along the highway to Mineralniye Vody. Behind the traffic police cars was the bus with the terrorists and the children, followed by about one hundred official and private cars: when the parents learned about the seizure of the schoolchildren they mobilized all the automobiles they could.

Each of us could understand what the parents were feeling. Some of them were crying and screaming. One of the fathers, an Ossetian, threatened to hack the perpetrators to death with an axe. It was in this atmosphere that the cavalcade of vehicles moved for many hours. Credit has to be given to the staff members of the KGB and the Interior Ministry, as they did everything in their power to prevent excesses from happening.

We were far from Mineralniye Vody, but reports from there seemed to make us eyewitnesses to what was happening on the road to the airport, and we realized how horrid and dangerous the developments there were. Three IL-76 airplanes had been made ready.

It was the Foreign Ministry's job to explore all possible ways for sending the plane abroad. First of all, we were to contact Pakistan and ascertain whether the government in Islamabad was prepared to help us. Secondly, we were to ensure the plane's overflight of Afghan territory.

Throughout the night we maintained constant communication

with our embassies in Pakistan, Afghanistan, and several other countries and with the General Consulate in Karachi.

At 2:50 a.m., I sent the first telegram to the Soviet Embassy in Islamabad. It read:

"Armed terrorists in Ordzhonikidze (approximately four or five persons) have seized a bus with thirty schoolchildren and at present it is proceeding in the direction of the town of Mineralniye Vody. Their demands: to be given two million U.S. dollars and the possibility to fly to Pakistan together with the children and the bus. It has been decided to accept their demands for the sake of the children."

Further on, the following instructions were given in the telegram:

"Immediately visit Pakistani officials at as high a level as possible and, citing the instructions of the Soviet leadership, urgently request that all manner of assistance be rendered in receiving the airplane and ensuring the children's safety and releasing them. You are to stress particularly that no actions be taken by the Pakistani side which could pose even the slightest threat to the lives of the children."

A telegram was also sent to the Soviet Embassy in Kabul requesting the Afghan authorities to clear the airplane for passage over Afghan territory to proceed to Pakistan. The wee hours of the morning notwithstanding, when the Soviet ambassadors received these telegrams they persistently and tactfully explored possibilities for meeting with the local authorities.

Meanwhile, the cortege of vehicles was approaching the Mineralniye Vody airport. It was decided not to allow the bus into the airport's main area, since there were thousands of people there. The column of cars and the bus were diverted to a special route a short distance from the air terminal building. The perpetrators did not notice this, however.

Interior Ministry troops were already at the airport. It had not been ascertained whether it was to Pakistan that the terrorists would be flying. To make sure, we sent telegrams to the Soviet embassies in a number of other countries. After the exposition of the essence of the matter, they read:

"If the terrorists choose your host country as their final destination, of which you will be informed later, you will have to immediately visit the leadership of the country at the highest possible level."

These telegrams, as well as the first, which was dispatched to Islamabad, underscored the need to pay particular attention to disallowing any actions that could pose the slightest threat to the children's lives.

The developments proceeded in two directions.

At the Mineralniye Vody airport the situation was still alarming. Negotiations were being held with the terrorists. Efforts were being made to convince them not to take the children. The authorities even met their demand to be provided with narcotics.

At the USSR Ministry of Foreign Affairs we continued studying options depending on which country the airplane would head.

Meanwhile the perpetrators scuttled their original plan of flying to Pakistan. "It's a mess there," their ringleader declared.

By that time we had received several telegrams from Islamabad and Karachi.

Throughout the night our diplomats worked energetically to meet with Pakistani officials. The Pakistani side was understanding toward our urgent request. Admittedly, their replies were not very definite, although, frankly, the situation itself was unclear and changeable, all the more so since the terrorists soon abandoned their plan to fly to Pakistan.

It was proposed to the perpetrators to fly to Finland. However, they knew that the Soviet Union and Finland have an agreement on extradition of terrorists and refused out of hand.

At 5:00 a.m. the bandits demanded to be sent to Israel or South Africa. Flying to South Africa was unrealistic, as the distance was very great and there were many landings; so it became obvious that the only option left was Israel.

The Foreign Ministry, the KGB, and the Civil Aviation Ministry began working urgently on this variant.

Since June 1987 a group of consular staff members of the USSR Ministry of Foreign Affairs headed by adviser Georgi Martirosov had been working in Tel Aviv at the Embassy of Finland, which represents the USSR's interests in Israel. It studies matters pertaining to the exchange of passports of Soviet citizens living in Israel and with Soviet real estate in this country. A team of Israeli consular employees led by Aryeh Levin has been in Moscow since the summer of 1988.

The problem immediately arose of how to inform our people in Tel Aviv of what had happened. Since there was no direct line of service communication with them, contact was maintained through the Soviet embassy in Nikosia, Cyprus, where our group went regularly.

If we acted formally, we would have to send a telegram to Nikosia and summon the group head there. But this was inexpedient—we had to act immediately. We decided to contact Tel Aviv by ordinary telephone. There has not been anything of the kind in our practice. Relatives and friends would ring Tel Aviv, but an official high-level call from the USSR Ministry of Foreign Affairs was an extraordinary happening.

We realized, of course, that this conversation could become known, yet we took it. My call to Tel Aviv at five o'clock in the morning woke up the head of the Consular Group. I told him: "Georgi Ivanovich, terrorists have seized a bus with children and are demanding to be sent to Israel. If they fly to Israel we will be forced to request the Israeli authorities to do everything to help get the children released. Don't move away from the telephone."

Then I added: "We know that they know how to do this well." Martirosov asked me whom he was supposed to contact, and I named the foreign minister, Shimon Peres.

Meanwhile, at the Mineralniye Vody airport the authorities had been able to persuade the bandits to release some of the hostages. The children raced over to their parents. The other children were still in the bus, however. The perpetrators were bargaining: they wanted bulletproof vests and foreign currency in exchange for the children.

I want to emphasize the point that the Soviet leadership constantly displayed concern for the schoolchildren. Early in the morning of December 2 Eduard Shevardnadze called. One of his first questions was: "Have the children been fed?" I regularly reported the situation to the minister.

We received a telephone message from Tel Aviv from our representative. It read:

"Today at 10:25 a.m. local time I was phoned by Yeshayahu Anug, the acting director general of the Ministry of Foreign Affairs of Israel, and informed that several hours ago the control tower of Lod Airport had received a report from the Aeroflot information service to the effect that the Aeroflot plane seized by the terrorists would possibly be flying in the direction of Israel. He inquired whether we knew anything about this matter. I replied that Moscow had informed us in principle and that we were awaiting additional information. Anug requested to be informed immediately of any developments, noting that the Israeli government was concerned and intended to act in accordance with international rules."

In reality the Soviet airplane had not left the Mineralniye Vody airport yet.

We reiterated to our representative that he should stay put and await our instructions. I contacted Anug and promised to inform the Israeli Foreign Ministry as fresh reports arrived from Moscow.

However, the Israeli officials were worried, and we soon received another telephone report from Tel Aviv:

"At 1:00 p.m. Anug phoned the head of the Consular Group in Tel Aviv. He reported that a telex had been received here. The report indicated that the Aeroflot plane seized by the hijackers would be departing at 12:00 p.m. and would arrive in Israel at 3:00 p.m.

Anug asked the following questions:

1. "Can the plane's departure be confirmed officially through the Soviet Consular group?

2. "By whom was the telex sent? Was it an official Aeroflot report or the result of pressure by the hijackers, or was the message sent by them?

3. "What time is meant (Moscow, Greenwich, or local)? Please inform us immediately.

"The head of the Consular Group will await a reply to Anug's questions and instructions.

"According to a telex received in Israel, the plane is already in the air. If the estimated flying time indicated is correct, the plane should be in Tel Aviv within an hour."

The Israelis were clearly hurrying—the plane was still on the ground. The IL-76 took off at 4:00 p.m. There were the four bandits and the ringleader's wife on it. The terrorists had released all the children and also the teacher. The hostages from that moment on were the members of the crew, commanded by Alexander Bozhkov.

Tamara Fotaki was also in effect a hostage of the bandits. She kept trying to convince them to release the children and surrender.

The plane maintained a course for Tel Aviv. The estimated time of arrival in Israel was 6:55 p.m.

A telegram had to be sent to the Soviet embassy in Ankara requesting the Turkish authorities to clear the plane for passage over Turkish territory. The message was sent, and Ankara immediately forwarded its consent. We contacted Tel Aviv and reported to our representative that the plane had taken off and that it had on board the terrorists and, as hostages, the crew members. The head of our consular group immediately informed the Israeli authorities of this.

From that time I kept constantly in contact with Tel Aviv. The sides exchanged reports on the developments. We soon learned that the Israeli authorities intended to have the plane land at the military airfield not far from Tel Aviv. I immediately informed Eduard Shevardnadze and Vladimir Kryuchkov and other officials. Our reply was sent to Tel Aviv within literally ten minutes.

Now imagine this unprecedented situation. The head of the Soviet Consular Group was at the Israeli military base observing troops being brought there, the plane appeared in the air, and all this time he was talking by phone to a deputy Soviet Foreign minister, briefing him on what was happening. I heard through the receiver: "The airplane has landed. The Israelis want to know what weapons the perpetrators have."

Hardly had the IL-76 landed than it was surrounded by special army units. On the control tower were Defense Minister Itzhak Rabin and the Israeli chief of staff, who was in charge of the operation.

Our representative was "broadcasting live":

After the plane landed it taxied onto a runway, came to a halt, and shut off its lights. It did not maintain radio contact. The entire lighting system at the airfield had been turned off; only the parking area of the plane was lit. The craft was immediately surrounded by special units of the Israeli Army. One of the plane's hatches opened, and a terrorist appeared in it. A small group of representatives of the Israeli authorities walked over to the plane. They were asked in English to surrender their weapons. A "talk" was begun. At this time the crew slowly came out of another hatch. It was immediately surrounded by a tight ring of Israeli submachine gunners. One of the terrorists shouted; "Don't let the crew out!" But it was already too late.

Meanwhile the "talk" between the ringleader and representatives of the Israeli authorities continued. "This isn't Syria?" he asked. "No, it isn't Syria." he was answered. "It isn't Palestine?" the bandit then asked. The Israelis remained silent. "Then show me some inscription in Yiddish or the Star of David," the bandit demanded. He was shown a Star of David drawn on one of the many ambulances standing nearby. The conversation was now being held in Russian. It is impossible to reproduce in detail what was said at the conclusion of it. However, the terrorists threw down their pistols and came out of the plane. They didn't forget to grab the money bags. They were then taken to be interrogated.

Meanwhile, our representative remained at the air force base. He was informed that the interrogation of the bandits had begun and that the crew members were in the officers' club where they were resting. We reported the latest details to Moscow and agreed that we would get in contact somewhat later. It had already been arranged that the crew would have free access to the city and would be accommodated at the hotel where the group was residing. We looked forward to meeting our people. Of course, we were also interested in the Israelis' first reaction from their encounter with the terrorists. Later we learned that the defense minister had spoken to them personally. The expression on the Israelis' faces after the first report on the contacts with the bandits could not but evoke smiles from us. Afterward we found out what the matter was. It turned out that the ringleader had figured out who the "chief" there was and without a moment's hesitation offered the defense minister a cool million—half of what the bandits had received as a ransom—in return for "good treatment." Nor were the Israelis pleased by the terrorists' reasons for choosing Israel. It turned out that there was where they had hoped to be accorded an especially warm and cordial reception. One of the Israelis present even made a bitter joke about what anti-Israeli propaganda leads to.

It was becoming increasingly clear that the bandits produced the impression they should have.

The meeting with the crew was a joyous one, our representative said, continuing his account. The courageous men were embraced and given congratulations form Moscow on a job well done. It was noticeable how the tension began draining out of them. The atmosphere was informal although, of course, there was some tension, but a joyful tension. The Israelis were shaking their hands, admiring their courage, stamina and poise, and asked for details about the terrorists' behaviour and the flight.

The flight commander briefed us on the developments. It was decided to go on board the airplane with two crew members. To ensure the plane's safety the Israeli side requested permission to inspect it for explosive devices. This request was met upon the agreement of the plane commander. However, it was not that simple to get to the plane. Probably no other IL-76 had enjoyed such attention from correspondents and news photographers and cameramen. Despite the fact that night had fallen, the location of the Soviet plane could be determined from the flashes and the buzzing of the cameras. In one of the hatches we could see the navigator, who was giving countless interviews. Subsequently these photographs were carried in many newspapers. Finally, after the airfield authorities had managed to move the pressmen out in three buses, we made our way through the dwindling crowd of correspondents to the airplane.

We could hardly believe that just a few hours before a tense drama that could have become tragic had been acted out here. It did not turn into a tragedy only because of the courage and poise of these men, of all the people in Moscow and in Mineralniye Vody who ensured precisely this outcome of the operation. On the floor there were scraps of paper—the wrappers from packets of Soviet and foreign currency, a Finnish knife and two cartridge clips form a Kalashnikov submachine gun. Clips from which not a single bullet was fired thanks to skillful handling of the situation.

Representatives of the Israeli airfield's authorities inspected the plane briefly. No explosives were found. Then we handled the technical matters of the taxiing of the plane. It turned out that here at the airfield there was no coupler for the tractor to tow the craft. We decided to use the plane's own motors. The crew joked to the Israelis that it had no intentions of taking off yet.

Of course, three or four years ago it would have been impossible to imagine that the USSR and Israel would be carrying out such an action together, but over this time perceptions of the world have changed drastically, and what took place on December 2 at the military airfield 20 kilometers from Tel Aviv graphically illustrated the changes that have occurred on the political scene.

The main task for us at that moment was to have the perpetrators extradited. We sent several telephone messages to Tel Aviv reporting that none of the terrorists were Jews and that the people who had seized the bus hardly acted out of political considerations but were repeat offenders—criminals who had treated the children cruelly, threatening and intimidating them.

Later we learned details which confirmed this assessment. That Yakshiyants has three convictions, the last for armed robbery, speaks volumes.

We received a telephone message from Tel Aviv which had been coordinated with the Israeli Foreign Ministry. It read:

"The Israeli side is prepared to ensure the airplane's departure with the crew at any time. The Israeli side is prepared to intern the hijackers at any time. If the Soviet side considers the return of the hijackers on this airplane inexpedient, the following options can be considered:

1. "The arrival in Israel from the USSR of a Soviet escort group, including a special flight.

2. "Escort of the hijackers by an Israeli special group up to an appropriate destination, e.g. Cyprus, to be replaced by a Soviet escort group.

We could sigh with relief.

The terrorists were immediately brought to a prison, and each was placed in an individual cell. They were convinced that Israel would not extradite them to the Soviet authorities.

On the morning of December 3 our representative sent a telephone message:

"At 9:00 a.m. Anug called and inquired whether Moscow had decided on a means to transfer the interned perpetrators to the USSR. He said that if it was decided to send the hijackers on the same plane (departure at 7:00 p.m. local time today) with an Israeli escort, say, to Cyprus, the perpetrators could be delivered to the airport in time for the flight with an escort consisting of two or three Israelis. He requested a reply as soon as possible."

The answer was not long in coming, of course, Anug was soon informed of the departure of a TU–154 plane with a special escort group to Tel Aviv. However, the developments that followed showed that it was still too early to breathe easy.

As was clear from the telephone message which we received from Tel Aviv, Anug told our representative the following:

"The Israeli side reaffirms in principle its readiness to intern the hijackers; however, the legal grounds are being studied here for extradition under Israeli law. This may take two or three days. In connection with the departure of the special flight today the legal procedures can be sped up; it is not an impossibility, however, that the return departure of the special flight will be determined by a procedural motion. The Israeli side is prepared to receive the special flight within the indicated time span, i.e., today, or at any later time, after the conclusion of the legal procedures."

We realized that although initially everything seemed to be going rather smoothly, it was not out of the realm of possibility that the Israelis would not hurry with the extradition of the perpetrators and that certain difficulties had arisen in this matter. Consequently, we had to work still more energetically for this.

At 11:00 a.m. on December 3, a press conference was given for Soviet and foreign journalists at the USSR Foreign Ministry Press Center. It was conducted by KGB Deputy Chairman Vitali Ponomaryov and myself. Both the journalists and we were very excited. Ponomaryov described how the operation to save the children had been carried out and reported information about the perpetrators. I announced that a special group was heading for Israel to take the offenders back. Satisfaction was expressed with the line of action taken by the Israeli authorities, who had agreed to extradite the terrorists and return the airliner and the money.

However, it still was not clear when the bandits would be turned over to us. The Israelis alluded to the need to study the legal grounds for this operation under their legislation, which could take two or three days. It was obvious that the Israeli government was divided on what to do with the terrorists.

We instructed our representative to urge the earliest extradition of the perpetrators.

Meanwhile the Soviet plane arrived in Tel Aviv. There were KGB officers, legal experts, and physicians aboard.

At 3:00 p.m. we at the Foreign Ministry received a report to the effect that the Israelis had supposedly agreed to turn over the bandits to the Soviet escort group without delay; however, the perpetrators were intending to seek legal aid to request political asylum. It could not be ruled out that this would delay the extradition.

An important development occurred at this time. The Soviet Foreign Affairs Minister received Aryeh Levin, the head of the Israeli Consular Group, which was in Moscow. Eduard Shevardnadze conveyed through Mr. Levin his gratitude to the Israeli government for the measures it had taken to apprehend and extradite the terrorists.

The Soviet Union, the minister said, has duly appreciated the fact that the Israeli side has urgently taken actions, as envisaged by international law, to return the airplane and its crew and also to extradite the persons who committed this grave crime. We are grateful to the Israeli authorities for the goodwill they have displayed and for having resolutely checked the illegal act. Such norms of civilized communication among states, the minister stressed, should be increasingly affirmed in today's world.

Eduard Shevardnadze also expressed gratitude to all the Israeli citizens who were instrumental to the successful outcome of the matter.

Aryeh Levin promised immediately to report this to the Israeli Foreign Ministry.

Eduard Shevardnadze's reception of Aryeh Levin evoked a veritable sensation in Israel, as the team of Israeli consular staff members in Moscow were engaged in purely technical matters. Israeli Foreign Minister Shimon Peres stated that this gesture "is virtually unprecedented in our relations with the Soviet Union in recent years."

This event, as well as the press conference we gave in Moscow, made a great impression on the Israeli side and helped eliminate the vacillations which were observed in it.

At 4:45 p.m., the following message came from Tel Aviv:

"At 3:15 p.m. (local time), a report was received through Anug to the effect that no legal procedures would take place. Both planes together with the hijackers will leave late tonight. The technical matters and the flight time are being specified.

"The special flight has arrived as planned. I intend to meet the crew and passengers.

"Permission for their passage to the city has been received.

"I will send additional information after returning from the airport."

Late in the evening of December 3, the bandits were turned over to the Soviet escort group. Operation "Grom" had come to a close.

What are the conclusions that can be drawn from what happened during these forty-eight hours?

First of all, it must be stated that we not only thought, we acted in a new way. Our actions in this emergency showed that we realize that people are more valuable than stereotypes and act accordingly. No child or adult was hurt as a result.

Operation "Grom" may not have been very massive but it is unquestionable proof that the new thinking is paving a way for itself in the international arena. Who could have guaranteed several years ago that Israel would have returned us the bandits? It is very important that the plans of the perpetrators failed, for if they had escaped retribution their example could have been followed by many other plotters; this would have been a signal of sorts for other terrorists.

We have before us a concrete contribution to the worldwide fight against terrorism. This fact has shown that no one can count on the impunity of acts of terror, that states are displaying an increasing readiness for joint actions and for effective cooperation to counter this evil.

The interaction between the Soviet and Israeli authorities and agencies in this matter was something new. I want to add in this connection that the consular groups—both the Soviet and the Israeli—proved their value in action. The former has already been devoted much attention in my article. The Israeli group also showed a vital interest in a successful outcome of the matter and promoted this.

All this points to the value of the constant presence of consular groups—ours and Israel's—in Tel Aviv and Moscow, respectively.

By and large, all these events have confirmed that today the principles of civilized communication among very different states are being increasingly consolidated across the globe, and it is thanks to this that it has become possible to check illegal actions and save people.

. . . Before leaving the Foreign Ministry building in Smoleskaya Ploshchad, I phoned the Vremya TV news program and named the precise times when the plane with the special escort group would cross the Soviet border and when it would land in Moscow.

I returned home at 10:00 p.m. on December 3. Exactly two days and nights had passed since the start of those dramatic events.

Intelligence and Foreign Policy

Oleg Kalugin

We have begun unraveling the inconceivably tight knots of blind enmity and confrontation that seemed to have been tied hard for endless years, and today the dialogue between the two superpowers has taken on unprecedented scope and intensity.

In the United States itself, public sentiments are also markedly changing in favor of the Soviet Union; people there having started to talk about the end of the postwar era and about new horizons in Soviet–American relations.

All the same, let us not delude ourselves. There still are forces capable of hindering mankind's incipient departure from the edge of the chasm, of again dragging the world into the long night of intoler-

OLEG KALUGIN, a former KGB major-general, was for a long time connected with diplomatic activities. He is now a USSR People's Deputy.

ance and enmity, and into a nuclear deadlock. And if we were to continue drawing on the old approaches, on the propaganda cliches of the past, buttressed by the well-known postulates of the classics, we would almost automatically point an accusing finger at the "U.S. ruling quarters, the military-industrial complex, the militarists from the Pentagon, the agents and provocateurs from the CIA who are safeguarding the moneybags of the overlords of imperialist bourgeoisie," etc.

The revamping of international relations and the affirmation of the new thinking require a fresh view of the many factors which exert an influence on relations among states, including the activity of special services.

A great deal has been written in this country about the activity of American intelligence. However, propaganda cliches have invariably dominated in all the literature on this subject accessible to the man in the street, and they are invariably painted one color—black. Less has been written about our own intelligence, and that in bright tones.

In the late 1970s, in the wake of the CIA exposures resulting from the Watergate scandal, the Soviet press wrote of the "repulsive bared teeth of the monster fed on the money of unsuspecting taxpayers, a monster which trampled underfoot all norms of morality and insulted the dignity of an entire nation." It was then said of CIA activity that these were political intrigues and conspiracies, corruption of foreign figures, from police chiefs to heads of state, tacit financing of election campaigns together with dirty methods of fighting opposition candidates, use of trade unions, student and charitable organizations and the church in covert operations, manipulation of the press, links with the criminal world and drug abuse, false propaganda, economic sabotage, subterfuge, abductions, and lastly, paramilitary operations and cloak-and-dagger murders using the most sophisticated means.

Brought up for decades on sensational exposures of provocations orchestrated by the imperialist special services, Soviet readers would hardly concur with a different characterization of the American espionage agency. And evidently they would be right. But the specifics of the moment lie precisely in the fact that unlike the past, we can now view many seemingly established notions not in a programmed dimension but in the broad spectrum of different approaches, in the light of fuller knowledge, in development.

In any event, when I see in *Literaturnaya Gazeta* a letter from a reader who complains that the showing of the Japanese film *The Legend of Narayama* in the Soviet Union adds grist to the CIA's mill, I feel embarrassment for our press which has worked hard to impress upon our people that this country's economic and social problems are associated with the intrigues of the special services. But not only the press is at fault for this. Just a few years ago those at the August rostrum would have us believe that the reasons for the different distortions in our lives lay not in the defects of the system but in hostile encirclement, in the intensifying pressure being brought to bear on socialism by the forces of imperialism, and that the antisocial activity of individuals and the crimes they committed against the state were a consequence of hostile propaganda and CIA provocations.

Unquestionably, stereotypes of imperialist agents who assumed, depending on the needs of the moment or the whims of the leaders, the identity of Trotskyites, kulaks, cosmopolitans, Titovites, Masons, and generally speaking, "enemies of the people"—legions of ordinary people who, by dint of circumstances, or, more often than not, of arbitrariness, were caught in the meat grinder prepared for them, are still strong in our everyday consciousness. Many from this unseemly contingent have disappeared, but they have been replaced by others: ideological saboteurs and omnipresent agents hunting for dissidents and duffers, not balking about using criminals and bums and prepared to do anything to corrupt our society from within. There is some truth to this. But is it the whole truth? Has it always been, and will it always be, this way?

Few people in this country know that until World War II the United States had virtually no intelligence service. That is, there were national heroes, intelligence officers of the period of the war for independence like Nathan Hale, or the scholarly Benjamin Franklin, who engaged in gathering information about the British in Europe. Even President George Washington himself was not averse to instructing scouts before they were infiltrated behind the frontline. But there was no intelligence service. There existed intelligence-gathering units in the troop armed services which handled purely applied, specialized tasks, and agents of the FBI, which was founded in 1908, who executed some intelligence functions in Latin America. In 1929 a deciphering service appeared in the armed forces.

Whatever we may write about the aggressiveness of the U.S. ruling quarters, isolationism and a reluctance to interfere in European developments were the prevailing sentiments during the prewar years. Cordell Hull, the U.S. Secretary of State during the Roosevelt administration, stated at the time: We recognize the right of all nations to decide their affairs as they see fit, irrespectively of whether their path may differ from our path or even be incompatible with our ideas. Even though one could find examples when the United States did not always act according to this principle in the prewar period, particularly during the Roosevelt administration, it generally paid more attention to its domestic problems.

The war that broke out in Europe forced Roosevelt to giver serious consideration to setting up an apparatus capable of providing the government with current and long-term intelligence. However, it was only after Pearl Harbor, in mid-1942, that the Office of Strategic Services (OSS) was formed on the basis of the information coordination department. The former became the main organizer of intelligence-gathering and subversive activity against the Axis powers and the prototype of the Central Intelligence Agency.

The OSS was disbanded in October 1945 and its 8,000 staff members went to work in closely related agencies—military intelligence, the State Department, and the FBI. Until 1947 complete disorder reigned, in the U. S. intelligence community, if it could be called that at the time. Attempts to recreate something like an independent organization encountered resistance from FBI director Herbert Hoover, who had become powerful. The State Department was not favorably disposed to this, either.

The cold war galvanized the projects to recreate a strong intelligence organization adapted to the new realities in the world. In the atmosphere of fear and suspicion with regard to Soviet intentions in Europe and Asia, the Truman administration veered sharply toward countering "Soviet expansion" by any means.

With the arrival of Allen Dulles as intelligence chief, this political task become the mainspring of CIA global operations, substantially elbowing out information-gathering and other functions devolving on intelligence. At the height of the cold war U.S. government sanctioned unlimited use of United States military might by the intelligence community and colossal outlays for covert operations. Under Richard Helms the outlays quadrupled. It was at this time that the powerful and dangerous cult of intelligence began to be formed in the United States.

Then came the Watergate scandal, one public exposure following another. Surmounting all barriers and legal squabbles, the memoirs of former CIA staff members, who revealed not only carefully protected secrets but also the amorality in the CIA and its cultivation of force, hit the bookshops.

The U. S. Congress and committees especially appointed by it were forced to examine the unseemly affairs of American intelligence. Many prominent public figures in the United States demanded that the activities of the CIA be monitored more closely and that it not be used for political purposes.

As a result of the disclosure of numerous facts of CIA involvement in the internal affairs of other states and its unconstitutional practice in the United States itself, the CIA's activities were scaled down considerably. According to expert data, the number of secret operations declined to between 20 and 30 a year on average, while in the 1950s and 1960s the mean figure approached 300.

The Soviet Union and the socialist community accounted for the lion's share of the covert operations that remained. In psychological warfare, which became the main province of CIA activities against the USSR, the slogan of struggle for human rights was held aloft.

One of the men who opposed the politicization of the CIA and favored it being returned to the framework of the traditional intelligence service was Admiral Stansfield Turner. When he took the oath in early 1977, he began his directorship of the CIA by dismissing almost 1,000 staff members from the covert operations department. In 1986, already retired, he recommended that the government narrow the CIA's scope in interfering in the internal affairs of other states and called for a fight against excessive secrecy. According to Turner, the fewer secrets in the country the more serious people will be about protecting real secrets. Turner, believed that America should be more open, for "openness is the main advantage which democracy has over totalitarianism."

Turner's advice was not destined to be followed. The power politics that predominated in the 1980s injected its inherent bellicosity into the U.S. foreign policy doctrine. Galvanization of the intelligence-gathering activities of the CIA, then headed by the OSS veteran William Casey, logically blended with it.

In different years Ronald Reagan signed a number of directives regulating the conduct of covert operations abroad. One of these directives was the creation of a $19 million fund for CIA secret operations in Nicaragua and the formation of a 500-man special unit to which at least 1,000 Nicacontras were to be attached.

In 1985 the conduct of similar operations by other governmental institutions aside from the CIA was sanctioned. And this happened after the Bowland amendments, which prohibited any military aid to the Nicaraguan contras by the U.S. intelligence agencies, had been in effect for some time. During the Reagan administration the invasion of Grenada was carried out, weapon supplies to Afghan counterrevolutionary bands were stepped up, and restrictions on subversive operations in Angola and military aid to the Pol Pot "partisans" in Kampuchea were lifted. During his term of office a real war against Libya and Nicaragua was organized and, lastly, there was the UN involvement in the conflict with Iran and then a hassle with the American Congress over arms deliveries to the Nicaraguan contras.

Unlike the situation in the past, when presidents easily took decisions on using the CIA and the Pentagon in foreign affairs, Ronald Reagan repeatedly came up against a reluctance on the part of Congress to toe the White House line.

In 1984, when the CIA mined Nicaraguan ports without the knowledge of Congress, the prominent conservative Barry Goldwater, who chaired the Senate Select Committee on Intelligence at the time, expressed his indignation in a letter to William Casey, calling the CIA's actions an "act of war which is hard to explain." It was then that the Senate condemned this CIA action by a vote of 84 to 12.

In 1988 the Senate passed by a majority vote a bill binding the government to inform the Congress on all covert operations being carried out within 48 hours after they have been begun.

Today the public at large realizes the threat to peace and civil freedoms that is posed by the special services, which are not controlled by legislative bodies and the public.

Whereas in the 1970s, when the first disclosures of the CIA's unseemly actions appeared, their authors, bold people working individually, were accused of betraying the American flag and all but being secret agents of the Kremlin. In the late 1980s there are different groups functioning in the United States that are demanding greater supervision over the special services' activities. Public attention was

drawn by the initiative of former staff members of the American intelligence service who announced this past January the establishment
of a new public organization opposed to secret operations as an instrument of foreign policy.

Explaining the reasons for the formation of the National Security
Services Veteran's Association, its head, Colonel (Ret.) Rottinger,
stated that the Iran–Contra scandal was still another foreign policy
failure of the United States caused by the use of clandestine operations. Our association he said, advocates a more open foreign policy
and will attempt to limit the possibilities of secret wars and to exert
an influence on the drafting of legislature in the national security
sphere.

The role and place of the intelligence service in the power structure and in the
pursuit of the foreign policy course is being analyzed more and more critically.
The appeal for a new political thinking coming from Moscow, the practical
actions of Soviet diplomacy, the numerous international accords and the favor
able prospects for other important agreements have unquestionably been power
ful catalysts in this process.

We have often been reproached, and rightly so—true, to a lesser
extent now than in the past—for our intolerance of the views of
others which do not coincide with the official line. The absurd
lengths we have gone to in protecting like-mindedness are best attested by the mass repressions of the 1930s through the early 1950s.
Today we honestly admit that in the following years as well, our
prisons, camps, and mental hospitals were not empty, that hundreds
of talented but different-thinking people were expelled from the
country or left it voluntarily, and not at all because they were in
pursuit of riches. In our day we cannot hush up any longer the little-
known remark of Lenin's in a letter to Felix Dzerzhinsky of November 23, 1920: the reason for the arrest is criticism of Soviet power. It
is an absurd reason. Nor is the fact likely to be overlooked that articles should disappear from the new criminal legislation that enabled
the authorities to interpret rather arbitrarily critical statements by
citizens against one institution or another regarding one outrage or
another.

In all fairness, we cannot overlook either some aspects of the international activities of our special services; for example, how tensions
mounted in spring and summer of 1968 over the alleged intervention

against Czechoslovakia being prepared by the NATO countries. The Afghan saga, in which, as can be guessed, the intelligence service was assigned far from the best role, still has to be told honestly. We are demonstrating an enormous amount of goodwill in the international arena today. Life has made adjustments in the long-standing image of the enemy and to our approach to cliches that set the teeth on edge. It is not fortuitous that "The Big Game," a TV series based on a novel by Yulian Semyonov, was dubbed the Big Boring Game by the Soviet press. Political detective novels of this type are losing their former attractiveness. The widespread stereotypes are disappearing from people's consciousness.

Agreeing with pluralism of views in our own country, we have the moral right today to ask how the situation stands in this sphere in the North American continent. How tolerant are American laws of views that do not jell with the ideology predominating there? How fair are local authorities to the bearers of these views, including foreigners who wish to visit the United States? The point at issue is not so much legislative acts similar to the notorious laws on internal security and control over communist activity as extending nonacceptance of dissidence to international affairs and elevating to the level of state policy denial of the right of other nations to live according to their own laws and proceeding along their own road.

Is dissidence to be further uprooted by force? Should marines and subversive groups be landed, unsubmissive politicians be killed, and naval squadrons sent to the shores of heretical governments and people? Perhaps there is good cause to check oneself against the thinkers of the Christian church, to whose aid American presidents have turned on occasion. For example, against the great reformer Martin Luther, who censured sovereigns for forcibly imposing the faith: "It is absurd and impossible to impel by commands someone to believe one way and not another. Heresies can never be stopped by force. A heresy is a spiritual thing . . . and it has to be conquered by treatises . . . If art consisted in destroying heretics by fire, hangmen would be the most learned doctors in the world."

The record of history has shown that even if power politics yields an effect it is usually illusory and of short duration. In reality it has unforeseen costly consequences that are often opposite to the original plan. One illustration is Iran, where in the 1950s the CIA toppled the Mossadegh government, while today the United States is reaping the fruits in the form of a storm of hostility and hatred. Or Chile, where the Pinochet junta that seized power with the CIA's aid is disdained not only by its own people but almost everywhere in the world. Or the murder by CIA agents of Che Guevara, whose name has become a symbol and banner of the struggle against imperialism.

In his first statement after George Bush announced that Webster was being appointed to the post of CIA director, the latter also expressed a much more optimistic view on the reforms under way in the USSR. Meaning, among other things, the declared reduction of Soviet armed forces by 500,000 effectives, Webster noted that Gorbachev had shown in word and deed that he wanted to see the USSR a more active and effective participant in events in the international arena and that this committed the American intelligence service to "exceptionally difficult tasks." Webster characterized the Soviet leader as "an extremely skilful politician" who "has injected new life and dynamism into Soviet politics by insisting on a whole series of reforms which none of them could have foreseen five years ago."

Soon after his election George Bush himself stated that, under the new distribution of duties in national security, the CIA is to play the role of an intelligence agency that has no political functions with the exception of those which are provided for by law for executing certain secret operations financed according to all the rules.

The American press is interpreting this and other statements by Bush as a sign that the CIA is duty-bound to provide the political leadership with intelligence but should not take part in the policy-making process. Brent Scowcroft, the new presidential national security adviser, has spoken out in the same vein. In a report from the American capital, Washington press corps veteran Henry Brandon notes: "As to covert operations, [Bush's] view of the CIA, in contrast to Reagan's, is that it should be an adjunct to foreign policy, not an instrument on its own."

It is a known fact that national security is ensured above all by a prospering economy and the well-being and moral health of the nation, not by a big army or a strong police force. However, since time immemorial humanity has used the services of intelligence agencies; it has reconciled itself to this inevitable evil because a society divided into states and classes cannot do without it. It is an open secret that the years of the cold war and confrontation led to an unprecedented ballooning of the special services and to an increase in expenditures for their maintenance and for clandestine operations which are not always justified from the standpoint of the present-day demands and the nature of the current stage in the development of international relations.

Today every government needs a compact, well organized information service, for it is capable of functioning effectively only when it has an opportunity to see, know, weigh, judge, and change.

The danger arises when this apparatus begins for various reasons to lose its original meaning and goals and gets out of control. This occurs in a society with an insufficiently developed system of democratic procedures where this system has not become fixed and where group and departmental interests take the upper hand. Largely determining the qualitative level of providing government instances with information, the intelligence service gravitates toward monopolizing information and creating curtains of secrecy behind which "policies are made." The instinct for self-preservation impels it to perpetuate bugbears, prejudices, and fears.

An exaggerated sense of its own importance and infallibility, especially if work is successful, ultimately leads to a narrowing of horizons and develops an attitude toward its own goals as ends in themselves.

The deeper the intelligence apparatus becomes involved in the shaping and pursuit of foreign policy, the more confidently it makes inroads into the sphere of general policy, domestic policy included, and the more dangerous it becomes to the constitutional foundations of any state.

Today, as a number of foreign policy priorities are being revised, it seems also that it is high time to take a fresh look at the role of the intelligence service in the modern world, revive its original purpose, and rid it of tasks not endemic to it. It is high time to refrain from self-righteous indignation every time some unsuccessful spy (a scout after all) is caught by counterintelligence. The Soviet side has already set an example of restraint in these matters a number of times. With rare exceptions Soviet press publications regarding "incompatible actions" by one diplomat or another have only been reactions to propaganda ballyhoos in the West bordering on a hysteria that end in mass expulsions of Soviet representatives without any concrete accusations made against them or in a hasty decision to tear gown an embassy building in Moscow.

A more civilized approach to such problems is necessary. What is needed is a greater sense of responsibility and objectivity in assessing events, as well as restraint in working out possible measures and countermeasures, and a realization of the growing interdependence and vulnerability of all the participants in secret clashes.

In a democratic society the intelligence service serves the people, but it is also a servant of the truth.

To suit the ruling elite and contrary to the truth, American intelligence has been lulling the people with cock-and-bull stories about the "light at the end of the tunnel," with which it prolonged the death throes of the Vietnam war for may years. Oriented more to the needs of the Pentagon than to a search for truth, U.S. military intelligence has with its biased appraisals and forecasts done much to prop up the myth of a Soviet threat and of violations of disarmament accords. Paradoxical as it may seem, the CIA and the State Department have often corrected their colleagues from the Department of Defense, surmounting opposition from above.

It is high time to revise the canons that took shape in the context of the bellicose rivalry between the two systems. Greater openness is needed in what pertains to the official activities of the special services as government bodies.

In the context of the scientific and technological revolution and reciprocal on-site inspections under INF agreements, the absurdity of numerous restrictions, closed areas, and stringent secrecy regimes, which are at odds with common sense, is obvious.

In an interview granted to the magazine *New Times* the French historian Alain Guérin notes that "the obsession with secrecy is not in any secret service's interests. A lot of information can be disclosed without detracting anything from a nation's security. The preoccupation with secrecy smacks of paranoia." While giving credit to the competence and high qualification of intelligence officers, Alain Guérin nevertheless notes that "while having more information than others they seek to keep it from the public eye.... This may prevent them from taking a sober view of the world around them."

Lastly, public control is imperative. Without even wanting to, the CIA is far ahead of us as far as openness is concerned. Its activities are monitored by several congressional committees and almost two hundred journalists specializing in covering the intelligence theme.

One more point. It makes sense to stop just blackwashing one another and try to communicate with one another, as our military people have already begun to do, and not secretively but openly, to solve problems of mutual interest.

On quite a few occasions I have had a chance to meet with CIA staff members, although they did not introduce themselves as such. They were highly refined and educated interlocutors who avoided extremes in their judgments. Although I did not delude myself over their friendly smiles, I was nevertheless inclined to perceive them as individuals who were not necessarily burdened by class hatred for everything Soviet.

In 1968, at a cocktail party given in the home of Joseph Harsch, a prominent political observer for *The Christian Science Monitor,* I met former CIA chief Allen Dulles. He was already gravely ill at the time, but he kept a stiff upper lip and even joked. Evidently the host had warned Dulles that a Soviet diplomat was among the guests, and he looked expectantly in my direction. I declined Harsch's offer to talk to Dulles. My apprehensions that something bad might come of it took the upper hand. Today I probably would have acted differently.

Diplomacy, Kremlin, and Republics

Introduction to Part V

The basic issue of the Soviet situation is whether this power would go on as a renovated Union of republics (at least, a majority of them), or whether the present USSR would disintegrate into a number of separate states. The controversy is heated. Under discussion are options of division of functions between the Center and the Republics in the area of foreign policy and diplomacy.

Neither the president nor other Kremlin leaders, still less the public, treat as doubtful the right of any Union republic to cede from the USSR and become a sovereign and independent state. The question is whether it should be done in accordance with the acting legislature, in a civilized and calm manner. Some republican figures, especially Baltic ones, say that there is no reason to wait for completion of legislative procedures, that the republics have declared their sovereignty and that is sufficient. Their formula is: no divorce is needed if there has never been a marriage.

Well, marriages without formal registration are known to be quite common in many states. But even partners of such marriages would hardly part ways overnight if they had many years of living together. A separation would most probably involve a long process of clarifying each other's positions; and, once the decision is made, some time will have to pass before separation becomes final in the matters of sentiment, relationship, and, naturally, property division.

This is all the more true of states. After seven decades of living within the USSR (half a century in the case of the Baltic Republics), all the republics surely find themselves bound in a thousand ways to other parts of the Union. Baltic leaders do not wish to wait out the necessary period; more than, some of them intentionally push on to bring matters to a head.

Up till now, far from providing an explanation, they deliberately throw a curtain of fog around some key issues of economic division and security. There is no respite in the tension around the Russian-speaking population there. What will be the lot of those people? Shall they be *Gastarbeiter*, unwelcome foreigners, or just inhabitants enjoying no rights? No adequate clarification has been forthcoming.

There are two clashing streams of claims, dissatisfaction, irritation, and power play, one originating with the Center, the other with the leadership of certain republics. This detonating mixture cannot fail to manifest itself in explosions of varying strength. Full truth of the Baltic situation, for one, could be grasped only if an account is taken of the sum total of all the factors involved.

So, where is a way out to be found? Surely, not in setting against each other shoulder to shoulder in an attempt to topple over the opponent, still less in taking up arms which are overabundant there. There is but one safe solution: to calm, down passions, restrain obstinacy, and sit down at a negotiating table to discuss the situation.

One cannot fail to see the risk involved in the schemes to push the problem out into the area of international politics as a lever against the Kremlin, with the hope of forcing concessions from the latter. That is the kind of pressure that would be eagerly played on by those far from negligible forces in Soviet politics who have never taken perestroika in earnest and who have launched a large-scale offensive against the democratic reform in the USSR. Any outside interference in the problem would provide such forces with a mighty trump card to deal still more painful blows against the center-left bloc. This is as perilous to perestroika and the Soviet Union as it is to international stability.

—BORIS PYADYSHEV

Who Does What Within the Echelons of Power

Alexander Dzasokhov

Boris Pyadyshev. The structure of state power in this country now contains many of the elements known in world practice: we have a President, a Presidential Council, a General Secretary of the CPSU Central Committee, a Politbureau, a Congress of People's Deputies, a Supreme Soviet, a Prime Minister and a government, so that a king with a privy council is, perhaps, the only institution we do not have. All of these operate simultaneously and in parallel. What is the role of

ALEXANDER DZASOKHOV was chairman of the USSR Supreme Soviet's Committee for International Affairs, Politburo member, and secretary of the CPSU Central Committee until August 1991.

the Supreme Soviet and its committees in this structure? Couldn't they be obscured within the power system?

Alexander Dzasokhov. Enough time has gone by since the formation of the present Soviet parliament, which arose on the crest of perestroika and which bears an imprint of the unprecedented upsurge in political activity in our society. Unfortunately, we have not as yet managed fully to assert the parliament's style and methods of work and decision-making or to elaborate the structures and forms of its cooperation with the various executive bodies, departments, and organizations. We are still at a crossroads. True, it is life itself which makes it impossible for us to put aside the slew of current work so as to get down to academic, so to speak, laboratory research in the seclusion of our offices.

We have a host of urgent problems on the agenda, many of which simply cannot be put off. I want to emphasize here that the foundation of our activity and our view of the existing problems has already taken shape: it is the new political thinking which has proclaimed the priority of universal human values and which animates the perestroika in the state and the society. This applies to the political superstructure as a whole. As for our committee, we attach great importance to the major philosophical-practical conclusion on the need to move away from the excessive ideologization of the Soviet state's foreign policy.

Another point is that there has been a fundamental regrouping in the higher echelons of power. It is common knowledge that administrative functions were for many years concentrated in the hands of the Party. All essential decisions, guidelines, and directives for all the existing structures first passed through the Party. While the Supreme Soviet, with all due respect to its status of supreme legislative power, for decades merely endorsed the decisions already made or, as diplomats put it, engaged in preordained ratification. No wonder one cannot recall a single debate on any issue, however controversial, held at the Supreme Soviet at the time. Serious discussions, let me repeat, were evidently confined to one sector of the political system, the Party, which had a special status under the Constitution, notably in mapping out our foreign-policy line. The country's political leadership at the time had in effect a free hand, making the most responsible decisions, like those on sending troops to Afghanistan or Czechoslovakia, without being accountable to any body, including the supreme legislative organ.

Now that democratic changes are under way, such things are no longer possible, for such a monopoly no longer exists. The newly formed and logically structured democratic system (Supreme Soviet—Congress of People's Deputies—President of the country—government) has been working to elaborate, realize, prognosticate, and control foreign policy. But even today many issues are being worked out by the CPSU, and this is easy to understand, for it is still the ruling party, and decisions on some matters have already been made. Hence some of the delicate issues in our work. In dealing with certain essential problems of world politics at the transitional stage, for instance, we realized that decisions on these problems had already been made by the Party's Central Committee. Nonetheless, by their very nature they are bound to come within the field of vision of the Supreme Soviet and our committee, where they are thoroughly worked up and edited together with the documents attached, like any other legislative initiative. In this way, the exclusive right to make the final decision is being handed over in practice to the legislators, and this is well in accord with the Party's own line. Or take another example. We have received an address (or, rather, a draft address) to the parliamentarians of the world on banning chemical weapons. Our consultants (a fairly large group of leading specialists) have studied the address and made some serious amendments and addenda.

B. Pyadyshev. Do you mean to say that the Supreme Soviet's address was drafted elsewhere? After all, it was only recently that the "top people" made speeches on international affairs without bothering to agree on these or to consult with legislative bodies, confronting them with a fait accompli.

A. Dzasokhov. Such things do happen. Let me note that this is a fairly widespread practice in other parliaments as well, when the initiators of this or that political act present a package containing documents of that kind. I mentioned the address merely to show that the decision-making mechanism is beginning to take effect in practice. But only just beginning, although the main document adopted by the First Congress of People's Deputies of the USSR requested the Committee for International Affairs to table its proposals for decision-making procedures on foreign-policy issues and preparation of decisions along the lines of the Supreme Soviet and the state.

Consideration and profound respect for the constitutional powers of the USSR president are an integral part of policy at every level, and parliament should set an example in this respect. I think it is important to synthesize supreme power so as to ensure through its various units a democratic dominant of social development and progress. Let us note here that the powers and prerogatives of the president in this linkage of legislative and executive power are a crucial element guaranteeing irreversible democratic gains and processes.

B. Pyadyshev. You used the word "synthesis," which is somewhat confusing: a synthesis of presidential power and the power of the Supreme Soviet?

A. Dzasokhov. A synthesis for implementing certain matters.

B. Pyadyshev. Yes, but this is something unstable, something with elements of uncertainty in it. In real practice much will depend on who is stronger—the president or the Supreme Soviet—and the balance will be established accordingly, whereas in a normal state both the philosophy and the conception of the balance between legislative and presidential power should be strictly defined. In the United States, for instance, the functions of the Congress and the Senate are strictly circumscribed.

A. Dzasokhov. Your question invites a philosophical comment. I think that all of us in the present Supreme Soviet are much too prone to back up our arguments by referring to foreign experience. This urge is for the most part perfectly sincere, but I think we should try to restrain it, for the overall intellectual potential and the record of our post-October and pre-October statehood enables us to draw on our own experience as well.

B. Pyadyshev. We do indeed tend to overdo the reference to foreign experience. In discussing fines on motorists, one deputy even said that, as he had learned on a recent visit to the United States, they had fines of up to 700 rubles (at the official exchange rate), and suggested we introduce a similar fine. But there is no denying that our own experience of relations between the legislative and the executive (presidential) power is far from copious: Before the revolution, there was the scant experience of mutual relations between the Duma and the emperor-tsar; then there was a short space between the revolution and the Constituent Assembly; and after the Constituent Assembly there was no such experience to speak of or else it was negative. So that in this specific case foreign experience could perhaps be of some help. But there is, of course, no need to overdo it.

A. Dzasokhov. Now that we have arrived at the only possible correct conclusion, we shall continue to advocate an open society. Since we as a society are heading toward openness, we should be receptive to positive foreign experience as well.

We should learn to borrow all that is best. Since we have mentioned Americans, I want to recall the May Soviet–U.S. summit, during which President Bush settled some matters with the U.S. Congress. Until the very last moment he could not be sure whether the U.S. legislators would support the Soviet–U.S. trade agreement. This was not reported in the press, but it was no secret either: The required approval was obtained by way of consultations over the telephone. Indeed, we could also do with something of this kind. As you see, "telephone law" American style, in contrast to our own, is not a bad thing at all. Here is another example. In speaking before both houses of Congress on the eve of his State of the Union message, the President traditionally puts forward a package of proposals, usually on the budget. We have also had such a precedent at the Supreme Soviet, but a further step could be taken by introducing question time. President Gorbachev and all of us feel this could be useful. A similar attitude is taking shape to the idea of reforming the Supreme Soviet, in one form or another, of any forthcoming foreign-policy initiatives from the "presidential platform."

Here is how this was done before. The corresponding state organ prepared proposals straight for the CPSU Central Committee, and also, but not always, for the Council of Ministers. Today, all foreign-policy documents (naturally, of a definite caliber) are always addressed to our committee, to the Supreme Soviet, and even to the Congress of People's Deputies. These include, first of all, international-law acts, to which we are gradually trying to comform our internal legislation.

B. Pyadyshev. In this context, the USSR Foreign Ministry has been the first executive organ to create a mechanism for linkage with the legislators. How useful has it proved to be? Are there any similar units in other departments? Has parliament come to exercise any real control over the activity of the executive in the foreign-policy and external economic field?

A. Dzasokhov. The Foreign Ministry is, so to speak, a close relative of ours. Its response to the formation of our committee was most dynamic indeed. Its team of "liaison officers" linking up Soviet diplomacy and the Supreme Soviet has been doing a good job. This practice has fully justified itself, and we want to spread it to other areas. But there are some reefs here as well. In comparison with us, the Foreign Ministry is a giant with immense possibilities and well-trained personnel, and if we take a consumer attitude toward it, using its readiness for cooperation and applying it here for some reference material and there for an explanation, we could soon find ourselves in the role of a diligent and attentive listener, but no more than a listener. What we need to have in the interests of our cause, just as the Foreign Ministry itself, is an exacting, fruitful, and constructive partnership, a partnership based on the laws that determine our mutual relations. I am happy to say that the Foreign Ministry is well aware of this, setting an example in this respect. I don't want this to sound as a bit of pleasantry, but I must say that we find the Foreign Ministry displaying the highest discipline in responding to our and the deputies' requests and paying the greatest attention to our recommendations, possibly because of its highly professional staff. Thus, we have recommended that they train not only politicians for diplomatic service, but politicians and economists at one and the same time.

B. Pyadyshev. Your optimism is only to be welcomed, but it is hard to get rid of the impression that the first meeting with the minister in your committee went off much too smoothly, that too many compliments were made at the meeting with his deputies, and that the confirmation of a group of ambassadors was no more than a ritual, with virtually no questions being asked.

A. Dzasokhov. As for Shevardnadze, he was indeed confirmed in his post in an atmosphere of full consensus. But that is hardly surprising when a candidate for the post of government member has a highly innovative approach and a broad view of the close connection between foreign policy and internal problems. But even he had to answer some very sharp questions. As for the ambassadors, it was not as simple as all that, although the candidates were well known. At that hearing, we raised one of the most essential and complicated questions, that of the Foreign Ministry's personnel policy. We took a firm stand on the simultaneous replacement of two of the Minister's first deputies and the departure of four other deputies for leading diplomatic work abroad. We set forth our approaches to the future nomination of candidates for ambassadorial posts, ruling out appointment of nonprofessionals, on the *nomenklatura* principle, or for "long service" in other departments. We spoke of joint action with the Ministry in the nearest future.

B. Pyadyshev. Judging by the press and by public opinion polls, the Committee for International Affairs has on the whole a good rating, while the Committee for Matters of Defense and State Security is so far viewed with reserve.

A. Dzasokhov. I wouldn't like to make any comparisons, I don't want to be misunderstood on this point, because maybe some of the committee's topics are more controversial. This is connected with the army, with fazing, the pressing problem of a military reform, conscription into the Soviet army, with the dilemma of whether our army should be built on the principle of compulsory service or be professional. In other words, maybe.

Our range of problems is, perhaps, most frequently conjugated with that of the USSR Supreme Soviet's Committee on Matters of Defense and State Security, and that is why we have held several joint sittings. We have jointly sent a group of deputies to Hungary, Czechoslovakia, Poland, and the GDR, from where Soviet troops are being withdrawn, in order to monitor implementation of the agreements on the spot, and to see what arrangements have been made for the return of our servicemen and their families. We have also had contacts with the USSR Ministry of Defense. For the time being, we apply to them for select information. We are also planning to exercise our functions of control over the fulfillment and observance of laws by a number of ministries, departments, and organizations within our competence.

B. Pyadyshev. Your committee has to not only deal with present-day problems or pave the way for the future, but turn to bygone days as well.

A. Dzasokhov. The past has numerous links with the present, sometimes slowing down or even predetermining future decisions and the future course of defense. We saw this for ourselves when we had to take a fresh look at one of the documents which had played an important role in international affairs on the eve of World War II, and to make a political assessment of it. What I mean is that the congress set up a special commission headed by people's deputy Alexander Yakovlev to reassess the Soviet–German treaty if 1939 known as the

Ribbentrop–Molotov pact. The Supreme Soviet and the Congress of People's Deputies also responded to more recent events; the dispatch of Soviet troops to Afghanistan and Czechoslovakia, as I mentioned earlier.

B. Pyadyshev. The debate on foreign-policy problems at the 28th Congress of the CPSU sometimes took a dramatic turn. One could recall an incident reflecting the conservative attitudes of many of its delegates. President Gorbachev remarked that one of CPSU CC secretaries had even advised him not to go abroad, and the audience responded in support of the secretary. Hardly believing his ears, the president asked: "Do you mean to say there is no need for state visits?" "No need!" chorused the hall.

Such views are most unfortunate, for a party claiming to be the vanguard party should be giving the lead instead of holding on to these views. The president was quite right in saying that from the standpoint of common sense, all we have done in foreign policy has been done correctly and meets the vital interests of our people and international moral standards.

A. Dzasokhov. No special study has ever been made by the United Nations or some other prestigious intergovernmental center as to which is the most politicized society in the world, but I am sure that a computer-aided study of our society would show it to be well ahead of the others. Hence also our highly politicized parliament, As we discuss and ponder over affairs, our generation and the country's future, all our deputies—and I am no exception—differ from each other at least on some points, each taking his own stand. I have a stand of my own as well: I try to avoid hasty assessments and extreme views, and I cannot accept a blanket rejection of the past. They say that negative experience is experience as well, but we have never had that kind of experience alone. Indiscriminate criticism is the latest fad in certain quarters, and some have got into a rut with this kind of criticism, refusing to look around and saying that the CPSU's activity has been nothing but a sting of blunders. My view is that the party has been drawing its conclusions, even if somewhat belatedly, and that power is being actually transferred to the Soviets, albeit slowly and not without difficulty. And it is hardly surprising that the mechanism which has not as yet been tried out by anyone cannot function without a hitch. There is no time to be lost, but the changes are bound to take time. We cannot be without criticism and self-criticism, without a truly exacting attitude up to a very high standard, but only if it is constructive and creative. There is no need at all to turn down all we have done and how we have done it.

In foreign policy we simply cannot do without a past. Whenever we try to substantiate our present policy, to correct and find arguments in its favor, we cannot operate in a historical vacuum, arbitrarily severing the connections between past and present. We cannot avoid resorting to documents and international agreements that determined the postwar setup in the world, notably in Europe. Take our approach to Germany's unification. Why should we be ashamed of saying that we were always opposed to the division of the German nation until the emergence, not on our initiative, of the two German states? There are many examples of this kind. Thus, on the issue of nuclear weapons tests, the Soviet Union firmly declared back in 1963 that these had to be banned in all three environments. How that was done and what we have actually achieved is another matter. I think these questions should henceforth be vigorously taken in hand by our legislative power.

B. Pyadyshev. On the eve of the Congress and at the Congress itself, we heard allegations that questions relating to disarmament, and troop withdrawal from Eastern Europe were being settled behind the backs of the military. These allegations were shown to be false, in particular, by the USSR Minister of Defense who made it perfectly clear that the military had played a leading role at all negotiations, with a collective discussion and solution of all problems. Nevertheless, such views distorting the actual picture still persist.

A. Dzasokhov. As for our present practice, it is being constantly improved, and I am sure that we shall manage to perfect it. Disarmament talks are under way in different areas and not concurrently, but there is a standing Soviet–U.S. institution at Geneva, where we formulated the idea of eliminating two classes of missiles, and where we are now drawing close to a 50 percent cut in strategic offensive arms and to the elimination of chemical weapons. At another European capital, Vienna, we have been working to reduce armed forces and conventional arms. In short, political, diplomatic, and military issues at these talks are closely intertwined, and we decided to take a look at the whole complex. With the Supreme Soviet's consent, we invited both Soviet delegations (which consist, as you know, of diplomats and military men, practitioners and theorists) and heard them at the committee. In the course of a spirited debate, which sometimes took a sharp turn, we examined the whole package of disarmament problems, discussed them in the light of the need to ensure complete security of our country and its allies, fully adhering to the line toward parity disarmament. On behalf of the Supreme Soviet, we adopted a decision and attached a detailed letter expressing our ideas and our concern on various problems. All these materials were dispatched to the Council of Ministers, the Foreign Ministry, the Defense Ministry, the military-industrial complex, etc.

Such is roughly the mechanism of our activity, which, of course, is just beginning to take shape; such is the tendency in the assertion of our committee within the present power structures.

Priorities

B. Pyadyshev. World politics, like any other serious business, rests on its own pillars, or priorities, as foreign affairs analysts put it. We obviously tended to abuse the word "priority," announcing ever new priority lines, whose number kept swelling out of all proportion, so that virtually everything came to be regarded as being of special importance, paramount, etc. Is there any reappraisal of values in this sense? And if there is, couldn't our relations with the East European countries be pushed into the political background? What place will they take?

A. Dzasokhov. It is bound to be an important one, and I am not afraid of sounding retrograde, because, for one thing, we have too much in common, both objective and subjective, and for another, we have good prospects for all-around and mutually advantageous cooperation.

Let us take a closer look at this matter. Trade with the East European group of countries comes to 65 percent of total Soviet trade, and it would be absurd to have this figure suddenly vanish into thin air. Just imagine the harm that would be done both to our country and to the East European states, especially now that after the serious turbulent processes our mutual interests in retaining and strengthening our relations has once again come to the fore. And in the case of the GDR, with which we have particular large-scale economic, scientific, technical, and trade cooperation, it is quite possible to prognosticate some of its new facets. Why should we rule out the prospect of a united Germany reaching out through its "Eastern wing" for close economic ties with the Soviet Union without neglecting its own interests?

B. Pyadyshev. Did the events in that region come as a surprise to the "fathers" and legislators of our foreign policy? How do you assess their development?

A. Dzasokhov. Contemporaries of epoch-making events usually find it hard to appreciate the full depth and importance of these events and the political, economic, and social changes in Eastern Europe are truly majestic. It is evident at first glance that what we have here is an expression of the people's will, a striving to find a way out of the blind alleys of the unitary and administrative-command system. In a sense, this is a return to the traditions that manifested themselves in this group of countries in the struggle for real, instead of nominal, people's democracy in the early postwar years.

At major historical turning points, democratic processes (When these are under way) and an emancipation of social thought often go hand in hand with events which harm democracy, and situations of extreme tension detrimental to the country and its economy may arise. All of that was in evidence in Eastern Europe.

Some think that the events in Eastern Europe are a product of the Soviet perestroika. But perestroika is primarily a constructive and not a destructive process, and the constructive element has been predominant in the East European countries. Nor can one question the objective character of the ongoing changes, the fact that these changes were long overdue, just as they were in our country. At the same time, there is an obvious link: The idea of perestroika, like any other idea, is not confined to the national framework. As foreign affairs specialists, we feel this very keenly.

One of the views expressed in the course of our discussions with Western parliamentarians is that, having put an end to Soviet domination, Eastern Europe no longer has any need of its neighbor at all. That is a narrow, hopeless, and, I would say, preperestroika view. Now that we are building a pluralistic, democratic and open society, we do not lay claim to any monopoly in our relations with this or that country, but the bonds we have should not be severed artificially, for this would harm the interests of the peoples. The most farsighted and realistically minded politicians in these countries are well aware of this truth: while supporting the idea of broader contacts with the West, they are in principle opposed to any attempts to turn one's back on the USSR and act against one's own interests. After all, there is much more at stake here than economic interests alone, since we have accumulated a solid store of experience in the field of science, technology, and culture, along the lines of creative unions, etc., and these are our common assets. Today, there is a wide spectrum of fresh opportunities.

B. Pyadyshev. Unfortunately, this idea has its opponents, to put it mildly...

A. Dzasokhov. Yes, you are right, and I do not want to avoid this question. Every country has its diplomacy, its parliament, its head of government, and its people. The people in the East European countries duly appreciate the Soviet Union's role. But there are also politicasters, and their attempts to spread anti–Sovietism, lies, and slander against our country, to poison our fraternal feelings, are bound to be a source of concern. They will go so far as to denounce and distort history, even the history of the struggle against fascism, and will stoop to defiling the graves of those who brought the peoples of these countries freedom and independence from Nazi slavery. They are trying to charge the USSR with those of our actions whose sole purpose was to ensure our common security in the divided postwar world, at the time of the cold war, which could have at any moment escalated into a "hot" war. And when some groups from parliamentary and other quarters talk of compensation for the "costs" of the stationing of our troops (Say, ecological costs), one may well ask, Where is the category of justice? On that logic, Soviet army veterans should, perhaps demand compensation for their wounds, for the loss of kin and property at a time when they stood guard on the peaceful life in other countries.

One should not yield to such temptations, for this could lead one far away from the goal of building a new society at home, of building a new Europe, a safe and prospering Europe free from the burden of past divisions. Together with our East European neighbors, we could do a great deal to attain this noble goal. Our peoples have sufficient reason to enter into a pan-European home, both historically and as a sum total of their present dimensions; even today, good neighborliness means cooperation and support for one another. I think this is a worthy task, and it is well within the power of our parliamentarians, whose cooperation should be constantly enriched and filled with new content.

Economic Integration Processes

B. Pyadyshev. One could recall many attempts to solve the problems of regulating our external economic ties. In one such attempt, former Foreign Minister Gromyko was concurrently appointed first deputy Prime Minister in order to coordinate our entire foreign policy and economic activity. But it appears that a solution has yet to be found.

A. Dzasokhov. The question of improving the whole system of our external economic and trade relations is now of exceptional importance in view of the obvious difficulties connected with the state of the Soviet economy, with our economic affairs. Over the past ten to fifteen years, all our higher organs—the government, the Foreign Ministry, the Supreme Soviet (very hesitantly), and the Party—tried to approach that issue. Economic integration processes in the international arena simply clamored for an adequate response, but we did not come up with such a response. Structural changes are long overdue, they can no longer be put off; but we should act in a calm and rational way, with due regard for past experience, both positive and negative.

Some time ago, a state external economic commission was set up to coordinate and accumulate the various economic ties. At the time of its formation, we had at least several state agencies and departments operating in this area: the old Ministry of Foreign Trade and the State Committee for External Economic Relations (SCEER), among others. The formation of the SCEER was largely due to the rapid process of decolonization, being the product of the illusory notions we had at the time that the whole postwar world was about to advance toward socialism. In fact, its main purpose was to render assistance, often free of charge. What is more, we often went along with the ambitious designs of the leaders of newly free states and helped them build showpiece projects, ranging from stadiums and hotels to political party schools and nuclear research centers, although there was no need for these from the standpoint of common sense. All of this is now being reviewed in a critical light. There are plans—and the government appears to have agreed with them—to do this analytical work together with the Supreme Soviet and with our committee in particular.

Another point is that when the old Ministry of Foreign Trade was disbanded, some of its employees specializing in foreign trade went to work elsewhere, while the associations and enterprises that are now entitled to maintain direct links with foreign partners are often helpless and lack professional skills. This is not doing the country any good; efficiency tends to decline, time is lost, and opportunities are missed. Here is an example. Last year, over 400 delegations visited the People's Republic of China to establish business contacts, but most of these were only partially successful and more than 100 delegations failed to achieve any results at all. Something like 130 high-ranking officials from ministries and departments went on business trips to the FRG, but the results are more than modest, while the financial expenses involved are considerable. The cooperatives have nothing to boast of either. Legislation in the area is a shambles. So, all these problems have to be sorted out in depth without delay. I think that even such an apparently minor question as teaching people the business ethic and training Soviet businessmen should not be overlooked, for this kind of activity should be viewed in all seriousness and, let me emphasize, with due respect. What we need here is a psychological and organizational breakthrough because otherwise hundreds and thousands of our people will have to go on dealing on the modern world market as some kind of provincial peddlers.

B. Pyadyshev. It was something of a revelation for most of us that our ideological confrontation with the West had added, over two decades, 700 billion rubles to the cost of the military rivalry, that apart from loss of life the war in Afghanistan had cost us 60 billion rubles, and that 200 billion rubles had gone to build up a powerful military infrastructure for a confrontation with China. On the other hand, as it was pointed out at the 28th Congress, the "peace dividends" from the foreign-policy line based on the new political thinking could amount to 240 to 250 billion rubles in the current five-year period.

Let us now take a look at our prospects in the Third World, where we have built quite a lot and have made large investments, though not all that rationally in every case.

A. Dzasokhov. A tough question. A heated debate is on in the society as to whether there is any need at all to develop economic and trade relations with the Third World countries. Some even think that the only thing we did was to give away assistance free of charge. But that is not the point now . Inveterate critics should come to realize that the developing world consists of more than ninety countries, with huge reserves of minerals and raw materials and an immense human political, which will come into play in the foreseeable future and which are already on the move. And we are being urged to come out in opposition to that world and isolate ourselves from it!

We think differently. We should review our strategy and conceptions at root and go over from prestigious shots-in-the-arm and one-time-only economic and other injections to solid economic, trade, scientific, and technical relations oriented toward the long term and meeting our national interests. That is also the Foreign Ministry's approach. Let us bear in mind that we are able to buy some of the goods the Soviet people badly need only on the markets of countries in that group, namely, tea, coffee, rubber, and many other things. One could find new forms of cooperation, including joint ventures with other partners, say, from Finland or from Eastern Europe.

B. Pyadyshev. Preperestroika foreign policy was mainly oriented toward relations with the West, with the United States. Don't you think that we have missed the emergence in the Third World of newly industrializing countries, the young "tigers of the economy?"

A. Dzasokhov. Here is how I would put it. There were traces of some kind of political philistinism in our behavior. We believed that it added to our prestige to put in an appearance on the markets of Western Europe, North America, and sometimes Japan, and we failed to notice the serious qualitative changes in other regions. There is now on these highly prestigious markets a great quantity of engineering products and computers, to say nothing of the boom in consumer goods, all coming in from the ASEAN countries. None of that is found on our markets. We often have to buy the goods they make in London or in Copenhagen. At an ASEAN conference in Manila, which was attended for the first time by people's deputies of the USSR, they were asked again and again, When are you going to do business directly with us? Who is to blame for this absurd situation? Could the USSR prefer to buy our goods at higher prices in the European countries?

Our public opinion is also distributed by the truly large debts accumulated in our favor. I, for my part, am sure that the prospects are not as dim as they are usually said to be. With a well-considered, differentiated approach, there are ways of having a large part of the debt redeemed through deliveries of goods we need.

It is worthwhile to look at the promising markets of Turkey, and here we have been moving in the right direction. The first few steps have been taken in establishing commercial contacts with South Korea.

B. Pyadyshev. Still, when are we going to cross the Rubicon? Our trade with Singapore, Malaysia, and Turkey has been marking time, although everyone seems to be in favor, and no one seems to be against. Haven't we taken much too long to surround this barrier in the case of South Korea, having announced five years ago the de-ideologization of our foreign policy and trade?

A. Dzasokhov. That is also the view taken in the Supreme Soviet and its Presidium. This problem will evidently be examined as a complex, and we shall eventually come to face the Asia-Pacific region, where major political and economic structures have been taking shape and where one half of mankind is concentrated. Politologists and futurologists make no mistake in saying that the Pacific is the ocean of the twenty-first century. The time has come to put this mentality behind us: since we are Europeans (and in fact we are not only Europeans), we must work and trade in Europe. Let me add that the Western Europeans have no such mind-sets. Their trade ties have carried them well beyond the boundaries of the Old World. In short, a balance must be struck. We shall clearly have to develop toward integration, and to seek modern technology in the developed countries, but that is not to suggest that our openness will be without the participation of the developing states.

Now in greater detail about debts and assistance. The first thing this matter requires is glasnost, and clarity is bound to follow. A full list of the debts on all the positions must be reflected in the budget as a separate item. Then people will know that 70 percent of the outstanding debts involve deliveries of special property, and that their consolidated amount does not at all add up to $300 billion, as some now and again irresponsibly declare, but about $80 billion. It is a fairly large amount, especially for us just now, but in the existing world system of economic relations, we are not an exception in any sense. The developing countries owe the United States more than $100 billion, and they owe a large debt to France and other developed countries, the total debt being expressed in figures that are more habitual for astronomers—over $1 trillion. This is a matter of concern for many statesmen and it has been discussed at major international conferences.

At home, in our own government, our positions have been clarified for each country, and we, too, as I have said, intend to address this problem. Some practical advances have been made in a number of cases. There has been a marked enlivening of trade with Egypt, trade with Syria has grown, our business relations with Vietnam are being improved or are on the way to improvement (and this is a country, incidentally, where some interesting processes have been under way in the basic structures with evidence of a commitment to alter the existing situation).

The question of aid in the form of grants has been raised in sharp terms in parliament and in the society. The term itself contains a solid share of misunderstanding. The aid and privileges accorded to this or that country are essentially different concepts. Besides, aid as such has long since become a norm of modern interstate relations. It is a manifestation both of farsightedness and of a certain philosophical and moral state of the international community. Each of its constituent states in this interconnected world does not want to take the way of self-isolation.

Our parliament has subjected this sphere to thorough examination and stocktaking, and it has reached this conclusion: we still have to give aid, but within reasonable limits; and the main thing is that it has to be given within the framework of our present possibilities.

B. Pyadyshev. How are we to react to attempts at discrimination in trade or attempts to lay down various conditions? Thus, the United States has linked the approval of a trade agreement with us in the Congress to our adoption of an emigration law. Does that not amount to interference in our internal affairs and in the legislative process? We seem to have accepted that.

A. Dzasokhov. "Accepted" is not the right word, in this case. Having signed an agreement on the level of the President, the American side appended a commentary that it would be passed on to the Congress after the adoption of our emigration law. We, for our part, will be adopting the law regardless of any agreement.

B. Pyadyshev. Let that be so, but this is not the first case. A similar "commentary" was made one day in the form of the Jackson–Vanick amendment, and a similar agreement turned out to be blocked for 15 to 16 years.

A. Dzasokhov. Elements of relapses into the past do, of course, appear here and there, and from the rostrum of the Supreme Soviet I drew the attention of the U.S. Congress to the destructive character of such an approach. But a look at the realities of the present day and an analysis of the principal trends in Soviet–American relations will show that U.S. policy has also been changing. Positive processes are under way. Take the field of disarmament and, indeed, the fact itself that a trade agreement has been signed. How is one best to act? Is one to strike the pose of some kind of controller of relations between the administration and the legislator? This is a fine matter. Or, in view of our common interest and the corresponding public frame of mind in our country and in the United States, is one to seek a consensus, to advance, even if only in terms of supporting the agreements signed by the presidents? In short, what is one to opt for? are we to take umbrage or strive for wisdom? One thing is certain: the Congress and the Supreme Soviet could make a greater contribution; our contacts must be more dynamic, more meaningful, and more productive.

B. Pyadyshev. Why is it then that a hiatus has occurred with the law on entries and departures? It was, after all, to have been considered before the summer talks and irrespective of them.

A. Dzasokhov. What is more, in practice these provisions are already in operation and the right to come and go is already being widely realized. In 1989, more than 240,000 persons left the country without undue formalities. We have had two readings of these laws, and have repeatedly examined them in Supreme Soviet committees and discussed them in the press. In view of all that, we had to defer them at the spring session because of the extreme lack of time. It was simply impossible to postpone other legislative acts, and their realization de facto without de jure recognition was unfeasible. There was the government's program, the law on property, and others of key significance for the perestroika as a whole.

The hiatus, as you put it, also occurred because the discussion brought out the need, after all, to pull up and orient the departments to practical steps in realizing the provisions of these laws. And if they are to traverse their established way, there is no need at all for anyone to be nudged or prompted, especially from abroad.

One has to admit that the interest in this part of our legislation is tremendous, but there is no need to dramatize the situation. Anyone wishing to be convinced of this can do so by making an objective assessment of the situation. The matter will altogether go away of itself somewhat earlier or somewhat later. Parliament is prepared to complete its work on it.

Parliamentary Latitudes and Longitudes

B. Pyadyshev. How fruitful are the contacts with our colleagues abroad, judging from the report in the press that last year members of parliament spent eighteen times more on trips abroad than they did in the past?

A. Dzasokhov. There has truly been a rapid growth of parliamentary ties, and their effectiveness should not be assessed according to financial accounts, but according to the much more meaningful political account. Let me say this right away, so as not to return to the matter later on. We must learn to economize on money, and this goes for our deputies as well.

Dozens of new and interesting men and women with original views, knowledge, and nonstandard approaches, have entered the arena of vigorous parliamentary political activity. Their speeches in the chambers and in the press are of intense interest to foreign observers, members of parliament, and representatives of political movements and forces, interest that is now and again close to sensational. Hence the urge of our partners to take a selective approach to invitations. This is, generally speaking, not a very widely accepted form, and we ourselves are unable in advance to decide whom to send to this or that forum or meeting. We are not guided by the popularity of this or that individual, but by his or her professional standards and many other things, including the knowledge of foreign languages and, indeed, the time they can spare. In this case, it is only right that we should have the last say, and we stand for serious specialization. Otherwise, it is only a short run to some mechanical rota system or the timing of trips to deputy vacations.

B. Pyadyshev. It is said that trips by members of parliament to many countries proceed along one and the same scheme. Everyone starts from scratch, without any information concerning the results achieved by his or her colleagues.

A. Dzasokhov. I can quite imagine something of the sort. I have been told that in Finland, where we have broad contacts, written answers in the Russian language have been prepared to questions which our compatriots ask them again and again. But seriously speaking, let me say this: We have complaints about Soviet representatives abroad when they fail to give the red light to "tourists" at the state expenses, when they do not take part in preparing the trips which could and should yield concrete results. But we, for our part, should also see to it that the embassy or other Soviet institution should not learn about the arrival of a parliamentary delegation or a deputy from the local press or after the visitors have departed.

B. Pyadyshev. Foreign policy is said to be a continuation of internal policy. Many things have been changing at home. Features of a renewed federation have been appearing. Union and autonomous republics, which are historically shaped regions of Russia, already insist on an extension of their rights and on participation in international affairs. The role of republican ministries of foreign affairs is being activated.

A. Dzasokhov. I think that it is with respect to this problem that we need to change most fundamentally. While being a federal state, we have grown accustomed, even psychologically, to assume that in practice, and not by declarations, external relations are a prerogative of the center. I know from my own experience that it is no easy thing to get rid of the habit. But then it is not all that hard either; after all, we do not have to alter our angle of vision by 180 degrees. The principled foreign-policy and external economic decisions bearing on the problems of ensuring peace and security, defense of the state borders, sovereignty of the Union, etc., continue to be the object of concern and responsibility of Union legislative and executive organs. On the other hand, many other things are taking their right place. The important thing is to make rational use of the new opportunities. Not everyone has been able to do so. One of my Supreme Soviet colleagues even raised, from the rostrum, the question of all our republics joining the United Nations, without having properly looked into the matter, nor into the effects of such a decision, say, from the standpoint of finance, advisability or, let us say, real possibility. Later on he himself explained in a personal conversation that his speech was simply a discourse on the subject. Needless to say, his choice of place and topic were clearly unfortunate.

The principled approach consists in all of us primarily seeking general national accord, for it alone makes our foreign policy powerful, strong, and dynamic. Generally speaking, a member of parliament working in the international section, a diplomat, a specialist in external economic relations finds it much easier to realize our challenging tasks when he feels that he has a country behind him that is united in a common quest for the right decisions. We must be a patriotic generation in the spirit of the times in which we live and which are oriented toward new world values, toward man and his wants. Indeed, those who want to establish a dual system of values—one for themselves, and another for others—are very, very wrong.

B. Pyadyshev. What is the atmosphere in the "team" you lead? Do you have a pluralism of views, and if you do, how does this tell on your work? Is it easy to get people to act in unison when there is a difference of views?

A. Dzasokhov. There is no unity of views today even in the society. Unfortunately, there is not always unity of action in its various sections. We, for our part, cannot afford that kind of luxury. We have the duty to find optimal decisions and act on them together in virtue of our responsibility to our electorate and to the Supreme Soviet. But it is also a consciousness of necessity. We have become convinced that truth does, indeed, emerge in a clash of opinions, in polemics, in discussions. That is something we are short of. And not on some particular matters or on tactical issues. Now and again there are diametrically opposite standpoints. Take Afghanistan. We have both those whom we call former "internationalist-soldiers" and those who adhere to the formula of the document adopted at the Congress in December and who are straightforwardly critical. Do we have to try to get them to think alike or is it better to take a decision with an eye to the existence of these views, regardless of whether they are written into the decision or not, but always bearing them in mind? After all, the members of the committee, the members of parliament come from the people and reflect the attitudes of this or that part of the people.

We have some very sharp discussions between professional politologists. We have on our committee academician Georgi Arbatov. He has his own concepts of the necessary scale of state orders to the arms industry for the armed forces, while V. N. Lobov, first deputy Chief of the General Staff, a member of the committee, may have another view. But that is not a cause for division, but only the sign of freedom of view. Nor are we hampered by the fact that some of our comrades represent the attitudes of definite social forces and groups. In the search for the truth they never resort to their assistance in order to put pressure on me or on the committee as a whole. We adhere to the principle that truth is the best proof.

We are short of professional diplomats specializing in international affairs. There is a clear shortage of them even in the country's corps of deputies. Even those who hold the rank of ambassador are now no longer directly connected with work at the Foreign Ministry. Let us bear in mind that within this whole powerful and authoritative department the minister alone, is according to the law, not entitled to be a member of parliament, because he is a member of the government. I am, on the whole, satisfied with the creative working atmosphere. As for personal characteristics, I am not entitled to give any, even if only for ethical reasons. Let me say this: I have had occasion to work with people endowed with the most important dignity for their activity—a supreme sense of civic responsibility.

The Ukraine, the UN, and World Diplomacy

A. Zlenko

The Ukraine Enters into Direct Contacts with the Outside World

B. Pyadyshev: Our conversation began in Kiev. It continued in New York when we met at the 45th Session of the UN General Assembly.

The Ukraine is one of the founding countries of the United Nations, and the UN direction has been of key importance throughout the postwar decades. Ukrainians took a direct part in the drafting of the UN Charter. Twice, in 1948–1949 and 1984–1985, the Ukraine was elected to the Security Council, this most important body of the world organization. The Ukraine is a member of fifteen international

---

A. ZLENKO is Foreign Minister of the Ukraine.

organizations and has taken part in over sixty permanent or temporary bodies of these organizations.

Presumably, the General Assembly session gives a chance for progress with the plans to raise Ukrainian diplomacy to a much higher level. Furthermore, the current session is unusual. A world meeting in the interests of children was held at UN headquarters. Aside from foreign ministers, several dozen presidents and prime ministers gathered in New York.

A. Zlenko: Reverting back to your words about the UN direction being of key importance for the Ukrainian Foreign Ministry, I want to say that it is still one of foremost significance for Ukrainian diplomacy, especially today, when the UN is gaining momentum and winning worldwide recognition. Over the decades of our participation in different forms of multilateral cooperation we have gained a taste for this work and amassed considerable experience. All this is helping us to better reanalyze the performance of the Ukrainian Foreign Ministry and reorient it to fresh approaches and chiefly to the establishment of bilateral relations with foreign states. I am proud to say that a collective of like-minded people has taken shape at the ministry. For us, there is no task more urgent and important than implementing the provisions of the Declaration on the State Sovereignty of the Ukraine. Section 10 ("International Relations") reads:

> The Ukrainian Soviet Socialist Republic as a subject of international law shall maintain relations with other states, conclude agreements with them, exchange diplomatic, consular and trade missions... and take a direct part in the European process and European structures.

B. Pyadyshev: Strictly speaking, there is nothing here that runs counter to the provisions of the present Ukrainian Constitution of 1978.

A. Zlenko: The structural forms are old but the ideas are new. We haven't the slightest doubt that full exercise by all the constituent republics of their constitutional rights not only did not run counter to the Soviet Union's interests in the past but also would protect it against many complexities today. But we will not recall the past—we must look ahead.

Over the three weeks of our stay in New York there were meetings with my colleagues from Australia, Hungary, Canada, Poland, Romania, Turkey, Czechoslovakia, and Yugoslavia and contacts with North Korea, the United States, and many other countries. I had a detailed talk with Foreign Minister Eduard Shevardnadze.

B. Pyadyshev: As far as I know, of the long line of meetings which Minister Shevardnadze had during his stay in New York, the one he held with you was his first.

A. Zlenko: This was a talk not about giving the facade a fresh coat of paint, but about giving the home a new layout. No one will be surprised if Portugal consults with Spain concerning its key foreign policy issues, and Austria, with Germany. Fate has determined that, geographically, we are neighbors, ethnically, relatives, and economically, partners. Just as no one will find it strange that the countries of the European community coordinate their stands prior to major international forums. We regard this as an example for relations among the republics in future.

Today the Ukraine is entering into direct contacts with the outside world. Hungarian president Arpad Göncz paid an official visit to the republic from September 27 to 29. We consider the Joint Statement which he and Chairman of the Supreme Soviet of the Ukraine L. Kravchuk made, a major event.

Polish Foreign Minister Krzysztof Skubiszewski, with whom I had a fruitful exchange of views, was in Kiev on October 13–14 on an official visit. We signed the Declaration on Principles and Guidelines for the Development of Ukrainian–Polish Relations. There are to be visits and meetings with ministers from other countries. A wide spectrum of issues are considered, and forms of diplomatic representations that accord with our needs and possibilities are usually discussed.

You know, during a talk with me Czechoslovak Foreign Minister Jiři Dienstbier declared for the establishment of diplomatic relations with all republics, and he added, "We'll be ruined otherwise." While being sympathetic to Czechoslovakia, I venture to assume that things are a bit worse in the Ukraine. Our foreign ministry simply does not have its own currency budget; in other words, it has nothing with which to pursue foreign policy as provided for by the Declaration. While not understating in the least the financial situation of the Ukraine and the need to meet the population's prime needs, I remain a committed supporter of developing direct bilateral ties between the Ukraine and foreign countries.

B. Pyadyshev: As an idea, this looks attractive. Are we talking about a necessity?

A. Zlenko: A common history existing a thousand years and a deep cultural, linguistic, and ideological closeness have linked us with neighboring Poland. The western regions of the Ukraine and eastern provinces of Poland are similar both in makeup of the population and economy. Are contacts between Kiev and Warsaw (800 kilometers as the crow flies) via Moscow (2,000 kilometers) justified? Aside from this, there are hundreds of thousands of Ukrainians living in Poland, and Poles in the Ukraine.

Our border with Czechoslovakia, Hungary, and Romania is shorter than that with Poland. But there are also ethnic mutual influences, economic ties, trade, mixed marriages, the common Danube waters and common Carpathian Mountains, the painful and common issue of ecology—in short, an indivisible knot which we frankly view as a shoot of the future, a sort of East European economic community, at first a partner of the Twelve and later a component of the whole of Europe in its present-day concept.

B. Pyadyshev: During the 45th session a meeting of the foreign ministers of the member states of the Conference on Security and Cooperation in Europe (CSCE) was held in New York. The ministers of thirty-three European states and also the United States and Canada finally reached an agreement on the time period—November 19 to 21—and the agenda for the conference in Paris of the leaders of the CSCE member countries. Through unbelievable efforts, above all those by Eduard Shevardnadze and U.S. Secretary of State James Baker, who met virtually every day, the tight knots which were beyond the powers of the delegations of the protracted Vienna talks on conventional arms reductions in Europe were unraveled. Was there talk of a representative of the Ukraine taking part in the ministerial meeting in New York as a major component of the European process? If so, what was the Western countries' attitude to this?

A. Zlenko: Our stand on this issue was set forth very explicitly at the General Assembly session: we are counting on our intention to take a direct part in the European process and European structures being understood and supported in the international community and being realized without superfluous delays. Of the meetings we had in

Kiev and here in New York, we can draw the conclusion that this hope was well-founded.

Believe me, this is not vanity on the part of a newly appointed minister, nor is it misunderstood national pride. Self-sufficing centralism has spent itself—this though belongs to the president of the USSR. The Ukraine sees its future as lying in a democratic, multi-party law-governed market society. It will be able to arrive at it only in cooperation with the peoples of the republics of the present-day Soviet Union, and only in harmony with neighboring countries. I think it is an insult to the reader to remind him or her that our republic is a European country both in terms of history and scope. During my time as the permanent representative of the Ukraine to UN-ESCO in Paris, I enumerated the dynastic ties of Grand Prince Yaroslav the Wise with the ruling houses of Norway, France, Sweden, and Denmark. And Ukrainian influence made itself felt in the later Middle Ages—from the Cossack campaigns against Turkey and France to the Ukrainian school of music in Italy and Russia.

The Ukraine at the Frontier of the New Diplomacy

B. Pyadyshev: The Declaration on State Sovereignty of the Ukraine, as well as analogous declarations of the Russian Federation and the other constituent republics, opens up vistas for an external political course which would best meet the interests of the republic and of the entire country. We can talk of a reassessment of the place and role of the new Ukraine in the outside world, of its being a subject of international law, and of recognition of the Ukraine being an equitable partner by the external world. However, it is obvious that the external political activity of the Ukraine can be effective if it is carried out in close contact with the other republics, in a union of sovereign Soviet states.

A. Zlenko: I must say that there was a very intense struggle around the Declaration. I know how it was conceived, how it was discussed, and what forces were concentrated around this Declaration. What is important is the result: despite the polemics in the parliament of different groups, groupings, parties, and deputies with differing views, the Declaration is acceptable to the majority; only four deputies voted against it. This document embodies the need for the further development of our society and the necessity of a new vision of the republic's future.

Compared to the Declaration of the Russian Federation, this document goes farther. The Ukrainian Declaration seems to be more voluminous. In the main areas, above all, the primacy of the constitution and the laws of the republic over the national laws, is enshrined in both declarations. The same applies to citizenship. The issues of economic independence or self-sufficiency are coincidentally interpreted in both declarations. Provisions touching upon international relations are expanded upon or presented in a new way. As I have already mentioned, the Declaration of the Ukraine goes farther in matters of external relations.

Furthermore, the Ukraine is declared a nuclear-free state. It must pursue its policies, proceeding from the three nonnuclear principles: not to use, develop, or stockpile nuclear weapons. The situation that has taken shape in the republic dictated the need to include sections on ecological security in the Declaration. These are already the serious consequences of the Chernobyl disaster. The point is also made that the Ukraine can be a neutral state.

B. Pyadyshev: Inasmuch as some time has already elapsed since the Declaration was adopted and discussion and analysis of it continue, how are views of relations with the Center, with the Union, taking shape? Is there a possibility for, say, a community of republics or is a line for the republic's independent status being pursued?

A. Zlenko: These views are in a state of flux. Initially there dominated sentiments to the effect that the Union should exist alongside an independent republic. It is expedient to turn over to the Union—in its renewed shape—such strategic matters as defense, global aspects of ecology, and the like. Then the discussion centered on the fact that yes, the Union should exist, but we should determine our participation in it only after the republic adopts a constitution and the corresponding normative documents which should serve as the foundation or a mandate for holding talks on the Union. To sum up briefly, I suppose there are forces that proceed from the need to preserve the Union, in the new form of course, with the understanding that there will be full decentralization, that there will be economic independence for the republic and full-fledged involvement in international relations. However, cautious approaches to how and in what form we would take part in talks are evident. After all, it has been decided to send a delegation to one of the sittings of the Council of the Federation, in effect deprived of its powers, that is, of observers.

This is a stand that must be taken into consideration. And, lastly, a decision was adopted by the Ukrainian Supreme Soviet on October 15 admitting the premature nature of the signing of the Union treaty prior to the adoption of the Constitution of the Ukraine.

B. Pyadyshev: You have diplomatically said "cautious approaches." Even from your replies it follows that the forces expressing these "cautious approaches" have been picking up the pace over a comparatively short period. Evidently their argumentation and ideas are attracting the public at large, and their arguments contain things that may be healthy or unhealthy, but they are alluring.

A. Zlenko: We have to give credit to the energy of these people, who are members of the democratic bloc, or Rukh. Despite their minority in the parliament, they are very noticeable there. Why is this so? It is due to the fact that parliament is coming under pressure both outside and inside it. Rukh supporters are en masse by the walls of parliament, conducting, with the national symbols, what I would call "slogan diplomacy." From their slogans and posters you can see these people's attitude to parliamentary decisions and to the leaders of a party and to events in the republic in general.

Another reason is the many problems, which they note—and they know how to show them. That is how public opinion is attracted, points are won, and the proceedings of parliament and its decisions influenced.

One other point. The decisions which are adopted in the Russian Federation Supreme Soviet exert a big impact on the atmosphere in our republican parliament. Much is taken into consideration of what is being done in the Russian Federation parliament, in terms of creating the groundwork for independence, strengthening the national self-consciousness, self-assertion, and, if you will, for possibly defending the republic's stand before the Union government.

B. Pyadyshev: As far as I know, all this is taking place against the background of the complicated political situation in the republic.

If you ask Russians, I am convinced that the overwhelming majority would declare for the preservation of the Union of republics. Not the one, however, which to this day, weighing heavily upon age-old Russian lands and regions, has ruined and exhausted them to the extreme. The community should be just and equitable. It goes without saying that it should have a central power—in the forms, scope, and functions which will be delegated to it by the members of the community.

The Slavic space of the current USSR is a natural foundation of the Union. In this sense I agree with Alexander Solzhenitsyn in his arguments about a union of the Russian Federation with the Ukraine and Byelorussia. "What will remain," he writes in his famous article "How Are We to Revitalize Russia?" "is what can be called Russ, as it was called from time immemorial (for the word "Russian" encompassed Little Russians, Great Russians, and Byelorussians) or Russia (the name since the eighteenth century), or, according to the correct meaning now—the Russian Union."

We hardly need to run away from the other twelve republics, as Solzhenitsyn insists, if they do not secede themselves, of their free will. There will be room for everyone in the community. But its fortress and viable bastion is Russia, the Ukraine, and Byelorussia.

A. Zlenko: Indeed, the situation in the republic is complex; it is developing differently in the western, eastern, and southern regions, and especially in the western ones. Lvov, Ivano-Frankovsk, Volyn, Rovno, and Ternopol are five regions where people from the opposition, from Rukh, have come to power. Difficult relations are taking shape between the new leadership which has come to power and the old, between the regional committees of the Ukrainian Communist Party and the regional Soviets. The situation, I repeat, is a complicated one. I don't want to say that it is close to a crisis. It is controllable, but very tense. No less tense is the situation that is being observed in Kiev. You are well familiar with the events associated with the student actions which in effect paralyzed the city for several days.

B. Pyadyshev: What are the centers of power in the Ukraine today? It is hard to figure this out nowadays.

A. Zlenko: They are the Supreme Soviet and the government of the Ukraine. Of course, the situation is changing, but I understand it as follows: As our state strengthens as a law-governed one, the full plentitude of power should belong to parliament, the Supreme Soviet, headed by the chairman or president. Here, we have a chairman. A balance of legislative, executive, and judicial power should be struck. Legislative—the Supreme Soviet, executive—the Council of Ministers, judicial—our judicial bodies.

B. Pyadyshev: To what extent is power concentrated in parliament today?

A. Zlenko: The process is taking place rapidly, but I would not say that power is already fully in the hands of parliament. It is a known fact that power used to belong to the Central Committee of the Party. Today we, for example, virtually do not feel intrusion from the Central Committee. This is the situation we are working in. We are directing our efforts to meet national interests. We are aware that today we need to do much more than yesterday, and tomorrow we must pose a task of still greater scope, promoting national and spiritual revival.

Ukrainian Diplomacy Today and in 1995

B. Pyadyshev: The Declaration on State Sovereignty is an epoch-making event for the Ukraine. It still has be to analyzed in detail. Since we are talking about Ukrainian diplomacy, my question is how is sovereignty in the sphere of international relations and foreign policy outlined in the Declaration itself in views and approaches?

A. Zlenko: If for decades we engaged chiefly in multilateral forms of cooperation which were implemented through participation in the UN and other international organizations, then today we are facing the task of developing bilateral ties.

To date, we have singled out three groups of states. Above all these are states where the republic's priority interests lie. To be more exact, they are neighboring states. The Ukraine borders on four East European countries: Poland, Romania, Czechoslovakia, and Hungary.

Then there are states where considerable interests of the republic lie, where large groups of people of Ukrainian descent live. There is a major Ukrainian diaspora in a number of countries. According to different sources, there are between 800,000 and 1 million Ukrainians living in Canada alone. This is the biggest settlement. In the United States, the estimate is a bit more difficult. If we go by ethnic origin, the figure is as high as 1.5 to 2 million. However, in the United States there are far fewer who have maintained their ethnic identity than in Canada. In Brazil there are between 300,000 and 500,000 persons. In Australia, there are 30,000. In short, there are approximately 5 million Ukrainians living in foreign countries. All told, 15 million Ukrainians reside outside the bounds of the republic, most of them in the Russian Federation and other Soviet republics.

We, of course, will be pursuing a lein for developing multifaceted economic and cultural contacts with Ukrainians living abroad. The first congress of the International Association of Ukraine Scholars was held in Kiev this past August. Representatives from all over the world were in attendance. Right before our meeting I received a group from Canada; they were in town for this congress and they had a host of questions. We believe that this is one of the important areas of our work.

Lastly, another level of bilateral relations, so to speak, is singled out—ties with territorial-administrative units of a number of federative countries. Interparliamentary and other agreements have been reached with Croatia, the Italian region of Tuscany, the Canadian provinces of Ontario and Alberta, the Slovak Republic, the state of Rio de Janeiro, Bavaria, the Chinese province of Hubei, and the land of Upper Austria. We have also received proposals from the states of New South Wales, Australia, and Pennsylvania and Indiana, in the United States, to establish bilateral ties. These relations are opening up rather broad vistas for Ukrainian enterprises at the current transitional stage for establishing direct economic ties with foreign firms and for gradually integrating into international economic relations. However, for all the substance of the aforementioned relations, we are aware that if the Ukraine wants to be a subject of international law, it must base these relations not with province of states but with the states themselves. Otherwise it will be perceived as a province itself.

B. Pyadyshev: Say, you and I meet five years from now, in 1995. With due account for current tendencies, and for the development rate of these processes—and this rate can well speed up—how do you visualize the republic's place in international relations and world diplomacy in 1995?

A. Zlenko: Let's try and dream. If we take into account the processes which you are talking about, I think that the Ukraine has possibilities for pursuing full-fledged foreign policy. I think that we will also be obliged to do so by the interest which is being showed by other states as well. Lying in this interest is consideration of the republic's potential and its geographical location in the heart of Europe, and a number of other circumstances.

I believe that the republic's foreign policy will establish itself, and I am certain that by that time we will have diplomatic, consular, and other relations with neighboring states. Thus far, we do not have diplomatic representations other than our missions to international organizations: at the UN in New York, UNESCO in Paris, and international organizations in Vienna and Geneva.

By 1995 the republic will be able to develop and ensure a large volume of external economic ties and broaden its participation in international organizations and in international legal practice. Most importantly, we would proceed from the republic's involvement in the European process.

As far as the possibility for establishing diplomatic relations is concerned, let me reiterate that I believe this is the end result of our work, not the beginning. It must be preceded by a prepared volume of cooperation, the requisite negotiating mechanism, a body of tiepinned diplomatic personnel, and the finances that could ensure such missions.

B. Pyadyshev: What will the future of the Ukrainian Ministry of Foreign Affairs itself be like?

A. Zlenko: If things go the way they are taking shape today, the Foreign Ministry structure will, of course, have to be brought in line with the tasks which we will be tackling. The underpinnings for such a structure have already been created. Such "attributes" of this structure as our own communications services and courier service will appear. We recently set up a bilateral ties and regional cooperation section and a contract and legal section. We will have to consolidate the international economic relations section and international organizations section. There is a Secretariat of the UNESCO Commission with the status of a section, and the Consular Service is even today handling a large volume of work—thousands of people go through this subdivision to obtain exit papers. We process only papers for business trips; nevertheless, this volume is increasing and the service is gaining momentum. Naturally, there is a protocol section, personnel department, and information section.

We have felt an extreme need for establishing a Press Center of the Ukrainian Ministry of Foreign Affairs.

B. Pyadyshev: I was invited to a meeting with Kiev journalists in this newly opened Press Center and I can confirm that the republic's Council of Ministers has assigned a wonderful mansion to it. The conditions for work with the press are excellent and one could feel that your staff members are prepared to use them to the best advantage.

Europe and Other Continents, and Problems

B. Pyadyshev: As you can understand, the idea is that without lessening attention to work in the UN, which provides unique chances for interstate interaction on a high level, we need to set up bilateral political ties with foreign countries, and also integrate ourselves into international cooperation in the trade and economic, scientific and technological, cultural, humanitarian and other spheres. This will likely affect Europe.

A. Zlenko: Yes, the significance of the European orientation of the Ukraine's foreign policy comes from economic and humanitarian circumstances as well as political ones. The Ukraine suffered from both world wars. So can it be indifferent to how affairs can take shape on the continent? Our principled stand consists in the inviolability of the borders of postwar Europe which were formalized in the Helsinki Final Act.

Above all, we need to ensure our stable relations with our neighbors—Poland, Hungary, Czechoslovakia, and Romania. The Ukraine also has a sea frontier with Turkey and Bulgaria. What should these relations be like? We view them as good-neighborly and free of any mutual claims and misunderstandings, relations that would best meet everyone's interests. It is important for us to have direct ties with our neighbors. The time will come also to think about signing treaties on good-neighborliness, friendship, and cooperation. All this would become an earnest toward ensuring the rights of the national minorities living in these countries. I think that in this way the Ukraine jointly with its neighbors would make a positive contribution to the consolidation of the political and juridical foundations of the new Europe.

There is another orientation of European policy—direct participation in the construction of a European home, which is taking place within the framework of the Conference on Security and Cooperation in Europe. This is linked with the solution of an entire series of problems—political, international-legal, financial, etc. A great deal will depend on the development of political processes in the Ukraine, the USSR, and the European continent as a whole. The Ministry of Foreign Affairs is duly preparing for this work.

A. Zlenko: From yesterday's *Izvestia* we found out that the third unit at the Chernobyl nuclear power station was shut down. I talked to the Deputy Chairman of Ministers of the Ukraine, who is in charge of the station. His state could be understood. How could they have done it, he asked, I am in charge of Chernobyl, but I don't know what is going on at the station. And this is because everything is done behind closed doors at the USSR Ministry of Nuclear Power Engineering.

B. Pyadyshev: Mentioning Chernobyl, we are steering this conversation toward ecology as one of the key areas of Ukrainian diplomacy.

A. Zlenko: I think that it is unnecessary to explain what the ecological problem means for the Ukraine after the Chernobyl disaster. For us Ukrainian diplomats, active involvement in multilateral environmental cooperation is not only our professional but also our moral duty. The Ukraine was one of the initiators of the elaboration of the concept of international ecological security. The resolution on international cooperation in the sphere of monitoring, assessment, and forecasting ecological threats and rendering aid in incidents of ecological emergencies was unanimously passed at the 44th Session of the UN General Assembly on a proposal tabled by the Ukraine and Czechoslovakia.

The new step in this direction was raising the issue of international cooperation in dealing with the Chernobyl disaster at sessions of ECOSOC, one of the main UN bodies. The energetic work done by the delegations of the Ukraine, the USSR, and Byelorussia, which tabled a draft resolution to the effect, ensured its passing by a consensus and the accession of sixty-three countries to it as co-authors. Many international organizations such as IAEA, WHO, ILO, UNDP, FAO, and EEC are becoming involved in the efforts to overcome the consequences of the Chernobyl disaster. The UN secretary general, in particular, will assist international specialized institutions in making an expert assessment of the aftermaths of the catastrophe and determining requirements for assuaging them. At the 45th Session of the UN General Assembly the secretary general presented a paper with recommendations regarding further practical steps toward extensive international cooperation not linked with ideological or bloc restrictions for dealing with the Chernobyl tragedy. The Chernobyl disaster has put before everyone a task of difficulty and depth, the accomplishment of which is possible only through the pooled efforts of the entire international community.

B. Pyadyshev: An important question is how our perestroika processes and the passions around the idea of sovereignty of the republics and the future of the USSR are perceived abroad, especially in Europe, the United States and Japan. We have seen for ourselves on the experience of the past few years that in today's interdependent world, one not divided into two ideological fortress-blocs, the position of an economically mighty and democratically strong West can be of very substantial importance to our domestic affairs. It turns out that Europe and the United States possess effective levers of influence.

Westerners are well suited by the current state of affairs. The acute domestic conflicts in the USSR remain within the framework of the country; the outside world is not affected or burdened by them. In international politics, a mechanism of cooperation has been worked out which is especially important in major problems such as disarmament, security, ecology, and the economy. In the dramatic and effective talks in September and October on conventional arms reductions in Europe and on the Persian Gulf crisis, Eduard Shevardnadze personified the authority and stability of power on which a great deal depends in the world. The West will appreciate our perestroika processes for as long as they are safe for the West militarily and politically, and are predictable and controllable. There should be no doubt about this; if events develop beyond this point, it will not remain indifferent.

West Germans and Americans, who have just calmed down with regard to the "menace from the East" and, beginning with Helsinki-75, have worked out a reliable mode of living with us, will hardly be prepared to agree to a situation where several tempestuous streams from the East bearing real dangers for well-being on the continent would flow into political and economic life.

The only reason I am saying this is that in our polemics we shouldn't lose an understanding of the importance of how we look from the side, how others perceive us. The idea of sovereignty is emerging victorious, but the practice of a Union of republics, or a community, or another form of unification and cooperation is viable, too. This will certainly render one and all more efficient, practical, and dependable, both in the foreign policy and diplomatic sphere.

A. Zlenko: I share your views about the difficult future of our state. In these issues I would like to avoid "roaming" ideas, which are born by chance and are immediately praised to the skies and served to society as virtually axiomatic and unconditional truths. Today it is more important than ever to understand the feelings and demands of the people and liberate its energies and possibilities—such is an earnest of the affirmation of universal values.

We republican diplomats do not claim to have all the answers to these highly complex questions; life will set everything in its proper place. But we are already doing the work entrusted to us by the highest body of power, the Ukrainian Supreme Soviet, and we are doing it professionally, giving it our all. And if we feel the benefit of our efforts—and, you know, we are beginning to feel it—we will do even more. We have set about a great cause—providing for the external political interests of the Ukraine. So, wish us luck!

Russian Diplomacy Reborn

Andrei Kozyrev

The appointment was seen by many as somehow unexpected. On October 11, 1990, the RSFSR Supreme Soviet named Andrei Kozyrev the new Russian Foreign Minister without holding any particular debate. This may be unprecedented in Russian diplomacy. The new minister, thirty-nine, is a graduate of the Moscow Institute of International Relations. A career diplomat, he rose from attaché to chief of directorate at the USSR Ministry of Foreign Affairs before assuming his new office.

Boris Pyadyshev, editor in chief of *International Affairs,* talked at the journal's Guest Club with the Russian Foreign Minister. The meeting was one in a series of meetings with the Soviet republics' foreign minsters.

Boris Pyadyshev. After decades of a rather nominal existence, Russian diplomacy appears to be acquiring substance as a real force.

It represents a mighty state taking up an area of 17 million square kilometers and inhabited by 147.3 million people. (The figures for the whole Soviet Union are 22.4 and 286.7 respectively). Russia's national wealth and industrial, scientific, technological, and other potentialities are equally impressive. The trend of development in the republic is bound to largely influence development in adjacent areas. This prompts me to ask: What are Russia's national interests? What are the objectives of its foreign policy and the guiding ideas of its diplomacy?

Andrei Kozyrev. You said that for decades there had practically been no such concept as Russian diplomacy. But what did we have seven decades ago? The Russian empire, a great power, had a highly experienced, centuries-old diplomatic school of its own. But does that mean the foreign policy of the Russian Federation is now going back to those roots?

The federation within its present-day boundaries has appeared on the political map of the world. It is a reality that may be regarded to a degree as a revival of the Russian statehood of the past. But this revival must take place within a renewed Union, for boundaries are indistinct and destines interwine. Thus the point is to conceive renewal as integration and transformation on democratic principles, not as a falling apart. This underlines the difference between our republic and the Russian empire. The federation isn't out to restore the imperial center, the *métropole*. What it wants is to get rid of the totalitarian legacy of the past seventy years.

Hence the great difficulty of both determining our place in the world and establishing proper, optimum relations between the Russian Federation and the regions that were part of the Russian empire and then became prisoners of totalitarianism along with Russia and are now searching for an identity as nation-states.

B. Pyadyshev. Excuse me for interrupting you, but I'd like to point to the term "empire," which is often applied nowadays to the Soviet Union. The allegation I hear that the Soviet Union is the last surviving empire puts me on my guard. I'm not sure the term is used correctly or is applicable to Russia, the Russian Republic, as a kind of center or *métropole* living at the expense of other constituent republics of the Union. How can anyone call Russia a "center" or "*métropole*," well knowing that throughout those seven decades its fertile regions bore the brunt of advancing the whole state? What kind of "empire" is it since its outlying areas were advanced at the expense of those Russian regions? Where does an empire or *métropole* come in, seeing that Russia's own original territories have turned out to be exhausted and ruined to the utmost? If we want to define somehow the situation prevailing in our state until recently, we ought to think of some other term. I don't find the term "empire" suitable. However, what I'm saying may sound like carping at terms while it's the essence that matters.

A. Kozyrev. That's just what I mean. We may be said to have had two predecessors: the Russian empire, which existed until 1917, and the totalitarian regime. Russia and other republics were victims of that regime. Assuming that the term "empire" is suitable to a degree, I would use it in the sense of a center oppressing the rest, meaning, however, not Russia or its regions but central departments, the supermonopolies that behaved and largely go on trying to behave like colonizers in Russia as well, without regard to ecology or demography.

B. Pyadyshev. The Soviet national anthem begins with the words: "The unbreakable Union of freeborn Republics Great Russia has welded for ever to stand." The words which a short time ago seemed above doubt. But the Union's unbreakability does not work out. Nor the freeborn republics. But what we have is choosing paths to a new union or community of republics—the name is beside the point. Lithuania's tragic developments last January must demonstrate, possibly for the last time, that political processes have a natural-born and delicate character, and cannot be interfered with through the use of force.

A. Kozyrev. You know what worries me most in the Lithuanian developments is a linkage of the protective structures of the Center with those of the "National Salvation Committee" on the "CPSU Platform" locally. The danger of restoration of what was inside and outside prior to 1985 is great as long as there are men in uniform ready to open fire if so ordered by those who have power against the will of the lawfully elected authorities. It should be remembered that the Supreme Soviets of both the Baltic republics and the RSFSR spoke against use of force and for troop withdrawal. Such danger would be perilous for Russia as well because the people would again be doomed to apathy, and tolerant of evil and arbitrariness, alcoholism, and deceit. That's the price to be paid for use of force to hold together the "unbreakable Union" and the leading role.

The historical analysis we've just made suggests the Russian Federation's primary concern: finding a new framework for relations with one-time parts of the Russian empire, in which Russia was the *métropole*, and those who for roughly seventy years were campmates under a totalitarian regime. I think there are some circumstances which nobody denies.

The second concern is the interdependence of economies, human destinies, and cultural links. Indeed, everything in this union is mixed together, and some of the mixing involved coercion. There were also friendly sentiments linking peoples. It remains a fact, however, that for all the conventionality of existing boundaries between republics, we may speak of primordially Russian territories, as you noted, and of concepts associated with Russia as home to the bulk of the Russian-speaking population. Most other republics, too, have a fairly distinct ethnic core. It follows that we really mustn't tear ourselves asunder. To do so would be an entirely unjustifiable, absurd step back to the last century or thereabouts. It would mean severing ties between people, redrawing boundaries, and so on. But can that serve as a reason for preserving an essentially totalitarian if refurbished central authority? Certainly not. That, too, would be a step back.

B. Pyadyshev. It is true that the republics making up today's Union want to keep up cooperation to one degree or another as equal and sovereign partners. It's also true that Russia, the Ukraine, and Byelorussia have always constituted a mighty Slavic massif. It's logical that Russia signed its early treaties with the Ukrainians and Byelorussians. Let me say in passing that Alexander Solzhenitsyn speaks of this course of development in his famous article about the future of Russia.

A. Kozyrev. I think Solzenitsyn has expressed a whole range of fundamental ideas that have yet to be fully appreciated. I mean above all the idea that we must concentrate on regenerating Russia and that this makes it absolutely necessary to renounce imperial thinking and destroy totalitarian rule. As regards the specifically Slavic area, I believe we may speak of two levels of perception.

First, there's the reflection of a certain reality, a universal phenomenon which consists in the existence of a definite unity of peoples based on ethnic cultures. There's of community among the Arab peoples, the Finno–Ugric peoples, the Francophone peoples, and so on, nor are the Slavic peoples any different in this respect. I consider that all people have legitimate reason to preserve and augment whatever they have in common. Incidentally, Yugoslavia, Bulgaria, and Czechoslovakia are in this category. In the case of Slavic republics, reciprocal ties can be closer than in other cases. Generally speaking, I don't think there can be a common pattern of relations. It would be unworkable. There may be peculiarities, and in some cases relations may be more extensive than in others. Life itself seems to offer solutions. I've said that the Russian Federation has signed bilateral treaties with two republics, the Ukraine and Byelorussia. Kazakhstan, where there are many Russians, became our third partner.

We must use the way out suggested by the late twentieth century. The world is a community of nation-states. The UN is an organization of sovereign states, and the EC is a community of such states. Thus it's logical that the republics should seek to regain their national identity. However, they need to preserve all sound links, primarily cultural and human contacts. This must be done without any orders from above, without the centralized control we are all used to. The republics themselves began right after declaring sovereignty to search for a path to reintegration, to unification, except that this time they want it to rest on new, horizontal, more democratic foundations. I've been involved in talks with republics ever since I took up my post. It isn't that the Russian Foreign Ministry's participation in them somehow underlines a differentiation between the republics. The task is to help base relations on standards and principles of international law that are universally recognized because they are universal in character.

B. Pyadyshev. *International Affairs* recently published a noteworthy document: the report on the work done in 1920–1921 which the RSFSR People's Commissariat of Foreign Affairs presented to the Ninth Congress of Soviets. Incidentally, Russian diplomacy at the time may have been closer in form and certainly was closer in content to the diplomatic service you now head. In addition to an account and analysis of relations with foreign countries, the report detailed the substance and lines of relations with other Soviet republics: the Baltic republics, the Ukraine, Byelorussia, the Transcaucasus, the Far Eastern Republic, Turkestan. And it's interesting to note that in 1921 the republics were independent and sovereign. Their peoples and leaders had already come to realize that the integral ties existing at the time were inadequate for the dynamic development of every one of them. So they set course for unification, for the formation of a union, which they brought into being in December 1922. Whatever the merits or demerits of the union, it is still there.

A. Kozyrev. That's really a very interesting historic starting point. But it may be useful to remark that the revolutions of 1917 signaled definite social requirements. One of them was the need to guarantee the right of nations to self-determination because the Russian empire was doomed like all others. But a democratic transformation never came about. The process wasn't completed. It got off to a start but was reversed by the rise of a totalitarian monster. It's true that the Russian Federation and its People's Commissariat of Foreign Affairs gave relations between republics as much if not more attention than international relations. Interestingly, the signing of the Treaty of Union in 1922 didn't end that.

The Treaty of Union, which we now seem to proceed from theoretically, provided for a union of sovereign states in the full sense of the term, not nominally. Years after the treaty was concluded, both the Russian Federation and other republics maintained international contacts of their own, especially with neighbors. Indeed, they had missions on one another's territory performing virtually diplomatic and consular functions. We still have a vestige of that in the form of the republics' permanent missions to the USSR Council of Ministers.

That model was defeated because power came to be concentrated in the hands of the central authority and degenerated into a dictatorial regime, into overcentralization. It's really open to question whether today's Soviet Union can be regarded as a state based on the 1922 treaty. I believe this is a moot point, if only because at that time the treaty was signed by four republics whereas we now have fifteen. In other words, most present-day members of the Union didn't sign the 1922 treaty, and so I strongly doubt the idea that they can and should live according to it. Besides, our life throughout the past years has by no means been based on a civilized principle, be it the social contract between citizen and state, so to speak, or the Treaty of Union between the republics. I agree, however, that it's useful to look back at that period.

Lenin and other Bolsheviks championed the idea of national self-determination and met, say, Finland halfway when it sought independence. That was a sphere in which democratic sentiments found their reflection. How the Bolshevik Party put the slogan of self-determination into practice afterward is another matter, but self-determination is a universally accepted concept.

B. Pyadyshev. I'm certain that the discord we are now witnessing in our state is aggravated by a fundamental reality, the current confrontation between the central and republican authorities over the fact that they can't come to terms on distributing responsibilities, powers, or functions. At the heart of the confrontation is opposition between the central authority and Russia, which has taken the biggest share of the confrontation, easing the burden of the other republics. Nothing could be sadder than the inability of two leaders enjoying the greatest prestige to reach an agreement calmly, in a businesslike manner.

Meanwhile the powers which the central authority would like to exercise in a number of spheres, including defense, foreign policy, environmental protection, transport, and communications, have been outlined.

Some republics, too, indicate in their program documents the powers they could delegate to the central authority. Speaking before the Russian Federation's Congress of People's Deputies, Boris Yeltsin said explicitly that Russia was for a Union without privileges, without important and less important peoples. It was for a Union because it considered that it should delegate some of the most important functions to the central authority. But the Russians were definitely against a Union at the expense of their republic's interests, against a Union to which Russia might be sacrificed, as had already been done before.

That brings us to the issue of foreign policy, of how far Russia would like to implement and control its foreign policy and what sectors, elements, or components of foreign policy activity Russia thinks it could delegate along with other republics to the central authority.

A. Kozyrev. The central authority opposes independence, including independence in seeking consolidation on a new basis, to the extent that it is still in the grip of authoritarian rule, that it is still influenced by the corporative interests of central departments, the supermonopolies lording it over the whole country. A sharp conflict is unavoidable to the extent that active at the center are vestigial totalitarian forces. Such a conflict may resolve itself into those forces establishing a dictatorship. Even if this threat isn't carried out by the time the next issue of the journal appears, it will still be there because dismantling the system will take considerable time.

But to the extent that the central authority is an exponent of perestroika ideas, there is hope for agreement. After all, these ideas are also conceived by central departments, as both of us know, if only because we've served in the Soviet Foreign Ministry. I feel that the President's statements contain very positive key propositions implying that the totalitarian, unitary state is bound to disintegrate. He said so at the CSCE meeting in Paris. The very first lines of the draft treaty proposed on his behalf stress that it envisages a voluntary agreement between republics. Those propositions show that while interests don't entirely coincide, they are very close to one another in many respects and have much in common.

I suppose there's going to be a gradual abolition of totalitarian rule and a parallel formulation of a new central authority really meeting the interests of the republics. I would jokingly compare that to matrimony. In one case the wedding took place in a camp hut and was imposed. This time we expect a wedding in a church and by reciprocal agreement. The former marriage is doomed and hence certain to end in divorce. As for the second one, I see the early signs of a love match. I'm an advocate of the closest possible integration, all the more since it's in keeping with international processes and is a universal trend.

B. Pyadyshev. The year 1991 is going to be decisive: either the state will succeed in reconciling divisive and integrational trends or its affairs will go from bad to worse. To be sure, Russia is itself a mighty state and can bear up under overloading for a long time but there's a limit to everything. Sometimes I get the impression that many complications are due to unwitting or possibly deliberate reticence. The main documents of both the Union and republics would seem to formulate fundamental provisions clearly enough. But when discussion moves on to concrete provisions to be put into practice, disagreement and discord set in. The main guiding principle is: "This is mine and so is that." It's above all on security issues, on issues of foreign policy and in the military area, that we need clarity.

A. Kozyrev. Not a single republic lays claim to dividing, say, military property, that is, the country's defense potential. On the contrary, all public statements, particularly by the Russian leadership but also by leaders of other republics, stress an awareness of the need to prevent any slackening of control, to say nothing of averting a spread or scattering of nuclear weapons. I find it very encouraging that the declarations of sovereignty and the very first documents adopted by, say, Byelorussia or the Ukraine, state a desire for neutrality. This is no obstacle whatever to their forming a union of community of sovereign states. Indeed, it shows that there is no intention at all to spread nuclear weapons or pull armed forces apart, as some in our country readily insinuate. And it's perfectly clear that this area will be under common jurisdiction. Of course, we could probably visualize several alternatives of a common army. But the principle itself is obvious. This suggests the primary common function of foreign policy. I mean all that concerns global security problems or disarmament talks.

It follows that security, above all the army, and, accordingly, talks on disarmament and security with other countries, must be made a sphere of common jurisdiction, with the central authority operating as a joint mechanism exercising control and negotiating on disarmament. This is indisputable because you can't negotiate with dozens of subjects simultaneously on limiting one and the same armory.

Therefore, the internal aspect of foreign policy, that is, the mechanism of working out directives and instructions for Soviet delegations entrusted with talks, will be of key importance. Why do I think all republics should participate? Not only because they need to have a say in, among other things, the formation of the armed forces and decision-making on their strategy and tactics. They need it also because any decision or agreement on disarmament will bear directly on the republics, Russia included. Russia accounts for 80 percent of the country's defense potential and, presumably, for the lion's share of military personnel, which means that any disarmament agreement directly concerns Russia, primarily in terms of conversion, of solving the social problems of officers and enlisted men.

The ecological situation is similar although environmental problems clearly have two or more levels. For instance, three republics have already reached an agreement on jointly organizing international cooperation in eliminating the effects of the Chernobyl accident. There are some other global environmental problems requiring both joint efforts by republics and cooperation with other countries. The UN plans to hold a world conference in 1992. Everybody realizes that in this case the more the central authority is involved and hence the more coordination there is, the better. But, of course, environmental problems also include purely local ones that should preferably be solved at the level of crossborder ties, as we and Finland do. There's no point in "dragging" the central authority into the solution of these particular problems, is there? Every republic can solve them in direct contact with the neighbor concerned. This also goes for other regions—meaning large ones—and for the economy. We have macroeconomic problems as well as microeconomic ones, so to say, or problems related to border areas, humanitarian activities, information order, and so on.

It seems to me that the pattern of solution should be as follows: what it's advisable to solve in common should be left to the central authority and what calls for a bilateral solution should be tackled by the republics concerned. I don't think this approach could harm anyone.

We must devise a mechanism enabling us to take advance account of interests and draw Russian departments and representatives into the solution of problems both before an agreement is signed and when we get down to carrying it out. I see nothing wrong with that. After all, even now we use a mechanism of interdepartmental coordination. The number of departments with which decisions must be agreed will increase somewhat but we won't be an exception in this respect. In many Western countries, including those that aren't made up of sovereign states but merely of democratically governed territories, things like that are agreed on with the territorial authorities both before an agreement is reached and when it has to be implemented.

During a recent trip to the Federal Republic of Germany, Russian Prime Minister Ivan Silayev and I told our hosts that the Russian authorities would like to join in settling the social problems of our withdrawal from Germany. They fully subscribed to our suggestion there and then. It wasn't a question of revising the terms of the agreement on the pullout of our troops. Needless to say, we support the agreement. What we meant was our participation in using the funds allocated by Germany itself for housing and other facilities for our servicemen. Now our troops must be fitted in with the Russian landscape, mustn't they? They will return into an existing environment, and this means that we mustn't treat them as if they were men from another planet sent by a mythical supreme authority. This is the problem. They'll need to be able to settle where they arrive, to find a job and home, to marry. To do that, they will first of all require contacts with the local as well as the republican authorities.

Our German interlocutors were amazed at the fact that the agreement had been drafted and signed without asking the republican authorities. I regret to say that the idea of the republican authorities' participation is appreciated in greater measure by the Germans than by people here at home. I'm sure that irrespective of the Germans' federal system, it would never occur to them to sign an agreement on stationing tens of thousands of troops in West German states without consulting those states' leaders. What we have in our case is, if you will, an army leadership proceeding against its own interests by creating an obviously unfavorable situation. I wonder why.

B. Pyadyshev. Statements by representatives of the republics give a reasonably clear idea of their diplomatic activity in the short term. There's no overlooking the fact that alongside an unquestionably sound approach they reveal a tendency toward traditional attitudes formed in the era of globalism, the cold war, and confrontation between the two superpowers. Yet sovereign republics are going to enter the foreign political scene in a new context. And this means that they should rid their diplomacy of traditional attributes as far as possible and concentrate on strictly concrete interests of their peoples.

I'll give some examples to illustrate what I mean.

We know from official quarters that 60 million Soviet people live outside their native republics, or their ethnic formations, to use the language of documents. But we estimate their number at as many as 73.7 million. Half of them—37 million—are Russians. Their situation is unenviable.

Seeing to the interests, rights, and human dignity of Russians hailing from the RSFSR are the destined task facing Russian diplomacy. This doesn't necessitate establishing contacts with faraway lands. The problem lies near at hand, in neighboring republics, except that nobody gives it serious attention.

A. Kozyrev. I can't agree that the Russian leadership gives the problem little attention. It treats the problem as a priority. What are we going to do? I think primarily what we've already begun doing. First, we want to ensure that whatever the trend of development, Russians don't feel like foreigners on the territory of other republics. What methods and mechanisms can we use to this end? We may be accused of wishful thinking on the ground that reality is evolving in a different direction. But I have certain reasons for optimism because, even after declaring sovereignty and before starting to really exercise it, Russia and other republics are negotiating between themselves at parliamentary level and thinking of how to integrate, how to prevent the boundaries between them from becoming Berlin Walls of sorts, how to stave off territorial disputes.

Ever since I was given my post, I've been engaged in this peculiar activity, which certainly isn't classical diplomacy. We've already signed treaties. They are interesting documents, and it's quite clear to me that my half-Ukrainian wife won't become a foreigner just because we've signed a treaty with the Ukraine. This also applies to all other republics, which assume a variety of obligations. One of them is to fully guarantee internationally recognized human rights and freedoms on their territory for their citizens, who are all Soviet citizens, free to choose the citizenship they prefer. Another obligation is to guarantee the citizens of the other contracting party full equality on its territory with its own citizens. Thus what we have here is a zero solution. All citizens enjoy equal rights, and the choice of citizenship is, in effect, a psychologico-cultural act fully guaranteed in terms of law.

We must see to it in practice that our union with the Ukraine and other republics, where there are millions of Russians, is in the nature of the European community, that is, of a common legal, humanitarian, and information area, and makes boundaries transparent and conventional.

Also to be put in operation under the treaties is the whole mechanism of civilized methods, such as interparliamentary commissions or permanent missions on one another's territory. Any Russian citizen who considers that he has been wronged or discriminated against can ask the Russian mission for protection. Lastly, there should be intergovernmental consultations. In other words, the methods should be the same as are current internationally. I believe they will prove far more effective than special militia or troop detachments and other components of an armory which, so far, has failed to safeguard anyone in our unitary state against persecution on ethnic grounds. It is to be hoped that our choice will prove better.

B. Pyadyshev. That's as far as the Ukraine, Byelorussia, and Kazakhstan are concerned. What about other republics? Some of them have passed laws making Russians second-rate citizens denied civil rights. How can anybody in Russia react calmly to the fact that today's leaders of the Baltic republics still haven't said anything coherent about the fate of the Russian-speaking population, their vanguard views notwithstanding? Or to the provocative treatment of "outsiders" in Moldova, which was the main reason for the formation of the Dniester Republic and for the unrest that's continuing there? And how are we to react to what Georgia's new leader, swept to the top by an upsurge in the struggle for human rights, states about Georgian citizenship? He said it could only be granted to those whose ancestors had lived in Georgia since the early nineteenth century and as for the rights of others, he said "we'll have to think about that."

A. Kozyrev. What can we do? Our treaties are open for signing to other republics. We're going to seek special agreements with them on protecting the rights of the population. I think introducing international norms and reaching agreements between governments and parliaments is the only method we have. I would say that there's also a reserve that we don't use to the full. It consists in eliminating or reducing sources of Russophobia created by the practices of the central authority and central departments. Take Georgia and the April 9 events there as an example. Of course that was a tragedy, and it's deplorable that some in Georgia refuse to distinguish between the Moscow that gave the go-ahead for those events and the other Moscow which is itself a victim of the totalitarian regime and which the departmental monopolies as heirs of that regime wouldn't mind punishing even now. And so I think we've got a reserve there, that is, a chance to rid Russia of totalitarian features, of being associated with the center of a *métropole* of sorts. This would lead to normalizing the psychological climate around Russians. Manifestations of Russophobia will be inevitable as long as the presence of Russians is associated with the presence of special forces and things like that.

B. Pyadyshev. What you call Russophobia is, among other things, an outgrowth of Stalin's diabolic nationalities policy. He proposed toasts to the great Russian people but throughout the years of his regime he made sure that other republics associated all negative things with the Russians: dictates of the central authority, crackdowns on ethnic traditions, the imposition of an amorphous internationalism. As a result, the Russians' plight was the worst. A. Nikolayev, a collective farm chairman from Kaluga Region, spoke bitter words at the latest Congress of People's Deputies of the USSR. "Some three thousand communities vanish from the map of Russia every year," he said. "Mortality exceeds the birthrate on roughly one-third of the republic's territory. We see this as an ethnic, political, economic tragedy. The deliberate ravaging of Slavic villages and destruction of the peasantry and Slavic roots along with it are continuing. The roots of the reverses which Russia suffers in every sphere lie right there, on abandoned lands."

And now for another, by no means traditional line of Russian diplomacy. I mean territorial issues, which may include territorial claims in relations between sovereign republics. Let my putting it this way not surprise you—Russia will come up against the problem sooner or later. A whole number of Russian territories are part of other republics today. As long as the Soviet Union was a unitary state, all discussion of the issue was veiled, being considered improper. But now that we're entering an era of sovereign republics, Russia must concern itself with the territories taken away from it at various periods. Nikita Khrushchev ceded the Crimea to the Ukraine without asking the Russians. What is to become of that territory? After Russia and the Ukraine signed their treaty, Boris Yeltsin was asked in parliament questions about the Crimea. He politely did not commit himself. Perhaps this is really no time for that kind of discussion.

Territories owned by Russia were incorporated in the past into the Lithuanian SSR. At the time of forming the Kazakh SSR, some Russian regions in the southern Urals were added to that republic.

In a word, those issues may assume the proportions of the big political problems. Besides, the territories in question aren't covered with either tundras or marshes, both of which Russia abounds in, but are fertile soil. And this makes them a further area of republican diplomacy.

A. Kozyrev. My activity over the past two or three months has consisted in a distinctive, peculiar kind of diplomacy relating to other republics. Its purpose is to contribute, not to centrifugal, but to centripetal trends between republics. And I must say that while the republics still haven't quite found their feet, they already take a stand against separating, against going back to the nineteenth century, against disputing boundaries. The treaties which Russia has signed with the Ukraine, Byelorussia, and Kazakhstan rule out territorial disputes.

The signatories have committed themselves on a reciprocal basis to guarantee boundaries on an internationally recognized level and to cooperate, each republic pledging to assure citizens of other republics complete equality on its territory with its own citizens.

The treaties contain many useful provisions. Regrettably, they get no coverage in the press, any more than, by the way, much else that the republics do without consulting the central authority but not against its will. Those are very interesting documents. They fully accord with international standards and specify the functions which the signatories—four central republics—have agreed to perform through a coordination mechanism. Please note the term "coordination mechanism."

B. Pyadyshev. Russia's leaders have become involved in debates over the islands claimed by Japan. It would be wrong to use an unfortunate tradition by attempting a solution in the form of a prize for Mikhail Gorbachev's visit to Japan.

A. Kozyrev. Quite right. I think it would be very strange if the Union leadership tried to settle all aspects of relations with Japan, including the issue of the islands, without the direct consent and participation of Russia. It's a question of our neighbor, primarily Russia's, and of territory to which Russia can't be indifferent, to put it mildly. I don't think the road to solving this set of problems lies through decisions made behind closed doors by apparatus methods at any level of authority. We've already had many decisions of that sort and are still paying for them. We've either ceded or tried to hold onto territory.

The only proper settlement of the problem, of all aspects of our relations with Japan, including the issue of the islands, is to reach a national consensus, primarily in Russia. I would therefore begin with the regions, with public opinion, so as to see clear in the whole process. The issue is burdened with a lot of misconception, myth, and biased information. Some of our people still take an ideologized approach to the matter, refusing to look at it in its concrete historical context. Yet reality offers solutions, except that they should be arrived at with help from an enlightened public opinion and in cooperation with Russian regions.

Boris Yeltsin has said on more than one occasion that Russia will refuse to recognize decisions made behind its back. I don't think that even Japan would accept such a decision. After all, it has a stake in a serious decision adopted by the peoples of both countries and resulting in durable peace between them. My contacts with Japanese colleagues have shown that they are interested in a much more serious approach.

B. Pyadyshev. Have you already come to any conclusions about the group of countries with which Russia or Russian diplomacy should develop relations first and foremost?

A. Kozyrev. The group we regard as a priority is our republics. We mentioned this earlier. Our next priority is Russia's neighbors in the northern hemisphere, that is, highly developed, pluralist, market-economy democracies in Western Europe, Japan as the number one country in the East, America, and, needless to say, China. Our third priority is all the countries with which we maintain traditional cultural and mutually beneficial economic relations. I believe this would help shift the emphasis from global military strategic to normal economic and geopolitical interests. For without success in precisely these areas, Russia may soon find itself among countries of secondary importance, from the economic point of view, while it should be a leading power.

B. Pyadyshev. You mentioned Soviet–American relations and their distinctive character. After 1945, they were the pivot of world politics. We still see them as such. That country still holds a leading position in the military sphere, and this translates into political influence. As regards America's economic leadership, however, it is no longer what it used to be, and the shrinking of the country's economic positions makes for reducing its political leverage. Both politically and economically, it is a uniting Europe, a powerful Germany and Japan that have surged forward. It's in them that we tend to see our priorities but, of course, without ignoring the United States. We also remember the "young dragons" of the Asia-Pacific region, the newly industrialized countries of other regions going from strength to strength. In the past, we "successfully" overlooked the appearance of the "dragons" and NICs on the world scene. Currently we're trying to make up for lost time, especially in regard to Korea, but we aren't moving very fast. Doesn't the glitter of America continue to blind us?

A. Kozyrev. Yes and no. I still think the United States retains its key position in the Western community, including Japan, New Zealand and Australia, that is, virtually in all the countries committed to a definite model of pluralist democracy and market economics. I think our relations with the United States are going to be of decisive importance. The point is that, historically, America really bears the brunt of responsibility for that group of countries. It helped most of them to their feet after the war. And it shouldered the burden of defending the whole Western community when the atmosphere was one of outright military confrontation. The United States is a great country which has scored remarkable successes in various fields. We can learn quite a lot from it and cooperate with it, and there's a basis for our contributing to each other's progress.

Nevertheless, we must remember that the world is becoming multipolar. Underestimation of the rise of new centers of economic power, cultural influence, and so forth, and, in general, underestimation of the Asian region used to create big problems for our earlier, ideologized foreign policy. And so I'd say that while continuing to respect the United States as a great country and the center of the Western community of nations, we need to cooperate as extensively as possible with all other members of that community. Speaking of Russia's long-term strategic interest, I believe it should consist in taking up a fitting place not only in terms of military policy but still more in other respects among the most developed and civilized countries in the Northern Hemisphere one of which Russia is by rights.

B. Pyadyshev. Let us turn to your experience as an authority on multilateral diplomacy and disarmament talks.

Five years have passed since the Soviet leadership put forward a program to make the world nuclear-free by the year 2000. I understand that you share in both theory and practice in drawing up that program. An analysis of the current situation in the area of nuclear arms shows that bulky global programs are a thing of the past and that plans aimed at solving really solvable problems are far more effective and concrete. Of course, we need to see the general outlook but we must firmly interlink our plans.

Concerning the general prospect of nuclear disarmament I think the program didn't quite make the right choice. A completely nuclear-free world is unattainable and even harmful. Why do I think it's unattainable? For pretty obvious reasons: the present attitude of France, and more importantly, the resolve of Israel, Iraq, Pakistan, and other countries to join the nuclear club, at whose door they are now knocking.

And why would a nuclear-free world be harmful in a sense? Because the world community of nations, however perfect relations between them may be, needs a big stick to maintain general order against adventurist regimes. There has to be an adequate quantity of superweapons at all times. They may be left in the hands of the UN or some major countries. The world can hardly do without reasonably sufficient nuclear arsenals or minimal nuclear deterrence in the period that is setting in and is already pregnant with a host of regional conflicts and wars.

A. Kozyrev. I beg to disagree with what I consider a certain underestimation of the program of January 15, 1986. It was messianic and somewhat utopian, all right. But it was important at the time because we were really emerging from an ideologized society. In such a society, its important to ensure that some outdated dogmas give way to others, meaning the former allegations to the effect that the world is split into two camps, that it's locked in an uncompromising class struggle, that imperialism is aggressive by its very nature. A new, pragmatic understanding of realities came in.

It follows that there was an element of a new mythology, except that it was positive, as it were. And it is important that it should not be exploited by reaction. I agree that we need to move on as fast as possible from those negative or positive ideological guidelines to realities. I call that opting for a policy of common sense. I fully accept the idea that we must give up the drive for parity, including parity in nuclear missilery. It is a universally recognized truth that achieving parity was seen as a key task in the seventies. I'm inclined to think, however, that if both Russia and the Union as a whole are to survive, the main task should be to achieve parity in quality and standard of life. Looking twenty years back, to the early seventies, we can't say that the strategic parity we've had with the United States since then is a great achievement. It cost us an enormous lag and is too heavy a burden for us. We bear it at the people's expense as in other cases. Besides, are we sure there's a threat of the United States attacking us in the absence of strategic parity? I think life itself answers this question.

Minimum deterrence is an idea I appreciate very much. It's the most realistic alternative today. The great powers of Europe, Russia's traditional partners whom it has always looked up—I mean France and Britain—can do quite well, not with nuclear parity with any country, including our country and the United States, but with a small nuclear arsenal. It would fully guarantee their sovereignty and security. I think that while no country seems to plan attacking us in the foreseeable future, we should keep, nonetheless, something of a superguarantee in the form of a minimal but radically reduced nuclear capability. I'm saying this with reference to the complexes and fears lingering in our society. Frankly, I don't think we should expect this process to take the form of talks with reciprocal commitments. That, too, is a correct path, but we ought to consider primarily not what's in the interest of the United States or what process of gradual reductions would suit that country but what our own national interests are and to define our possibilities accordingly.

You raised the subject of heading off a spread of nuclear weapons. I'm an adherent of the old school but not the one that views the problem through one ideological prism where it concerns, say, Israel or South Africa, and through another where it's question of India or our other friends, such as North Korea or Cuba, both of which have refused to sign the Treaty of Non-Proliferation. We should speak openly about the countries refusing to sign the treaty. But I stand for preventing the emergence of further nuclear states. It's important not to dilute the concept of the regime of nonproliferation from the moral, political, legal, and all other points of view, but to preserve in international affairs a climate not admitting of proliferation.

I must say, however, that this now applies to us, too. The West has misgivings about the fate of our nuclear capability: It fears that in a Union transformed from a unitary state into a community of sovereign states every republic may claim its share of nuclear weapons. The Russian leadership is well aware that this must not be allowed to happen. From what my contacts with representatives of other republics indicate, no one lays claim to nuclear weapons. All fears expressed on this score are groundless. I consider that our nuclear arsenal should be under a single command and that we must firmly uphold the national interest of our state, never allowing a proliferation even in theory.

B. Pyadyshev. It is not for nothing that Eduard Shevardnadze's resignation is worrying the West. While we stress that foreign policy is a prerogative of the President, everybody knows of the role which

Shevardnadze played in framing and implementing it.

A. Kozyrev. I have a high opinion of Eduard Shevardnadze's role. He really made an outstanding contribution at this transitional stage. I would like the effort begun by him to be carried forward. I favor an even more radical approach, a course taking us away from the policy of new thinking or based on new thinking to a policy of common sense. Shevardnadze's departure is no foreign policy problem. The issue was picked on as a pretext for attacking him over the Gulf, for one, or over foreign policy. But the real problem, which he made clear enough, has to do with home policy, that is, the threat of dictatorship. If we continue moving to reinforce or reanimate authoritarian structures and overcentralized monopoly formations, to revive the party and state *nomenklatura,* I believe we'll be in for hard times in foreign policy as well, for to justify such a policy, it will be necessary, as it has always been, to invent an external enemy. There will be a need for an international crisis, for tension. If we start getting involved in new round of emergency measures, we'll need noninterference in our affairs, just being closed.

Let us recall our past. After all, the proposition about the so-called intensification of the class struggle in the international arena was advanced in a most favorable period of Soviet foreign political history, that is, in the late twenties, when capitalism stabilized itself. Yet it was just then that the need arose to whip up passions over "espionage" with provocative intent, and party documents came to include the allegation that the class struggle in the international arena was intensifying. Yet it was merely a twin brother of the thesis about an intensifying struggle over the policy of compulsory collectivization.

A reversal of our home policy would therefore go inevitably hand in hand with regression in foreign policy. I don't think Western leaders and analysts are right to have forgotten the lessons of history so soon. Why is foreign policy under attack? For the simple reason that the attackers need conflicts and aggressors and want to prove that our state must allegedly wage an uncompromising ideological struggle on class lines. I don't feel like arguing with them but in the last fifteen to twenty years, during which Western society attained very high standards of civilization, the main threat to peace came from the preservation of the Stalin/Brezhnev model of totalitarianism.

I'm inclined to agree with those who consider that the concept of perestroika has largely outlived its usefulness. We need something new. It's time we moved on from reanimating the old model to thoroughly transforming it. I would describe the change we need as "transfiguration," meaning a transfiguration of Russia and the whole Union in the spiritual, economic and moral spheres. Its roots lie in Orthodox, Christian, Russian culture. Transfiguration is also a qualitative transition connoting continuity, not a razing to the ground. It is charged with spiritual energy.

International Affairs *Guest Club*

In Smolenskaya Square and Also in 128 Countries of the World

Alexander Bessmertnykh, First Deputy Minister of Foreign Affairs of the USSR; former Minister of Foreign Affairs

Felix Bogdanov, Ambassador Extraordinary and Plenipotentiary of the USSR to Belgium; now Ambassador in Romania

Nikolai Neiland, former Deputy Minister of Foreign Affairs of the Latvian SSR, People's Deputy of the USSR

Boris Pyadyshev, USSR Ambassador Extraordinary and Plenipotentiary, member of Collegium, Ministry of Foreign Affairs of the USSR, editor in chief of *Mezhdunarodnaya Zhizn* magazine

Mikhail Shatrov, author, State Prize winner

B. Pyadyshev. The year 1951 saw the completion on Moscow's Smolenskaya Square of what was a fine, mighty skyscraper by the standards of the time. When construction started it was not clear which of the ministries would be housed in the prize building. The arguments given by diplomats won the upper hand, and the Foreign Ministry moved in from Kuznetsky Most Street. However, it only got a section of the building, from the seventh to the twenty-fourth floor. The other floors went to the Ministry of Foreign Trade. This coexistence has gone on to this day although both ministries have expanded in the meantime by taking over further premises in various parts of the capital.

Diplomats associate the high-rise building on Smolenskaya Square with the Foreign Ministry's central apparatus. Reaching out from the skyscraper's floors are invisible but strong, pulsating threads and information channels linking the Ministry with 128 Soviet embassies, 6 permanent missions (New York, Geneva, Paris, Vienna, Brussels, Nairobi), 75 consulates-general and 7 consulates. Besides, each of the fifteen Union Republics has its own Foreign Ministry and diplomatic service. We will probably agree that to choose the main line correctly, it is important to define something which is both simple and tremendously complicated, namely, the essence of the Soviet Union's national interest in the area of foreign policy. Once we've defined it, we can search for effective solutions to subordinate problems.

And so, let us discuss our national interest in international affairs. To make a start, I wish to quote a reader from Leningrad. "We have been talking about a balance of interests in an interdependent world," he writes. "But what is the Soviet Union's foreign political interest? Has it changed in comparison with the past? Shouldn't we ease the burden of this 'great power'?"

A. Bessmertnykh. It all comes down to a correct definition of the interest which the state defends and upholds, to bringing it into line with the country's potentialities. Strictly speaking, this is the point of departure for any policy, for its success or failure. It is easy enough to imagine a situation where foreign policy is trying to uphold and defend too ambitious an interest even though that is more than can be done. Such cases have actually occurred.

On the other hand, the interest being pursued may be too modest, with considerable loss for the state at world level as a result. I would say, therefore, that the national interest upheld by Soviet foreign policy today consists in ensuring the vital activity of this country on the international scene as an independent, sovereign, and territorially integral state. This is a general statement.

But there is another general requirement that is equally important and has emerged in recent years. I mean the need to guarantee progress in perestroika in the Soviet Union, that is, to provide favorable external conditions for our reformative activity.

Behind these general statements are perfectly concrete national interests in various sectors. We have, say, a special interest in developing relations with European countries, that is, both neutral states and NATO members. An interest differing from it in character is what may be called our natural Russian interest in promoting ties with neighbors. It can only follow the principle of neighborliness, which must daily be given substance. A further interest is our stake in maintaining strategic parity with the United States, etc.

B. Pyadyshev. I like Alexander Alexandrovich's idea that one of the essentially new objects of Soviet foreign policy today, a new aspect of our national interest, is to provide guarantee for our internal perestroika. We must carry on our foreign policy in a way that will help us in internal affairs. It is already estimated that by adopting new political thinking in our international affairs, we've saved around 30 billion rubles, which we can spend for our domestic needs. If we succeed in cutting military spending by 25 or 50 percent of the present amount as we want to we can get another 20 to 30 billion rubles. This is a road leading to the solution of many of the country's internal problems.

I don't mean economic problems alone. Right now our new foreign policy is helping raise Soviet society to universally accepted international standards in the legal, humanitarian, information, and many other spheres. Since we've put our signature to the Vienna accords, are a party to the London Information Forum, and the Paris Humanitarian Conference and have joined the Council of Europe, if as a "special guest" for the time being, we must work—regardless of whether or not this suits some in our country—to bring our internal standards, traditions, and regulations into harmony with existing high international standards.

F. Bogdanov. One of the meanings of the Russian word for interest is "benefit," "gain," or "profit," according to Vladimir Dal's dictionary. It follows that we need not be excessively modest on this point. Interest in foreign policy should really be beneficial and profitable to our country. Yet what we had more than once in the past was that our policy in this or that region was not really our own but that of a foreign country or rather of its leadership because we were linked with it by friendly relations. We ought naturally to reckon with the interest of other countries but should probably treat our own national interests as decisive.

Dal's dictionary says that the Russian word for interest also means "sympathy" and "care." This has a direct bearing on foreign policy activity, as when it is a sympathy with the national liberation struggle of other peoples or just with people in trouble. And this raises the question of the relationship between the international and the human ties. We often regard the former as a kind of political game in which one side understandably wants to defeat the other. We may be said to ignore the connection between international relations and human behavior and nature. Hence a biased attitude to each other, the emergence of an "enemy image," a tendency to regard even a sincere concession as a trick or fraud. Hence also the fear of making concessions lest you should be accused by people at home of antipatriotism, of a departure from ideals or, indeed, of betrayal. It's extremely important for us to have a better understanding of the worldview of other nations, whose history, geography, experience of life, and present situation differ greatly from ours. It we do we may be able to realize why capitalism is still there notwithstanding our repeated announcements of its failure. And when we've realized this we will be able to shape our foreign and domestic policy, our propaganda and much else, more correctly.

A. Bessmertnykh. Speaking of the "burden of a great power," isn't it too heavy for us?

I suppose being a great power is very burdensome. I mean primarily the degree of responsibility which a great power is compelled to assume, both for the fortunes of its people and for the evolution of the situation on the planet. For a great power to set aside its burden is to renounce part of its great responsibility. This would hardly be right.

However, there is another aspect to the matter. Is there nothing in our activity on the world scene that we could renounce without detriment to our national interest? I think there is. And this brings us to the concept of the dimensions of the national interest. Due to much too broad an interpretation of it, we proceeded at times without regard to our potentialities. Occasionally we did so because we were prompted not so much by our national interest but by our ideological conception of it. This is something we can renounce in some cases. We have no need for excessive involvement in regions where no direct interest of ours is at stake and where involvement is onerous both politically and economically. And so, being at the state of new thinking, we see one of our tasks in framing our policy pragmatically, in pursuing it on a realistic basis. As soon as policy goes beyond that, it becomes onerous.

M. Shatrov. In carrying on our policy, we used to forget for a long time that the principal method of influencing the world was our own example, primarily a strong economy. True, we were talking about it constantly, quoting sources, which we are very good at.

A. Bessmertnykh. You are right.

F. Bogdanov. Don't let us talk here about the historical reasons for that approach, reasons that may be called objective. It wasn't typical of us alone but of many other nations which had accomplished revolutions and lived through decisive changes in their destinies. Think of the great French Revolution, the American War of Independence, the Chinese revolution. Our greatest trouble was obviously our conviction that we had a monopoly on the truth and that this faced us with a missionary's task: preaching our faith, converting others to it, and thus doing the world a great favor. We proceeded from theoretical propositions about the superiority of our system. I say "theoretical" because we had yet to prove it in practice. We were only just beginning to build our "new world" and were genuinely surprised because others didn't realize that it was the most just of all worlds, the most humane, and so on. We mistook that incomprehension, that reluctance to regard us as a model, for immaturity or, worse still, an ill-intentioned attitude and intrigue. But there really was no model as yet, nor is there any even now, from what has come out.

N. Neiland. Our country is still called a superpower. I remember how this definition was played up in the seventies. On one hand, it sounds like a compliment. But on the other hand, let us say frankly that even if we do lay claim to being defined as a great power, it is only from the point of view of the country's area, population, resources, military strength. Let us recall that there are quite ironical opinions, to put it mildly, of what our power is like otherwise. To be a real superpower, our country must become strong not only militarily but economically as well, for it cannot remain a great power for long if it has nothing but a powerful military capability.

A. Bessmertnykh. Yes, we owe our superpower status chiefly to the outcome of World War II, to our victorious military power. Many countries having larger populations that ours aren't considered great powers. We may ask ourselves whether we cannot give up some plans we regrettably made in the past, plans which are exaggerated and exceed our possibilities, as we now realize. We would stand to gain, not lose, if we discarded them. Such plans increase the burden of military spending.

M. Shatrov. Indeed, it's the burden of expenditures for military purposes that we must get rid of to begin with. Incidentally, this applies to great powers and small countries alike. I would go as far as to say that the burden of armaments has a more tragic effect on small and developing countries than on others. The Middle East, for one, ranks third after NATO and the Warsaw Treaty as to saturation with armaments. How is any country to sustain such overburdening? By contrast, West Germany and Japan don't spend much on defense and have become economic superpowers.

A. Bessmertnykh. Was participation in the arms race a mistake in all circumstances? I feel that we need clarity on this point. My opinion is that, up to a definite historical juncture, the Soviet Union had to participate in the arms race. When the United States became an atomic monopoly while we lagged behind in strategic offensive weapons, with the ratio during, say, the Caribbean Crisis being 9:1, the very need to guarantee the country's survival compelled us to participate. It was also a moral task because the survival of a whole nation was at stake. But when strategic parity was achieved, which came at the very beginning of the seventies, both our participation in the arms race and America's became meaningless, as I see it. Both countries ought to have stopped and said it was enough because they had reached parity and that to make more missiles meant merely exhausting the resources of both sides. But, unfortunately, the arms race went on in spite of talks over many years and the signing of SALT-2 in 1979.

N. Neiland. Alexander Alexandrovich, you lived in America for many years. Did you never have a feeling that the United States deliberately "invited" us to the arms race, seeing it as a means of exhausting our economy?

A. Bessmertnykh. I believe that aim was there and still is. But it wasn't the only one. The main spiral of the strategic arms race began when the Americans adopted a program to make a thousand ICBMs.

When the program was announced the Soviet Union was forced to get involved in a new spiral.

B. Pyadyshev. To confirm that the "ceiling" approach of the other side was occasionally countered in the past by a similar approach on our part, I can give you a story told by somebody who heard a conversation between Leonid Brezhnev and Dmitry Ustinov. Brezhnev: "Why do we need so many missiles in Europe, Dima?" Ustinov: "Let them stay there. We don't have to feed them, do we?"

A. Bessmertnykh. The trouble is they have to be "fed."

N. Neiland. Yes, it often costs less money to manufacture arms than to keep them at the ready.

B. Pyadyshev. And then to scrap them.

N. Neiland. I can say as a deputy that our country's foreign policy enjoys very great confidence among people's deputies. This is one reason why they mention it fairly seldom. But the important thing is something else: we've discovered that the "enemy" is within ourselves, inside our country. And it is for us to defeat him, with foreign policy providing external conditions for this. Everybody realizes that the war menace has diminished and that we've made big gains in foreign policy.

M. Shatrov. There's a problem that is worrying me in this connection. New ideas are undoubtedly gaining ground in international relations. At home, however, we are still floundering. Don't you think ideas cannot win by just being proclaimed? They can only win through people. Our foreign service now includes many new people free from the burden of the past. But in home policy we've been shy of promoting new people, and this is why our cart is creaking. You will recall that Mikhail Gorbachev said in Leningrad that we should allow people one year to decide whether they could join in and were willing to. Many of the people in question found those words idealistic and so decided that they could but wouldn't and stayed where they were. Four and a half years on, we have achievements in so complex a sphere as international relations but inside the country things are still going poorly, with people refusing to make way for new thinking.

B. Pyadyshev. Mikhail Filippovich was right in saying that there is much that's novel in the high-rise building on Smolenskaya Square. Beginning with the new minister. Of the twelve deputy ministers now serving, ten have been appointed in perestroika years.

The situation is similar in the Ministry Collegium, which is headed by the minister and includes deputy ministers and the heads of key echelons of the Ministry. At present Collegium meetings on the seventh floor bring together twenty-nine members, who discuss fundamental aspects of the Ministry's activity, and work out and approve various measures, plans, and proposals covering a wide range of international and diplomatic activities. Most of those who sit at the Collegium table are newcomers.

The meetings themselves differ from what they were like a few years ago. They are now characterized by lively yet substantive discussions, and concrete opinions and decisions. Whereas earlier meetings took place sporadically and didn't last long because many participants preferred to keep silent, the situation is different now, so that the chairman is even compelled to restrict the number of speakers according to an unannounced time limit. They include both Collegium members and invited directorate chiefs and department heads of the Ministry plus experts. Participants advance many new, nonstandard ideas concerning the most diverse problems, such as preparations for a further round of Soviet–American talks, the situation in the Asia–Pacific area, environmental protection, relations with specific countries, further steps to guarantee the rights and dignity of Soviet citizens abroad, and so on.

A. Bessmertnykh. That's right. I think there is yet another circumstance. Few are those who realize that the Foreign Ministry is no administrative body. While other ministries are linked with groups of interest and may be described as something of a lobby, the Foreign Ministry is different. We don't control anybody except ourselves. And we owe our "output" to ourselves. We can't push a button and tell somebody to do this or that and then to submit reports and figures. In other words, the Foreign Ministry isn't represented in the 18-million-strong administrative apparatus still existing in our state. Our Ministry is more like a production unit.

Secondly, I believe the reason why foreign policy is the sphere in which we have made more active moves than in other fields is the differing perception of the danger threatening our country. In foreign policy you are constantly aware of a risk because it is close at hand. Where something isn't done properly the result tells on the whole country. It is sad that there should be those who don't realize how risky it is for the country to be in bad shape economically or to have to wrestle with acute inner political problems. The risk in this case is as great as the threat from without. We must mobilize our energies and tackle internal problems in good earnest.

M. Shatrov. It is more than some can do—they've got the wrong genes.

A. Bessmertnykh. Many believe there are things that can still be postponed and put right under plans to be made for the twenty-first century. Perestroika allows us no such time limit. We must proceed most purposively. Mikhail Gorbachev told the Supreme Soviet that new thinking must pervade our entire effort at home in the same way as it pervades our foreign policy activity.

F. Bogdanov. We need common principles. We cannot base economic relations at home on principles differing from those we are following abroad. Our failure to do so accounts for the lack of dovetailing with the world economic complex and for the biggest of the shortcomings, difficulties, and problems we come up against in our foreign economic effort. You cannot encourage democracy and glasnost at home and yet approve, if tacitly, of the approach of some countries which has nothing to do with universally accepted legal, humanitarian, interethnic, and other standards. This is bound to tell sooner or later on both the internal policy and the leadership of the country concerned, which it may deprive of support from the progressive forces of society advocating its transformation on democratic principles.

Our past knew such things. Take, for example, the period after the 20th CPSU Congress. Our reaction to the events in Hungary revealed the limitations of our "thaw" policy and had its effect on the subsequent evolution of the situation inside the country. As for our reaction to the 1968 events in Czechoslovakia, it was rightly described recently by someone as a watershed marking a turnaround toward stagnation. He who uses force and not dialogue outside the country as a means of resolving contradictions comes to the false conclusion that he can resort to the same device at home, and vice versa.

N. Neiland. As a spokesman for one of the republics, I wish to point out that new thinking in foreign policy is also translating into a bigger role for the Foreign Ministries of the republics. Whereas previously the existence of our ministries was more form than substance, currently their role is changing.

The constitution entitled the Baltic republics, like the rest of Union republics, to establish consular and diplomatic relations with foreign countries. But while this was put on paper and sounded fine, it only went as far as that. At present Sweden is setting up a branch of its Leningrad Consulate–General in Riga and Tallinn. In April 1990 the Danes plan to open their seventh cultural center abroad, this time in Riga. Also in April, passenger services are to be started by SAS and Aeroflot between Stockholm and Riga.

The time has come to extend our representation abroad. Latvia and Estonia have traditionally had representatives in the Soviet Embassy in Sweden. A question under discussion now is whether they should perform the duties of both diplomats of the Soviet Union and consuls of the Latvian and Estonian SSRs, with the Swedish Foreign Ministry registering this in its diplomatic list. Contacts between our republics now involve mostly Baltic states. This is only natural, for the problem of, say, conserving the Baltic Sea by combating pollution is primarily a task facing the countries of the Baltic region and uniting them. We are really in one boat in this respect. There are also many problems such as can be solved through cross-border ties,

We are well aware, of course, that we can have no foreign policy of our own. Our federal state can only have one foreign policy. We may and do have particular interests stemming from our geographic location and the distribution of our emigrants, who have settled in the course of history in the United States, Canada, Sweden, Britain, Australia, and West Germany.

A. Bessmertnykh. Perestroika has made big demands not only on the Moscow apparatus of the Foreign Ministry but also, on our embassies. The embassies are part of our Ministry. This is why, in speaking of perestroika, we also mean perestroika in our embassies. Some changes have already come about there.

B. Pyadyshev. It's important to stress that the Soviet diplomatic service today has a solid basis and sound professional traditions. Postwar decades in Soviet diplomacy have seen the rise of a generation of experienced, knowledgeable people, professionals who may be said to know the fine points of international affairs. In short, we now have a diplomatic school of our own. In any case, it it nothing short of the diplomatic schools of countries having a centuries-long record.

As far back as the war years and the early postwar period, prominence in world politics was gained by Andrei Gromyko, Valerian Zorin, Arkadi Sobolev, Georgi Pushkin, and some other Soviet ambassadors. They made up a constellation of diplomats operating in extraordinary conditions. They contributed to the drafting of so unique a historic document as the UN Charter, treaties and other documents relating to the postwar organization of Europe and the world.

Our diplomatic school in later years had its peculiarities.

A rule repeated for decades at Foreign Ministry meetings implied that it was better not to say a hundred times what should be said than to say once what should not be said. Diplomats were taught very well not to say what should be said, but then they were also weaned away from speaking, reasoning, and putting forward and upholding new ideas.

Nevertheless, by and large, we had reason to be at least satisfied with the standard of the Soviet diplomatic service in earlier decades, if not to be proud of it. Most officials were well-trained people who spoke foreign languages, were cultured, and had a capacity for contact as well as for analysis and for the proper formulation of political texts.

In that constellation of diplomats, which immediately preceded the present generation, much was done by Vasily Kuznetsov, Alexander Dobrynin, Georgi Kornienko, and some other veterans of Smolenskaya Square.

In the course of complicated diplomatic talks held in recent years, with the Ministry's central apparatus working hard to formulate and then implement foreign policy decisions, new people entered the scene to become Soviet diplomats, deputy ministers, ambassadors, experts at conducting negotiations. With regard to new trends on Smolenskaya Square and in our missions abroad, it is fair to say that perestroika in the diplomatic service made rapid progress precisely because it had a solid basis and able people waiting for their chance.

A. Bessmertnykh. One would like our embassies to show greater imagination, to extend the range and depth of their effort, to grapple with their tasks in a more creative spirit. There is still a tendency to see and report primarily what appears on the surface. As for things lying deeper down, they are occasionally overlooked. But, of course, this depends on the training received by ambassadors, councillors, specialists serving in embassies. Also, our embassies are committed to quantity, which is a trouble typical of our economy. There are ambassadors who believe for some reason that their work will be considered particularly fruitful if they send as many dispatches as possible every month. Our cryptographic equipment is often overheated by an avalanche of unnecessary messages. Yet, it's better to receive one really useful dispatch than ten descriptive ones, as has been the case. Over the past three or four years, however, our embassies have been approaching their job more creatively. Besides, many ambassadors have been replaced by younger people. These new people are competent and imaginative.

F. Bogdanov. Basic to perestroika in our missions abroad is the adoption by their staffs of the principles of glasnost and democracy that are now coming into their own at home. One-man management is all right but surely we cannot leave command methods in missions abroad intact at a time when we are combating them at home. One must reckon with people's opinions. There is no tolerating a situation where the atmosphere in an embassy isn't very healthy because the ambassador does as he pleases. I think the key to perestroika lies in our people participating extensively in decision-making on all official, social, party and everyday matters.

N. Neiland. When you served in the United States prior to perestroika, Alexander Alexandrovich, I often heard you speak in English over the Voice of America when you held debates with Americans. That was something sensational at the time. Working over there today is easier in some respects because we are now seen as human beings.

A. Bessmertnykh. These are normal human relations.

N. Neiland. I suppose the new situation connotes a change in the role of our diplomats abroad. Formerly a diplomat could live peacefully in a country for three to five years without trying too hard to learn the language because he sought no contacts. He read the press but spoke neither on the radio nor on television and never joined in discussions. Nowadays every diplomat worth the name must speak well the language of the country of residence. He has ample opportunities to help form a better opinion of the Soviet image. He can grant TV interviews, contribute articles, join in discussions, give a talk. Our diplomats are in high demand today. The question is how far we meet it.

A. Bessmertnykh. It's more difficult and risky for mediocre diplomats to work today because they are out in the open. And as exigencies have increased immensely, diplomats are expected not only to speak the language of the foreign country but to mix with the most diverse people there to spell out our policy to them in plain terms and have a proper knowledge of the public mood. The diplomat's tasks now extend beyond political issues, which we used to be concerned with most of all. They cover economic, military, cultural, and many other spheres. We tackle not only general problems but specific problems of promoting trading, economic, scientific, and technological ties; and we also recommend as reliable partners as possible to our governmental agencies.

Our embassies receive numerous Soviet people. This is a welcome reality but I regret to say that many of the business trips made abroad by our specialists are meaningless. Our representatives in the United States repeatedly witnessed, as I know by personal experience, a situation where one and the same firm or farm was visited over, say, two or three years, by dozens of delegations that asked for and were supplied with one and the same kind of documentary information. The heads of the firms or farms wondered what that could mean, why visitors kept arriving although our centralized economy had obtained the same information a dozen times before. Americans just simply can't understand so typically Soviet a phenomenon as our glaring departmental approach to things.

One of our ambassadors' tasks today is to keep tabs on this, to take a critical view of everything and assess our ties correctly and objectively.

The job is certainly harder now because the world has really become more diversified and colorful, and sometimes it isn't easy to see the crux of the matter amid its political and other intricacies. But the main purpose of ambassadorial work is unchanged—objective information. The ability to be objective is very difficult to develop for any analyst, scholar, diplomat, or people's deputy, and it takes years provided that he is loyal to principle.

B. Pyadyshev. One of the new lines that has emerged in our diplomatic service in this period of perestroika is that we now have more embassies playing a key role. What I mean is that until recently we only had from five to ten leading diplomatic missions abroad—I don't know exactly how many. They included our missions in, say,

Washington, Bonn, London, the UN, Tokyo—

A. Bessmertnykh.—Vienna.

B. Pyadyshev. Yes. But we regarded vast areas as just a remote periphery. After all, it is a fact that Eduard Shevardnadze didn't go to Latin America until recently and that it was the first visit to be paid to the region by a Soviet Foreign Minister. Nor did any Soviet Foreign Minister visit Australia and Southeast Asia until Eduard Shevardnadze did so not long ago. Incidentally, I don't think we've yet visited Africa at the level of minister.

A. Bessmertnykh. I would add that the Soviet Foreign Minister didn't visit Mongolia and the DPRK until recently.

F. Bogdanov. There are "unexplored areas" in Europe as well. Vienna was mentioned here as an important center of international activity. I believe we have every reason to put Brussels on the same list. It is a really unique center, and I hardly need demonstrate that. Suffice it to name two international organizations headquartered in Brussels: NATO and the European Community. But that's what lies on the surface, if I may say so, whereas there is also Belgium itself, a small European country with its own history, culture, political system, and a corresponding foreign policy. Belgium has its own interests and priorities and takes an original approach to a number of international problems. Yet we haven't been there since 1976. I don't think this is normal.

B. Pyadyshev. The responsibility, and role of our embassies are also growing in other countries in addition to those of our traditional centers in Washington, New York, Bonn, Paris, London, and a few other capitals, for the world is really becoming more and more interdependent and interconnected. Of course, the United States, the Soviet Union, and other big powers are very vocal in world politics. But they aren't alone. Other countries are gaining in leverage irrespective of their size and the distance separating them from world political centers. This means that our embassies in those countries must review their role and accomplish their tasks with a particular sense of duty and in a statesmanly manner. They mustn't mark time as if they were several light-years away from Moscow and Smolenskaya Square, mustn't expect Moscow to "forget" about them. This is a time when our country is making foreign policy there as well.

A. Bessmertnykh. Absolutely everywhere. Indeed interdependence implies that if something positive occurs somewhere it will reverberate in other parts of the globe, and as for something negative, its repercussions are even stronger. This is one reason why all ambassadors are responsible no matter where they are. A crisis even in a very distant region may have a direct impact on our interests and the interests of our allies. I consider your comment quite correct.

And here is another point. You were right in saying that formerly the trouble with our ambassadors and embassies was that they bore our interests in mind only within the framework of the country they were accredited to. Yet a country may be small, and its interest may be narrow accordingly. We insist on our ambassadors taking a broader look at things, on approaching them in regional and global terms, because an analytical view from any point is likely to contribute to an overall assessment of the world situation. I'm sure our embassies in any small country would show a better performance if the ambassadors went about their job energetically, creatively, and on a broad basis.

N. Neiland. I would like to call attention to the change in our stand on emigrés. Our relations were confrontational for years but now they are assuming the character of dialogue. We've jettisoned a principle which says that he who isn't with us is against us.

B. Pyadyshev. I wonder how correct it is to say that now is the time to change our approach to evaluating the importance of information from embassies. Many of our government departments, including the one on Smolenskaya Square, now have in some offices TV sets broadcasting CNN program live. In other words, they are in a position to learn instantly what's going on in America, to get prompt information from all over the wide world. The world is becoming transparent. There is less and less need for ambassadors to supply current news on a regular basis. The task is to move on to deeper-going analysis, to ascertaining fundamental aspects of the situation in any given country. And then, we should take better care of Soviet citizens abroad.

A. Bessmertnykh. You are right. In this age of information technology, the problem doesn't lie in a shortage of information, but in the fact that we are being overwhelmed by information. This applies to the highest leadership of the Soviet Union as well as to the Foreign Ministry and other entities. The flow of information is truly tremendous. We now have not only TV sets but telefaxes and teletypes installed by major news agencies of the world. I have computers in my office. Our offices are quite different today, and this means a different style and different standard of work.

Ambassadors lacking a capacity for analysis often conceal that lack by pouring in information of middling value. A gifted and competent ambassador never goes in for nonsense, never makes his subordinates copy articles from the press. He does his best to analyze events in depth and to visualize their likely evolution, which is what we need. To adopt foreign policy decisions, it is necessary to have objective, reliable information. If the information we get lacks authenticity and is therefore unreliable, we risk failing in our search for the right solutions.

B. Pyadyshev. The words "information" and "press" uttered here prompt me to read to you a letter received by *International Affairs* from Belozerskaya, a Moscow reader. "Our press has lately been taken to task," she writes, "mainly over our internal affairs. But now criticism, is also reaching out for those who cover international problems. They are said to do that insipidly and often euphorically."

M. Shatrov. She is probably right. The year 1985 was a definite watershed for our journalists dealing with international problems. I would say that formerly our press reverted time and again to two subjects: a further drop in the rate of the dollar and moral degradation in the West. It did so every year. True, the dollar is still going strong for all that its decline has been announced a thousand times.

We are now in the presence of quite serious changes. Journalists who have made a name for themselves as analysts of internal or international problems have been enabled to write as they see fit. We have a fairly interesting group of journalists who analyze developments and are unafraid to criticize the Foreign Ministry or even the leadership. In other words, life is getting normal, with common sense prevailing. I don't think this is a crisis—it's simply that life is putting everything where it belongs. We have midling ambassadors who ply the Foreign Ministry with information, and there are also quite a few journalists who keep writing about moral degradation and a declining dollar. Well, that's the way it is.

N. Neiland. Nearly every issue of *Izvestia, Moscow News, New Times* and other publications carries what I see as very interesting and profound articles. I wish to thank such noted and serious commentators as Kondrashov and Bovin. I read everything they write. And

I've completely changed my opinion of *International Affairs*. Time was when it occasionally took me a mere ten to fifteen minutes to study the journal from cover to cover. But now it takes me days to read, red pencil in hand, Not long ago, I was strongly impressed by Alexei Arbatov's and Andrei Kozyrev's articles. I could name many other articles. I note with satisfaction that the editor-in-chief of the *International Affairs* offers a topical commentary on the last page, possibly after the longstanding example of *U.S. News & World Report* or according to his own idea.

A. Bessmertnykh. I consider that most of our commentators, too, are clever and gifted. They've begun to express their own views. Occasionally they may be wrong, but a wrong opinion can be used as the starting point to arrive at the right opinion. The only thing I regard as intolerable in the work of any journalist is inaccurate facts.

M. Shatrov. Information.

A. Bessmertnykh. Inaccurate information. That won't do at all. As for dissenting opinions, they are welcome. We can argue with those who express them but we must in all circumstances respect them whether they are right or wrong.

Journalism is the complement of diplomacy, isn't it? It lends color to events, shows the reader what is really going on, and occasionally digs deeper and describes the atmosphere more exactly than a diplomatic document does. These two teams—diplomats and journalists specializing in international problems—are linked by common interests and are doing a common job, international politics.

N. Neiland. I sympathize with journalists because certain themes are still half forbidden, especially those relating to our allies. I believe the Foreign Ministry and Soviet diplomats must help eliminate stereotypes both we and some allies of the Soviet Union still have. Besides, what a journalist writes or a Soviet newspaper publishes isn't the voice of Moscow or the Kremlin. It merely states the opinion of the journalist and the paper. Needless to say, stereotypes handicap many of our journalists and commentators, with the reader as the loser because he is thus denied complete and objective information on developments in, say, the DPRK, Romania, and other countries. I hope we can also overcome this hurdle.

A. Bessmertnykh. I subscribe to Nikolai Vasilyevich's comments. For all our openness, for all the journalism concerned with international problems has undergone a tremendous change, we still have "gray," half-closed zones of sorts.

M. Shatrov. Our press is doing a big, important job. It is helping advance perestroika. The 19th CPSU Conference put it correctly when it stated: "The press is and will be a socialist opposition. It will criticize party and other officials. It will show how they work, what they are doing, the mistakes they make and the shortcomings they have, the positive experience of work gained by them."

One witnesses a bit too frequent attacks on the press, many of them unfounded. And one is really struck by words like the following: "I must say that some media are trying to get away from Party control. They discredit our sociopolitical system under the guise of criticizing past mistakes. Actually they are out to influence people's thinking. The press and television are using the most diverse forms to defame our achievements and set off the people against the Party. And they are scoring some gains in this." These words didn't come from a chance speaker but from the first secretary of a republic's Communist Party CC. How can anyone lump things together by smearing all mass media? What kind of democracy or glasnost is that?

F. Bogdanov. Boris Dmitrievich, you led the Soviet delegation to the London Information Forum. Speakers insisted on improving the situation in the information sphere within the framework of the European process. Has anything specific been done yet?

B. Pyadyshev. At the Information Forum, both delegations and individual participants submitted about seventy proposals. Most of the proposals were useful because they were aimed at extending glasnost and informing people more objectively. There was no call for proceeding immediately to implement the proposals. They are to be examined at the next CSCE meeting in Helsinki.

The Soviet leadership has adopted a decision of principle intended to carry out a series of measures extending the range of glasnost for Soviet people and for foreign journalists who arrive in our country. I mean such things as, say, giving greater access to sources of official and unofficial information, and allowing contacts with official institutions, private individuals, and nongovernmental organizations with the aim of obtaining data wanted by the press. Or giving Soviet citizens unhampered access to the foreign press, foreign satellite television programs, copying machines, audiovisual aids. Perestroika has a stake in enabling the press to fully play its role as part of civil society, to renounce prohibitive and restrictive procedures running counter to international law and militating against the obligations assumed by the Soviet Union in accordance with the documents of the European process.

M. Shatrov. All that is correct. But diplomacy involves the relationship between politics and morality, between diplomacy and morality.

A. Bessmertnykh. It is an exceptionally important subject. I've been struck by few publications that may be said to question the correctness of the trend of development of our relations with some countries. I feel that in this period of pluralist opinion, every point of view is entitled to be heard. I don't want to guess at the motives of the authors of particular articles, nor do I want to create the impression that they are all completely wrong.

Aristotle said that intentions brought out people's moral qualities. Applying this principle to our foreign policy activity and diplomacy, we can say without hesitation that they are motivated by noble aspirations. I know this exactly because I see the mechanism of decision-making from within, so to speak. For instance, the Soviet Union's effort to promote ties with the most diverse neighboring countries is prompted by the intention to create something of a zone of good-neighbor relations around us. Does this imply that, being prompted by national interests, we must shut out eyes to what goes on in this or that country, must ignore violations of the laws of morality and humaneness? Of course not. No country must have interests going beyond moral ideals. Politics today are less cynical than in the past centuries, when political achievements were measured by the proportions of seized territory.

The moral dimension of our foreign policy is becoming more explicit because the tasks of Soviet diplomacy fuse increasingly with the spiritual requirements of both the Soviet Union and humanity as a whole. Indeed, our country is championing the ideals of peace, freedom, democracy, prosperity, and tranquillity not only for its own sake but for the sake of all. I don't mean to say that the altruism of a country's foreign policy is proportional to its morality. There is no doubt that reasonable selfishness remains a component of foreign policy. But this aspect of it shouldn't outweigh universal interests.

In upholding the ideas of perestroika, a phenomenon of truly historic magnitude, on the international scene as well, our foreign policy and diplomacy show high moral qualities that I trust will characterize them at all times.